KEN WILBER, JOSEPH CAMPBELL & THE MEANING OF LIFE

Volume 2: Foundations of 'The Human Odyssey'

Proof & Review Copy

This is a pre-publication proof and review copy of this book, and is not intended for general sale. Please send your comments, suggestions, corrections, and reviews to <u>MartinHughCo@Gmail.com</u>. Permissions for some illustrations are pending.

AK Publishing
P.O. Box 1736
Sebastopol, CA 95473
MartinHughCo@Gmail.com

© January 29, 2015 Hulbert Martin and Amalia Kaye Martin

All rights reserved. No part of this book may be reproduced in any form, or by any means, electronic or mechanical, including photocopying, recording, or by any information storage and retrieval system, without permission in writing from the publisher.

Third B&W Proof Edition
Printed in the United States of America

Library of Congress Cataloging-in-Publication data
Martin, Hulbert
Ken Wilber, Joseph Campbell, & The Meaning of Life:
Volume 2: Foundations of the Human Odyssey
/Hugh Martin and Amalia Kaye Martin
ISBN-13: 978-1500659219
ISBN-10: 1500659215
Psychology (Developmental, Lifespan)
Cover design & photographs: Hugh Martin
Drawings & illustrations: Hugh Martin

Hugh Martin is listed in Who's Who in America and Who's Who in the World. Mr. Martin received his degrees and credentials from Swarthmore College, University of Pennsylvania, and University of California, Berkeley -- with emphasis on symbolic literature and early childhood education. Mr. Martin is past president of the investment brokerage and advisory firm, Hugh Martin & Co. Hugh has appeared on numerous talk shows, led seminars at many colleges and corporations, and spoken at many professional conferences.

Amalia Kaye Martin is an early-education specialist in the Sonoma County Public Schools, a community activist, and a member of the Occidental, California city council. Kaye received her degrees and training from California State College Fullerton and Baumann College.

Hugh and Kaye are best qualified as integral practitioners and theorists because they have lead integral lives. Both have richly diverse backgrounds in a multitude of fields, including: Personal growth & transformation, natural medicine & health, teaching from preschool through college, artistic & creative expression, influencing societal change, diverse natural & cultural environments, advanced academics, and spiritual exploration. They have been married for over 30 years, and have five highly-independent, multi-gifted children with close family ties. (For biographical details, see Appendix C1.)

Modern Artists represented in the Human Odyssey series: Pablo Amarindo, Julia Becker, John Blumen, Marc Chagall, Robert Connett, Salvador Dali, Jakob Eirich, M. C. Escher, William Etty, Kim Gamble, Paul Gauguin, Cameron Gray, Alex Grey, Scott Gustafson, Simon Haiduk, William Holman Hunt, Heri Irawon, JLof, Thomas Kinkade, Jan Patrik Krasny, Vladimir Kush, Daniel Leiske, Luches, Ilene Meyer, K. Madison Moore, Edvard Munch, Plisyuk Nataliya, Pablo Picasso, Alex Piexoto, Max Qin, Dante Gabriel Rossetti, Ruth Sanderson, Mario Sotelo, Flamenco Sun, Pavel Tchelitchew, Stephanie Tihanyi, Roland Tomayo, Vincent Van Gogh, Voitv, Josephine Wall, John William Waterhouse, Jacek Yurka. *** **Cartoonists:** Berke Breathed (*Opus*), Al Capp (*Li'l Abner*), Jim Davis (*Garfield*), Walt Disney (*Donald Duck*), Cathy Guisewite (*Cathy*), Jim Henson (*Muppets*), Bill Keane (*Family Circus*), Walt Kelly (*Pogo*), Hank Ketchum (*Dennis the Menace*), Gary Larson (*Far Side*), Looney Tunes (*Bugs Bunny*), New Yorker, Nick Park (*Wallace & Gromit*), Dan Piraro (*Bizarro*), Hal Roach (*Our Gang*), Charles M. Schultz (*Peanuts*), Bill Watterson (*Calvin & Hobbes*). *** **Movies, TV, Media:** African Queen, Alice in Wonderland, Art of Self Defense, Big Fat Greek Wedding, Casablanca, Chronicles of Narnia, Dead Poets' Society, Four Freshmen, Gladiator, Gladiator, Golden Compass, Gone With Wind, Graduate, Harry Potter, Hook, Hook, Horatio Hornblower, I Am Sam, Indiana Jones, Les Miserables, Life Magazine, Little Mermaid, Little Women, Lord of Rings, Monty Python's Meaning of Life, National Lampoon's Vacation, Odd Couple, Odyssey, Office, Pinocchio, Pirates, Pirates of Caribbean, Play It Again Sam, Pride & Prejudice, Quiet Man, Seven Years in Tibet, Simpsons, South Pacific, Star Trek, Star Wars, Sword & Stone, Ten Commandments, Thomas Crown Affair, Time Magazine, Up, Way Out West, West Side Story, West Wing, Wizard of Oz, Wormworld. Permissions for some illustrations pending. *** **Cover Illustration:** *Millennium Tree*, Josephine Wall. **Frontispiece:** *Nautilus Evolution*, Josephine Wall. **Title page:** *The Odyssey*, Armand Assante (1997), American Zoetrope Pictures.

KEN WILBER, JOSEPH CAMPBELL & THE MEANING OF LIFE

Volume 2: Foundations of 'The Human Odyssey'

Hugh Martin

Amalia Kaye Martin

AK Publishing
Sebastopol, CA
2014

FOUNDATIONS OF *THE HUMAN ODYSSEY*

These Appendices contain important supplementary information that explains and expatiates on key concepts from the authors' landmark study on Human Development, *Ken Wilber, Joseph Campbell, & The Meaning of Life (aka 'The Human Odyssey')*. The Appendices are divided into three sections – those pertaining primarily to Ken Wilber, those pertaining to Joseph Campbell, and those that combine both Wilber and Campbell.

These Appendices are relegated to the back of this book, because they contain unusually complex material, or might otherwise impede the narrative flow of the text. However, the material they present is essential to a full understanding of the ADAPT Model and the Life Journey Archetype. In fact, **these Appendices are almost as important as the Main Text itself.** Among other things, the Appendices contain the following:

✸ **Derivations and explanations of fundamental concepts**
   ➢ The ADAPT Model. (A2)
   ➢ The Internal Developmental Sequence. (A7)
   ➢ The Hero's Journey. (B1)
   ➢ The Life Journey Archetype. (B2)

✸ **Detailed Stages of major Developmental Sequences**
   ➢ Wilber's Fundamental Sequence. (A7b)
   ➢ The extended and condensed Internal Developmental Sequence. (A7d)
   ➢ Arenas of Life Passages. (A8a)
   ➢ Arenas of Psyche Passages. (A8b)
   ➢ Arenas of Spirit Passages. (A8d)

> Nothing in these Appendices should be construed as a denigration, criticism, bashing, or debunking of the work of Ken Wilber or Joseph Campbell. These great men are both titans on which all our efforts stand: 'We see further because we stand on the shoulders of giants.'

FOUNDATIONS OF *THE HUMAN ODYSSEY* (cont.)

- ❁ **Important supporting data and arguments for key contentions**
  - ➢ Why Wilber's IOS is actually a very extended (though incomplete) version of ADAPT. (A3)
  - ➢ How ADAPT improves on Wilber. (A6b)
  - ➢ How Wilber's AQAL inhibits inquiry into the study of Human Development. (A4)
  - ➢ Why ADAPT is the appropriate foundation for the next generation of AQAL. (A5)

- ❁ **Application of the Hero's Journey and the Life Journey to key works of literature and film, and to Personal Growth**
  - ➢ The Hero's Journey in literature and film. (B1b, d-e, h)
  - ➢ The Hero's Journey of Personal Growth. (Bf-g)
  - ➢ The Life Journey Archetypes in Homer's *The Odyssey*. (B3)

- ❁ **Background data for important concepts**
  - ➢ Wilber's Processes for Actualization and Restoration Growth. (A9a-b)
  - ➢ Anodea Judith's Balancing the Chakras. (A9c)

- ❁ **Complete diagrams of Domains, Sectors, and Models**
  - ➢ Circle diagrams of ADAPT – along with Wilber's AQAL and IOS. (A, C3, C5d)
  - ➢ Quick Reference Guides for ADAPT and the Life Journey. (C4a-c)

- ❁ **Essential reference resources**
  - ➢ Glossary of terms, with Wilber equivalent. (C2)
  - ➢ Resources for Study, annotated and evaluated. (C3)

On occasion, these sections also include personal Explorations to help you understand key concepts, and to apply them in your own life.

THE HUMAN ODYSSEY
Volume 2: Foundations
TABLE OF CONTENTS

KEN WILBER APPENDICES 12

APPENDIX A1. CIRCLE DIAGRAMS 14
- A1a. Ken Wilber's AQAL — 14
- A1b. Ken Wilber's Integral Operating System (IOS) — 14
- A1c. The ADAPT Model of Human Development — 14

APPENDIX A2. BEYOND KEN WILBER: HOW AQAL BECAME ADAPT 18
- A2a. From AQAL to IOS — 21
- A2b. From IOS to ADAPT — 22
- A2c. The Domains and Sectors of Wilber's AQAL — 23
- A2d. The Domains and Sectors of Wilber's IOS — 24
- A2e. The Formulation of ADAPT — 26
- A2f. Fine-Tuning ADAPT — 27
- A2g. The Domains and Sectors of ADAPT — 28
- A2h. The Systems of ADAPT — 29
- A2i. The Eight Systems: Circle Diagram — 30
- A2j. The ADAPT Model: Circle Diagram — 31
- A2k. ADAPT vs. Wilber: How Do They Compare? — 32
- A2l. From Concept to Archetype: Domains — 34
- From Concept to Archetype: Sectors — 35
- A2m. From Abstract Theory To Personal Revelation — 36
- A2n. From Revelation To Application — 37

APPENDIX A3. KEN WILBER'S ADAPT: How Wilber's *Integral Psychology* Parallels ADAPT   38

Appendix A4. THE TYRANNY OF AQAL:
Ken Wilber's AQAL Now Inhibits Free Inquiry into Human Development 48

Appendix A5. TOWARD A NEW AQAL:
How the Next Generation of AQAL Will Be Birthed 52
- A5a. The Evolution of AQAL, Version One. — 52
- A5b. The Need for a New Model — 52
- A5c. Why ADAPT Provides the Basis for the New AQAL — 53
- A5d. AQAL, The Next Generation — 53

Appendix A6a. HOW ADAPT IMPROVES ON WILBER 54

    A6aa. ADAPT & Wilber Compared   *55*

    A6ab. 12 Degrees of Divergence: How ADAPT and Wilber Differ   *56*

Appendix A6b. COMPARISON TABLES: ADAPT VS. WILBER --
87 MAJOR WAYS ADAPT IMPROVES ON WILBER 58

Appendix A7. THE INTERNAL DEVELOPMENTAL SEQUENCE:
How Wilber's FDS Became ADAPT's IDS 92

    A7a. External & Internal Passages of Growth   *96*

    A7b. Wilber's Fundamental Developmental Sequence   *97*

    A7c. Correlations Among Researchers: Self & Ego   *100*

    A7d. The Chakras – A Simplified FDS   *102*

        The Chakras – West and East   *103*

    A7e. Correlations Among Researchers: Chakra Version   *106*

    A7f. Two Forms of Growth: Succession & Accumulation   *108*

    A7g. Two Models of Self: Layered and Retrofit   *110*

    A7h. Two Modes of Treatment: Archeology & Architecture   *112*

Appendix A8. THE PROGRESSIONS OF HUMAN DEVELOPMENT:
Developmental Sequences -- Arenas of Life Passages, Psyche, Spirit 114

    A8a. Arenas of Life Passages   *115*

    A8b. Arenas of the Psyche   *129*

    A8c. Arenas of the Spirit   *132*

APPENDIX A9. THE PROCESSES OF KEN WILBER & ANODEA JUDITH 142

    A9a. Integral Life Practice: Wilber's Specific Processes   *142*

    A9b. Wilber's Pathologies & Treatments   *145*

    A9c. Anodea Judith's Balancing the Chakras   *146*

CAMPBELL APPENDICES   148

APPENDIX B1. THE HERO'S JOURNEY:
How Joseph Campbell's Archetypal Journey Manifests itself in Human Culture 150

    B1a. The Campbell Persona   *153*

    B1b. The Hero's Journey: Myth & Legend   *154*

    B1c. The Hero's Journey: Campbell Version   *156*

    B1d. Hero's Journeys: The Five Types   *158*

    B1e. The Hero's Journey: Literature & Movies   *160*

    B1f. Your Inner Hero's Journeys: Their Scope   *162*

    B1g. Your Inner Micro-Journey: Its Steps   *164*

    B1h. Archetypal Characters of the Hero's Journey   *166*

Appendix B2. BEYOND JOSEPH CAMPBELL:
How the Hero's Journey Became the Life Journey 172

    B2a. From ADAPT to Life Journey: Domains   *173*

    B2b. From ADAPT to Life Journey: Sectors   *174*

    B2c. From Life Journey to Hero's Journey   *180*

Appendix B3a. HOMER'S *THE ODYSSEY*: SYNOPSIS	184
Appendix B3b. ADAPT AND HOMER'S *THE ODYSSEY*: PARALLELS	188
Dimensions	*189*
Participants	*190*
Processes	*192*
Pathfinders	*194*

WILBER + CAMPBELL APPENDICES   196

Appendix C1. HUGH AND KAYE MARTIN: BIOGRAPHICAL BACKGROUND	197
Appendix C2. GLOSSARY OF TERMS AND CONCEPTS	198
Appendix C3. READING SYSTEM-BY-SYSTEM: THE STUDY PROGRAMS	220
S1-8. The Complete ADAPT Study Program	*221*
Study Program S1. Individual Growth	*222*
S1a. Diagram of System 1	224
S1b. Quickstart Study Program for Individual Growth	225
S1c. Full Study Program for Individual Growth	227
Study Program S2. Collective Growth	*230*
S2a. Diagram of System 2	232
S2b. Study Program for Collective Growth	233
Study Program S3. Actualization Growth	*234*
S3a. Diagram of System 3	236
S3b. Study Program for Actualization Growth	237
Study Program S4. Restoration Growth	*238*
S4a. Diagram of System 4	240
S4b. Study Program for Restoration Growth	241
Study Program S5. Horizontal Growth	*242*
S5a. Diagram of System 5	246
S5b. Study Program for Horizontal Growth	247
Study Program S6. Perspective Growth	*248*
S6a. Diagram of System 6	252
S6b. Study Program for Perspective Growth	253
Study Program S7. Evolution & Involution	*254*
S7a. Diagram of System 7	258
S7b. Study Program for Evolution & Involution	258
Study Program S8. Spiritual Growth	*260*
S8a. Diagram of System 8	262
S8b. Study Program for Spiritual Growth	263
Appendix C4. RESOURCES FOR PERSONAL EVOLUTION	264
Hugh & Kaye Martin: Books, Studies, Educational Materials	*266*
Ken Wilber: Books and Other Resources	*268*
Joseph Campbell: Books and Other Resources	*271*
Dimensions	*274*
Participants	*284*
General Processes	*286*

Specific Processes   288
Pathfinders   298

Appendix C5. Quick Reference Guides: The Domains & Sectors of ADAPT 305

C5a. ADAPT Quick Reference: Dimensions, Participants, General Processes, Pathfinders   306

C5b. ADAPT Quick Reference: Systems, Specific Processes   308

C5c. Life Journey Quick Reference:
Dimensions, Participants, General Processes, Pathfinders   310

C5d. Circle Diagram: The ADAPT Model Of Human Development   312

The Human Odyssey Series: Three Versions

The books of *The Human Odyssey Series* are available in three versions:

- The stripped-down, streamlined **Quickstart Version** (~170 pages).
- The abbreviated, one-volume **Introductory Version** (~300 pages).
- The complete, comprehensive, two-volume **Advanced Version** (~700 pages). The Advanced Version has the long title *Ken Wilber, Joseph Campbell, and the Meaning of Life*.

The Quickstart Version is the best place for any reader to begin their explorations of this fascinating, but complex, perspective on human life. The Advanced Version is for those who have already assimilated the Quickstart or Introductory Version. The book you are now reading is Volume 2 of the Advanced Version.

What This Book Contains

This book, Volume 2 of *The Human Odyssey*, is comprised of Appendices to the Main Text. These Appendices contain important supplementary information that explains and expatiates on key concepts from the Main Text. The Appendices are divided into three sections – those pertaining primarily to Ken Wilber, those pertaining to Joseph Campbell, and those that combine both Wilber and Campbell.

WILBER APPENDICES (page 12)

How the ADAPT Model derives from, illuminates, and extends the Integral Theory work of philosopher and systems theorist Ken Wilber.

- **A1. Circle Diagrams: AQAL, Wilber, & ADAPT** (page 14)
  The entire ADAPT Model displayed as one grand, multi-colored diagram. Along with a comparable diagrams for Wilber's AQAL and Integral Operating System (IOS).

- **A2. Beyond Ken Wilber: How AQAL Became ADAPT** (page 18)
  The ADAPT Model of Human Development, one of the twin foundations of this book: How it was derived from the AQAL/IOS Models of Ken Wilber, and other sources.

- **A3. Ken Wilber's ADAPT** (page 38)
  Quotes from Wilber's own works – showing that Wilber's Model is actually a very extensive (though incomplete) version of the ADAPT Model itself.

- **A4. The Tyranny of AQAL** (page 48)
  How Wilber's great AQAL Model now diverts and inhibits open inquiry into the nature of Human Development.

- **A5. Toward a New AQAL** (page 52)
  The evolution of Wilber's AQAL and IOS Models. Why ADAPT is the appropriate next step in that evolution.

- **A6. ADAPT and Wilber Compared** (page 54)
  The 12 fundamental ways the ADAPT Model diverges from Wilber's IOS. Includes a detailed table of comparisons -- showing at least important 87 positions where ADAPT differs from and improves on Wilber.

- **A7. The Internal Developmental Sequence (IDS)** (page 94)
  The Developmental Sequence that shows the progressions of Growth for the Internal Realms of Psyche, Body, and Spirit: How it was derived. What it consists of. What it tells us about Human Development.

- **A8. The Progressions of Human Development** (page 114)
  Full sets of Developmental Sequences showing the progressions of Growth for all the Arenas in the Realms of Life Passages, the Psyche, and the Spirit.

- **A9. The Processes of Ken Wilber & Anodea Judith** (page 142)
  Ken Wilber's program for Actualization Growth: Integral Life Practice. Wilber's program for Restoration Growth: Pathologies & Treatments at various Stages of Development. Anodea Judith's program for Restoration Growth: Balancing the Chakras.

What This Book Contains. Page 11.

CAMPBELL APPENDICES (page 148)

How the Life Journey Archetype derives from, illuminates, and extends the Hero's Journey 'Monomyth' of scholar and mythologist Joseph Campbell.

❂ B1. Joseph Campbell's Hero's Journey (page 152)
Eight ways Campbell's Hero's Journey manifests itself in myth, literature, movies, the media, and one's own inner life.

❂ B2. Beyond Joseph Campbell: How the Hero's Journey Became the Life Journey (page 172)
The Life Journey Archetype, one of the twin foundations of this book. How it was derived from the Hero's Journey of Joseph Campbell, and other sources.

❂ B3. Parallels to Homer's *The Odyssey* (page 184)
The premier example of the Life Journey Archetype. An outline of the many parallels between the ADAPT Model and that greatest and most complete of all mythic Life Journeys, *The Odyssey* by Homer. Includes a synopsis of epic itself.

WILBER + CAMPBELL APPENDICES (page 196)

How the ADAPT Model (from Wilber) and the Life Journey Archetype (from Campbell) combine to form a fully-rounded conception of Human Development. Plus additional general background information necessary to understand these concepts.

❂ C1. Biographical Background (page 197)
Biographical background and professional qualifications of the authors, Hugh and Kaye Martin.

❂ C2. Glossary of Terms and Concepts (page 198)
Definitions of all the key terms and concepts of this book – along with the closest equivalent in Wilber's work. Serves also as an index: Contains references to key sections of the Main Text.

❂ C3. Reading System-by-System: The Study Programs (page 220)
Detailed Lesson Plans for the study each of the eight Systems of Growth – showing what parts of this book should be read, and in what order. Also includes the portion of the ADAPT Circle Diagram (Appx A1c) that pertains to each System.

❂ C4. Resources for Personal Evolution (page 264)
Annotated outline of important books, research studies, and other resources that explore the various facets of Wilber, Campbell, ADAPT, and the Life Journey.

❂ C5. Quick-Reference Guides (page 305)
Outlines and thumbnail descriptions of every Domain and Sector of the ADAPT Model and the Life Journey Archetype. Plus a Circle Diagram for the ADAPT Model, showing the full model condensed into a single one-page diagram.

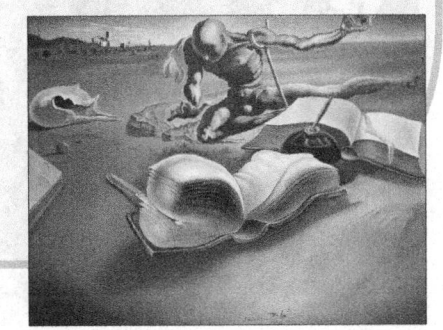

A: KEN WILBER APPENDICES

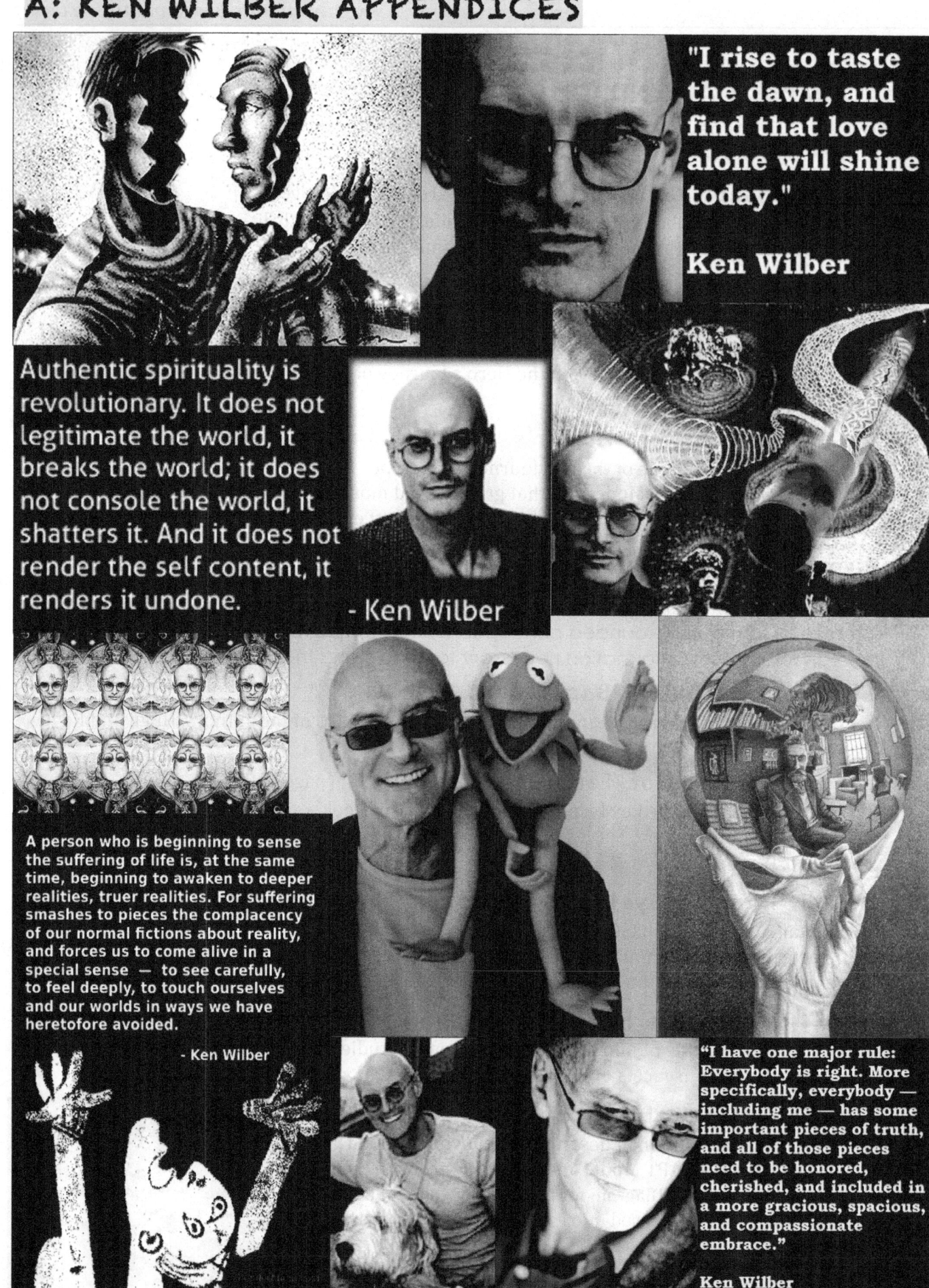

"I rise to taste the dawn, and find that love alone will shine today."

Ken Wilber

Authentic spirituality is revolutionary. It does not legitimate the world, it breaks the world; it does not console the world, it shatters it. And it does not render the self content, it renders it undone.

— Ken Wilber

A person who is beginning to sense the suffering of life is, at the same time, beginning to awaken to deeper realities, truer realities. For suffering smashes to pieces the complacency of our normal fictions about reality, and forces us to come alive in a special sense — to see carefully, to feel deeply, to touch ourselves and our worlds in ways we have heretofore avoided.

— Ken Wilber

"I have one major rule: Everybody is right. More specifically, everybody — including me — has some important pieces of truth, and all of those pieces need to be honored, cherished, and included in a more gracious, spacious, and compassionate embrace."

Ken Wilber

WHEN WE TRANSFORM OUR SELVES...

...WE TRANSFORM THE WORLD

Page 14. Wilber Appendices

Appendix A1.
Circle Diagrams

The three Circle Diagrams in this section illustrate how the concepts of this book developed: We began with Ken Wilber's AQAL (A1a). Then we progressed to Wilber's IOS (A1b). Finally, we arrived at our own ADAPT Model of Human Development (A1c). Here is a brief introduction to these Diagrams:

A1a. Ken Wilber's AQAL (facing page)

The concepts of this book originally arose Ken Wilber's AQAL Model. Wilber's famous and elegant AQAL Diagram illustrates only the two Parameters: Perspectives [*Quadrants*] and Stages [*Levels*]. The somewhat expanded version of the AQAL Model (not pictured in the Diagram) includes four other Parameters: Lines, States, Self, and Types

A1b. Ken Wilber's Integral Operating System (IOS) (page 16)

Wilber's Integral Operating System (IOS) is the most extended version of his AQAL Model (A1a). This IOS Model is never explicitly described in Wilber's work, but can be derived from all the Parameters of Human Growth described in Wilber's *Integral Psychology*, and other works (over two dozen Parameters in all). For comparison purposes, we arrange Wilber's Parameters in the same configuration as our ADAPT Circle Diagram (A1c). [Brackets indicate Parameters that are implicit in Wilber.]

A1c. The ADAPT Model of Human Development (page 17)

The ADAPT Circle Diagram incorporates all the Domains, Systems, and major Sectors of the ADAPT Model presented in this book. The four quadrants of the Diagram represent the four Domains; the eight concentric circles are the eight Systems of Growth; the items within each circle are the Sectors for that System; the items outside the circles pertain to all eight Systems.

When we compare the IOS Diagram (A1b) to the ADAPT Diagram (A1c), it's clear that **Wilber's Integral Operating System (IOS) is actually a highly-developed (though incomplete) version of the ADAPT Model itself.***

The Circle System. A Circle Diagram is a way of conveying that a particular collection of parts is all one big System.

A1. Circle Diagrams. Page 15

Circle Diagram A1a.
KEN WILBER'S AQAL

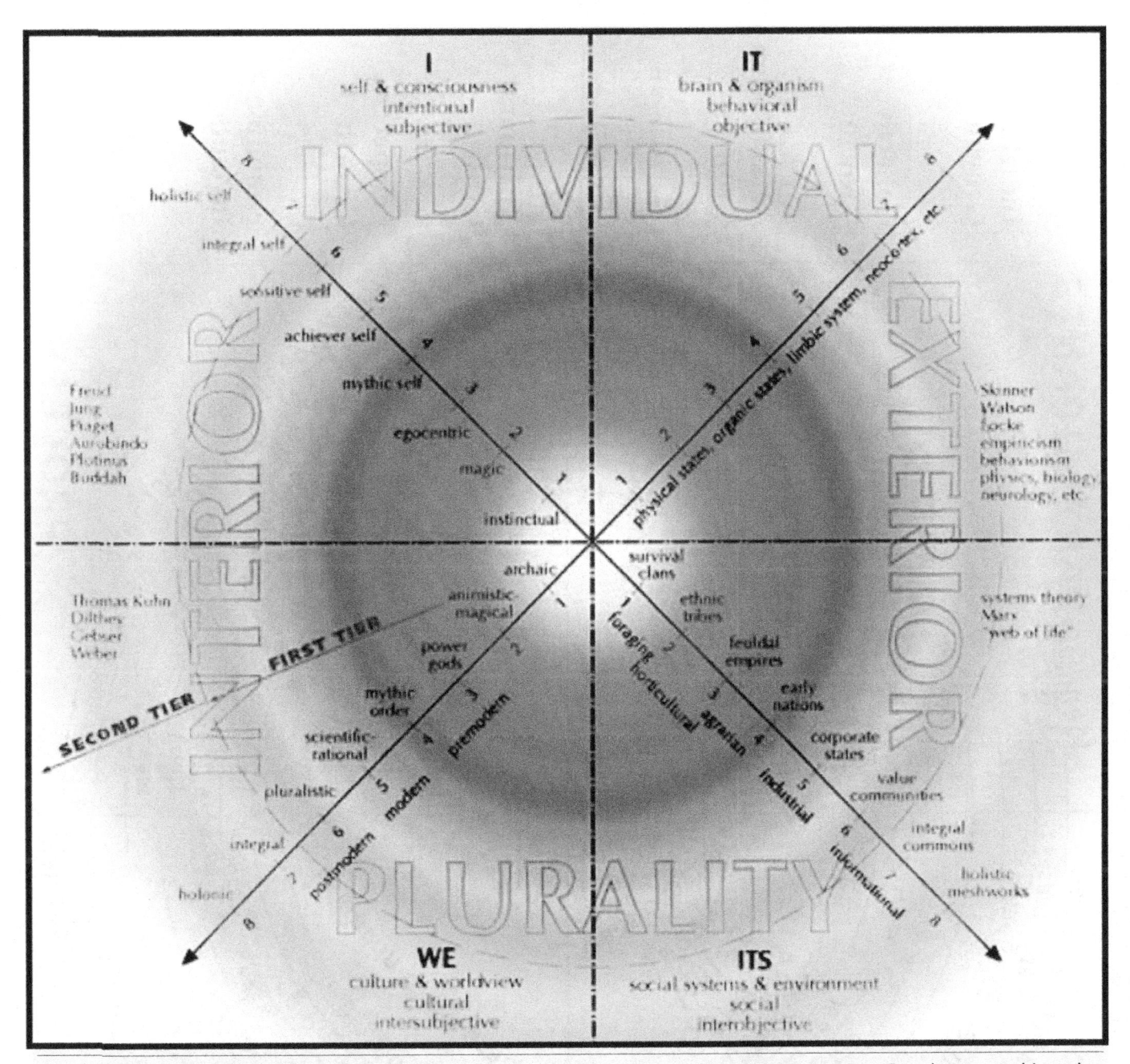

I — self & consciousness / intentional / subjective
IT — brain & organism / behavioral / objective
WE — culture & worldview / cultural / intersubjective
ITS — social systems & environment / social / interobjective

Individual (top) / Plurality (bottom); Interior (left) / Exterior (right). First Tier / Second Tier diagonals.

Upper-Left (I) levels: instinctual, magic, egocentric, mythic self, achiever self, sensitive self, integral self, holistic self.
Upper-Right (IT) levels: physical states, organic states, limbic system, neocortex, etc. Associated: Skinner, Watson, Locke, empiricism, behaviorism, physics, biology, neurology, etc.
Lower-Left (WE) levels: archaic, animistic-magical, power gods, mythic order, scientific-rational, pluralistic, integral, holonic. Associated: Thomas Kuhn, Dilthey, Gebser, Weber. Also: Freud, Jung, Piaget, Aurobindo, Plotinus, Buddah.
Lower-Right (ITS) levels: survival clans, ethnic tribes, feudal empires, early nations, corporate states, value communities, integral commons, holistic meshworks. Associated: systems theory, Marx, "web of life". Stages: foraging, horticultural, agrarian, industrial, informational.

Ken Wilber's AQAL. Wilber's famous AQAL Diagram illustrates only two Parameters: Quadrants and Levels. Wilber's more extended IOS Model (A1b) covers over two dozen Parameters. The ADAPT Model presented in this book (A1c) covers the broadest and most comprehensive range of Human Development Parameters.

---

*For details on the passages from Wilber's *Integral Psychology* that substantiate these comparisons, see Appendix A3. To compare Wilber's terms to those of ADAPT, see the tan textboxes in each section of the Main Text. *** Circle Diagrams A1b and A1c summarize the entire Models of Human Development for both Ken Wilber and ADAPT. Each Parameter of the Diagrams is explained in detail in the Main Text. *** The ADAPT and Wilber Circle Diagrams are derived in Beyond Ken Wilber (Appx A2). The ADAPT Circle Diagram is derived circle-by-circle under Systems (S1-8). The information in the ADAPT Circle Diagram is outlined more extensively in the Quick Reference Guides (Appx C4).

Page 16. WILBER APPENDICES

Circle Diagram A1b.
KEN WILBER'S INTEGRAL OPERATING SYSTEM (IOS)

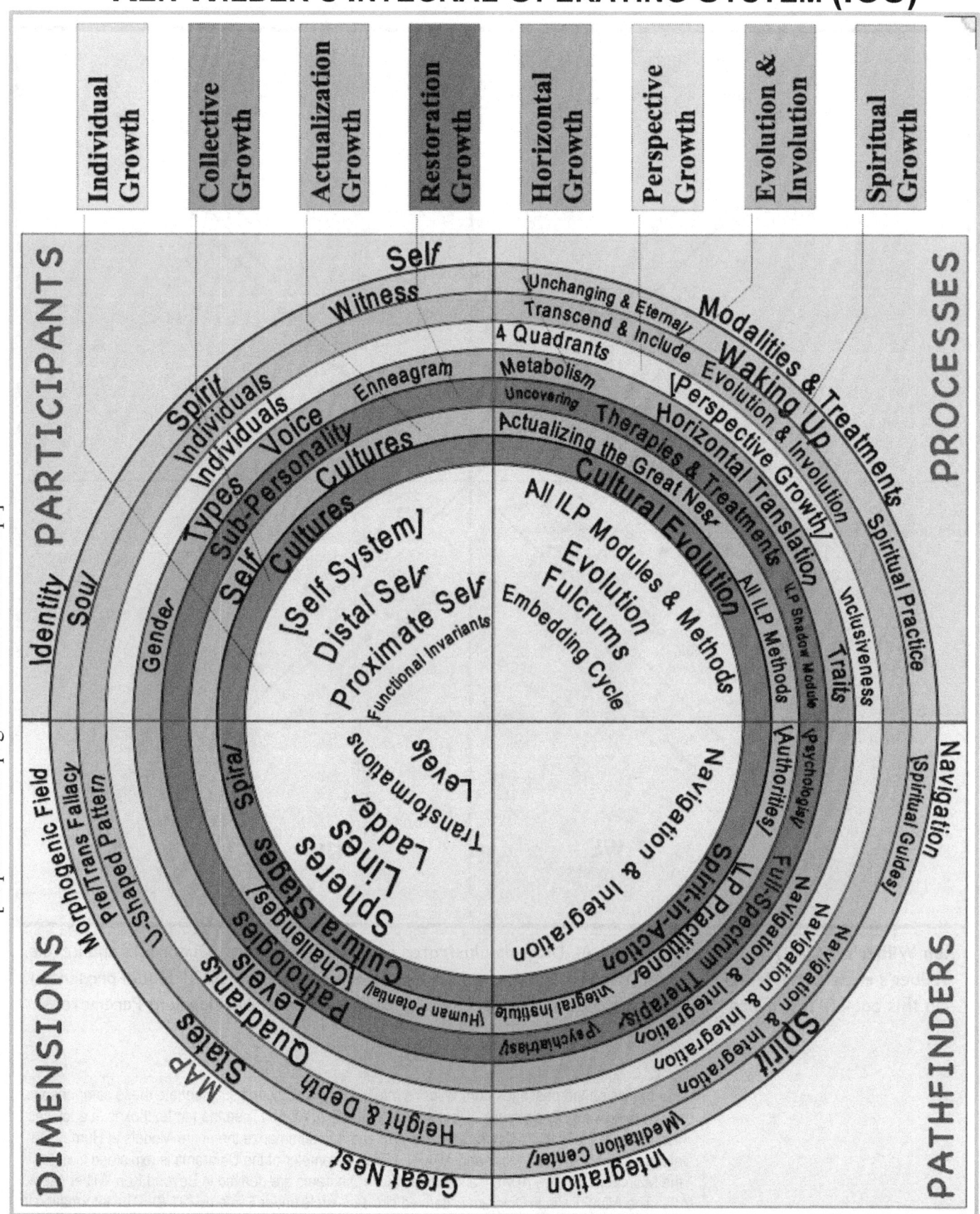

[Explanation on page 21. View this side up.]

PROCESSES: Individual Growth, Collective Growth, Actualization Growth, Restoration Growth, Horizontal Growth, Perspective Growth, Evolution & Involution, Spiritual Growth

PARTICIPANTS: Self, Witness, Spirit, Individuals, Individuals, Types, Voice, Sub-Personality, Enneagram, Cultures, Self, Cultures, Identity, Soul, Gender, [Self System], Distal Self, Proximate Self, Functional Invariants

PROCESSES (inner): Unchanging & Eternal, Transcend & Include, 4 Quadrants, Metabolism, Uncovering, Therapies & Treatments, Actualizing the Great Nest, All ILP Modules & Methods, Evolution, Fulcrums, Embedding Cycle, Modalities & Treatments, Waking Up, Evolution & Involution, Horizontal Translation, [Perspective Growth], All ILP Methods, [ILP Shadow Module], Inclusiveness, Traits, Spiritual Practice

DIMENSIONS: Morphogenic Field, Pre/Trans Fallacy, U-Shaped Pattern, Levels, Pathologies, [Challenges], Cultural Stages, Spheres, Lines, Ladder, Transformations, Levels, Quadrants, Height & Depth, States, Map, Great Nest

PATHFINDERS: Navigation, [Spiritual Guides], [Psychology], [Authorities], Full-Spectrum Therapist, ILP Practitioner, Spirit-in-Action, Navigation & Integration, Navigation & Integration, Navigation & Integration, [Psychiatry], Integral Institute, [Human Potential], Spirit, [Meditation Center], Integration

A1. Circle Diagrams. Page 17

Circle Diagram A1c.
THE ADAPT MODEL OF HUMAN DEVELOPMENT

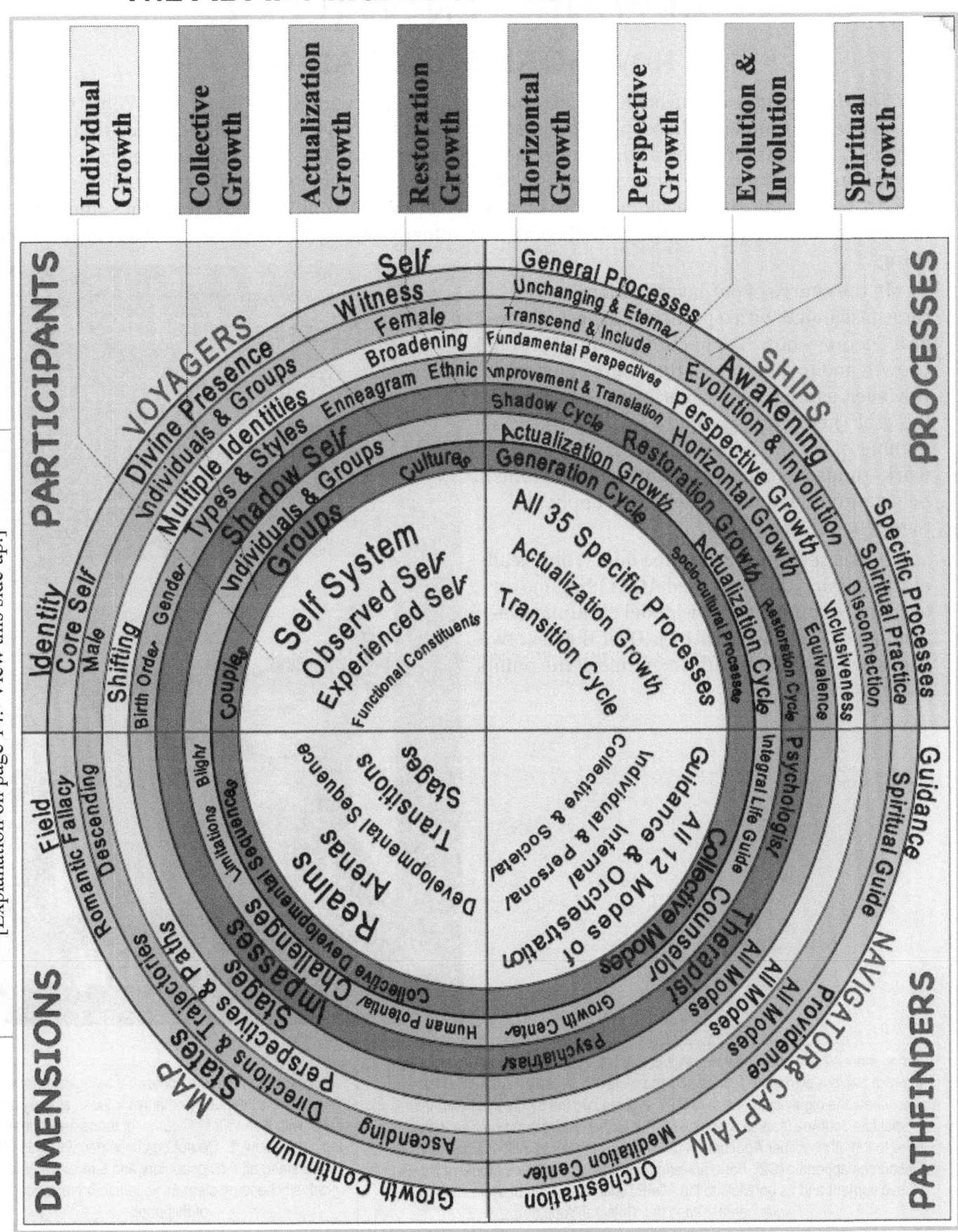

[Explanation on page 14. View this side up.]

Growth types (top banners): Individual Growth · Collective Growth · Actualization Growth · Restoration Growth · Horizontal Growth · Perspective Growth · Evolution & Involution · Spiritual Growth

PARTICIPANTS / VOYAGERS
- Self — Witness — Divine Presence
- Female / Male — Broadening — Individuals & Groups
- Multiple Identities — Enneagram — Ethnic
- Types & Styles — Shadow Self
- Individuals & Groups — Cultures
- Groups — Couples — Birth Order — Gender — Shifting — Core Self — Identity

PROCESSES / SHIPS
- General Processes — Unchanging & Eternal
- Transcend & Include — Awakening
- Fundamental Perspectives — Evolution & Involution
- Improvement & Translation — Perspective Growth — Horizontal Growth
- Shadow Cycle — Restoration Growth
- Actualization Growth — Socio-cultural Processes
- Generation Cycle — Restoration Cycle
- All 35 Specific Processes — Equivalence — Inclusiveness — Disconnection
- Actualization Cycle — Spiritual Practice — Specific Processes
- Transition Cycle

Center: Self System · Observed Self · Experienced Self · Functional Constituents

DIMENSIONS
- Field — Romantic Fallacy — Guiding — Descending — Blight — Limitations — Initiations — Developmental Sequences — Collective developmental sequences — Human Potential
- Arenas — Realms — Challenges — Impasses — Stages — Perspectives & Trajectories — Directions & Paths — Ascending — States — Growth Continuum — MAP

PATHFINDERS / NAVIGATORS
- Individual & Personal — Internal — Guidance & Orchestration — Collective & Societal
- All 12 Modes of Collective Modes — Counselor — Therapist — All Modes — All Modes — Providence
- Psychiatrist — Growth Center — Integral Life Guide — Psychologist
- Mediation Center — Orchestration — Spiritual Guide — Guidance — CAPTAIN — NAVIGATOR

Appendix A2.
Beyond Ken Wilber:
How AQAL Became ADAPT

The Human Odyssey, the book you are now reading, began with Ken Wilber. Ken Wilber is a very hip and popular modern philosopher and systems theorist – a very bright, self-educated thinker (now in his 50's) who has founded a whole movement called **Integral Theory**. Integral Theory in simplest terms is an effort to merge and synthesize all systems of Development (ranging from biological growth, to psychological development, to human evolution) into one grand system that summarizes the fundamental nature of reality. To its devotees, Integral Theory is known as the '**Theory of Everything**.'

In the course of our investigations, we became fascinated with a particular aspect of Integral Theory -- how it applies to our own Personal Growth and to all forms of Human Development. However, as we began exploring the nuances of Integral Theory in this context, we discovered a number of potential improvements on Wilber's work – improvements that help to explain human behavior better, and that help us to apply the theory in our own lives.

In this section, we describe how Wilber's all-encompassing theory (called **AQAL**) became an even more comprehensive Model of Human Development (our own **ADAPT**). Over the next two pages, we first begin with an outline of the points we will cover.

In Appendix A2, we show how Ken Wilber's AQAL Model of Human Development evolved into our own more refined and complete Model, called ADAPT. Then we show how the highly conceptual ADAPT evolved into the highly symbolic Archetypal Life Journey (see also Appx B2). For further background on Ken Wilber, refer to the other Wilber Appendices (A1, A3-9) – as well as Wilber's books in the Resources appendix (C2). For a full-length treatment of Wilber's Model of Human Development and its parallels to the ADAPT Model, see the authors' study *The Fundamental Ken Wilber* (IntegralWorld.net)

This section can seem somewhat technical and abstruse. It is intended primarily for those already familiar with Ken Wilber's work – or interested in learning more about it. Do not be concerned if you do not understand all the vocabulary and terms. They will gradually become clear as you absorb the concepts of this book.

Appendix A2.
The ADAPT Model of Human Development:
How It Was Derived, How We Can Use It

In Appendix A2, we describe how Wilber's all-encompassing theory (called **AQAL**) evolved into the authors' even more comprehensive Model of Human Development (called **ADAPT**). We will then explore the implications of ADAPT: Its parallels in the study of archetypal mythology, its application to our own Personal Growth, its broader applications in many spheres of human culture. We address these topics in the following order:

- **A2a. From AQAL to IOS.** Ken Wilber's famous AQAL Model of Human Development is just an abbreviation of his far more comprehensive Model, which we call his Integral Operating System (IOS). (page 21)

- **A2b. From IOS to ADAPT.** The many Parameters of Wilber's IOS break down conveniently into four categories, or Domains: Dimensions, Participants, Processes, and Pathfinders (page 22)

- **A2c. The Domains and Sectors of Wilber's AQAL.** When applying this four-part categorization, Wilber's more limited AQAL Model consists of four Dimensions and two Participants. (page 23)

- **A2d. The Domains and Sectors of Wilber's IOS.** Using the same form of categorization, Wilber's more extended IOS Model contains approximately 23 parameters from Dimensions, 18 from Participants, 18 from Processes, and five from Pathfinders. (page 24)

- **A2e. The Formulation of ADAPT.** The four Domains of this Model can be summarized by the acronym ADAPPPT: **A**ll **D**imensions, All **P**articipants, All **P**rocesses, All **P**athfinders, **T**ogether (**ADAPT** for short). (page 26)

- **A2f. Fine-Tuning ADAPT.** Once the basic ADAPT Model is established, it can be find-tuned by modifying some Parameters, adding others, and consolidating yet others. (page 27)

- **A2g. The Domains and Sectors of ADAPT.** The result is the comprehensive ADAPT Model described in this book – consisting of eight Dimensions, seven Participants, nine General Processes, and 12 Pathfinders. (page 28)

[continued next page]

Theory of Everything. "Wilber's Theory of Everything seeks to merge and synthesize all systems of Development (ranging from biological growth, to psychological development, to human evolution) into one grand system that summarizes the fundamental nature of reality."

ADAPT: How It was Derived, How We Can Use It (cont.)

✤ **A2h. The Systems ADAPT.** To complete the Model, one additional Domain is needed: Systems. Systems are eight ways that the other four Domains can combine to produce Growth. (page 29)

✤ **A2i. The Eight Systems: Circle Diagram.** To make the Domains and Systems easier to visualize, they can be depicted as a Circle Diagram – where the Circles are the Systems, and where the four quadrants of the Circles represent the four other Domains. (page 30)

✤ **A2j. The ADAPT Model: Circle Diagram.** With the basic form of the Circle Diagram established, it can now be filled in with the various Sectors that pertain to each Domain. The result is the entire ADAPT Model depicted as one grand Circle Diagram. (page 31)

✤ **A2k. ADAPT vs. Wilber: How Do They Compare?** With the ADAPT Model now complete, we now compare it point-for-point with Wilber's IOS. Of 443 points of comparison, the two Models differ in 256 instances – and the ADAPT Model is assessed to be an improvement in at least 169 cases. (page 32)

✤ **A2l. From Concept to Archetype.** Once the configuration of ADAPT was established, we made one more surprising discovery: Every Domain and Sector of the ADAPT conceptual model has a symbolic equivalent in the fundamental Archetype of human life – the Life Journey, or Human Odyssey. (page 34)

✤ **A2m. From Abstract Theory to Personal Revelation.** In the process of deriving ADAPT, we found it transformed from a stimulating intellectual exercise into a detailed blueprint on how to live a life that is richly satisfying and rewarding. (page 36)

✤ **A2n. From Revelation to Application.** Aside from its personal benefits, we found the ADAPT Model to have important real-world applications: Real-life applications for parents, teachers, counselors, etc. Broader societal applications in such diverse

The Power of AQAL. "The AQAL Model created a sensation in the intellectual world, because of its vast explanatory power."

A2a. From AQAL to IOS

WILBER'S AQAL

Ken Wilber's famous **AQAL Model** has been the source of much confusion. The AQAL acronym is not (nor was it intended to be) an adequate summary of Wilber's Model of Human Development. It is merely a convenient and catchy enumeration of two of its more prominent features – *Quadrants* and *Levels* (with *Lines*, *States*, *Self*, and/or *Types* often added in).

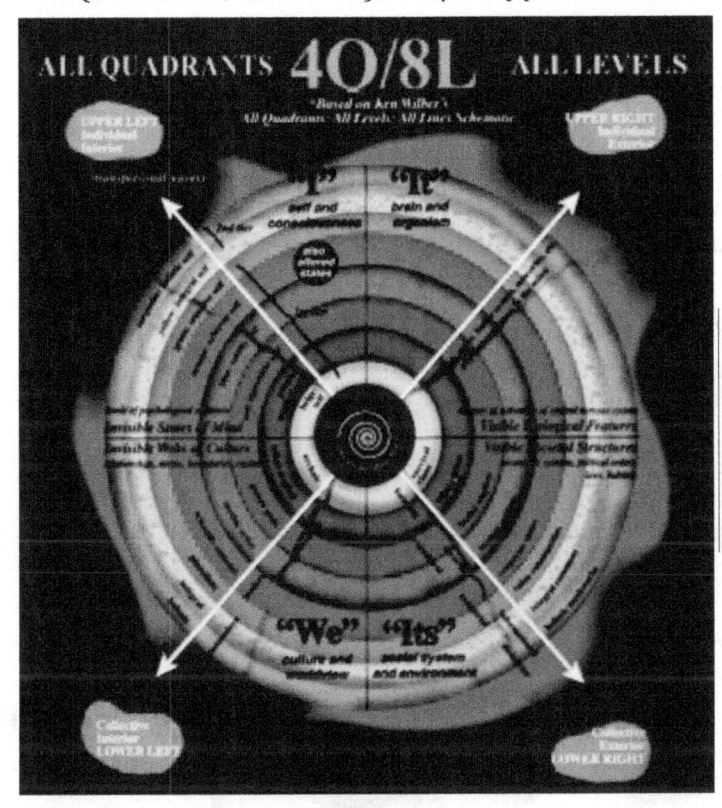

Ken Wilber's AQAL. Ken Wilber's basic AQAL Model ('All Quadrants, All Levels') is often depicted as a circle diagram – where the circles are the Levels (our 'Stages') and the four sections are the Quadrants (our 'Perspectives')

WILBER'S IOS

Behind Wilber's AQAL is a far broader, more comprehensive Growth Model. That Model is never explicitly defined in Wilber's work, yet serves as the basis for many of his pronouncements. We refer to that Model as Wilber's **Integral Operating System** (or **IOS**).

So, what is Ken Wilber's Integral Operating System? What is Wilber's fundamental, all-inclusive conceptual platform for the study of Human Development? To answer these questions, we combed Wilber's *Integral Psychology* and other seminal works – finding over 50 distinct concepts Wilber considers essential for explaining Human Growth. Then, much like Wilber himself, we wrote these concepts on yellow pads, laid them out on the living room floor, and rearranged them in various combinations until they formed meaningful patterns.

A2b. From IOS to ADAPT

When we laid out Wilber's many concepts on Human Development where they could all be viewed, we made a surprising discovery. Each of Wilber's Developmental Parameters falls into one of four fundamental **Domains**:

- **Dimensions**. Where does the Growth take place? Where is our Growth headed? What are the various ways we can grow? The **Dimensions** are the various areas of human experience where Development can occur.

- **Participants**. Who does the growing? What aspects of our Identity, or Self, take part in our Growth? The **Participants** are the various aspects of Identity or Self that participate in the Growth process.

- **Processes**. How can our Growth be accomplished? By what Methods and Techniques do we implement our Growth? The **Processes** are the means by which our Growth takes place.

- **Pathfinders**. With whose assistance? Who can guide us through the maze of Growth possibilities? Who can help us coordinate and orchestrate the many strands of our Growth? The **Pathfinders** are the people and other resources that aid us in our Growth process.

Dimensions	**Participants**
Pathfinders	**Processes**

A2c. The Domains and Sectors of Wilber's AQAL

Using this mode of categorization, the six Parameters of Wilber's expanded AQAL Model consist of four Dimensions (*Quadrants*, *Levels*, *Lines*, and *States*) and two Participants (*Self* and *Types*).

DIMENSIONS
- Quadrants
- Levels
- Lines
- States

PARTICIPANTS
- Self
- Types

Pathfinders

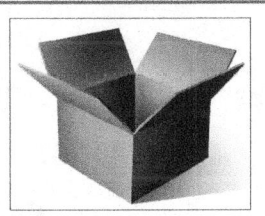

Processes

A2d. The Domains and Sectors of Wilber's IOS

The additional Parameters and concepts of Wilber's far more extensive Integral Operating System (IOS) likewise fall into these four categories. The four Domains of Dimensions, Participants, Processes, and Pathfinders encompass the following Wilber terms. (Original AQAL Parameters shown in blue. IOS Parameters are categorized according to the ADAPT Model.)

DIMENSIONS

- D. Great Nest
- ⊛ Map
- D1. Level, Stage, Wave
- ⊛ Trait
- D2. Transformation
- D1+2. Ladder
- ⊛ Correlative Structure
- ⊛ Holistic Pattern
- ⊛ Chakra
- ⊛ Cultural Stages
- ⊛ Spiral
- D3. Realm, Plane, Sphere, Domain, Ax-
- ⊛ Physiosphere/ Noosphere/ Theosphere
- ⊛ Terrestrial Realm/ Plane of Existence
- ⊛ Bodyself, Felt Body
- ⊛ Celestial Plane
- D4. Line, Stream
- D5. Quadrant
- D6. Height & Depth
- ⊛ U-Shaped Pattern
- D7. Pathology
- D8. State
- ⊛ Pre/Trans Fallacy

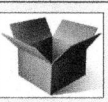

PATHFINDERS

- PF. Navigation
- ⊛ Integration
- PF9. Integral Institute
- PF10. Full-Spectrum Therapist
- PF12. Spirit-in-Action

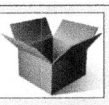

PARTICIPANTS

P1. Proximate & Distal Self
- Self-System

P2. Self, Ego
- Culture

P3. Type, Role
- Gender Type
- Voice
- Agency vs. Communion
- Eros vs. Agape
- Enneagram Type

P4. Subpersonality
- Shadow Self

P5. Functional Invariant

P7a. Core Self
- I-I Self, True Self
- Ultimate Subject, Antecedent Self

P7b. Witness
- Seer, Pure Consciousness, Spirit

PROCESSES

PPR1. Fulcrum, Milestone, Round
- Embedding
- Vertical Transformation

PPR3. Actualizing the Great Nest
- Evolution

PPR4. Uncovering
- Archeology of Self

PPR5. Socio-Cultural Evolution

PPR6. Horizontal Translation
- Metabolism

PR7. Inclusiveness

PPR8. Evolution & Involution
- Transcend & Include

PPR9. Waking Up
- Mysticism

PR1-35. Methodology
- Modules of Integral Life Practice (ILP)
- Therapies, Treatments

A2e. The Formulation of ADAPT

Thus, Wilber's own Integral Operating System is actually a very highly-developed (though incomplete) version of a new Developmental Model that is much more inclusive and far more integrated. Using an acronym based on the four Domains, we call this Model **ADAPPPT** (**'ADAPT'** for short*):

- **All Dimensions**
- **All Participants**
- **All Processes**
- **All Pathfinders**
- **Together (All Domains combined in one System**)**

(*For simplicity, the acronym **ADAPPPT** is condensed to **ADAPT**, and pronounced **"A'-Dapt"**. **The Domain of Together-ness ('Systems') will be discussed on page 29.)

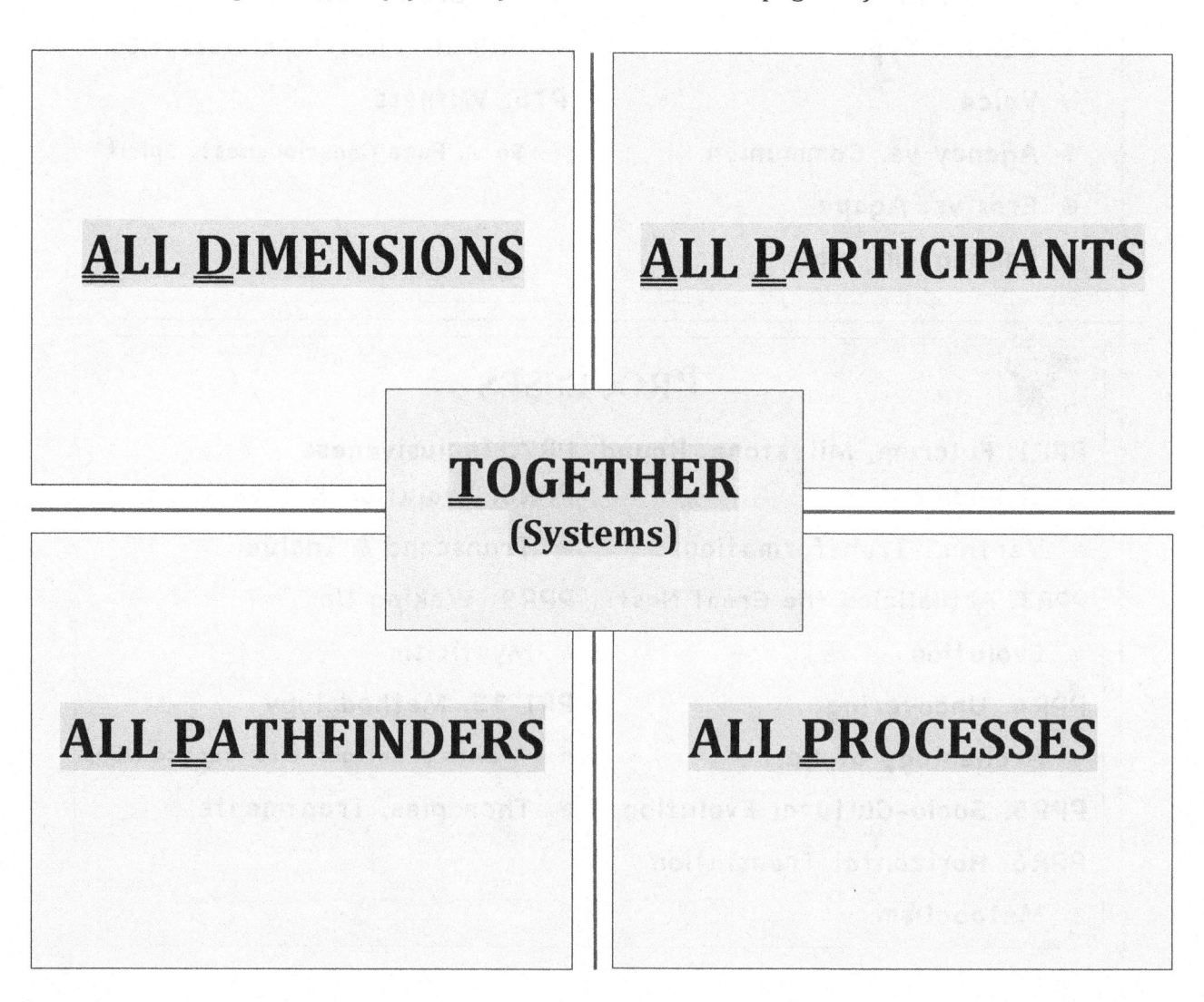

ALL DIMENSIONS	**ALL PARTICIPANTS**
ALL PATHFINDERS	**ALL PROCESSES**

TOGETHER (Systems)

A2f. Fine-Tuning ADAPT

The establishment of the basic ADAPT Model brought forth more questions: In addition to Wilber's concepts, were there any other Parameters that should be included? Were Wilber's pronouncements sufficiently clear, consistent, and correct? Were his concepts adequately organized, prioritized, and differentiated? By fine-tuning Wilber's Parameters and adding new Parameters from our own research and life experience, we completed the ADAPT Model.

THE CREATION OF ADAPT

In assembling, modifying, and expanding Wilber's IOS to create our ADAPT Model, we proceeded through the following steps:

- **Include All Wilber's Parameters**
  We searched Wilber's writings to find all his Parameters pertaining to Human Growth.

- **Categorize by Domain**
  We then categorized those Parameters according to the four Domains – Dimensions, Participants, Processes, and Pathfinders.

- **Sub-Categorize Within Each Domain**
  Within each Domain, we clustered Parameters that were related or similar.

- **Modify & Fine-Tune Some Parameters**
  Based upon additional research and our own personal experience, we modified some Parameters that appeared to need improvement.

- **Add New Parameters**
  Where gaps or discontinuities appeared within the set of Parameters, we added new Parameters to complete the picture.

The result was the complete and comprehensive ADAPT Model we display on the next page.

For details on the many improvements we made, see Appendix A6.

A2g. The Domains and Sectors of ADAPT

When we made the necessary modifications of Wilber, the result was the comprehensive ADAPT Model described in this book – a Model consisting of 8 Dimensions, 7 Participants, 9 General Processes, and 12 Pathfinders:

8 DIMENSIONS

D1. Stages
D2. Transitions
D3. Realms
D4. Arenas
D5. Perspectives & Paths
D6. Directions & Trajectories
D7. Impediments
D8. Transcendent States

7 PARTICIPANTS

P1. Self System
P2. Individual & Collective Selves
P3. Types & Personae
P4. Shadow Self
P5. Functional Constituents
P6. Multiple Identities
P7. Divine Presence

12 PATHFINDERS

PF1. Parents & Family
PF2. Society & Culture
PF3. Holistic Growth Situations
PF4. Authorities
PF5. Long-Term Partner
PF6. Counselor, Coach, or Therapist
PF7. Spiritual Guide
PF8. Mentor
PF9. Growth Centers
PF10. Integral Life Guide
PF11. Internal Navigator
PF12. Providence

9 GENERAL PROCESSES

PPR1. Transition Cycle
PPR2. Shadow Cycle
PPR3. Actualization Growth
PPR4. Restoration Growth
PPR5. Collective Growth
PPR6. Horizontal Growth
PPR7. Perspective Growth
PPR8. Evolution & Involution
PPR9. Awakening

A2h. The Systems of ADAPT

It's all well and good to enumerate the factors that contribute to Growth. But how do these factors relate to each other? How does each factor contribute to the Growth process? How do the various factors combine to produce Growth?

In answer to these questions, we discovered a fundamental mechanism of Human Growth we call the System. A **System** is a set of Dimensions, Participants, Processes, and Pathfinders that work together to produce Growth.

As it turns out, there are eight different Systems – each of which generates its own kind of Growth. These Systems are described in detail in the *Systems* section (S1-8). In the table below, we briefly outline these eight Systems. On the following two pages, we show how all eight Systems can be depicted visually on a single Circle Diagram.

THE EIGHT SYSTEMS OF ADAPT

❀ **Individual Growth**
The System that moves Individuals from one Stage to the next.

❀ **Collective Growth**
The System that moves Groups from one Stage to the next.

❀ **Actualization Growth**
The System that takes us through a whole series of Stages and Transitions.

❀ **Restoration Growth**
The System that returns to an earlier Stage to restore functioning – so that normal Actualization Growth may resume.

❀ **Horizontal Growth**
The three sub-Systems that facilitate Growth within a Stage.

❀ **Perspective Growth**
The two sub-Systems that implement Growth by shifting or broadening one's Perspective.

❀ **Evolution & Involution Growth**
The three sub-Systems that involve Growth that is not only Upward & Outward, but also Downward & Inward.

❀ **Spiritual Growth**
The System that enables us to Awaken to universal truths that unchanging and eternal.

A2i. The Eight Systems: Circle Diagram

In an effort to convey the unity of our conception, we found that we could display every feature of the Model on a single Circle Diagram. In this Diagram, each concentric circle represents one of the eight Systems, while the quadrants of those circles represent the four Domains – Dimensions, Participants, Processes, and Pathfinders:

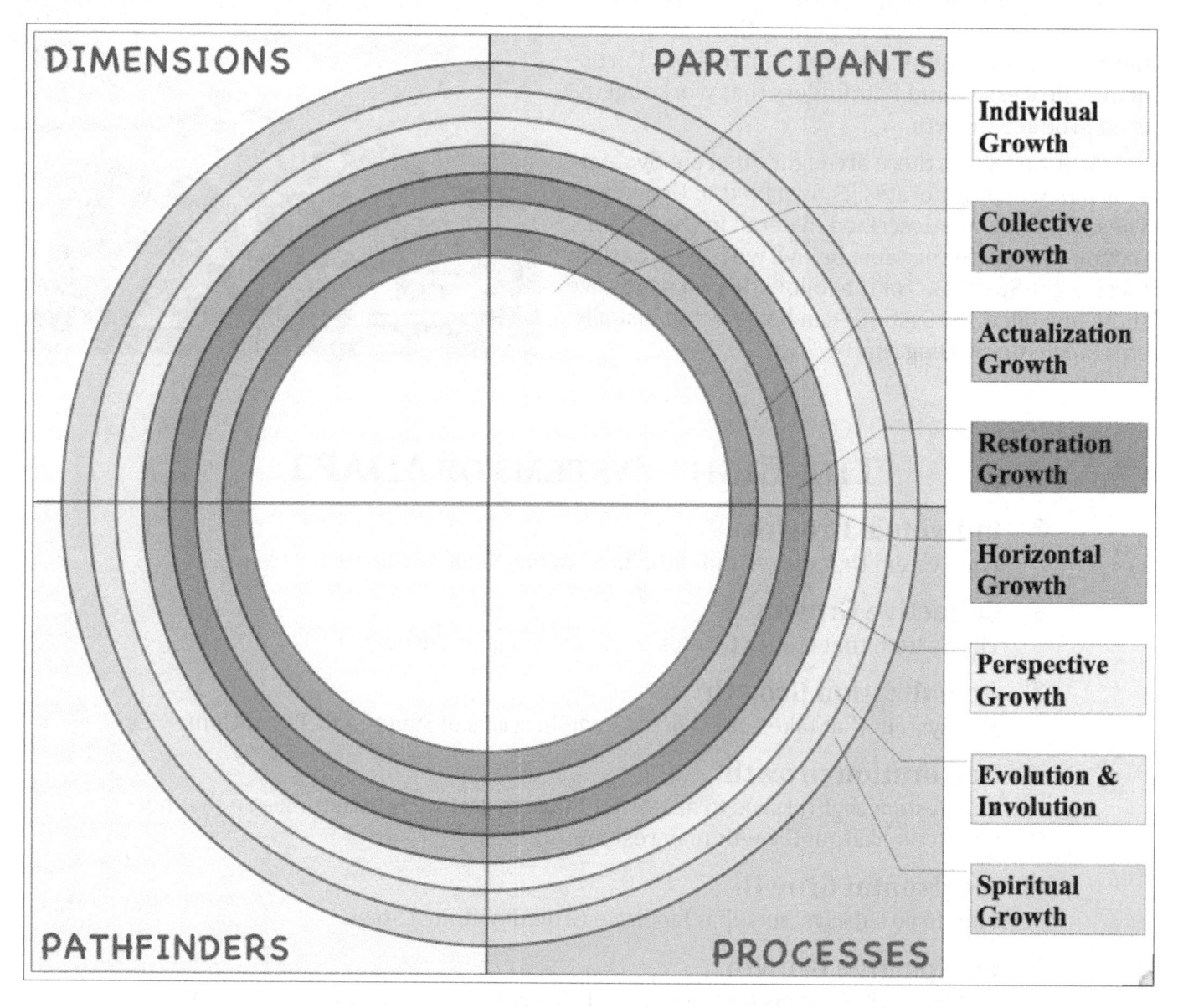

DIMENSIONS | **PARTICIPANTS**

- Individual Growth
- Collective Growth
- Actualization Growth
- Restoration Growth
- Horizontal Growth
- Perspective Growth
- Evolution & Involution
- Spiritual Growth

PATHFINDERS | **PROCESSES**

A2j. The ADAPT Model: Circle Diagram

We then filled in the various Parameters that pertain to each Domain and Sector (p. 28). The result is a comprehensive Diagram that summarizes the entire ADAPT Model.

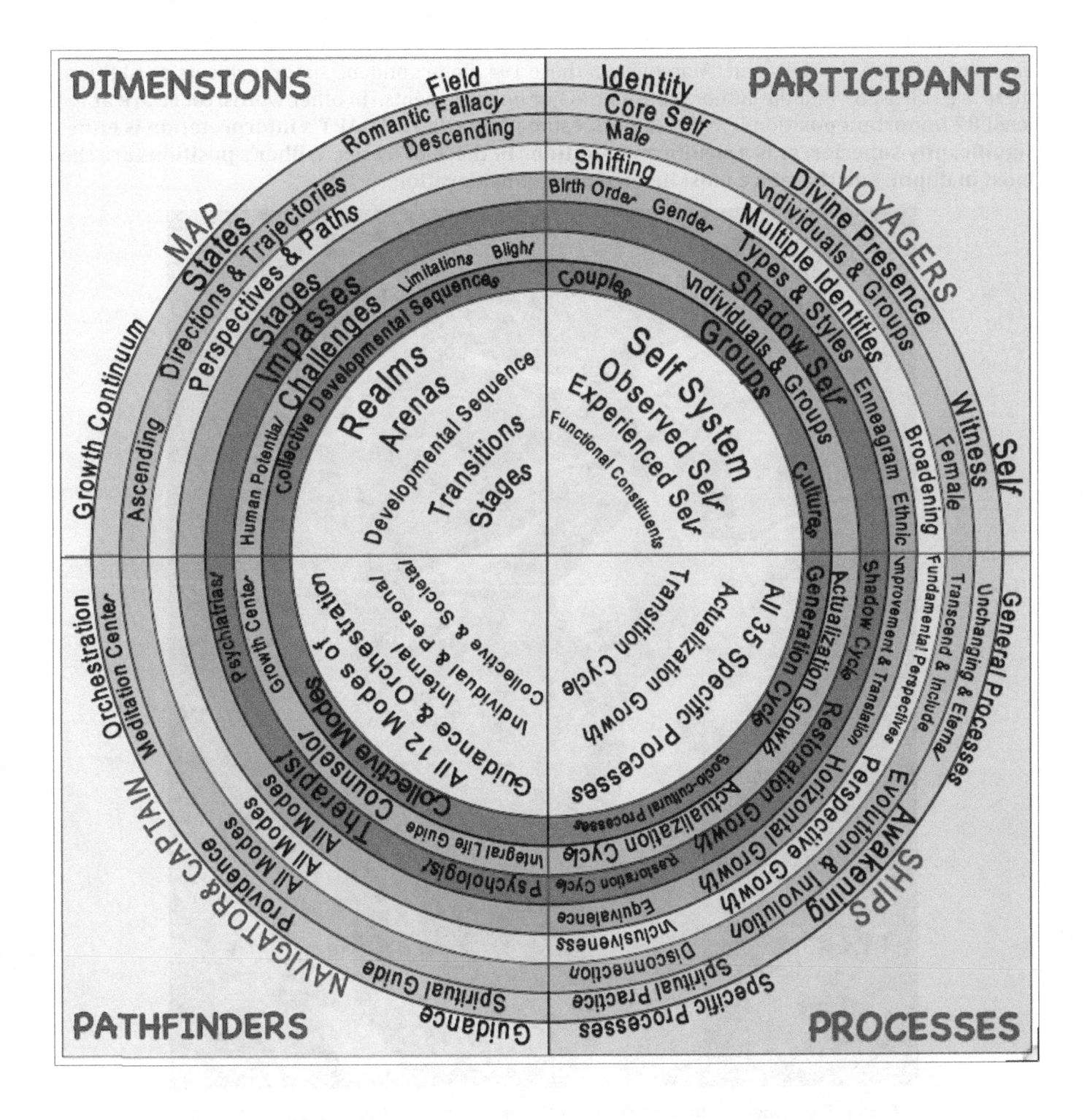

The full Circle Diagrams for both ADAPT and Wilber are presented in Appx A1. For further details on the construction of this Circle Diagram, refer to the Systems section (S1-8).

A2k. ADAPT vs. Wilber: How Do They Compare?

With the ADAPT Model complete, we wanted to assess its validity. To do so, we performed point-by-point comparisons between Wilber's positions and those of ADAPT. Of 491 points of comparison, we found 292 conceptions where the two Models take significantly differing positions. Of these, we found at least 194 instances where (in the authors' opinion) ADAPT's position has at least a 90% likelihood of being an improvement. Moreover, of those 194 high-confidence improvements or additions, there are at least 87 that the authors consider major improvements. In other words, **there are at least 87 important positions** (in the authors' estimation) **where ADAPT's interpretation is either significantly superior, or is a significant addition. In these 87 cases, Wilber's positions are the most in doubt, and therefore most in need of re-consideration.**

Comparing Models. The best Model is the one that simplifies and clarifies – yet retains the most accuracy and accounts for the most detail.

For a full set of comparisons between the two Models, including statistics on differences, see *ADAPT and Wilber Compared* (Appx A6).

A2. How AQAL Became ADAPT. Page 33.

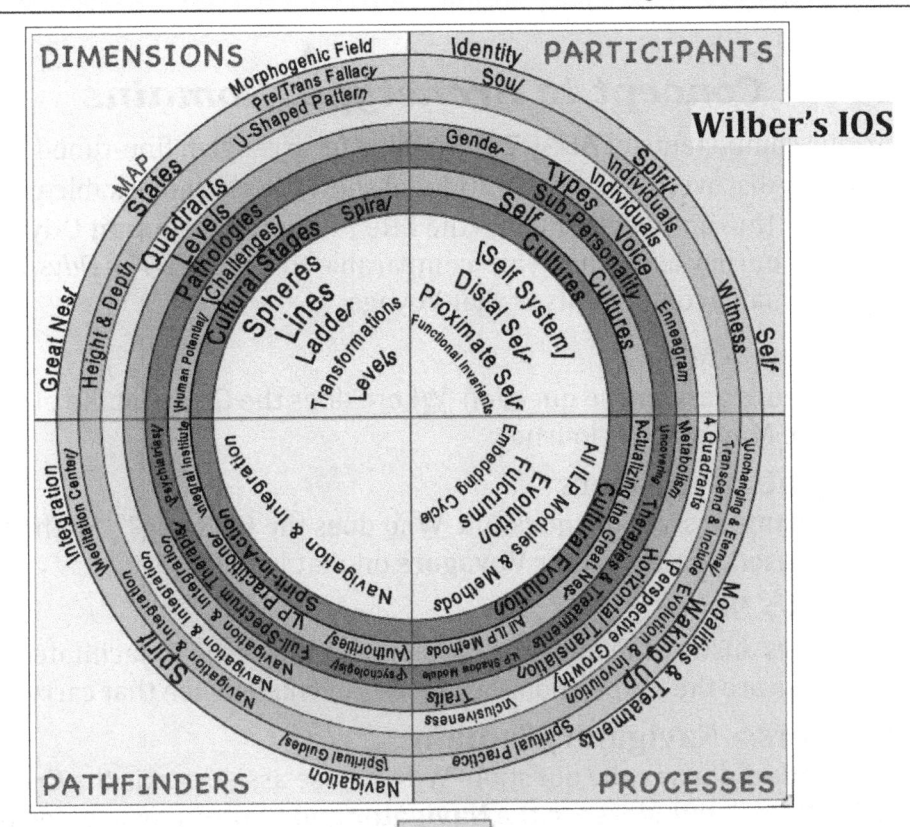

Wilber's IOS

DIMENSIONS	PARTICIPANTS
PATHFINDERS	PROCESSES

491 Comparisons
292 Improvements
194 Most Certain Improvements
87 Major Improvements

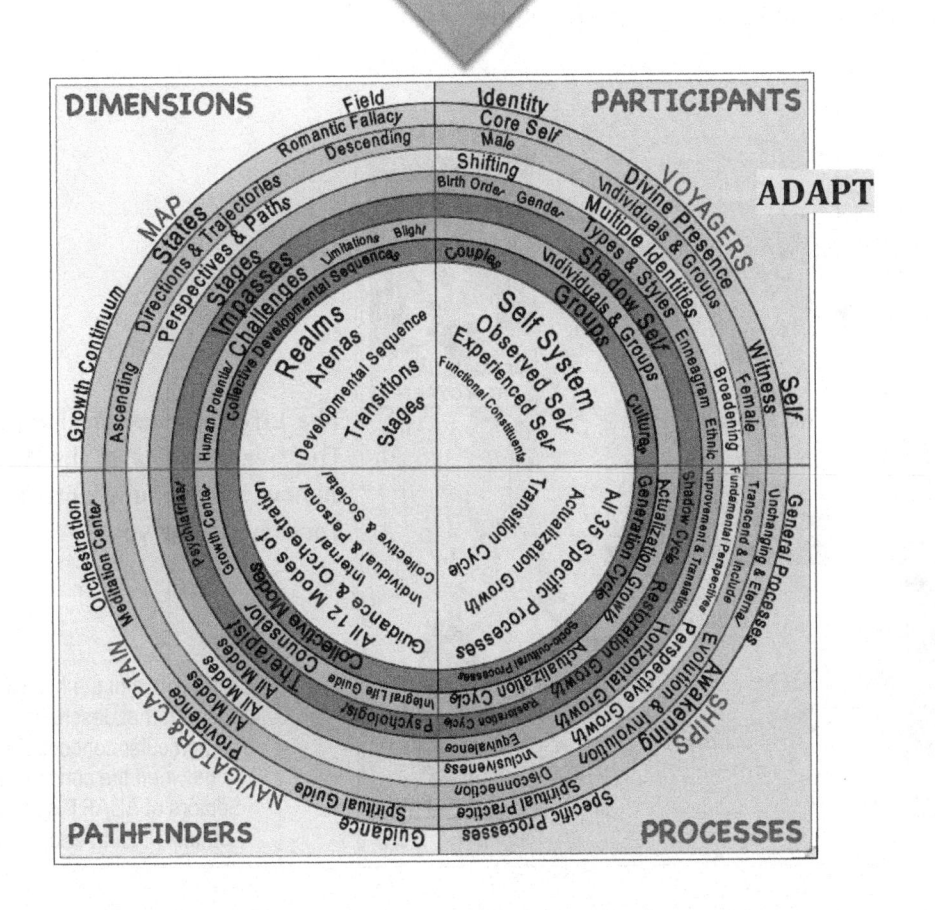

ADAPT

DIMENSIONS	PARTICIPANTS
PATHFINDERS	PROCESSES

A2l. From Concept to Archetype: Domains

As the various components of ADAPT were filled in, arranged, fine-tuned, and evaluated, we made one more surprising discovery: The ADAPT Model shows some remarkable parallels to the fundamental Archetype of Human Development – the **Life Journey**, or **Human Odyssey**. For instance, if we conceive of the Life Journey as a sea voyage comparable to Homer's *The Odyssey*, the five Domains of ADAPT become the major components of that Voyage:

- **Dimensions > Map**
  The Dimensions answer the question 'Where does the Growth take place?'. So the Dimensions are the **Map** of Life's Journey.

- **Participants > Voyagers**
  The Participants answer the question 'Who does the Growing?'. So the Participants are the crew, passengers, and other **Voyagers** on that Journey.

- **Processes > Ships**
  The Processes answer the question 'What means are used to facilitate the Growth?'. So the Processes are the **Ships** and other modes of conveyance that carry us on that Voyage.

- **Pathfinders > Navigator/Captain**
  The Pathfinders answer the question 'With whose assistance is the Growth brought about?'. So the Pathfinders are the **Navigator** and **Captain**, who guide our Ships and orchestrate our Journey.

- **Systems > Shipping System**
  The Systems answer the question 'How do the various factors work together to produce Growth?'. So the Systems are the **Shipping System** (docks, warehouses, shipyards, port officials, administrative personnel, etc.) that provides the coordination and support necessary to make such Voyages possible.

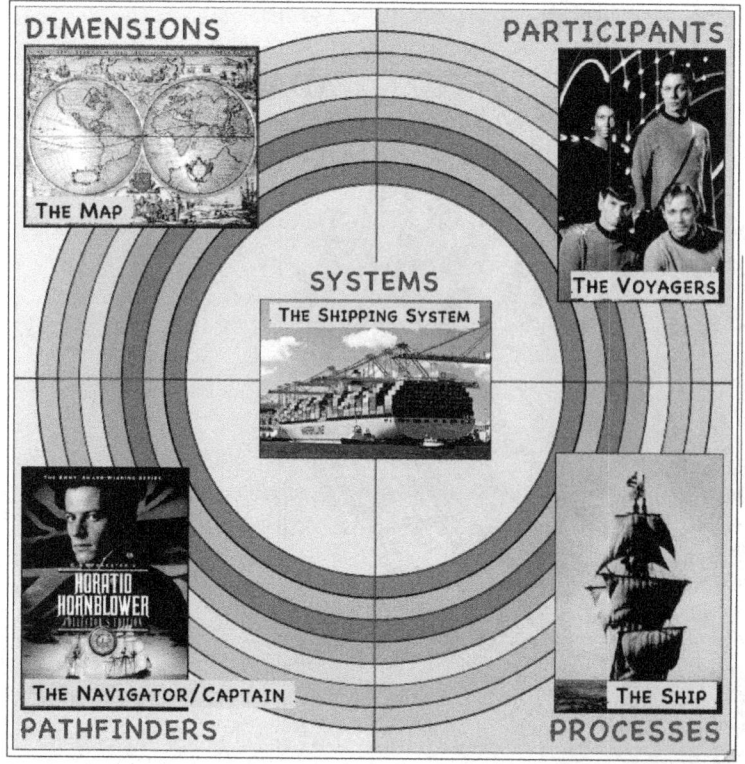

The Life Journey Archetype: Domains. The five Domains of the ADAPT Model all have their equivalents in the Life Journey Archetype.

Each section of the Main Text includes a textbox in the upper-left that describes the Life Journey equivalent to that particular concept. The full set of correspondences between the conceptual and symbolic Domains & Sectors of ADAPT is presented in the Campbell Appendix (B2a-b) and in the Overview section (OV).

A2. How AQAL Became ADAPT. Page 35.

From Concept to Archetype: Sectors

Once we had discovered the symbolic equivalents of the five Domains, we then expanded the Life Journey Archetype to encompass all the Sectors of ADAPT. Using Homer's *The Odyssey* as our primary mythic example, we asked: 'For each Sector of ADAPT, what is the symbolic or archetypal equivalent?' When we did so, we discovered a remarkably exact set of correspondences between the conceptual and the symbolic versions of ADAPT.

These and many other parallels between model and Archetype suggest that ADAPT is not just one theory among many that purport to describe Human Development. Rather, **ADAPT is the abstracted version of a <u>universal</u> model that people have used since the dawn of time to describe the progressions of human life.** These parallels to the Archetype confirm the validity of the ADAPT Model, and also provide an analytic source for further insights about that Model.

The Life Journey Archetype: Sectors. The 40+ Domains and Sectors of the ADAPT Model all have their equivalents in the Life Journey Archetype.

A2m. From Abstract Theory To Personal Revelation

As the various components of ADAPT were filled in, arranged, fine-tuned, and evaluated, we made one more surprising discovery -- a very personal one: As children of the 1960's, we have always been bold experimenters. Over the course of 30+ years, we have continually explored a dizzying array of alternative lifestyles, advanced academics, cutting-edge therapies, innovative methods of raising children, alternative forms of medicine and healing, a succession of colorful careers and business ventures, radical political movements, and esoteric religious practices – all with an insatiable drive to become healthier, happier, clearer, wiser, more successful, more influential, more authentic, more free.

With a rush of self-revelation, we discovered that our ADAPT Model explained, illuminated, and unified all these diverse experiments in life improvement. Through ADAPT, we could reflect back on our frenetic quest for Nirvana – using our Model to understand how to build a strong and supportive marriage; how to raise happy, healthy children; how to pursue a successful and significant career; and how to orchestrate our own Growth and self-improvement. In short, **the ADAPT Model was transformed from a stimulating intellectual exercise into a detailed blueprint on how to live a life that is richly satisfying and rewarding.**

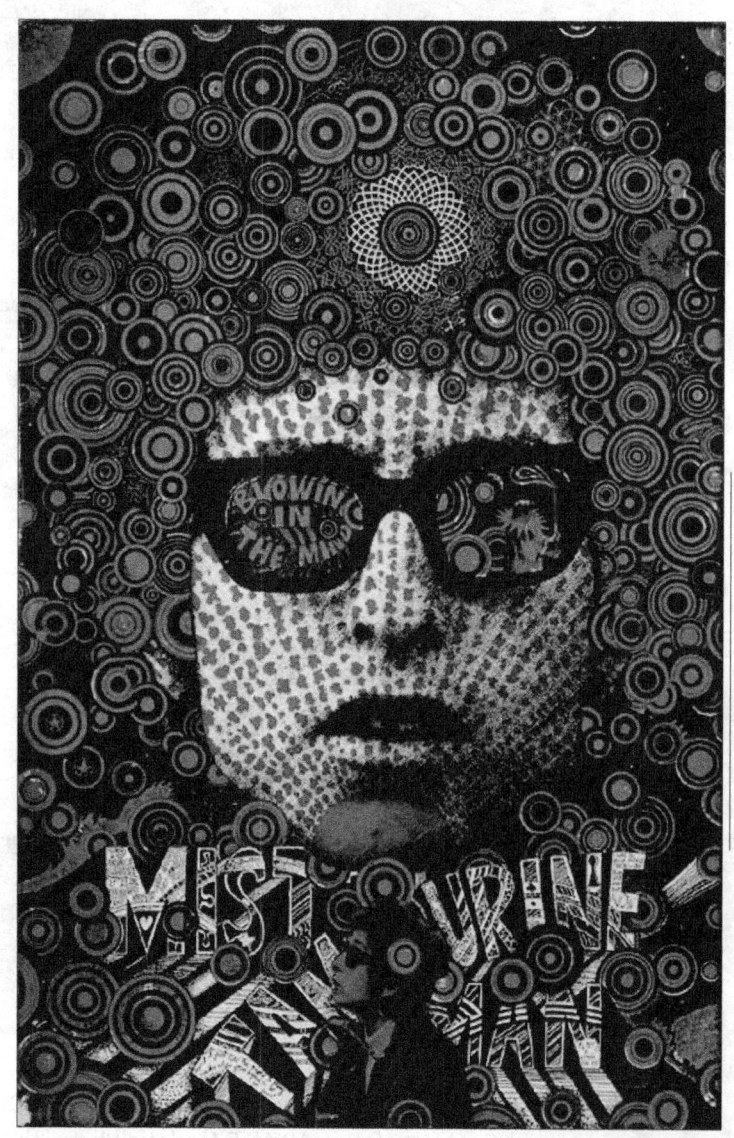

Hey Mr. Tambourine Man
As children of the 60's, we followed our Tambourine Man through innumerable experiences in personal growth, self-exploration, and lifestyle experimentation. As the Life Journey Archetype has shown us, our search was all part of one grand Quest – our personal Hero's Journey.

For details on the parallels between the ADAPT Model and the personal Life Journey, see *Overview of ADAPT* (OV) and the Campbell Appendices (B1-2). For details on Hugh Martin's personal journey, see the Preface to the Main Text of this book -- as well as the authors' book-length study *The Processes According to Esalen* (IntegralWorld.net).

A2n. From Revelation To Application

Any theory that yields so many original insights on the human condition will also have many valuable applications. Thus, we found the ADAPT Model to be an indispensable tool for the crucial, real-life applications of Integral Theory. At an individual and personal level, those applications include Personal Growth, parenting, teaching, counseling, organizational consulting, and academic research. At a social and cultural level, the range of applications is immensely broader – including psychology, history, science, economics, ethics, art, literature, health, and worldview. In the course of this book, we will present concepts that explain and illuminate all these important fields.

For further details on the breadth, depth, and meaning of Human Development, see *The Scope of Human Development* (IN1).

Appendix A3.
Ken Wilber's ADAPT:
How Wilber's *Integral Psychology* Parallels ADAPT

Although AQAL gets most of the attention, Ken Wilber propounds a far more complex and sophisticated Model of Human Development we call his Integral Operating System (IOS). Wilber's IOS consists of over 50 Parameters he considers important for describing Human Growth (see Appx A2d). Although the IOS is never explicitly defined, its components may be derived from Wilber's writings – especially his seminal work, *Integral Psychology* (*IP*).

The following tables present a representative selection of Wilber's pronouncements on Human Development (shown in *italics*). Those pronouncements are matched to the corresponding Domains and Sectors of the ADAPT Model (shown in **bold**). **As these tables demonstrate, Wilber's IOS is actually a very extensive (though incomplete) version of the ADAPT Model itself.**

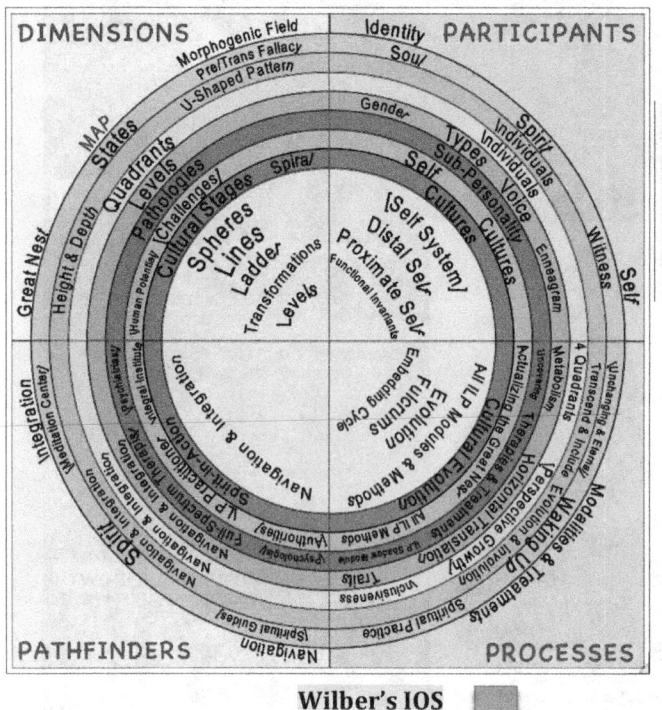

Wilber's ADAPT. Ken Wilber's pronouncements on Human Development correspond to the ADAPT Model almost point-for-point.

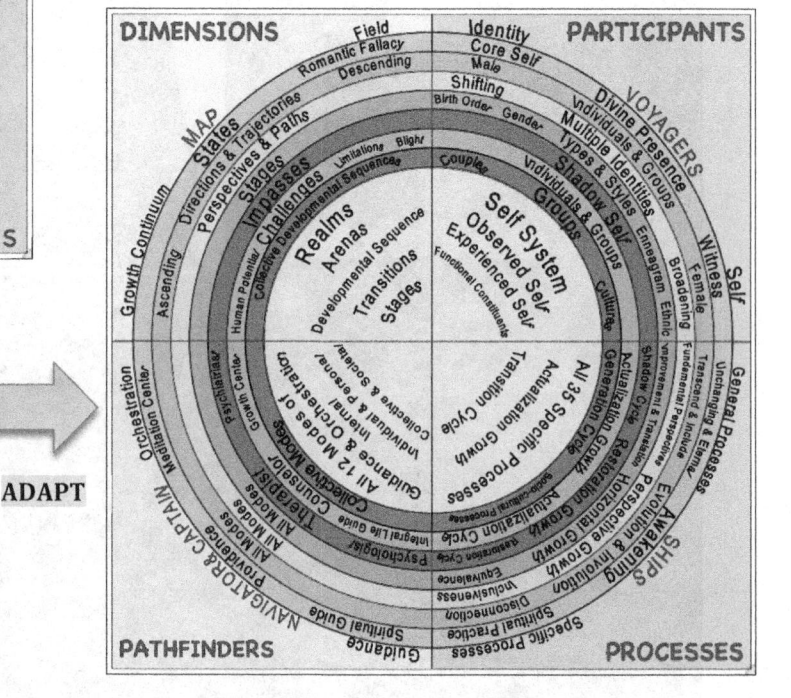

Wilber's IOS

ADAPT

In this Appendix, by quoting from Wilber's own writings, we demonstrate that Wilber's IOS is actually a very extensive (though incomplete) version of ADAPT. These parallels are also shown throughout the Main Text – in the tan textboxes that accompany each feature of the ADAPT Model. For a more complete collection of parallels, see the authors' study *The Fundamental Ken Wilber*, on IntegralWorld.net. *** For full-size versions of the above Circle Diagrams, see Appx A1.

WILBER'S ADAPT

ADAPT. In devising an effective program of Personal Growth, we need four Domains -- Dimensions (of the Growth Continuum), Participants (in the Growth process), Processes (of Growth), and Pathfinders (who guide and orchestrate our Growth process).

... the major components... of the evolution of consciousness: the basic levels, structures, or waves in the Great Nest (matter, body, mind, soul, spirit); the developmental lines or streams (moral, aesthetic, religious, cognitive, affective, etc.) that move relatively independently through the great waves; the states, or temporary states of consciousness (such as peak experiences, dream states, and altered states); the self, which is the seat of identity, will, and defenses, and which has to navigate, balance, and integrate all the various levels, lines, and states that it en-counters; and the self-related lines, which are the developmental lines most intimately connected with the self (such as the self's central identity, its morals, and its needs). In short: waves, streams, states, self, and self-streams. (IP 89)

WILBER'S DIMENSIONS

HUMAN GROWTH. Moving and progressing along the Growth Continuum.

...a person's deepest drive -- the major drive of which all others are derivative -- is the drive to actualize the entire Great Nest through the vehicle of one's own being, so that one becomes, in full realization, a vehicle of Spirit shining radiantly into the world, as the entire world. (IP 190)

D1-8. GROWTH CONTINUUM. A field consisting of the eight Dimensions of Growth.

What the Great Nest represents, in my opinion, is most basically a great morphogenetic field or developmental space -- stretching from matter to mind to spirit -- in which various potentials unfold into actuality. (IP 12)

D1-8. DIMENSIONS. The various areas of our life where our Growth takes place – and the various features of that Growth.

[Wilber refers to the Dimensions as a Map of Consciousness.]

D1. STAGES. The levels of development, maturity, enlivenment, or enlightenment through which we pass as we grow.

[See Developmental Sequence (D1+2).

D2. TRANSITIONS. The quantum leaps that take us from one Stage to the next.

[Wilber refers to Transitions as Vertical Transformation. See Developmental Sequence (D1+2).]

D1+2. DEVELOPMENTAL SEQUENCE. An alternating series of Stages and Transitions.

The traditions often divide life's overall journey into the "Seven Ages of a Person," where each age involves adaptation to one of the seven basic levels of consciousness (such as the seven chakras: physical; emotional-sexual; lower, middle, and higher mental; soul; and spirit), and each of the seven stages is said to take seven years. (IP 17-18)

These three early waves of self-development can be summarized fairly simply. The self starts out relatively undifferentiated from its environment That is, it cannot easily tell where its body stops and the physical environment begins (this is the start of fulcrum-1). Somewhere during the first year, the infant learns that if it bites a blanket, it does not hurt, but if it bites its thumb, it hurts: there is a difference between body and matter. The infant differentiates its body from the environment, and thus its identity switches from fusion with the material world to an identity with the emotional-feeling body (which begins fulcrum-a). As the conceptual mind begins to emerge and develop (especially around 3 to 6 years), the child eventually differentiates the conceptual mind and the emotional body (this is fulcrum-3). The proximate self's identity has thus gone from matter to body to early mind (and we can see that it is well on its way through the waves in the Great Nest). (IP 92-96)

D1+2. DEVELOPMENTAL SEQUENCE. An alternating series of Stages and Transitions. (cont.)

The worldview of both late F-3 and early F-4 is mythic, which means that these early roles are often those found displayed in the mythological gods and goddesses, which represent the archetypal roles available to individuals. That is, these are simply some of the collective, concrete roles available to men and women -- roles such as a strong father, a caring mother, a warrior, a trickster, the anima, animus, and so forth, which are often embodied in the concrete figures of the world's mythologies (Persephone, Demeter, Zeus, Apollo, Venus, Indra, etc.)...

With the emergence of formal-reflexive capacities, the self can plunge yet deeper, moving from conventional/conformist roles and a mythic-membership self (the persona), to a postconventional, global, worldcentric self -- namely, the mature ego (conscientious and individualistic, to use Loevinger's version). No longer just us (my tribe, my clan, my group, my nation), but all of us (all human beings without exception, regardless of race, religion, sex, or creed). Consciousness cuts loose from its parochial surfaces and dives into that which is shared by a global humanity, insisting on forms of compassion that are universal, impartial, just and fair for all...

As vision-logic begins to emerge, postconventional awareness deepens into fully universal, existential concerns: life and death, authenticity, full bodymind integration, self-actualization, global awareness, holistic embrace -- all summarized as the emergence of the centaur (e.g., Loevinger's autonomous and integrated stages). In the archeological journey to the Self, the personal realm's exclusive reign is coming to an end, starting to be peeled off a radiant Spirit, and that universal radiance begins increasingly to shine through, rendering the self more and more transparent... (IP 102-108)

D1+2b-c. INTERNAL DEVELOPMENTAL SEQUENCE. The Stages & Transitions we proceed through in the Internal Realms of Psyche, Body, and Spirit.

... although around two dozen basic structures can be readily identified (e.g., form, sensation, perception, exocept, impulse, image, symbol, endocept, concept, rule . . .), nonetheless they can be condensed into around seven to ten functional groupings which reflect easily recognizable stages... These functional groupings of basic structures I represent with some very general names: (1)sensorimotor, (2) phantasmic-emotional (or emotional-sexual), (3) rep-mind (short for the representational mind, similar to general preoperational thinking, or "preop"), (4) the rule/role mind (similar to concrete operational thinking, or "conop"), (5) formal-reflexive (similar to formal operational, or "formop"), (6) vision-logic, (7) psychic, (8) subtle,) (9) causal, and (1o) nondual. (IP 18-19)

DD1+2. COLLECTIVE DEVELOPMENTAL SEQUENCE. The Developmental Sequence for Groups, ranging from Couples to whole Cultures.

... Graves proposed a profound and elegant system of human development… "Briefly, what I am proposing is that the psychology of the mature human being is an unfolding, emergent, oscillating spiraling process marked by progressive subordination of older, lower-order behavior systems to newer, higher-order systems as man's existential problems change. Each successive stage, wave, or level of existence is a state through which people pass on their way to other states of being. When the human is centralized in one state of existence… he or she has a psychology which is particular to that state. His or her feelings, motivations, ethics and values, biochemistry, degree of neurological activation, learning system, belief systems, conception of mental health, ideas as to what mental illness is and how it should be treated, conceptions of and preferences for management, education, economics, and political theory and practice are all appropriate to that state." ... (IP40)

DD1+2b. CULTURAL EVOLUTION. The Developmental Sequence that occurs in whole Cultures.

The magical/shamanic mode was the dominant form of consciousness for the largest period of humanity's stay on earth thus far, reigning from perhaps as early as 500,000 years BCE to around 10,000 BCE, with its peak period probably from around 50,000 to 7000 BCE. As the average mode evolved from magic into mythic (beginning roughly around 10,000 BCE), and nature elementals and polytheistic figments increasingly gave way to a conception of one God/dess underlying the manifold world, the figure of the saint eventually became the dominant spiritual realizer...As the average, collective mode of consciousness evolved from mythic to mental (beginning around the sixth century BCE), the most advanced mode evolved from subtle to causal, and the sage, more than the saint, embodied this growing tip of consciousness ...The great Nondual traditions began around 200 CE, especially with such figures as Nagarjuna and Plotinus; but these traditions, particularly in their advanced forms as Tantra, began to flower in India around the eighth to the fourteenth century (coincident with the first collective or average-mode glimmers of vision-logic, exemplified in the West with Florence and the rise of Humanism, circa fourteenth century). (IP 154-156)

D3. REALMS. The four major spheres of human experience where Growth can occur – Everyday Life, Psyche, Body, Spirit.

... as Huston Smith pointed out (Forgotten Truth), the body level of consciousness corresponds with the terrestrial realm or plane of existence; the mind level of consciousness corresponds with the intermediate realm or plane of existence; the soul level of consciousness corresponds with the celestial plane of existence; and the spirit level of consciousness corresponds with the infinite plane of existence... in Eye to Eye I refer to them using the terms sensibilia, intelligibilia, and transcendelia (i.e., the objects in those planes or realms). The eyes of flesh, mind, and contemplation are the epistemological levels correlated with (and disclosing) those ontological planes of sensibilia, intelligibilia, and transcendelia. (IP Note 8:2)

D3a. REALM: EVERYDAY LIFE. The external phases of accomplishment or achievement that occur as we progress through the biological Life Cycle.

Several stage conceptions, such as Levinson's, deal with the "seasons" of horizontal translation, not stages of vertical transformation... (IP Note 4:3)

D3c. REALM: BODY. The internal phases of physical Enlivenment that occur as we activate and connect the Energy Centers of our body.

..."body" can mean the biological organism as a whole, including the brain (the neocortex, the limbic system, reptilian stem, etc.) -- in other words, "body" can mean the entire Upper-Right quadrant, which I will call "the organism." I will also refer to the organism as the "Body," capital B... Thus, the brain is in the Body, which is the commonly accepted scientific view (and an accurate description of the Upper-Right quadrant). But "body" can also mean, and for the average person does mean, the subjective feelings, emotions, and sensations of the felt body. When the typical person says "My mind is fighting my body," he means his will is fighting some bodily desire or inclination (such as sex or food). In other words, in this common usage, "body" means the lower levels of one's own interior. ...I have labeled this as "body" in the Upper-Left quadrant, which simply means the feelings and emotions of the felt body (versus the Body, which means the entire objective organism). (IP 177-178)

D3d. REALM: SPIRIT. The internal phases or modes of spiritual Enlightenment that occur as we awaken ourselves to the Divine Presence or open ourselves to the Holy Spirit.

One of the thorniest of questions is whether spirituality itself necessarily unfolds in stages. This is an extremely touchy issue. Nonetheless, as I have often suggested, this question depends in large measure on how we define "spirituality." There are at least five very different definitions, two of which seem to involve stages, and three of which do not. (1) Spirituality involves the highest levels of any of the developmental lines. (2) Spirituality is the sum total of the highest levels of the developmental lines. (3) Spirituality is itself a separate developmental line. (4) Spirituality is an attitude (such as openness or love) that you can have at whatever stage you are at. (5) Spirituality basically involves peak experiences, not stages. (IP 129-134)

D4. ARENAS. The specific areas of activity within each Realm where Growth takes place.

Through the basic levels or waves in the Great Nest flow some two dozen relatively independent developmental lines or streams. These different developmental lines include morals, affects, self-identity, psychosexuality, cognition, ideas of the good, role taking, socio-emotional capacity, creativity, altruism, several lines that can be called "spiritual" (care, openness, concern, religious faith, meditative stages), joy, communicative competence, modes of space and time, death-seizure, needs, worldviews, logico-mathematical competence, kinesthetic skills, gender identity, and empathy ... These lines are "relatively independent," which means that, for the most part, they can develop independently of each other, at different rates, with a different dynamic, and on a different time schedule. (IP 28)

D5. PERSPECTIVES & PATHS. The four basic points-of-view from which any Growth experience can be observed.

... these four classes represented the interior and the exterior of the individual and the collective... The upper half of the diagram is individual, the lower half is communal or collective; the left half is interior (subjective, consciousness), and the right half is exterior (objective, material).

Thus, the Upper-Left quadrant represents the interior of the individual, the subjective aspect of consciousness, or individual awareness, which I have represented with the cognitive line, lead-ing up to vision-logic. ... The full Upper-Left quadrant includes the entire spectrum of consciousness as it appears in any individual, from bodily sensations to mental ideas to soul and spirit... The language of this quadrant is I-language: first-person accounts of the inner stream of consciousness. This is also the home of aesthetics, or the beauty that is in the "I" of the beholder.

D5. PERSPECTIVES & PATHS. The four basic points-of-view from which any Growth experience can be observed. (cont.)

The Upper-Right quadrant represents the objective or exterior correlates of those interior states of consciousness. ... simple cells (prokaryotes and eukaryotes) already show "irritability," or an active response to stimuli. Neuronal organisms possess sensation and perception; a reptilian brain stem adds the capacity for impulses and instinctual behavior; a limbic system adds emotions and certain rudimentary but powerful feelings; a neocortex further adds the capacities to form symbols and concepts, and so on. ...The language of this quadrant is it-language: third-person or objective accounts of the scientific facts about the individual organism. But individuals never exist alone; every being is a being-in-the-world. Individuals are always part of some collective, and there are the "in-sides" of a collective and the "outsides." These are indicated in the Lower-Left and Lower-Right quadrants, respectively. The Lower Left represents the inside of the collective, or the values, meanings, world-views, and ethics that are shared by any group of individuals. ... I have represented all of these with worldviews, such as magic, mythic, and rational...

The language of this quadrant is we-language: second-person or I-thou language, which involves mutual understanding, justness, and goodness -- in short, how you and I will arrange to get along together. This is the cultural quadrant.

But culture does not hang disembodied in midair. Just as individual consciousness is anchored in objective, material forms (such as the brain), so all cultural components are anchored in exterior, material, institutional forms. These social systems include material institutions, geopolitical formations, and the forces of production (ranging from foraging to horticultural to agrarian to industrial to informational). Because these are objective phenomena, the language of this quadrant, like that of the objective individual, is it-language. (IP 61a)

D6. DIRECTIONS & TRAJECTORIES. The two major vertical Directions our Growth can take – Ascending & Descending.

Huston Smith, in Forgotten Truth, points out that the traditions usually refer to greater levels of reality as higher, and greater levels of the self as deeper, so that the higher you go on the Great Nest of Being, the deeper you go into your own selfhood. I have just taken that approach in the Archeology of the Self... Sometimes this ascent is also felt concretely, as when, for example, Kundalini energy literally moves up the spinal line. The metaphor of vertical height also works well because in many spiritual experiences, we sense that Spirit is descending from above into us (a factor emphasized in many spiritual practices, from Aurobindo's descent of the supermind to the Gnostics' descent of the holy spirit). We reach up to Spirit with Eros; Spirit reaches down to us with Agape. (IP 110-111)

D7. IMPEDIMENTS. The two major ways the Growth process can be impeded or obstructed – Challenges & Impasses.

[See Shadow Self (P4).]

D8. TRANSCENDENT STATES. The higher levels of consciousness experienced by mystics, translucents, and others encountering the Divine Presence.

...the path of shamans/yogis deals with the energy currents in the gross realm and gross bodymind (exemplified in nature mysticism), leading up to the sahasrara (i.e., the energy cur-rents or shakti from the first to the seventh chakra, at the crown of the head). The path of saints plumbs the interior depths of the psychic and subtle realm, often beginning at the fourth or fifth chakra, moving into the sahasrara, and then into numerous, more "within-and-beyond" spheres of audible illuminations and haloes of light and sound (exemplified in deity mysticism), occasionally culminating in pure formless absorption. The path of sages plumbs the pure emptiness of the causal domain (exemplified in formless mysticism), and often pushes through it to completely dissolve the subject-object dualism in any form (including that between self and God), to resurrect the nondual. The path of siddhas plays with nondual mysticism, which is al-ways already accomplished in each and every gesture of this ever-present moment. (IP Note 8:34)

D8a. ROMANTIC FALLACY. The condition where we interpret the primitive, immature, or infantile Stages as higher Stages or States.

Many psychological theorists who are investigating the subtle line of development -- e.g., the Jungians, Jean Bolen, James Hillman -- often confuse the lower, prepersonal levels in the subtle line with the higher, transpersonal levels in that line, with unfortunate results. James Hillman, for example, has carefully explored the preformal, imaginal levels of the subtle line, but con-stantly confuses them with the postformal levels of the subtle line. Just because theorists are working with dreams/images/visions does not mean they are necessarily working with the higher levels of that line... (IP Note 9.16)

WILBER'S PARTICIPANTS

P1-8. PARTICIPANTS. The aspects of Identity, or Self, that partake in the Growth process.
[No general term in Wilber.]

P1. SELF SYSTEM. A combination of the Experienced Self and the Observed Self – the two entities that engage in a dialectic by which the Self grows.
[There are] at least two parts to this "self": one, there is some sort of observing self (an inner subject or watcher); and two, there is some sort of observed self (some objective things that you can see or know about yourself -- I am a father, mother, doctor, clerk; I weigh so many pounds, have blond hair, etc.). The first is experienced as an "I," the second as a "me" (or even "mine"). I call the first the proximate self (since it is closer to "you"), and the second the distal self (since it is objective and "farther away")... (IP 33-37)

P2. INDIVIDUAL & COLLECTIVE SELVES. Individual Self: The aspect of Self that identifies and grows as an Individual. Collective Self: The aspect of Self that identifies and grows as a Group.
Individual: ...I generally use the term "ego" in three different ways, reflecting common uses in the literature: (1) the ego is the sense of self or "I-ness" at any of the personal (or frontal) stages, from the material ego to the bodyego to the rational ego; (2) the ego is more narrowly the per-sonal self that is based on formal-rational-reflexive capacities, which I also call "the mature ego"; (3) the ego is the separate-self sense or self-contraction in general, body to mind to soul. (IP Note 8:7)

Collective (cultural): ... Spiral Dynamics—and developmental studies in general—indicate that many philosophical debates are not really a matter of the better objective argument, but of the subjective level of those debating. No amount of orange scientific evidence will convince blue mythic believers; no amount of green bonding will impress orange aggressiveness; no amount of turquoise holarchy will dislodge green hostility—unless the individual is ready to develop forward through the dynamic spiral of consciousness evolution. This is why "cross-level" debates are rarely resolved, and all parties usually feel unheard and unappreciated. (IP Note 3:22)

P3. PERSONALITY TYPES & PERSONAE. Personality Type: A profile of Personality that recurs in human populations with significant regularity. Persona: Our public face. Enables us to play a part in the drama of existence.
... "horizontal" typologies, such as Jungian types, the Enneagram, Myers-Briggs... For the most part, these are not vertical levels, stages, or waves of development, but rather different types of orientations possible at each of the various levels.... these "horizontal" typologies are of a fundamentally different nature than the "vertical" levels -- namely, the latter are universal stages through which individuals pass in a normal course of development, whereas the former are types of personalities that may -- or may not -- be found at any of the stages. ...[They] simply outline some of the possible orientations that may, or may not, be found at any of the stages, and thus their inclusion is based more on personal taste and usefulness than on universal evidence. (IP 53)

P3a. GENDER TYPES. The attitudes and modes of behavior that originate from one's sexual Gender.
...men and women can negotiate these same structures and stages "in a different voice" (which is usually summarized by saying men tend to translate with an emphasis on agency, women on communion, although both use both). (IP 120)

P3b. ENNEAGRAM TYPES. A widely-recognized system that classifies human personalities into nine basic Types.
Various horizontal typologies -- such as the Enneagram -- can also be used to elucidate the types of defenses used by individuals. Each type proceeds through the various fulcrums with its own typical defense mechanisms and coping strategies. (IP Note 8:28)

P3e. ARCHETYPES. The characters from our Collective Unconscious that populate our Hero's Journey.
Joseph Campbell... has given a wonderful summary of the general Jungian approach: "Briefly summarized, the essential realizations of this pivotal work of Jung's career were, first, that since the archetypes or norms of myth are common to the human species, they are inherently expressive neither of local social circumstance nor of any individual's singular experience, but of common human needs, instincts, and potentials [again, "common" or "collective" does not necessarily mean transpersonal, any more than the fact that human beings collectively have ten toes means that if I experience my toes, I am having a transpersonal experience; the mythic archetypes are simply some of the deep features of the late preop and early conop mind, and thus they are basic forms at those levels, which are devoid of content but fleshed out by particular cultures and individuals; in other words:]; second, that in the traditions of any specific folk, local circumstance will have provided the imagery through which the archetypal themes are displayed in the supporting myths of the culture; third, that if the manner of life and thought of an individual so departs from the norms of the species that a pathological state of imbalance ensues, of neurosis or psychosis, dreams and fantasies analogous to fragmented myths will appear; and fourth, that such dreams are best interpreted, not by reference backward to repressed infantile memories (reduction to autobiography), but by comparison outward with the analogous mythic forms (amplification by mythology), so that the person may see himself de-personalized in the mirror" of the collective human condition. In other words, the aim is to differentiate from (and integrate) these mythic forms and roles. (IP Note 8:27)

P4. SHADOW SELF. Our Inner Saboteur or Gremlin -- any disattached scrap of Identity that impedes or distorts the Growth process.
Subpersonalities, in their benign form, are simply functional self-presentations that navigate particular psychosocial situations (a father persona, a wife persona, a libidinal self, an achiever self, and so on). Subpersonalities become problematic only to the degree of their dissociation, which runs along a continuum from mild to moderate to severe... These submerged personae -- with their now-dissociated and fixated set of morals, needs, worldviews, and so on -- set up shop in the basement, where they sabotage further growth and development. They remain as "hidden subjects," facets of consciousness that the self can no longer disidentify with and transcend, because they are sealed off in unconscious pockets of the psyche, from which they send up symbolic derivatives in the form of painful symptoms. (IP 100-102)

P5. FUNCTIONAL CONSTITUENTS OF SELF. The fundamental components from which the Self is built. The fundamental mechanisms that enable the Self to grow.
...the self has numerous crucial functions: the (proximate) self is the locus of identity (an annexing of various elements to create a self-sense); the seat of will (the self is intrinsically involved in the good); a locus of intersubjectivity (the self is intrinsically a social, dialectical self, involved in justice and care); the seat of aesthetic apprehension (the self is intrinsically involved in the beautiful); the seat of metabolism (the self metabolizes experience to build structure); a locus of cognition (the self has an intrinsic capacity to orient to the objective world); the seat of integration (the self is responsible for integrating the functions, modes, states, waves, and streams of consciousness). These are largely functional invariants... (IP Note 3:9)

P6. MULTIPLE IDENTITIES. Situations where healthy Individuals can assume more than one Identity – either by Shifting or by Broadening their Identity.
[Discussed in Wilber as Inclusiveness.]

P7. DIVINE PRESENCE. The spiritual entity that presides over our lives – in its two manifestations: the Core Self and the Witness.
... at the very upper reaches of the spectrum of consciousness, your individual I -- your separate self or inner subject -- becomes an object of the ultimate I, which is none other than radiant Spirit and your own true Self. According to the mystics, you are one with God as ultimate Subject or pure Consciousness -- a pure Emptiness that, as absolute Witness, I-I, or Seer, can never itself be seen, and yet paradoxically exists as Everything that is seen... (IP 33-37)

Wilber's Processes

PPR1-9, PR1-35. PROCESSES. The Methods and Techniques that move us along the Growth Continuum.
[No general term in Wilber.]

PPR1-9. GENERAL PROCESSES. The Processes that are available to implement Growth at any Stage, Realm, Arena.
[No general term in Wilber. See sections below.]

PR1-35. SPECIFIC PROCESSES. The Methods and Techniques that promote specific kinds of Growth in specific Stages, Realms, or Arenas.
[Referred to in Wilber as Methodologies. See Wilber's Processes (Appx. A9).]

PPR1. TRANSITION CYCLE. The four-phase process of Metamorphosis by which we Transition from one Stage to the next.
During psychological development, the "I" of one stage becomes a "me" at the next. That is, what you are identified with (or embedded in) at one stage of development (and what you there-fore experience very intimately as an "I") tends to become transcended, or disidentified with, or de-embedded at the next, so you can see it more objectively, with some distance and detachment. In other words, the subject of one stage becomes an object of the next... Each time the self (the proximate self) encounters a new level in the Great Nest, it first identifies with it and consolidates it; then disidentifies with it (transcends it, de-embeds from it); and then includes and integrates it from the next higher level. In other words, the self goes through a fulcrum (or a mile-stone) of its own development. (IP 33-37)

PPR2. SHADOW CYCLE. A malfunction of the Transition Cycle, which can produce a pernicious Shadow Self that is the source of neurosis.
Each of those self-stages (or fulcrums) ideally involves both differentiation and integration (transcendence and inclusion). The self differentiates from the lower level (e.g., body), identifies with the next higher level (e.g., mind), and then integrates the conceptual mind with the feelings of the body. A failure at any of those points results in a pathology -- a malformation, crippling, or narrowing of the self in its otherwise ever-expanding journey. Thus, if the mind fails to differentiate from bodily feelings, it can be overwhelmed with painfully strong emotions (not simply feel strong emotions, but be capsized by them), histrionic mood swings are common, there is great difficulty with impulse control, and developmental arrest often occurs that that point. On the other hand, if mind and body differentiate but are not then integrated (so that differentiation goes too far into dissociation), the result is a classic neurosis, or the repression of bodily feelings by mental structures (ego, superego, harsh conscience). (IP 92-96)

PPR3. ACTUALIZATION GROWTH. Actualizing qualities for which we have an innate potential, by moving progressively to higher and higher Stages of development.
... this is an archeology that unearths the future, not the past. This profound archeology digs into the within in order to find the beyond, the emergent, the newly arising, not the al-ready buried. These ever-deeper sheaths pull us forward, not backward; they are layers of Eros, not Thanatos; they lead to tomorrow's births, not yesterday's graves. (IP 108-11)

PPR4. RESTORATION GROWTH. Revisiting past Stages to resolve Impasses, so that normal Actualization Growth (PPR3) can resume.
In this unfolding of higher potentials, should any aspect of the Self that has already emerged be repressed, lost, or alienated, then we need, therapeutically, to "regress in service of the self" -- we need to return to the past, return to the more superficial and shallow layers -- to the material self, the libidinal self, the early distorted scripts, and so on -- and recontact those facets, release their distortions, reintegrate them in the ongoing stream of consciousness unfolding, and thus resume the voyage to the real depths undistracted by those surface commotions... (IP 108-11)

PPR5. COLLECTIVE GROWTH. Growth that occurs among Groups of people – ranging from Couples to Cultures.
[See Collective Developmental Sequence (DD1+2).]

PPR6. HORIZONTAL GROWTH. Growth that occurs within a Stage.
[See Types & Personae (P3).]

PPR7. PERSPECTIVE GROWTH. Growth that occurs as we broaden the Perspectives from which we view and orchestrate our lives.
[See Perspectives & Paths (D5).]

PPR8. EVOLUTION & INVOLUTION. The twin processes of Directional Growth – Ascending and Descending.
[See Directions & Trajectories (D6).]

PPR8b. LIFE TRAJECTORIES. The developmental pattern -- consisting of Ascending and Descending periods, with intervening Mid-Life -- that takes place over the course of a whole lifetime.
... subtle-cognition shows a U-development, being more present in early childhood and then temporarily waning as conop and formop come to the fore, then picking up prominence again in the postformal stages, up to the causal. (IP 124)

PPR9. SPIRITUAL GROWTH. The process of Awakening to universal spiritual truths that are unchanging and eternal.
...looking deep within the mind, in the very most interior part of the self, when the mind becomes very, very quiet, and one listens very carefully, in that infinite Silence, the soul begins to whisper, and its feather-soft voice takes one far beyond what the mind could ever imagine, beyond any-thing rationality could possibly tolerate, beyond anything logic can endure. In its gentle whisperings, there are the faintest hints of infinite love, glimmers of a life that time forgot, flashes of a bliss that must not be mentioned, an infinite intersection where the mysteries of eternity breathe life into mortal time, where suffering and pain have forgotten how to pronounce their own names, this secret quiet intersection of time and the very timeless, an intersection called the soul.
In the archeology of the Self, deep within the personal lies the trans-personal, which takes you far beyond the personal: always within and beyond. Experienced previously only in peak experiences, or as a background intuition of immortality, wonder, and grace, the soul begins now to emerge more permanently in consciousness. Not yet infinite and all-embracing, no longer merely personal and mortal, the soul is the great intermediate conveyor between pure Spirit and individual self. The soul can embrace the gross realm in nature mysticism, or it can plumb its own depths in deity mysticism. It can confer a postmortem meaning on all of life, and deliver grace to every corner of the psyche. It offers the beginning of an unshakable witnessing and equanimity in the midst of the slings and arrows of outrageous fortune, and breathes a tender mercy on all that it encounters. ...
When the soul itself grows quiet, and rests from its own weariness; when the witness releases its final hold, and dissolves into its ever-present ground; when the last layer of the Self is peeled into the purest emptiness; when the final form of the self-contraction unfolds in the infinity of all space; then Spirit itself, as ever-present awareness, stands free of its own accord, never really lost, and therefore never really found. With a shock of the utterly obvious, the world continues to arise, just as it always has.(IP 102-108)
In the deepest within, the most infinite beyond. In ever-present awareness, your soul expands to embrace the entire Kosmos, so that Spirit alone remains, as the simple world of what is. The rain no longer falls on you, but within you; the sun shines from inside your heart and radiates out in-to the world, blessing it with grace; supernovas swirl in your consciousness, the thunder is the sound of your own exhilarated heart; the oceans and rivers are nothing but your blood pulsing to the rhythm of your soul. Infinitely ascended worlds of light dance in the interior of your brain; infinitely descended worlds of night cascade around your feet; the clouds crawl across the sky of your own unfettered mind, while the wind blows through the empty space where your self once used to be. The sound of the rain falling on the roof is the only self you can find, here in the obvious world of crystalline one taste, where inner and outer are silly fictions and self and other are obscene lies, and ever-present simplicity is the sound of one hand clapping madly for all eternity. In the greatest depth, the simplest what is, and the journey ends, as it always does, exactly where it began. (IP 102-108)

WILBER'S PATHFINDERS

PF1-12. PATHFINDERS. The means by which our Growth process is put into effect – combining Guidance & Orchestration.
[Not explicitly discussed by Wilber as a general concept.]

PF1. PARENTS & FAMILY. The original, the most influential, and potentially most beneficial Guides of our Journey of Growth.
[Very limited discussion in Wilber, except implicitly as source of Pathologies.]

PF2. SOCIETY & CULTURE. The set of role models and the lessons on living life we receive from our Society & Culture.
[Implicit in Wilber's extensive discussions of Socio-Cultural Evolution.]

PF3. HOLISTIC GROWTH SITUATION. A cluster of experiences that offers many diverse opportunities for Growth in a single integrated activity.
[Discussed in Wilber only by way of Growth Centers like Integral Institute (PF9).]

PF4. AUTHORITIES. People with exceptional wisdom whose works sheds light on and contributes to our Growth.
[Wilber's whole body of work is a compilation and synthesis of the work of innumerable Authorities.]

PF5. LONG-TERM PARTNER. The special person we choose to share our Journey through life.
[Wilber's *Grace and Grit* is a moving testimony to the importance of a Long-Term Partner.]

PF6. COUNSELOR OR THERAPIST. A Growth Practitioner specially trained to implement some aspect of Actualization or Restoration Growth.
[Discussed in Wilber primarily as Integral Life Guide (PF10).]

PF7. SPIRITUAL GUIDE. A counselor or master with extensive personal experience navigating the higher realms of consciousness (or encountering the Divine Presence) and guiding others to do so.
...authentic spirituality does involve practice. This is not to deny that for many people beliefs are important, faith is important, religious mythology is important. It is simply to add that, as the testimony of the world's great yogis, saints, and sages has made quite clear, authentic spirituality can also involve direct experience of a living Reality, disclosed immediately and intimately in the heart and consciousness of individuals, and fostered by diligent, sincere, prolonged spiritual practice. ...Therefore, don't just think differently, practice diligently. My own recommendation is for any type of "integral transformative practice" ... but any sort of authentic spiritual practice will do. A qualified teacher, with whom you feel comfortable, is a must. (IP 136)

PF8. MENTORS. People other than Counselors, Therapists, Spiritual Guides, etc. who endeavor to help us grow.
[The presence of Alex Grey (art) and Steward Davis (music) as affiliates of Integral Institute indicates Wilber's recognition of the importance of Mentors in the growth process.]

PF9. GROWTH CENTER. A place where people gather to cultivate a particular aspect of their Growth.
[Integral Institute is Wilber's conception of the ideal Growth Center.]

PF10. INTEGRAL LIFE GUIDE. A Growth Practitioner whose work encompasses all five Domains of the ADAPT Model, or equivalent
... the average adult comes to therapy with, to use a simplified version, a physical body, a libidinal/emotional body, one or more body-images, one or more personae or conventional roles, one or more ego states -- with dissociations at any of those levels producing dissociated complexes and subpersonalities at those levels -- and a fledgling soul and spirit awaiting a more genuine birth. A full-spectrum therapist works with the body, the shadow, the persona, the ego, the existential self, the soul and spirit, attempting to bring awareness to all of them, so that all of them may join consciousness in the extraordinary return voyage to the Self and Spirit that grounds and moves the entire display. (IP 108-110)

PF11. INTERNAL NAVIGATOR. The Guide we form within ourselves by internalizing the various forms of Guidance we receive from outside.
[Implicit in Wilber, but not specifically discussed.]

PF12. PROVIDENCE. The Guidance & Orchestration we receive from the Divine Presence.
[The Witness:] this Self is responsible for the overall integration of all the other selves, waves, and streams. It is the Self that shines through the proximate self at any stage and in any domain, and thus it is the Self that drives the transcend-and-include Eros of every unfolding. And it is the Self supreme that prevents the three realms -- gross, subtle, and causal -- from flying apart in the first place. (IP 125-127)

The Witness. "[The Witness] is responsible for the overall integration of all the other selves, waves, and streams. It is the Self that shines through the proximate self at any stage and in any domain, and thus it is the Self that drives the transcend-and-include Eros of every unfolding. And it is the Self supreme that prevents the three realms -- gross, subtle, and causal -- from flying apart in the first place."

Appendix A4.
THE TYRANNY OF AQAL:[1]
Ken Wilber's AQAL Now Inhibits Free Inquiry into Human Development

When you play the game of Scrabble, do you notice how play sometimes gets scrunched down into one small corner of the gameboard? People keep coming up with ingenious new words, but they are confined to a shrinking and increasingly congested space. That's the way we often felt about the July 2010 Integral Conference at JFK University. Stimulating and often brilliant, but generally limited to one small (but highly important) section of the Integral gameboard.

At a conference with so many enticing speakers, we like to browse. To get the lay of the land, we circulated among three or four presentations during each workshop session, gleaning the essence of the speaker's presentation. Then we supplemented those initial impressions by reading the appropriate papers, and later listened to the recordings of each speaker who seemed to have something especially valuable to say. In the course of those three days, we surveyed some remarkable presentations by Kegan, Smith, Cook-Greuter, Forman, Esbjorn-Hargens, Visser, Combs, Marquis, Hubbard, Ganti, Parlee, Roy, Whetton, Golin, Fuhs, Zeitler, Ingersoll, Meyerhoff, Reams, Gafni, Hamilton, Schlitz, Fischler, Laske, Smith, Walsh, Anderson, Ross, O'Fallon, Patten, Winton, and Stein, among others. In almost every case, the underlying subject was AQAL, and the underlying assumption was that some version of AQAL was representative of or virtually equivalent to Integral. In other words, the primary or exclusive subjects of inquiry in most of these presentations were the Parameters of Quadrants and Levels – with Lines, States, Self, and/or Types occasionally thrown in for good measure.[2]

> In this Appendix, we describe how Ken Wilber's AQAL Model has now become an impediment to broad-based research on Integral Theory.

WILBER'S FULL RANGE OF PARAMETERS

We found ourselves asking throughout these presentations, 'All well and good, but what about Wilber's other Parameters?' 'What about all the factors of Human Development[3] delineated in *Integral Psychology* and other seminal works that constitute Wilber's extended Integral Operating System (or IOS)?'[4]

---

[1] AQAL is a 'tyranny' in the metaphorical sense. That is, the AQAL paradigm is unnecessarily becoming so narrow and restrictive that it inhibits inquiry into a broader range of Integral distinctives and alternative models. 'Tyranny' is used here, not in the polemical sense, but as a quasi-technical term that describes the fourth stage of the four-generation cycle of cultural Development, as outlined by Strauss and Howe. (See the section 'The Evolution of Integral' later in this article.)

[2] Throughout this article, key terms are capitalized where necessary to distinguish the technical form of a given word from its corresponding generic. This approach is less cumbersome than enclosing each such term in quotes. (For instance, the field of Integral Theory, as contrasted to an 'integral theory.') For definitions and explanations of these terms, see the Glossary (Appx C2).

[3] Yes, Integral Theory is more than Human Development. But not a whole lot more. Human Development is a very comprehensive field that subsumes many other more specialized fields – such as parenting, teaching, counseling, therapy, organizational consulting, academic research on Human Development, and the orchestration of one's own Personal Growth and self-improvement. From a wider perspective, Human Development encompasses all areas of human endeavor where people grow and evolve – fields as diverse as psychology and education, history and economics, science and technology, art and music, literature and film, ethics and social activism, health and sexuality, worldview and religion. The great majority of conference presentations applied Integral Theory to one or more of these topics.

Yes, Quadrants, Levels, Lines, and States are extremely important, but what about other Wilber concepts relating to the Dimensions of the Growth process? What about the Great Nest, Map, Wave, Trait, Transformation, Ladder, Correlative Structure, Chakra, Spiral, Realm, Plane, Sphere, Physio-Biosphere/ Noosphere/ Theosphere, Terrestrial Realm, Plane of Existence, Celestial Plane, Stream, Height & Depth, U-shaped Pattern, Pathology, and Pre/Trans Fallacy?

Yes, Self and Types are important, but what about other Wilber concepts pertaining to the Participants in the Growth process? What about Proximate & Distal Self, Self-System, Archeology of Self, Ego, Bodyself, Felt Body, Culture, Role, Voice, Gender Type, Agency vs. Communion, Eros vs. Agape, Enneagram, Subpersonality, Shadow Self, Functional Invariant, I-I Self, True Self, and Soul?

What about Wilber concepts that are aspects of the Processes by which Growth takes place? What about Fulcrum, Embedding, Metabolism, Horizontal Translation, Vertical Transformation, Actualizing the Great Nest, Uncovering, Methodology, Modules of Integral Life Practice (ILP), Treatment, Therapy, Evolution & Involution, Transcend & Include, Sociocultural Evolution, and Waking Up?

What about Wilber concepts that are features of the Guidance and Orchestration of the Growth process? What about Navigation, Integration, Spirit-in-Action, Integral Institute, Full-Spectrum Therapist, Witness, Seer, Pure Consciousness, and Spirit?

We grant that at least some additional topics beyond the AQAL matrix were covered in the conference. However, we would contend that the preponderance of talks accepted the AQAL Model as the central organizing principle of Integral Theory ('forms the basis for much of our shared vocabulary,' in the words of one commentator) -- and that in fact many presentations treated AQAL as the very definition of Integral itself.

Ken Wilber is one of the great generalists of our time. He may not get all the particulars right, but he is terrific at sketching out all the elements worthy of consideration. Wilber's *Integral Psychology* is perhaps the most structurally-sophisticated of his works. Despite its apparent simplicity, this remarkable book goes furthest in delineating all the factors that constitute a complete theory of Human Development. If we ignore or underestimate a significant portion of those factors, we run the risk of overlooking some of Wilber's main contributions to human thought. Moreover, if we fail to incorporate that broader range of factors into a comparably broad system, we are contravening the central principle of Integral – i.e. that all the factors we are considering are 'integrated' into a single, comprehensive Model.

IF NOT AQAL, WHAT?

At this point, a question naturally arises in the reader's mind: "If not AQAL, what?" If AQAL is not to be the central organizing principle of Integral Theory, what can we offer to replace it?

We ourselves began asking that question about seven years ago. After careful study of *Integral Psychology* and other important works by Wilber and other Integral thinkers, we began to recognize the limitations of AQAL. It became clear that AQAL was only one important aspect of Wilber's own extended Model of Human Development – what we call his Integral Operating System (or, IOS). At the same time, we became increasingly aware that the AQAL mindset is extremely pervasive in the Integral community. Then, very gradually, in the course of publishing a series of six book-length studies

---

Thus, Human Development in some form was by far the most commonly-addressed topic of the conference. But more generally, Human Development is in our estimation the most fruitful field for Integral investigation. Human Growth is the Developmental system we know most about. Therefore, it yields the most detailed set of Parameters upon which to base any Integral model that aims to be comprehensive.

[4] Wilber's IOS is described in the next section, *If Not AQAL, What?*

on *IntegralWorld.net*, the outlines of a revised and expanded Model[5] began to take shape. That Model incorporates all the Parameters that Wilber explored in *Integral Psychology*, adds a few more to fill in the gaps, and organizes all those Parameters into a simple but comprehensive system called ADAPT – All Dimensions, All Participants, All Processes, Together.[6]

Thus, to continue the Scrabble metaphor, AQAL is just one important corner of a much broader Integral gameboard. Wilber's expanded IOS enumerates many of the other important squares on the gameboard. The ADAPT Model endeavors to show how <u>all</u> those squares can be arranged into a cohesive gameboard pattern.

Any new system, especially one that challenges a Model as beloved as AQAL, inevitably encounters much resistance. Here are some representative objections, critiques, and suggestions we received[7] regarding our own system, along with our rejoinders:

- **Too big a playing field.** 'That's just too big a playing field for Integral Theory to absorb right now.' Our response: You don't have to play on the bigger field until you need it. In the meantime, just acknowledge it's there.

- **Too AQAL-phobic.** 'Your approach is too AQAL-phobic. You attack or denigrate a line of inquiry that has proven immensely fruitful.' Our response: On the contrary, we consider AQAL a magnificent contribution to human thought. Now we can use that great example to become even more comprehensive.

- **Too Wilber-centric.** 'This approach is too Wilber-centric. Concentrating on Wilber is passé.' Our response: Any good theory builds on the best work that's gone before. The colossal contribution of Ken Wilber is the place all of us have to start. In the words of the Great One, before we can 'transcend' Wilber, we must 'include' him.

- **Too complicated.** 'Your new theory is complicated and hard to follow.' Our response: Every new theory seems complicated at first, because it is unfamiliar. However, the basic Model of ADAPT is simplicity itself: Life is a journey by sea, or 'Human Odyssey'; that journey has a Map, a set of Voyagers, a Ship, and a Navigator/Captain. The complexity comes only as we drill down into the nested holons beneath the main concept to explore the details.

- **Requires too much retooling.** 'Your approach would require too much reconfiguring and retooling.' Our response: You have the option of retooling, but you don't have to. If you concentrate on AQAL, just recognize that you're specializing in one very important niche.

- **Broader than Human Development.** 'Integral Theory is broader than Human Development alone.' Our response: see Footnote 3.

- **Different objectives.** 'Your aims and objectives are much different from ours.' Our response: Very true. Integral Theory as an academic discipline often seeks to identify the fundamental structures of reality. Integral Theory from our perspective seeks to identify the structures, sequences, and systems that make human life significant and rewarding. (See Footnote 3.)

- **Not rigorous.** 'This approach is not meta-theoretically rigorous enough.' Our response: Like any social science, a full-bodied Integral Theory will always be half-science, half-art. The rigor of meta-theory is extremely important. But that level of rigor can sometimes inhibit the flashes of brilliant intuition that brought us Integral in the first place.

---

[5] We do not consider ADAPT an 'alternative model' or 'competing model,' because it is derived from Wilber's own model and consists primarily of Wilber's own Parameters. That is why we call ADAPT the 'next generation' of AQAL.

[6] For details, see our conference presentation, *AQAL, the Next Generation*, or the more extended version presented in this book. We refer to our studies, not as a form of self-promotion, but to show that it is indeed possible to devise a viable Integral model that is far more comprehensive and far more 'integrated' than AQAL.

[7] From over a dozen conference speakers and many attendees, not verbatim.

- **Not academic.** 'Your Model is not framed in language and argumentation that is sufficiently academic.' Our response: 'Wilber himself was often judged not sufficiently academic by many speakers and panelists at his own conference! What chance have we got?'

The foregoing objections may all have some validity. However, the central issue remains: Integral Theory is concentrating its attention almost exclusively on one small corner of a much broader field of inquiry. By limiting itself to a few major concepts, Integral becomes not a 'Theory of Everything,' but a 'Theory of a Few Very Important Things.' By failing to show how the full range of concepts fit together, it ceases to be 'Integral' at all.

We are not claiming that our ADAPT Model is the answer. Any valid revision of Wilber's AQAL and IOS will ultimately require the collaborative efforts of many authorities on the Integral worldview. However, we are confident that we have struck upon some key points of discussion that must be addressed before Integral Theory can evolve to its own next level.

THE EVOLUTION OF INTEGRAL

According to Strauss & Howe (*Generations* (1991) and sequels), cultures may evolve over decades of time through a mechanism we call the Generation Cycle. A Generation is the biological period of life, normally about 20-25 years, between the time one is born and the time one first procreates. According to the authors, dynamic cultures repeatedly pass through a Generation Cycle consisting of four characteristic Generations: 1) <u>Prophetic Generation</u>: Conceives a new cultural vision and a new impetus for change; 2) <u>Reactive Generation</u>: Reacts against or detaches from the dominance of the Prophetics; 3) <u>Civic Generation</u>: Fills out and implements the vision of the Prophetics; 4) <u>Bureaucratic Generation</u>: Institutionalizes and standardizes what once was the prophetic vision. After the four Generations are complete, the cycle repeats all over again – but at a higher level of development, and with a new prophetic vision.

The transition from old to new vision is sometimes an arduous and painful one. Adherents to the old system experience its departure as the death of an old and dear friend. The original prophetic vision that began as a force for expansion and liberation can become in its later stages an entrenched 'tyranny' that must be resolved before the next vision can be embraced.

Integral Theory is itself a culture that is progressing through a Generation Cycle – in this case telescoped into 40-50 years, instead of the normal 80-100. In this schema, Wilber is of course the Prophetic; incisive critics and skeptics like Visser and Meyerhoff are the Reactives; brilliant actualizers like Cook-Greuter, many other speakers at the conference (as well as the JFK Conference itself) are the Civics; and the Bureaucratics are the natural tendency in all of us to cling to familiar, established truths.

We by no means presume to see ourselves as the next Prophetics. However, we may be among the first to see the glimmering outlines of a new vision. We hope through our work to stimulate broader discussion on a topic of central importance – the very structure and scope of the field of Integral Theory itself.

The Next AQAL? Ken Wilber once said, "When they lay me in the ground, the words I'd like engraved on my tombstone are, 'He was right, but partial.'" As we now know, AQAL itself is very right – but also very partial. Is it time to move on?

Appendix A5.
Toward a New AQAL:
How the Next Generation of AQAL Will Be Birthed

A5a. The Evolution of AQAL, Version One.

According to Brad Reynolds' *Embracing Reality* (2004), Ken Wilber's AQAL has evolved through five phases:

- **Phase 1. The Spectrum of Consciousness** (1973-77). Outlined Stages and States of Development from conception to enlightenment.
- **Phase 2. Transition** (1978-83). Discovered the Pre/Trans Fallacy: Overthrew the 'recaptured goodness' or 'return to Eden' Model of the Romantics.
- **Phase 3. The Integral Vision** (1983-94). Created the first Integral Model – consisting of three Dimensions (Levels, Lines, States) and one Participant (Self).
- **Phase 4. The Four Quadrants & the Post-Modern Critique** (1995-2000). Added the Dimension of Quadrants, and applied the Quadrants to the misconceptions of Post-Modernism.
- **Phase 5. Public Outreach** (2000-on). Began promoting the Integral revolution through education and training.

These phases represent a series of upgrades to Wilber's basic conceptual software. In these upgrades, the fundamental components remain intact -- and new features, emphases, and applications have been added. It appears that AQAL Version One is now essentially complete. Furthermore, Wilber's long-promised, extended treatise on Integral Psychology* has not come forth after more than ten years. Therefore, we can assume that Wilber's IOS is as complete as we can expect it to be.

A5b. The Need for a New Model

However, as these Appendices demonstrate (esp. Appx A2, 4, 6), the present versions of both AQAL and IOS are showing numerous signs of age – everything from annoying glitches to fundamental design flaws. At this point, Integral Theory needs more than another upgrade. It needs a new Model that is thoroughly overhauled and radically reconceived. The new Model must overcome the glitches and flaws of the old system, encompass all known Parameters, and rearrange those Parameters in a new configuration that explains Human Development more clearly and completely. In our estimation, the natural basis for that new Model is **ADAPT**.

The Evolution of Ken Wilber. "Wilber's AQAL Model has itself gone through at least five Stages of Develop-

*Wilber's book *Integral Psychology* was originally intended merely as an outline for this far more expansive work. *** In Appendix A4, we showed how the old AQAL Model impedes further research in Integral Theory. In this Appendix, we show how AQAL developed, why a new Model is now needed, and why ADAPT is the best basis for that new Model.

A5c. Why ADAPT Provides the Basis for the New AQAL

There are eight major reasons why ADAPT is the appropriate basis for a radically-revised AQAL. (See Appendix A6 for details on these comparisons.)

1. **All Parameters.** ADAPT incorporates all the concepts and Parameters Wilber considers important for explaining Human Growth. (A2c-d)
2. **Extensive fine-tuning.** ADAPT extensively revises and fine-tunes Wilber's positions on at least 292 points. (A2f, k)
3. **Substantial improvement.** ADAPT significantly improves Wilber's positions in at least 194 cases. Of those, at least 87 are improvements in major positions(A2k)
4. **New Parameters.** ADAPT adds many new or substantially expanded Parameters that are essential for a complete and comprehensive Model. (A2k)
5. **Unified configuration.** ADAPT organizes these many diverse Parameters into a unified configuration of four Domains that is simple, elegant, and intuitively obvious. (A2e)
6. **Embodies the fundamental Archetype.** The validity and universality of the ADAPT Model is confirmed by its many parallels to the fundamental Archetype of Human Development – the Life Journey, or Human Odyssey. (A2l)
7. **A better tool.** In the authors' opinion, ADAPT is a substantially more effective framework for applying Integral Theory to the practical concerns of Human Development. ADAPT is a comprehensive and accurate blueprint for parenting, teaching, counseling, organizational consulting, and for orchestrating one's own Growth and self-improvement. (A2m-n)
8. **Wilber's Own Model.** Our final reason is a particularly telling one: Compare the two Circle Diagrams in Appendix A1: Ken Wilber's IOS (A1b) and the ADAPT Model (A1c). In these diagrams, Wilber's IOS Model is shown to be literally a highly-developed version of ADAPT itself. That is, all the Parameters of Wilber's IOS are Dimensions, Participants, Processes, and modes of Togetherness of the ADAPT Model. Therefore, at least implicitly, Wilber and the authors agree that ADAPT is the most satisfactory Model. The authors merely rearrange and fine-tune Wilber's ADAPT for greater completeness and clarity. Thus, in the authors' estimation, ADAPT is the next AQAL, because **ADAPT is in many ways the logical extension and completion of Wilber's own work.** (A3, A6)

We are no match for the legendary Ken Wilber and his stellar array of colleagues. However, as we see it, ADAPT is a clear improvement on the versions of Integral Theory most widely used today.

A5d. AQAL, The Next Generation

Ken Wilber is the Big Kahuna of Integral Theory. Everything Integral that we have today, we owe to him. However, as Ken once mused, "... When they lay me in the ground, the words I'd like engraved on my tombstone are, 'He was right, but partial.'" As this book demonstrates, Wilber's AQAL and IOS Models are both right, but partial. Wilber's pronouncements in the field of Human Growth are outstanding and impressive – but seriously limited and significantly incomplete. Perhaps it's time to give Wilber's venerable and revered AQAL a new face-lift? Maybe even a complete make-over? Maybe we're ready for Integral Operating System, Version Two. Perhaps it's time for AQAL, The Next Generation.

Appendix A6a.
HOW ADAPT IMPROVES ON WILBER

ADAPT sounds like a great new Model. But, why do we need such a Model at all? Why can't we just use the Integral Model Ken Wilber has already provided? Because, in our view, Wilber's system is no longer adequate to the task. Ken Wilber's Model of Human Development is highly impressive and extremely valuable. However, even his extended IOS Model is not sufficiently inclusive, organized, balanced, differentiated, clear, consistent, unambiguous, explicit, complete, or correct (see the table A6ab, *12 Degrees of Divergence*). If a Model lacks any of these qualities, it is not adequate for the crucial, real-life applications of Integral Theory – for parenting, teaching, counseling, organizational consulting, academic research, or for orchestrating one's own Growth and self-improvement (IN1a). Nor is it adequate for describing the phenomenon of Human Development in such diverse fields as: Psychology, History, Science, Economics, Ethics, Art, Literature, Religion, and so forth (IN1b).

Comparing Models
Through our 12 Degrees of Divergence, we show that Wilber's IOS Model is not sufficiently inclusive, organized, balanced, differentiated, clear, consistent, unambiguous, explicit, complete, or correct.*

Apples to Oranges. "Hmm... Well, these are red and have a smooth skin. And these are orange and have a rougher texture." ADAPT is actually just a new and improved strain of the same IOS apple.

*None of the comparisons in this section imply any disrespect for the work of Ken Wilber -- or any claim to superiority over that work. This whole book is only possible because of the monumental pioneering efforts of Wilber and Campbell. "We can see further, because we stand on the shoulders of giants."

In Appendices A6a/b, we show in detail all the ways ADAPT differs from and improves upon Ken Wilber's AQAL and IOS. In this way, we demonstrate that ADAPT is an appropriate successor to Wilber's models (A5).

A6aa. ADAPT & Wilber Compared

To substantiate these bold contentions, we have made meticulous Parameter-by-Parameter comparisons between Wilber's IOS and the ADAPT Model. Of the total **491 comparisons**, our analysis shows 199 points (categories 1-2, below) in which the two Models are in total or substantial agreement – but at least **292 points** (categories 3-12, below) where the two Models present significantly differing positions, or where Wilber's position is absent. As we see it, those 292 divergent positions are especially deserving of further examination, reconsideration, revision, or inclusion.

Further, of these 292 divergent points, there are 194 instances where the authors have a Confidence Level of 90% or better in the ADAPT position. Moreover, of those 194 high-confidence improvements or additions, there are at least 87 that the authors consider major improvements. In other words, **there are at least 87 important positions** (in the authors' estimation) **where ADAPT's interpretation is either significantly superior, or is a significant addition.** The existence of so many divergent interpretations on so many different issues is itself strong evidence that Wilber's conceptions are in serious need of reexamination.

To make more refined comparisons, we categorized the differences between ADAPT and Wilber into 12 degrees of Divergence – ranging from total agreement to significantly differing conceptions. An outline of these 12 points of comparison is shown on the following two pages.

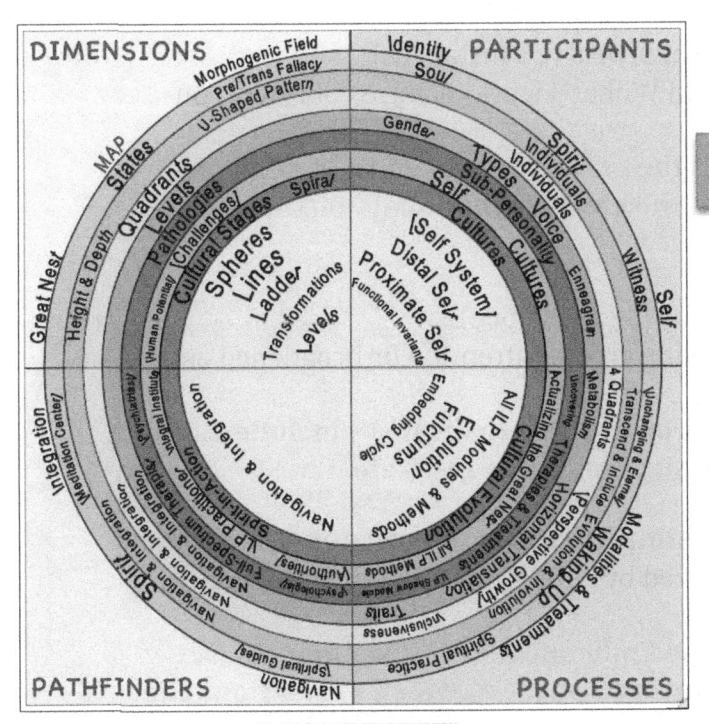

Wilber's IOS

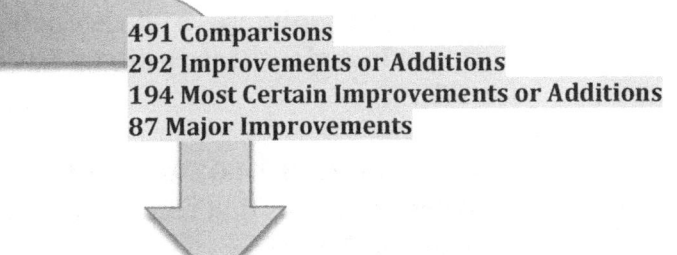

491 Comparisons
292 Improvements or Additions
194 Most Certain Improvements or Additions
87 Major Improvements

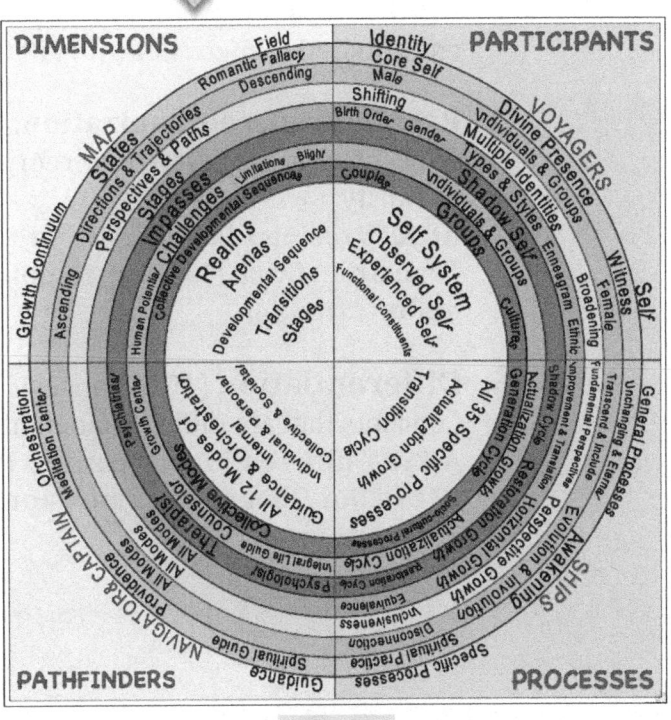

ADAPT

This section supports the contentions made in *Beyond Ken Wilber* (Appx A2k) – that Wilber's AQAL and IOS are significantly incomplete and are in need of serious overhaul. For details of parallels between ADAPT and Wilber, refer to *Ken Wilber's ADAPT* (Appx A3) and in the authors' book-length study, *The Fundamental Ken Wilber* (IntegralWorld.net).

The comparisons made in this section are very detailed and voluminous. For most readers, it is sufficient to sample a representative number of comparisons from each Domain and Parameter, to get a flavor of just how Wilber might be improved.

A6ab. 12 Degrees of Divergence: How ADAPT and Wilber Differ

1. **Substantial agreement** (109 instances)
Wilber positions with which ADAPT is in total or substantial agreement.
ADAPT and Wilber are in substantial agreement that Individual Growth occurs through a dialectic between the Experienced & Observed Selves (P1a-b). ADAPT changes the names from Wilber's *Proximate* and *Distal Selves* to better characterize their functions in the Transition Cycle (PPR1).

2. **Rendering explicit** (90 instances)
Positions implicit in Wilber's work that are rendered explicit by ADAPT.
ADAPT makes explicit what is implicit in Wilber's Famous Tables – that Growth occurs through a series of alternating Stages & Transitions (D1+2).

3. **Consolidation of concepts or versions** (23 instances)
Concepts or versions scattered about in Wilber's work that are collected, consolidated, and reconciled by ADAPT.
ADAPT consolidates and reconciles the many versions of Wilber's Functional Invariants into a single list of the eleven Functional Constituents (P5).

4. **Increased or broadened emphasis** (2 instance)
Wilber positions that receive significantly greater attention or broadened emphasis in ADAPT.
ADAPT broadens Wilber's emphasis on Integral Institute to include many established Growth Centers (PF9f), such as Esalen Institute.

5. **Restatement, reorganization, or simplification of concept** (9 instances)
Concepts that are restated or reorganized by ADAPT for greater completeness or clarity.
ADAPT restates Wilber's three-phase Embedding Cycle as a four-phase Transition Cycle (PPR1) – to point up each phase at which Transitions can malfunction.

6. **Differentiation** (45 instances)
Concepts that are differentiated into multiple levels or structures by ADAPT.
ADAPT differentiates the many Parameters of Growth in Wilber's IOS into five major Domains – Dimensions, Participants, Processes, Pathfinders, and Systems.

12 DEGREES OF DIVERGENCE (cont.)

7. **Expanded or reinterpreted conception or scope** (106 instances)
   Features whose scope or function is significantly expanded or extended by ADAPT.
   ADAPT expands Collective Growth to include not just Cultures, but Groups of all sizes – from Couples and Families to Ethnic Groups and Generations (P2b).

8. **Modified or alternative methodology** (28 instances)
   Occasions where ADAPT uses a significantly different or modified methodology for deriving information and interpreting concepts.
   ADAPT introduces the Life Journey Archetype as a consistent, overarching metaphorical parallel to the Growth process – both to illustrate important points and as an analytical source for further insights.

9. **Shift in emphasis or conception** (3 instances)
   Occasions where ADAPT substantially shifts the emphasis from one concept or theme to another.
   In Therapies (PF6b), ADAPT shifts the emphasis from mainstream psychiatry and clinical psychology toward Growth Modalities that are often non-traditional, non-Western, Humanistic, and/or body-inclusive.

10. **Elevation of role, importance, or validity** (15 instances)
    Concepts whose significance, role, or status in the Development process is significantly elevated (or reduced) by ADAPT.
    ADAPT elevates the external process of Life Passages (D3a) to the status of true Growth – that is, an alternating Sequence of Translation and Transformation (Stages and Transitions) -- rather than Translation alone.

11. **Added concept, Parameter, or characteristic** (52 instances)
    Concepts and Parameters introduced by ADAPT which have no parallel in Wilber.
    ADAPT introduces the Generation Cycle (PPR5b) – a Collective Process of Growth by which dynamic Cultures may evolve.

12. **Substantially differing conception** (9 instances)
    Substantially differing or conflicting positions between Wilber and ADAPT.
    ADAPT introduces an 'Architectural' model of Self – where Growth occurs simultaneously and reciprocally in the Realms of Body, Psyche, and Spirit. This differs from and supplements Wilber's 'Archeological' model of Self – where Growth proceeds sequentially from Body, to Psyche, to Spirit (Appx A7f).

Appendix A6b.
COMPARISON TABLES: ADAPT VS. WILBER
-- 87 MAJOR WAYS ADAPT IMPROVES ON WILBER

The Table on the following pages is designed to help the reader recognize the fine points of Ken Wilber's positions on Human Growth – and to reveal instances where they may due for reexamination. The Table shows a point-by-point comparisons of the Correspondences and Divergences between Wilber's positions (as defined primarily by his statements in *Integral Psychology*) and the ADAPT Model – organized by Domain and Sector.

Below, we show a summary of the comparisons to be found on the table. As you will note, the authors made a total of **491 comparisons** (col. 2). Of those comparisons, we found 292 cases where ADAPT's position diverged significantly from Wilber (col. 3), or where Wilber's position was absent. Of those **292 Divergences**, there were 194 instances where the authors' confidence in the ADAPT position is at least 90% (col. 4). Moreover, of those **194 High-Confidence Divergences**, there were at least **87 that the authors consider Major Improvements**. In other words, **there are at least 87 instances where** (in the authors' estimation) **a major ADAPT position is either significantly superior, or is a significant addition.**

ADAPT vs. WILBER: Comparisons

DOMAINS	COMPARISONS	DIVERGENCES	90%+ CONFIDENCE IN DIVERGENCE	MAJOR IMPROVEMENTS
Preliminaries	12	10	10	2
Introduction	16	9	8	2
Overview	31	24	23	10
Dimensions	144	73	36	13
Participants	63	27	9	3
Processes, General	50	26	12	8
Processes, Specific	9	8	7	2
Pathfinders	47	23	21	8
Systems	18	16	10	5
Conclusion	9	7	7	3
Wilber Appendices	62	47	34	19
Campbell Appendices	30	22	17	12
TOTALS	491	292	194	87
% OF TOTAL	100%	59%	39%	18%

ADAPT vs. WILBER COMPARISONS

The comparisons in the table that follows are divided into 12 sections, corresponding to the sections of this book:

- **PL. Preliminaries** (page 61).
- **IN. Introduction** (page 61)
- **OV. Overview** (page 62).
- **D. Dimensions** (page 64).
- **P. Participants** (page 73).
- **PPR. Processes, General** (page 77).
- **PR. Processes, Specific** (page 80).
- **PF. Pathfinders** (page 81).
- **S. Systems** (page 84).
- **CL. Conclusion** (page 85).
- **Appx A. Wilber Appendix** (page 85).
- **Appx B. Campbell Appendix** (page 90).

The entries in this table may be supplemented by the parallels between ADAPT and Wilber that are shown in the tan textboxes in each section of the Main Text. As you peruse the table, follow along in the appropriate section of the Text.

ADAPT vs. Wilber: Your Comparisons

Consider this very extensive table comparing ADAPT to Ken Wilber. *** Begin by reviewing the 12 degrees of Divergence or Modification ('Mods') between ADAPT and Wilber (page 56). *** Now turn to the Dimensions section of the Table, and select one Comparison for exploration. *** Begin by selecting a Comparison with a Mod #1 or 2 (column 4) – Stages (D1), for example. These are areas where ADAPT and Wilber agree, at least implicitly. In what ways do the positions agree? How is the ADAPT position 'implicit' in what Wilber believes? *** Next, select a Comparison with a Mod #3-6 – ADAPT's differentiation (#6) of Wilber's 'Lines' into 'Arenas' and 'Lines of Inquiry,' for example (D4). In what way is ADAPT differentiating a Wilber concept into multiple parts? How does this differentiation clarify the concept? *** Now select a Comparison with a Mod #7-12, and ask similar questions. *** Now select a Comparison (other than Mod #1 or 2) where the authors' Confidence Level is 90% or better. These are conceptions where ADAPT and Wilber differ – <u>and</u> where the authors are most sure their modification is correct. *** Which improvements are the authors most sure of? Which ones are most open to debate? *** As time permits, select Comparisons from each of the other Domains, and ask similar questions. *** As you explore various Comparisons, does it become more obvious why Wilber's Model needs fine-tuning? Maybe a complete overhaul?

ADAPT vs. Wilber Comparisons Table

This table of comparisons* between ADAPT and Wilber contains six columns:

- **Column 1. Parameter Number**
  The letter/number of the Parameter from the ADAPT Model of Human Growth. For all Major Parameters,** the Parameter Number is highlighted in yellow.

- **Column 2. Parameter Name**
  The name of the Parameter from the ADAPT Model of Human Growth.

- **Column 3. Type of ADAPT Modification**
  The type of modification made by ADAPT in Wilber's position.***

- **Column 4. Divergence Number**
  A number indicating which of the 12 type of modification ('Divergence') applies.***

- **ADAPT Modification of Wilber**
  How ADAPT's position on this Parameter differs from Wilber's.*

- **Confidence in the ADAPT Position**
  The authors' degree of Confidence in the validity of ADAPT's position – expressed as a percentage.****

*For simplicity, we merely describe the differences between the two positions, without any attempt to defend or justify either one. Comments are necessarily abbreviated and simplified.

**Major Parameters are positions of particular importance in the ADAPT Model. Where the table shows similar or related positions on successive lines, only one such position is chosen, to avoid redundancy.

***See table of *12 Degrees of Divergence*, page 56.

****This percentage represents the authors' subjective assessment of their Level of Confidence in the validity of ADAPT's position. This number helps the reader assess how much weight or credibility to give to any proposed modification. For example, if we propose a substantial revision in feature A, and at the same time have a 90%+ Confidence Level in ADAPT's position on that feature, that revision may deserve especially high consideration. The highest Confidence Level we have assigned to any position is 95%, the lowest 60%.

*****The four numbers included in the heading of each section are: Total number of comparisons, number of Divergences (not 1 or 2), number of High-Confidence Divergences (90% or better), number of Major Positions with High-Confidence Divergences. (See summary table, page 58.)

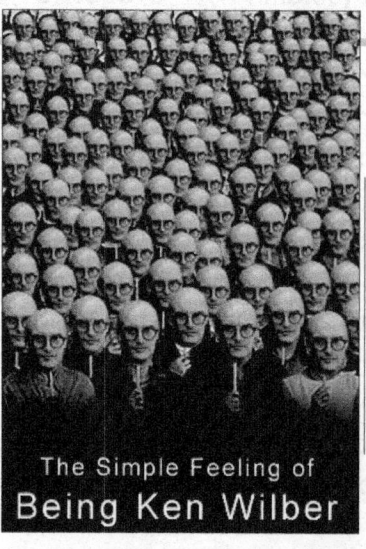

What Does Ken Say?
Despite the immense popularity of Ken Wilber, it's surprising how few people actually read him really carefully. These comparisons will help you make a very careful reading of Wilber's key pronouncements on Human Growth.

ADAPT & WILBER COMPARED

Letter/Number	Parameter	Type of ADAPT modification	Mod #	ADAPT Modification of Wilber	Confidence in ADAPT position
PL	PRELIMINARIES			Totals: 12, 10, 10, 2	
PL	Preface	Rendering explicit	2	ADAPT and Wilber both ground the study of Human Development in the Meaning of Life.	95%
PL	Preface	Added concept	11	ADAPT proposes to integrate two strands of thought on Human Development – the conceptual form Ken Wilber, and the symbolic from Joseph Campbell.	90%
PL	Preface	Added methodology	8	ADAPT adds the cartoon, and other forms of illustration – not just for entertainment, but to elucidate concepts that cannot be adequately conveyed through words alone.	95%
PL	Preface	Elevation of role	10	ADAPT proposes that the adventures of childhood prepare us for the Adventure of Life of adulthood.	90%
PL2	How to Read	Added methodology	8	ADAPT suggests three different reading methods as alternatives to reading cover-to-cover: Reading for fun, for insights, for understanding.	95%
PL2	How to Read	Added methodology	8	ADAPT proposes System-by-System as the best reading method for full understanding.	90%
PL3	Page Layout	Added methodology	8	ADAPT proposes an set of modes for conveying information on the printed page – based upon the various ways people actually learn.	95%
PL3	Page Layout	Added methodology	8	ADAPT outlines six alternative modes of conveying information: The conceptual, the visual, the mythic, the analytical, the systematic, and the experiential.	95%
PL3	Page Layout	Added methodology	8	ADAPT observes that the six alternative modes of conveying information do not just describe an Integral model, but are themselves Integral.	90%
PL3	Page Layout	Added methodology	8	ADAPT introduces the Personal Exploration as a particularly effective method for understanding complex concepts and applying them to one's own life.	95%
PL4	How Benefit	Added methodology	8	ADAPT offers a mode of presenting Human Development that is relevant to people of many different ages, stages of life, occupations, and interests.	90%
PL5	Previews	Rendering explicit	2	Both view Human Development as a vehicle for answering some of life's most vexing questions.	90%
IN	INTRO: HUMAN DEVELOPMENT			Totals: 16, 9, 8, 2	
IN1	Human Development	Substantial Agreement	1	ADAPT and Wilber agree that Human Development is the study of how human beings change and grow over the course of a lifetime.	95%
IN1	Human Development	Rendering explicit	2	ADAPT makes explicit that Human Development is a huge field that encompasses all areas of human endeavor where people grow and evolve.	95%
IN1	Human Development	Differentiation	6	ADAPT differentiates the vast applicability of Human Development into three major categories: Breadth, Depth, and Meaning	90%
IN1a	HDev: Breadth	Rendering explicit	2	ADAPT renders explicit that the individual applications of Human Development to include parenting, teaching, counseling, organizational consulting, academic research, and orchestrating one's own personal growth and self-improvement.	95%

ADAPT & Wilber Compared

Letter/Number	Parameter	Type of ADAPT modification	Mod #	ADAPT Modification of Wilber	Confidence in ADAPT position
IN1a	HDev: Breadth	Substantial Agreement	1	Both substantially agree that the collective applications of Human Development to include all areas of human endeavor where people grow and evolve – fields as diverse as psychology and education, history and politics, science and technology, economics and business, ethics and social activism, art and music, literature and film, health and sexuality, worldview and religion.	90%
IN1b	HDev: Depth	Rendering explicit	2	ADAPT makes explicit that the study of Human Development includes multiple levels of inquiry: in the four Domains of Dimensions, the Participants, the Processes, and the Pathfinders.	95%
IN1c	HDev: Meaning	Rendering explicit	2	ADAPT makes explicit that Human Development is ultimately the study of the Meaning and Purpose of Life.	90%
IN1c	HDev: Meaning	Differentiation	6	ADAPT differentiates questions as to the Meaning of Life into ten common answers.	85%
IN1c	HDev: Meaning	Differentiation	6	ADAPT differentiates those ten common answers into two broad categories: Life has no or limited meaning. Life has higher meaning.	90%
IN2	Growth Mentality	Rendering explicit	2	ADAPT makes explicit the concept Growth Mentality – the disposition of some people to seek and participate in personal growth and evolution.	90%
IN2	Growth Mentality	Differentiation	6	ADAPT differentiates between the Cultural Creatives who seek growth, and the Droids who don't.	90%
IN2	Growth Mentality	Expanded conception	7	ADAPT observes six benefits that accrue from Growth.	90%
IN3	How Grow	Expanded conception	7	ADAPT observes six factors that are necessary for people to grow.	90%
IN3	How Grow	Added Concept	11	ADAPT identifies the Moment of Truth as the decision point where Growth has an opportunity to occur.	90%
IN3	How Grow	Expanded scope	7	ADAPT identifies classic movies that contain a Moment of Truth that serves as a pivot point for action.	90%
IN3	How Grow	Differentiation	6	ADAPT identifies two points in life where Moments of Truth are most likely to present themselves and have significant impact: Nudge-from-the-Nest and Mid-Life.	90%
OV	**OVERVIEW**			**Totals: 31, 24, 23, 10**	
OV	Paths	Rendering explicit	2	ADAPT renders explicit that Personal Growth is fundamentally a matter of the Path we choose in life.	90%
OV	Paths	Substantial agreement	1	ADAPT identifies three periods in life when we pay particular attention to the Path we will taken (or have taken): Youth, Middle Age, and Maturity.	90%
OV	ADAPT & Life Journey	Differing conception	12	ADAPT posits two equally important modes of understanding Human Development: The conceptual mode of Ken Wilber, and the symbolic mode of Joseph Campbell.	90%
OV	ADAPT & Life Journey	Consolidation of concepts	3	ADAPT identifies the integration of the conceptual and symbolic models of Human Development as The Human Odyssey.	90%
OV	ADAPT & Life Journey	Expanded conception	7	ADAPT identifies the twin sources of the need for a new life paradigm: Increased lifespan, reduced attention to material needs.	85%

ADAPT & WILBER COMPARED

Letter/Number	Parameter	Type of ADAPT modification	Mod #	ADAPT Modification of Wilber	Confidence in ADAPT position
OV	ADAPT	Substantial agreement	1	ADAPT and Wilber substantially agree on the content of Wilber's AQAL and IOS.	90%
OV	ADAPT	Expanded conception	7	ADAPT expands Wilber's AQAL and IOS to become ADAPT.	90%
OV	ADAPT	Differentiation	6	ADAPT identifies three features whereby ADAPT is defined: Domains, Sectors, Scenarios.	90%
OV	ADAPT	Substantial agreement	1	ADAPT and Wilber substantially agree that Human Development is 'actualization of the Great Nest' of Human Potential.	90%
OV	Life Journey	Substantial agreement	1	ADAPT and Wilber substantially agree on the content of Campbell's Hero's Journey.	90%
OV	Life Journey	Expanded conception	7	ADAPT expands Campbell's Hero's Journey to become the Life Journey Archetype.	90%
OV	Life Journey	Differentiation	6	ADAPT identifies three features whereby the Life Journey is defined: Domains, Sectors, Scenarios.	95%
OV	Life Journey	Added Concept	11	ADAPT adds Campbell's Archetype of the Labyrinth as a metaphor for the circuitous pathways of the human Soul.	90%
OV1a	Domains: ADAPT	Methodology	8	ADAPT identifies the five questions that must be posed, when devising a Model of Human Development.	90%
OV1a	Domains: ADAPT	Methodology	8	ADAPT posits the answers to those questions as the five Domains of ADAPT: Dimensions, Participants, Processes, Pathfinders, and Systems.	95%
OV1a	Domains: ADAPT	Consolidation of concepts	8	ADAPT consolidates the five Domains into the acronym ADAPT.	95%
OV1a	Domains: Life Journey	Methodology	8	ADAPT identifies the five questions that must be posed, when devising a Life Journey Archetype.	90%
OV1a	Domains: Life Journey	Methodology	8	ADAPT posits the answers to those questions as the five Domains of the Life Journey Archetype.	95%
OV1a	Domains: Life Journey	Methodology	8	ADAPT identifies the five Domains of the Life Journey Archetype: Map, Voyagers, Ship, Navigator/ Captain, Shipping System.	95%
OV1a	Domains: ADAPT & Life Journey	Consolidation of concepts	3	ADAPT consolidates the ADAPT Model and the Life Journey Archetype as conceptual and symbolic formulations of the same concept.	90%
OV1a	Domains: ADAPT & Life Journey	Consolidation of concepts	3	The twin conceptions of ADAPT and Life Journey are presented in parallel for all five Domains.	90%
OV	ADAPT & Adaptation	Consolidation of concepts	3	ADAPT notes the coincidental similarity between the ADAPT acronym and Darwin's evolutionary principle of 'Adapt-ation' to changing life conditions.	90%
OV1b	Sectors: ADAPT & Life Journey	Rendering explicit	2	ADAPT makes explicit that the Sectors are the sub-categories of each Domain.	95%
OV1b	Sectors: ADAPT & Life Journey	Differentiation	6	ADAPT differentiates each Domain into seven or more Sectors.	95%
OV1b	Sectors: ADAPT & Life Journey	Consolidation of concepts	3	The twin conceptions of ADAPT and Life Journey Archetype are presented in parallel for all Sectors in all five Domains.	90%
OV1c	Systems	Rendering explicit	2	ADAPT makes explicit that the various Domains and Sectors work together as a System to produce Growth.	90%

ADAPT & WILBER COMPARED

Letter/Number	Parameter	Type of ADAPT modification	Mod #	ADAPT Modification of Wilber	Confidence in ADAPT position
OV1c	Scenarios: ADAPT & Life Journey	Expanded concept	7	ADAPT posits that Systems may be combined to produce Scenarios that encompass all factors of the Growth process.	90%
OV1c	Scenario: ADAPT	Consolidation of concepts	3	The Domains and Sectors of ADAPT are combined into a single Scenario of Growth.	90%
OV1c	Scenario: Life Journey	Consolidation of concepts	3	The Domains and Sectors of the Life Journey Archetype are combined into a single Scenario of Growth.	90%
OV1c	System: Cultural Evolution	Elevation of role	10	Noah's Ark is shown to be the original System of Cultural Evolution.	90%
OV1c	System: Life Journey	Elevation of role	10	This book itself is shown as a System of Growth, of which the Personal Exploration is an essential part.	90%
D	**DIMENSIONS**			**Totals: 144, 73, 36, 13**	
D	Growth Continuum	Rendering explicit	2	ADAPT makes explicit that Growth is the process of moving and progressing along the Growth Continuum.	90%
D	Growth Continuum	Expanded conception	7	ADAPT expands Wilber's *Morphogenic Field* to become the Growth Continuum -- a Field of developmental Parameters (called Dimensions), Parameters that describe the various areas where growth takes place.	90%
D	Growth Continuum	Rendering explicit	2	ADAPT makes explicit that humankind's greatest drive is to actualize the Growth Continuum by developing at a personal and collective level.	80%
D	Dimensions	Consolidation of concepts	3	ADAPT identifies the various areas of our life where Growth takes place -- and the various features of that Growth -- and consolidates them as Dimensions..	85%
D	Dimensions	Added and expanded parameters	11	ADAPT expands the total Dimensions to eight – and adds several sub-Dimensions. (see D-sections below) [Wilber's AQAL contains just four of these Dimensions – *Levels*, *Quadrants*, *Lines*, and *States*.]	85%
D1	Stages	Substantial agreement, differing terms	1	Both agree that Human Development occurs primarily by progression through a series of Stages.	95%
D1	Stages	Rendering explicit	2	ADAPT makes explicit that Stages are the levels of development, maturity, enlivenment, or enlightenment through which we pass as we grow.	90%
D1	Stage Growth	Substantial agreement, differing term	1	Both agree that Stages are like rungs on a Ladder, or steps of a stairway, that we ascend as we grow.	95%
D1	Stage Growth	Substantial agreement, differing term	1	Both agree that Stages are periods of Assimilation – times when we digest and metabolize the Discoveries of the previous Transition, turning them into established Traits.	95%
D1a	Stage Growth: Life Passages	Expanded role	7	ADAPT expands the role of Growth through Stages to include the Realm of Life Passages – the Stages of Everyday Life (see Realms, D3).	95%
D1a	Stage Growth: Life Passages	Elevated role	10	ADAPT elevates the role of Stages of Everyday Life from repeating cycle to progressive development.	90%
D1a	Stage Growth: Life Passages	Differentiation	6	ADAPT divides Life Passages into 15 Stages (see Realms, D3).	85%

ADAPT & Wilber Compared

Letter/ Number	Parameter	Type of ADAPT modification	Mod #	ADAPT Modification of Wilber	Confidence in ADAPT position
D1a	Stage Growth: Life Passages	Differentiation	6	ADAPT differentiates the 15 Stages of Life Passages into four Phases – Earlier Childhood, Later Childhood, Earlier Adulthood, and Later Adulthood (see Realms, D3).	85%
D1a	Stage Growth: Life Passages	Expanded conception	7	ADAPT describes the physical and psychological characteristics of each Stage of the four Phases of Life Passages.	85%
D1-2	Stage & Transitions	Rendering explicit	2	ADAPT makes explicit what is implicit in Wilber's Tables – that his Stages are actually two alternating phases of the growth sequence, Stages and Transitions. (see D2 and D1+2)	95%
D1-2	Stage & Transitions	Substantial agreement	1	ADAPT and Wilber agree that, whereas Stages are periods of stability and consistency, Transitions are periods of movement and change.	95%
D2	Transition Growth	Substantial agreement	1	Both agree that Transitions are Vertical Transformation – periods where we become something we've never been before.	95%
D2	Transitions	Substantial agreement, new term	1	Both agree that Transitions are Bridges that take us from one Stage to the next.	95%
D2	Transitions	Substantial agreement, differing terms	1	Both agree that Transitions are the Quantum Leaps that take us from one Stage to the next.	95%
D2	Transitions	Substantial agreement, new term	1	Both agree that Transitions are periods of Discovery – occasions when we encounter situations and insights we will assimilate during our next Stage of Development.	95%
D2	Transition Growth	Substantial agreement, new term	1	Both agree that Transition Growth occurs as we leave the familiar comfort of past (often-surmounted) Challenges, and venture into the unknown territory of strange and daunting new Challenges.	95%
D2	Transition Growth	Substantial agreement	1	Both agree that Transition Growth may be experienced as an ordeal of Death and Rebirth.	95%
D2	Transitions	Added concept	11	ADAPT adds that Transitions may be symbolized by the Arch, the Tunnel, or the Birth Canal.	95%
D2a	Transitions: Life Passages	Expanded role	7	ADAPT expands the role of Growth through Transitions to include the Realm of Life Passages – the Transitions of Everyday Life (see Realms, D3).	95%
D2a	Transitions: Life Passages	Added characteristic	11	ADAPT divides Life Passages into 14 Transitions, separating the 15 Stages (see Realms, D3).	85%
D2a	Transitions: Life Passages	Added characteristic	11	ADAPT divides Transitions of Life Passages into four Phases – Earlier Childhood, Later Childhood, Earlier Adulthood, and Later Adulthood (see Realms, D3).	85%
Da	Transition Growth: Life Passages	Expanded conception	7	ADAPT describes the physical and psychological characteristics of each Transition of the four Phases of Life Passages.	85%
D1+2	Developmental Sequence	Rendering explicit	2	ADAPT makes explicit what is implicit in Wilber's work (especially in his Tables): Growth occurs primarily through a Developmental Sequence – a series of alternating Stages and Transitions.	95%
D1+2	Developmental Sequence	Rendering explicit	2	ADAPT makes explicit that the Developmental Sequence is like a Ascending Spiral – with each turn of the Spiral representing one Stage, plus its corresponding Transition.	95%

ADAPT & WILBER COMPARED

Letter/Number	Parameter	Type of ADAPT modification	Mod #	ADAPT Modification of Wilber	Confidence in ADAPT position
D1+2	Developmental Sequence	Expanded conception	7	ADAPT expands the concept of the Ascending Spiral as a fundamental form of growth – to be found at every level from DNA to our galaxy.	90%
D1+2	Developmental Sequence	Added conception	11	ADAPT adds that, in an additional symbolic form, the Developmental Sequence is the Tree of Life.	90%
D1+2	Developmental Sequence	Added conception	11	ADAPT adds that the Tower of Babel is symbolically the original dysfunctional Developmental Sequence.	90%
D1+2a	Developmental Sequence: Life Passages	Expanded role	7	ADAPT expands the role of the Developmental Sequence to include the Realm of Life Passages – the Stages and Transitions of Everyday Life (see Realms, D3).	95%
D1+2a	Developmental Sequence: Life Passages	Consolidation of concepts	3	ADAPT combines the 15 Stages and 14 Transitions to form the Developmental Sequence for the Realm of Life Passages.	85%
D1+2b	Developmental Sequences: Internal vs. External	Differentiation	6	ADAPT distinguishes between an External Developmental Sequences (like Physical Growth and Life Passages), and the Internal Developmental Sequences (like Psyche, Inner Body, Spirit).	90%
D1+2c	Internal Developmental Sequence	Substantial agreement	1	ADAPT and Wilber agree that Wilber's Fundamental Sequence (FDS) is the most detailed and complete version of the IDS.	80%
D1+2c	Internal Developmental Sequence	Rendering explicit	2	ADAPT derives the Chakras from Wilber's FDS (Appx A7d).	80%
D1+2c	Internal Developmental Sequence	Expanded conception	7	ADAPT proposes the Chakras of Wilber and Anodea Judith as an abbreviated and less cumbersome version of the FDS – to be used as the Developmental Sequence for Internal Realms.	75%
DD1+2	Collective Developmental Sequence	Rendering explicit	2	ADAPT renders explicit that Groups can follow a Developmental Sequence comparable to the Sequence for Individuals. (see P2)	85%
DD1+2	Collective Sequence: Groups	Expanded role	7	ADAPT expands the role of the Collective Developmental Sequence to include Groups of all sizes and complexity – from couple and families to ethnic groups and whole Cultures.	90%
DD1+2a	Collective Sequence: Relationships	Differentiation	6	ADAPT differentiates the Collective Developmental Sequence to include all the Arenas (like Relationships) within a particular Realm. (see Realms and Arenas, D3 & D4)	85%
DD1+2a	Collective Sequence: Relationships	Differentiation	6	ADAPT differentiates the Relationships Developmental Sequence in the same 15 Stages and 14 Transitions of the Life Passages Sequence (D1+2a).	85%
DD1+2b	Collective Sequence: Cultures	Substantial agreement	1	Both agree that Cultures, like Individuals, can develop and evolve over time.	80%
DD1+2b	Collective Sequence: Cultures	Substantial agreement	1	Both agree that Cultures can follow a Stage-related path of Development similar to individuals, but spread over eons of time. (see P2b)	75%
DD1+2b	Collective Sequence: Primitive Cultures	Differentiation	6	ADAPT differentiates between Static and Dynamic Cultures.	90%
DD1+2b	Collective Sequence: Primitive Cultures	Rendering explicit	2	ADAPT makes explicit that Primitive Cultures and traditional Agrarian Societies generally do not progress and evolve – but do change in accordance with natural cycles	90%

ADAPT & WILBER COMPARED

Letter/Number	Parameter	Type of ADAPT modification	Mod #	ADAPT Modification of Wilber	Confidence in ADAPT position
DD1+2 b	Collective Sequence: Static Cultures	Rendering explicit	2	ADAPT makes explicit that Static Cultures (like tyrannies and bureaucratic societies) generally do not evolve – because their natural process of growth is suppressed.	90%
DD1+2 b	Collective Sequence: Dynamic Cultures	Rendering explicit	2	ADAPT makes explicit that Dynamic Cultures (like Western Civilization) can evolve through a Cultural Developmental Sequence called Cultural Evolution.	80%
DD1+2 b	Collective Sequence: Spiral Dynamics	Substantial agreement	1	Both agree that Spiral Dynamics is a prime example of Collective Development for Cultures.	80%
DD1+2 b	Collective Sequence: Spiral Dynamics	Substantial agreement	1	Both agree that human culture has gone through approximately ten major Stages of Cultural Development, as described by Spiral Dynamics.	70%
DD1+2 b	Collective Sequence: Spiral Dynamics	Rendering explicit	2	ADAPT makes explicit that many of the previous Stages of our Culture still exist as remnants or Cultural Layers in our present-day society.	85%
D3	Realms	Rendering explicit	2	ADAPT makes explicit that Realms are the major spheres of human experience in which growth can take place – by progression through Stages and Transitions.	90%
D3	Realm Growth	Expanded application	7	ADAPT emphasizes the potential for growth in all four Realms. [Wilber focuses almost exclusively the two Realms of Psyche and Spirit.[8]]	90%
D3	Realms: Passages	Rendering explicit	2	ADAPT names and makes explicit that Passages are the processes of moving through the Stages of the Growth Continuum in each Realm.	90%
D3a	Realms: Life Passages	Added Realm	11	ADAPT adds a fourth Realm of Life Passages – the Realm of everyday Life. [the external manifestation of Wilber's *Gross* realm]	95%
D3a	Realms: Life Passages	Added conception	11	ADAPT defines Life Passages as the external phases of accomplishment or achievement that occur as we progress through the biological Life Cycle.	90%
D3a	Realms: Life Passages	Elevation of role or status	10	ADAPT elevates Life Passages to the status of true growth – i.e. an alternating Sequence of Translations and Transformations, rather than Translation alone.[9]	90%
D3b	Realms: Psyche Passages	Substantial agreement, new term	1	Both agree that Psyche Passages are the internal phases of mental Maturation that occur as we progress through the Stages of psychological Development.	95%
D3b	Realms: Psyche Passages	Rendering explicit	2	ADAPT makes explicit what is implicit in Wilber's Tables – that his psychological 'Lines' may be conveniently collected into the Realm of Psyche Passages.	95%
D3c	Realms: Physical Body Passages	Substantial agreement	1	Both agree that the Physical Body grows and changes over the course of a lifetime.	95%

---

[8] The huge assemblage of Wilber's Tables in the authors' study *Arrays of Light* contains only two sparsely-populated Tables for Life Passages (Table 3) and Body Passages (Physical Development, Table 5). All the remaining Tables focus on Psychological Development (Tables 4), Spiritual Stages and States (Tables 6), Spectrum of Consciousness (Tables 2), and Socio-Cultural Development (Tables 7).

[9] Wilber largely ignores the external Realm of Life Passages, relegating it to the status of 'horizontal translation.' Regarding Yale professor Daniel Levinson's influential *The Seasons of a Man's Life*, for example, he comments, "Several stage conceptions, such as Levinson's, deal with the 'seasons' of horizontal translation, not stages of vertical transformation" (*IP* 227). Neither Levinson nor his prolific popularizer, Gail Sheehey, rate even an index reference in *Integral Psychology*.

ADAPT & WILBER COMPARED

Letter/Number	Parameter	Type of ADAPT modification	Mod #	ADAPT Modification of Wilber	Confidence in ADAPT position
D3c	Realms: Body Passages	Added conception	11	In consonance with the Eastern conception of the Chakras (D1+2c, Appx A7d), ADAPT proposes to add Body Passages as a separate Realm of Growth. (See also PR 6/29)	80%
D3c	Realms: Body Passages	Added conception	11	ADAPT conceives of Body Passages as the internal phases of physical Enlivenment that occur as we awaken and connect to the Energy Centers of our body.	75%
D3d	Realms: Spirit Passages	Substantial agreement	1	Both agree that Spirit Passages are the internal phases of spiritual Enlightenment that occur as we as we Awaken to spiritual truths that are unchanging and eternal.	75%
D3d	Realms: Spirit Passages	Rendering explicit	2	ADAPT makes explicit that modes of spiritual Development may be collected into a distinct Realm (but see D8). [A substantial proportion of Wilber's Tables outline 'spiritual' phases or sequences.]	75%
D3d	Realms: Spirit Passages	Differing conception	12	ADAPT conceives of Spirit Passages as an awakening to an actual, objective Divine Presence (P7). Wilber is ambiguous as to whether the spiritual experience is purely subjective and internal – or whether it has an external, objective component.	65%
D3d	Realms: Spirit Passages	Expanded conception	7	ADAPT interprets Van Gogh's *Starry Night* as a depiction of the Spirit Realm in harmony with the Realm of Everyday Reality.	85%
D3b-d	Internal Realms	Substantial agreement, differing terms	1	ADAPT and Wilber substantially agree that our inner world of consciousness can be divided into three Realms [Wilber's *Realms, Planes, Domains, Spheres,* or *Axes*]	80%
D3b-d	Internal Realms	Restatement and Simplification	5	ADAPT restates and simplifies the three internal Realms as being Psyche, Body, and Spirit.[10]	80%
D3b-d	Development in the Internal Realms	Shift in conception	9	In consonance with the Eastern conception of the Chakras (Appx 7d), ADAPT views growth in Body, Psyche, and Spirit as taking place simultaneously in all three Internal Realms. [In contrast to Wilber's view of their growth as sequential -- from body, to psyche, to spirit. See also Appx A7f-h.]	75%
D4	Arenas	Rendering explicit	2	ADAPT makes explicit that Arenas are the specific areas of activity within each Realm where growth takes place.	95%
D4	Arenas	Differentiation	6	ADAPT differentiates Wilber's 'Lines' into three levels of inquiry: The broader category of Arenas, to the more specific Lines of Inquiry within that Arena, to the Studies within those Lines.	95%
D4a	Arenas Internal	Expanded conception	7	ADAPT expands the Internal Developmental Sequence for Psyche, Body, and Spirit Passages (i.e. the Chakras) to be applicable to all the Arenas of those three Realms.	85%
D4	Arenas: Differential Growth	Substantial agreement, added term	1	Both agree on Differential Growth: That growth may take place at different rates in different Arenas, and that one may therefore be at different Stages in each.	95%
D4a	Life Arenas	Added concept	11	Corresponding to the added Realm of Life Passages, ADAPT posits a set Life Arenas – spheres of activity in which we live our Everyday Life.	95%
D4a	Life Arenas	Elevation of role	10	ADAPT elevates the Life Arenas from the level of Horizontal Translation to vertical Transformation.	95%

---

[10] ADAPT may not incorporate in Realms all implications of Wilber's three 'spheres.'

ADAPT & WILBER COMPARED

Letter/Number	Parameter	Type of ADAPT modification	Mod #	ADAPT Modification of Wilber	Confidence in ADAPT position
D4a	Life Arenas	Added set of features	11	ADAPT names 12 different Life Arenas – using categories familiar to the counseling and coaching professions.	95%
D4a	Life Arenas	Added methodology	8	ADAPT adds Wheel of Life – as a tool from the counseling and coaching professions to implement the 12 Life Arenas.	95%
D4a	Life Arenas	Expanded conception	7	ADAPT expands the External Developmental Sequence for Life Passages to be applicable to all the Arenas of Life Passages.	95%
D4a1	Life Arenas: Growth	Expanded conception	7	In Career & Calling, an Arena of Life Passages, ADAPT shows an abbreviated System: How Stages, Transitions, Realm, and Arena work together to produce growth.	95%
D4b	Psyche Arenas	Rendering explicit	2	Corresponding to the Realm of Psyche Passages, ADAPT posits a set Psyche Arenas – themes of psychological Development that characterize our inner life.	90%
D4b	Psyche Arenas	Consolidation of concepts	3	ADAPT derives a set of nine Psyche Arenas by consolidating the psychological studies from Wilber's Tables (*IP*).	90%
D4b	Psyche Arenas	Substantial agreement	1	Wilber and ADAPT substantially agree as to the content of each Psyche Arena.	90%
D4b	Psyche Arenas: Growth	Substantial agreement	1	Wilber and ADAPT substantially agree on the roughly parallel growth takes place in the various Psyche Arenas.	85%
D4c	Realms: Body Passages	Substantial agreement	1	Both agree that the body can be conceived in two ways -- the Physical Body (upper-right) and the Internal Body (upper-left). [Wilber's *Felt Body* or *Body Self*][11]	85%
D4c	Body Arenas	Added conception	11	Corresponding to the Realm of Body Passages, ADAPT proposes a set of Body Arenas – regions or functions of the body where we experience growth internally.	60%
D4c	Body Arenas: Growth	Added conception	11	ADAPT proposes that growth in the Body Arenas consists of activating and enlivening the regions of the Chakras. (See Appx A7d.)	70%
D4c	Body Arenas	Expanded conception	7	ADAPT observes that the seven anatomical Chakras are associated with corresponding nerve ganglia, bodily organs, and states of wellbeing.	70%
D4c	Body Arenas	Added methodology	8	ADAPT proposes that the Body Arenas be drawn from the five groups of body-oriented growth practices that employ them.	75%
D4c	Body Arenas	Expanded conception	7	ADAPT proposes as possible Body Arenas, Anodea Judith's categories of bodily Chakras: Bodily locations, bodily systems, sets of organs and functions, glands, spinal and skeletal parts, bodily senses, types of physical malfunction, etc.	70%
D4d	Spirit Arenas	Substantial agreement	1	Both agree that there may be several Arenas in which spiritual growth takes place. (see also D8)	90%
D4d	Spirit Arenas	Rendering explicit	2	ADAPT observes that Spirit Arenas are modes by which we experience Transcendent States (D8)..	75%

---

[11] Wilber tends to assign the body to the Upper-Right Quadrant. See for instance Wilber's comments on Michael Murphy's *The Future of the Body* (*SES*, p. 579): "Murphy almost single-handedly has been representing the great importance of the Upper-Right quadrant in human transformation…" [underline ours] We would characterize Esalen's attitude toward the body (not necessarily Murphy's) as predominantly Upper-Left.

ADAPT & WILBER COMPARED

Letter/Number	Parameter	Type of ADAPT modification	Mod #	ADAPT Modification of Wilber	Confidence in ADAPT position
D4d	Spirit Arenas	Differing conception	12	ADAPT conceives of Spirit Arenas as modes by which we also experience the objective reality of the Divine Presence (P7) or Providence (PF112).	65%
D4d	Spirit Arenas	Substantial agreement	1	ADAPT agrees with Wilber's suggestion of five possible Spiritual Arenas – Care, Openness, Concern, Religious Faith, and Meditative Stages.	70%
D4d	Spirit Arenas	Consolidation of concepts	5	ADAPT consolidates Sequences from two major categories from Wilber's Tables as potential Spirit Arenas: Spectrum of Consciousness and Transcendent States & Stages	80%
D4d	Spirit Arenas	Expanded conception	7	ADAPT adds seven additional Spirit Arenas, for a total of nine.	65%
D4d	Spirit Arenas	Differentiation	6	ADAPT differentiates between the first two Spirit Arenas, which manifest only in the Crown Chakra – and the remaining seven, which manifest in all seven Chakras.	75%
D4d	Spirit Arenas	Substantial agreement	1	Both differentiate between Life or Psyche Arenas, where we grow from Stage and Stage – and Spirit Arenas, where we expand our capacity to awaken to a truth that is unchanging and eternal.	85%
D5a	Perspectives of Growth	Substantial agreement, differing term	1	Both agree that any growth experience may be viewed from four different Perspectives; Inner/individual, outer/individual, inner/collective, and outer/collective.	95%
D5a	Perspectives of Growth	Substantial agreement	1	Both agree that a complete and Integral Development program must approach growth from all four Perspectives.	95%
D5b	Paths of Growth	Expanded concept	7	Corresponding to the four Perspectives, ADAPT posits four Life Paths – or types of life activity we may choose to focus our attention on.	90%
D5b	Paths of Growth	Expanded concept	7	ADAPT characterizes the four Paths as manifestations of the four Perspectives -- the inner and outer Realms, combined with the Individual and Collective Participants	90%
D5a-b	Perspectives & Paths	Rendering explicit	2	ADAPT makes explicit that we grow best when we include all four Perspectives and all four Paths.	95%
D6	Directions & Trajectories	Substantial agreement, differing terms	1	Both agree that growth can be experienced in two contrary Directions. Either Ascending: Upward & outward. Or Descending: Downward & inward.	90%
D6	Directions & Trajectories	Substantial agreement	1	Both agree that the Ascending & Descending Directions can be manifested either in present-day activities (Directions) or in activities that span a lifetime (Trajectories).	90%
D6	Polarities	Rendering explicit	2	ADAPT makes explicit that the two Directions correspond to the two fundamentally opposing forces that characterize the universe -- variously called yang and yin, male and female, spirit and flesh, etc.	65%
D6a	Directions	Expanded conception	7	For the four Realms, ADAPT characterizes the Ascending Direction as Achievement, Maturity, Aliveness, and Enlightenment, respectively	80%
D6a	Directions	Expanded conception	7	For the four Realms, ADAPT characterizes the Descending Direction as Fulfillment, Authenticity, Grounding, and Compassion, respectively.	80%

ADAPT & WILBER COMPARED

Letter/Number	Parameter	Type of ADAPT modification	Mod #	ADAPT Modification of Wilber	Confidence in ADAPT position
D6a	Directions	Substantial agreement	1	Both agree that the Ascending Direction is characteristic of the male, while the Descending Direction is characteristic of the female.	85%
D6b	Trajectories	Substantial agreement	1	Both agree that the full course of our existence follows a sequential pair of Trajectories. Our life first traces an Ascending arc of Evolution; later, our life follows a Descending arc of Involution.[12] (See PPR8b.)	80%
D6b	Trajectories	Expanded conception	7	While Wilber focuses on the spiritual aspect of Evolution/Involution, ADAPT applies this concept to the four basic Realms.	85%
D6b	Trajectories	Added conception	11	Between the arcs of Evolution and Involution, ADAPT adds a difficult Transition called Mid-Life. (See D2d.)	80%
D7	Impediments	Substantial agreement, differing term	1	Both agree that Impediments are all the ways the growth process can be limited, diverted, or obstructed.	95%
D7	Impediments	Rendering explicit	2	ADAPT makes explicit that Impediments may be differentiated into Challenges and Impasses.	95%
D7a	Impediments: Challenges	Added concept	11	ADAPT defines Challenges as overt difficulties, demanding tasks, or tests of one's abilities and resolve faced by relatively healthy people.	95%
D7a	Impediments: Challenges	Expanded conception	7	ADAPT observes that failure to address Challenges can cause the growth process to become limited, restricted, diverted, denied, neglected, un-actualized, or avoided.	95%
D7a	Impediments: Challenges	Expanded conception	7	ADAPT observes that Challenges are places where Actualization may fail to take place -- and where we may thus be left with Unrealized Opportunities, or Un-actualized Potential.	95%
D7a	Impediments: Challenges	Expanded conception	7	ADAPT observes the conception that, when Challenges are not engaged and overcome, they may become Limitations, and may eventually result in atrophy or Blight.	90%
D7a	Impediments: Challenges	Added methodology	8	ADAPT observes that Challenges can often be surmounted by Actualization Growth (PPR3), with the help of a Counselor or Coach (P6a-b).	95%
D7a	Impediments: Challenges	Rendering explicit	2	ADAPT makes explicit that Challenges of specific types are likely to occur at specific Stages of life.	90%
D7a	Impediments: Challenges	Expanded conception	7	ADAPT identifies specific Challenges a person might face over the course of a lifetime.	90%
D7b	Impediments: Impasses	Substantial agreement, differing term	1	Both agree that Impasses are submerged or subconscious difficulties suffered by people with 'problems.' [Wilber's *Pathologies*]	95%
D7b	Impediments: Impasses	Substantial agreement, differing term	1	Both agree that Impasses are Blocks, Hang-ups, or Pathologies – any condition that causes the growth process to become obstructed, thwarted, blocked, repressed, distorted, split off, repressed, or damaged.	95%

---

[12] Trajectories: Wilber's 'U-shaped pattern.' ADAPT may not incorporate in this all the implications of Wilber's formulation. The cycle of Evolution and Involution is a highly-complex and esoteric subject covered at length in Wilber's earlier works – especially *The Atman Project* (185-203), *Up From Eden* (299-313), and *Eye of the Spirit* (55-6, 62-3).

ADAPT & WILBER COMPARED

Letter/Number	Parameter	Type of ADAPT modification	Mod #	ADAPT Modification of Wilber	Confidence in ADAPT position
D7b	Impediments: Impasses	Substantial agreement	1	Both agree that Impasses can be symptoms of a pernicious Shadow Self (P4), which can be created by a Shadow Cycle (PPR2).	85%
D7b	Impediments: Impasses	Substantial agreement	1	Both agree that Impasses may sometimes be resolved by Restoration Growth (PPR4), with the assistance of a trained Therapist (PF6d).	90%
D7b	Impediments: Impasses	Rendering explicit	2	ADAPT makes explicit that Impasses of specific types are likely to have been created at specific Stages of life.	85%
D7b	Impediments: Impasses	Expanded conception	7	ADAPT identifies specific Impasses a person might face over the course of a lifetime.	90%
D7a-b	Impediments: Challenges & Impasses	Extended conception	7	ADAPT observes that virtually every Sector in each Domain has potential Challenges, but that there are relatively few types of Impasse.	80%
D8	Transcendent States	Substantial agreement	1	Both agree that Transcendent States are the higher levels of consciousness experienced by mystics and translucents.	90%
D8	Transcendent States	Expanded interpretation	7	ADAPT interprets Moses's episode with the Burning Bush as a Transcendent State (D8), where the blinding light of the bush represents Moses's actual encounter with the Divine Presence (P7).	85%
D8	Transcendent States	Substantial agreement	1	Both agree that Transcendent States are not progressions from one truth to a higher truth. They are phases of Awakening – of increased awareness, illumination, and revelation of a central unchanging truth.	90%
D8	Transcendent States	Substantial agreement	1	ADAPT accepts Wilber's view that there are four higher States of consciousness – Psychic, Subtle, Causal, and Non-dual.	80%
D8	Transcendent States	Substantial agreement	1	Both substantially agree that State Growth occurs as we increase our capacity to attain and move fluidly among the higher States of consciousness.	85%
D8	Transcendent States	Substantial agreement	1	Both agree on the five typical conceptions of Transcendent States.[13]	90%
D8	Transcendent States	Added conceptions	11	In addition to Wilber's five possible conceptions of States, ADAPT offers two others: That States may be a distinct Realm (D3d), and a distinct Dimension (D8) within that Realm.	70%
D8	Transcendent States	Differing conception	12	ADAPT views Transcendent States, not only as an subjective, Internal Experience [upper-left], but as an encounter with an objective, External Reality [upper-right].	70%
D8	Transcendent States	Expanded conception	7	ADAPT expresses the conviction that we may awaken to the Divine Presence (P7) [Wilber's *Spirit*] by moving through a series of Transcendent States, whereby the Divine Presence is progressively revealed.	70%
D8	Natural States	Substantial agreement	1	Both agree on the existence of Other States: Natural States, Altered States, and Peak Experiences.	80%

---

[13] According to Wilber, there are five common conceptions of 'spirituality': "(1) Spirituality involves the highest levels of any of the developmental lines. (2) Spirituality is the sum total of the highest levels of the developmental lines. (3) Spirituality is itself a separate developmental line. (4) Spirituality is an attitude (such as openness or love) that you can have at whatever stage you are at. (5) Spirituality basically involves peak experiences, not stages." (IP, p. 129-35) We substitute the words Transcendent States for Wilber's 'spirituality.'

ADAPT & WILBER COMPARED

Letter/ Number	Parameter	Type of ADAPT modification	Mod #	ADAPT Modification of Wilber	Confidence in ADAPT position
D8a	Romantic Fallacy	Substantial agreement, differing term	1	Both agree on the Romantic Fallacy -- that primitive, archaic, or mythic Stages may be mistaken for Transcendent Stages or States. [Wilber's Pre/Trans Fallacy]	90%
D8a	Romantic Fallacy	Differentiation	6	ADAPT differentiates the Romantic Fallacy into a pair of misconceptions – the Romantic Fallacy *per se* and the Inverse Romantic Fallacy.	90%
D8a	Romantic Fallacy *per se*	Substantial agreement	1	Both characterize the Romantic Fallacy *per se* as mistaking low-level Stages or Pathologies for genuine Transcendent Stages and States.	90%
D8a	Romantic Fallacy	Substantial agreement	1	Both agree that the Romantic Fallacies *per se* are serious misconceptions, which cause much confusion and misdirection in the Counter-culture, Human Potential, and New Age Movements.	90%
D8b	Inverse Romantic Fallacy	Expanded Conception	7	ADAPT characterizes the Inverse Romantic Fallacy as mistaking genuine Transcendent Stages and States for low-level Stages or Pathologies.	90%
D8b	Inverse Romantic Fallacy	Expanded Conception	7	ADAPT observes that Inverse Romantic Fallacies are serious misconceptions, which cause much confusion and misdirection in the Conservative, Fundamentalist, and Rational/ Scientific camps.	90%
D8a-b	Romantic/Inverse Fallacy	Rendering explicit	2	ADAPT renders explicit that both the Romantic Fallacy and the Inverse Romantic Fallacy can be Impediments of the Challenge variety (D7a).	90%
P	**PARTICIPANTS**			**Totals: 63, 27, 9, 3**	
P	Participants	Rendering explicit	2	ADAPT makes explicit that Participants are the aspects of Identity or Self that participate in the Growth Process.	95%
P	Participants	Consolidation of concepts, differing term	3	ADAPT collects and consolidates into Participants the seven entities described by Wilber that partake in the growth process.[14]	95%
P	Participants	Rendering explicit	2	ADAPT makes explicit that the Self is 'cubist' -- a composite of many interrelated parts.	90%
P1	Self System	Substantial agreement, differing term	1	Both agree that the Experienced & Observed Selves are the twin components of our Self System.	90%
P1	Experienced & Observed Selves	Substantial agreement, differing term	1	Both agree that the Self System represents the two parts of a dialectic by which the Self grows.	90%
P1	Experienced & Observed Selves	Substantial agreement	1	Both agree that the Experienced & Observed Selves are the central figures in our Developmental process.	90%
P1	Experienced & Observed Selves	Substantial agreement	1	Both agree that the Experienced & Observed Selves proceed through the Stages & Transitions, using the mechanism of the Transition Cycle (PPR1).	90%

---

[14] References to these elements of Identity can be found, for example, in *IP*: Proximate/Distal, pp. 333-36; Personae, Enneagram Types, and other Types, pp. 53-54; Gender, pp. 120-21; Sub-Personalities, pp. 100-02; Functional Invariants, pp. 37-7, 226; Witness, pp. 126-27.

ADAPT & Wilber Compared

Letter/Number	Parameter	Type of ADAPT modification	Mod #	ADAPT Modification of Wilber	Confidence in ADAPT position
P1	Experienced & Observed Selves	Expanded conception	7	ADAPT observes that the Experienced & Observed Selves are the central figures in other General Processes of Growth -- including the Shadow Cycle (PPR2), Actualization Growth (PPR3), Restoration Growth (PPR4), etc.	90%
P1a	Experienced Self	Substantial agreement, differing term	1	Both agree that the Experienced Self is the observing, subjective, inside, I-Self -- the Self that identifies with our current Stage of Development.	90%
P1b	Observed Self	Substantial agreement, differing term	1	Both agree that the Observed Self is the detached, objective, outside, Me-Self -- the Self from a prior Stage of Development that we have transcended, or otherwise ceased to identify with.	90%
P2	Individual & Collective Selves	Substantial agreement	1	Both agree that we can participate in the growth process both individually and collectively.	95%
P2a	Individual Self	Substantial agreement	1	Both agree that the Individual Self progresses through the Stages and Transitions individually -- makes its own decisions, takes its own actions, and bears the consequences of its own behavior.	95%
P2b	Collective Self	Substantial agreement	1	Both agree that the Collective Self progresses through the Stages and Transitions as a member of a Group -- shares in Group decisions, participates in Group actions, and bears collective responsibility for its behavior.	90%
P2b	Collective Self	Expanded concept	7	ADAPT expands the Collective Self from Culture alone[15] to include all Groups – including Couples, Families, Teams, Workgroups, Communities, Sub-Cultures, Ethnic Groups, Nations, Generations, and whole Cultures. (see also DD1+2)	90%
P3	Personality Types	Substantial agreement	1	Both agree that Personality Types are profiles of personality that recur in human populations with a significant degree of regularity.	90%
P3	Persona	Substantial agreement	1	In the more restricted sense, both agree that Persona refers to the Membership-Self (conformist Role-Self).[16]	90%
P3	Persona	Differing conception	11	In a broader sense, ADAPT views the Persona as our 'public face' -- the set of attributes and behaviors we construct to enable the Self to play a part in the drama of existence.[17]	90%
P3	Types	Substantial agreement	1	Both agree that Types include Gender Types, Enneagram Types, and Personality Assessment Systems like Jungian and Myers-Briggs.	95%
P3	Types	Expanded conception	7	ADAPT expands the varieties of Types to include: Ethnic Types, Birth-Order Types, Comic Stereo-types, and Arche-types. (See each below.)	90%
P3	Types: Styles	Substantial agreement, differing term	1	Both agree that each Type proceeds through the Stages & Transitions in a Style characteristic of that Type.	85%
P3a	Gender Types	Substantial agreement	1	Both agree that Gender Types are the attitudes and modes of behavior that originate from one's sexual Gender – the primary Gender Types being male and female.	95%

---

[15] In discussing Collective Participants, Wilber's emphasis is almost exclusively on Cultures. See *IP* 145-49, 154-55.

[16] The Rule/Role region of Wilber's 'correlative structures' (Steps 12-18 in the FDS). (see *IP* 91, 126, 240-41, and 198 -- self-sense column)

[17] From this perspective, a Persona is not Stage-specific, but can be manifested at any Stage of Development to deal with real-life circumstances.

ADAPT & WILBER COMPARED

Letter/Number	Parameter	Type of ADAPT modification	Mod #	ADAPT Modification of Wilber	Confidence in ADAPT position
P3a	Gender Types	Substantial agreement	1	Both agree that females go through Stages of growth comparable to males, but in a different Style.	90%
P3a	Gender Types	Substantial agreement	1	Both agree that Stage Growth occurs in men primarily through Agency, in women through Communion.	85%
P3a	Gender Types	Substantial agreement	1	Both agree that Transition Growth occurs in men primarily through *Eros*, in women through Agape.	85%
P3a	Gender Types	Rendering explicit	2	ADAPT renders explicit how males and females differ at each Stage of Development.	85%
P3b	Enneagram Types	Substantial agreement	1	Both accept the Enneagram as a widely-recognized system for typing personalities.	95%
P3b	Enneagram Types	Substantial agreement	1	Both agree that there are thought to be nine different Enneagram Types. [May differ as to the exact names and characteristics of those Types.]	95%
P3b	Enneagram Types	Elevation of validity and status	10	ADAPT views as credible the evidence that Enneagram Types represent distinct and fundamental Types – not just arbitrary personality categories.	85%
P3b	Enneagram Types	Differentiation	6	ADAPT distinguishes between Enneagram Types that are Dominant and others that are Contributing.	85%
P3b	Enneagram Traits	Added characteristic	11	ADAPT observes that, although Enneagram Types do not grow, they can improve within Type. That is, a particular Type can progress from Fixated Traits to Evolved Traits.	85%
P3c	Ethnic & Cultural Types	Added Parameter	11	ADAPT adds a Type called Ethnic & Cultural – a personality profile that derives from the order of one's ethnic and/or cultural origins and identification.	90%
P3d	Birth-Order Types	Added Parameter	11	ADAPT adds a Type called Birth Order – a personality profile that derives from the order of one's birth among siblings.	80%
P3e	Comic Stereo-Types	Added Parameter	11	ADAPT adds a Type called Comic Stereotypes – an quirky and unchanging personality profile that makes a character funny.	90%
P3g	Arche-Types	Added Parameter	11	ADAPT adds a Type called Arche-types – stock characters that recur in archetypal stories with significant regularity.	90%
P4	Shadow Self	Substantial agreement, added terms	1	Both agree that the Shadow Self is the Inner Saboteur or Gremlin -- any disattached, distorted scrap of identity that impedes or distorts the growth process.	90%
P4	Shadow Self	Substantial agreement	1	Both agree that the Shadow Self can be created at any Stage of Development.	90%
P4	Shadow Self	Substantial agreement	1	Both agree that the appropriate mode of Treatment will differ for Shadow Selves created at each Stage.	85%
P4	Shadow Self	Substantial agreement	1	Both agree that the difficulty of Treatment increases as we go back to Shadow Selves created at earlier and earlier Stages.	90%
P4	Shadow Self	Expanded conception	7	ADAPT expands the Shadow Self to include various types: Lonely, Destructive, Creative, etc.	85%
P4	Shadow Self	Expanded conception	7	ADAPT expands the Inner Gremlin to include various types: Demon, Saboteur, Hero, Tame, etc.	85%

ADAPT & WILBER COMPARED

Letter/Number	Parameter	Type of ADAPT modification	Mod #	ADAPT Modification of Wilber	Confidence in ADAPT position
P5	Functional Constituents	Rendering explicit	2	ADAPT makes explicit that the Functional Constituents are the fundamental attributes of human nature -- the components from which the Self is built and the mechanisms that enable the Self to grow.	90%
P5	Functional Constituents	Consolidation of versions, differing names	3	ADAPT collects and consolidates the many versions of Wilber's *Functional Invariants* into a single list of the eleven Functional Constituents.[18]	85%
P5	Functional Constituents	Reorganization of concept	5	ADAPT ranks the Functional Constituents from the most primitive to the most advanced.	85%
P5	Functional Constituents	Substantial agreement	1	Both agree that some Functional Constituents are primarily rational left-brain activities, while others are primarily emotional right-brain.	90%
P5	Functional Constituents	Rendering explicit	2	ADAPT makes explicit that the Functional Constituents do not themselves undergo Stage-like Development, but that they do enable such Development to take place.	90%
P5	Functional Constituents	Extended conception	7	ADAPT observes that the functional efficacy of Functional Constituents can be strengthened and improved through proper use.	90%
P6	Multiple Identities	Expanded conception	7	ADAPT broadens the conception of Identity to include Multiple Identities -- situations where healthy Individuals can assume more than one Identity.	80%
P6	Multiple Identities	Differentiation	6	ADAPT differentiates Multiple Identities into two types – Shifting and Broadening Identities.	80%
P6a	Multiple Identities: Shifting	Added characteristic	11	ADAPT observes that we Shift our Identity when we shift our view among any of the four Fundamental Perspectives (D5a), and/or follow any of the four Fundamental Life Paths (D5b).	75%
P6b	Multiple Identities: Broadening	Added characteristic	11	ADAPT observes that we Broaden our Identity when we become more Inclusive as to who or what we Identify or empathize with.	80%
P6b	Multiple Identities: Broadening	Substantial agreement	1	ADAPT and Wilber substantially agree that Broadening involves expanding one's Moral Span.	90%
P6b	Multiple Identities: Broadening	Substantial agreement	1	Both ADAPT and Wilber differentiate Moral Span into several levels – nine levels in ADAPT's case.	85%
P7	Divine Presence	Substantial agreement, differing term	1	Both agree on the existence of a spiritual entity at the center of our being, which ADAPT calls the Divine Presence. [Wilber's *Spirit*]	80%
P7	Divine Presence	Substantial agreement	1	Both agree that the Divine Presence does not Transition from one Stage to the next, but is revealed through a process of Awakening (PPR9).	85%
P7	Divine Presence	Differing conception	12	Wilber considers Spirit to be primarily a subjective, Internal Experience (upper-left) – whereas ADAPT views the Divine Presence as also an objective, External Reality (upper-right).	70%

---

[18] Wilber's 'functional invariants' of the Self comprises a similar list of up to seven entities: metabolism, tension regulation, defenses, will, intersubjectivity, identity, cognition, navigation, and integration (*IP* 36-37, 226).

ADAPT & WILBER COMPARED

Letter/ Number	Parameter	Type of ADAPT modification	Mod #	ADAPT Modification of Wilber	Confidence in ADAPT position
P7	Divine Presence	Differing conception	12	ADAPT considers The Divine Presence in the form of Providence (PF12) to be our highest form of Pathfinder – the ultimate Guide & Orchestrator of our Life Journey.	70%
P7a-b	Divine Presence	Differentiation	6	ADAPT differentiates the Divine Presence into two separate manifestations, Core Self and Witness – corresponding to the Immanent and Transcendent. (see also T12)	80%
P7a-b	Divine Presence	Differentiation	6	ADAPT differentiates the Divine Presence between the Eastern conception of Spirit and Western conception of the Christian Trinity.	75%
P7a-b	Divine Presence: Immanent/ Transcendent	Extended conception	7	From a Western perspective, ADAPT equates the Immanent Presence to Christ (or His surrogate, the Holy Spirit), the Transcendent Presence to God.	75%
P7a	Divine Presence: Core Self	Rendering explicit	2	ADAPT makes explicit that the Core Self is our pure Identity – unaffected by material concerns, physical discomforts, or psychological obsessions and compulsions.	70%
P7a	Divine Presence: Core Self	Rendering explicit	2	ADAPT makes explicit that the Core Self is traditionally known as the Soul.	70%
P7b	Divine Presence: Witness	Substantial agreement	1	Both agree that the Witness (from an subjective point of view) is the experience of reality from the perspective of the all-seeing, all-knowing Observer.	70%
P7b	Divine Presence: Witness	Differing conception	12	ADAPT views the Witness (from an objective point of view) as the pervasive, overarching Presence that presides over all aspects of our existence -- observing, guiding, cherishing, and protecting us.	65%
PPR	**GENERAL PROCESSES**			**Totals: 50, 26, 12, 8**	
PR	Processes	Rendering explicit	2	ADAPT makes explicit that the Processes are all the Methods and Techniques that move us along the Growth Continuum.	95%
PPR/ PR	Processes: General and Specific	Differentiation	6	ADAPT differentiates between two types: General Processes that are always in available at any Stage, Realm, or Arena. Specific Processes that implement specific kinds of Growth at specific Stages, Realms, or Arenas.	95%
PPR	General Processes	Rendering explicit	2	ADAPT renders explicit that the General Processes are available to implement Growth at any Stage, Realm, or Arena.	90%
PPR	General Processes	Consolidation of concepts	3	ADAPT consolidates the various General Processes to nine different Processes.	90%
PPR1	Transition Cycle	Substantial agreement. Differing terms	1	Both agree that transition from one Stage to the next takes place through a Process of Metamorphosis, which ADAPT calls the Transition Cycle.[19]	90%
PPR1	Transition Cycle	Expanded conception	7	ADAPT expands Wilber's 3-phase Embedding Cycle into a 4-phase Transition Cycle -- consisting of Identification, Differentiation, Re-identification, and Integration.[20]	90%

---

[19] Wilber characterizes this metamorphosis as a *Fulcrum* -- which he considers either a 'milestone' (Stage) or a pivot point (Transition), but which is actually a combination of both.

[20] Wilber's *Fulcrum* consists of three phases: differentiation, identification, and integration (*IP*, p. 93. See also *IP*, pp. 35-36, 92-108, and *BHE*, p. 131.). Wilber's *Embedding* cycle drawn from Kegan, *The Evolving Self* (1992) and other works.

ADAPT & WILBER COMPARED

Letter/Number	Parameter	Type of ADAPT modification	Mod #	ADAPT Modification of Wilber	Confidence in ADAPT position
PPR2	Shadow Cycle	Rendering explicit	2	Both agree that a traumatic phase or episode can sometimes cause the Transition Cycle to malfunction.	90%
PPR2	Shadow Cycle	Expanded conception	7	To characterize that malfunction, ADAPT describes a distortion of the Transition Cycle, called the Shadow Cycle.	85%
PPR2	Shadow Cycle	Expanded conception	7	ADAPT describes the five phases of the Shadow Cycle: Identification, Detachment, Re-identification, Disassociation, and Di-sattachment.	80%
PPR2	Shadow Cycle	Rendering explicit	2	ADAPT makes explicit that the Shadow Cycle can produce a pernicious Shadow Self (P4), which in turn creates the Impasse (D7b) that blocks the Growth process. [see P4]	85%
PPR2	Shadow Cycle	Rendering explicit	2	ADAPT makes explicit that the Shadow Self can sometimes be resolved through Restoration Growth (PPR4).	80%
PPR2	Shadow Cycle	Rendering explicit	2	ADAPT makes explicit that malfunctions in the Transition Cycle (primarily Impasses, D6b) often originate in the earliest Stages of life – when the child is least defended and has the fewest tools for correct interpretation.	90%
PPR3-4	Actualization & Restoration Growth	Rendering explicit	2	ADAPT makes explicit that there are two distinct approaches to the Growth process – Actualization Growth for basically healthy people, and Restoration Growth for people with entrenched 'problems.'[21]	95%
PPR3	Actualization Growth	Rendering explicit	2	ADAPT makes explicit that Actualization Growth is 'growing forward' – meeting the normal Challenges of life through a series of healthy Transition Cycles.	95%
PPR3	Actualization Growth	Rendering explicit	2	ADAPT makes explicit that Actualization Growth is actualizing qualities for which we have an innate Potential, by moving progressively to higher and higher Stages of Development.	90%
PPR3	Actualization Cycle	Expanded conception	7	For Actualization Growth, ADAPT reformulates the Transition Cycle as the four-phase Actualization Cycle – consisting of Recognition, Engagement, Breakthrough, and Integration.	90%
PPR3	Actualization Growth	Expanded scope	7	ADAPT expands Actualization Growth to encompass other forms of growth beyond the individual Transition Cycle – including Collective Growth, Horizontal Growth, Evolution & Involution, and Awakening (PPR5-9).	90%
PPR4	Restoration Growth	Substantial agreement, differing term	1	Both substantially agree that Restoration Growth means 'growing backward' -- revisiting past Stage/s to resolve Impasses, so that normal, forward-directed Actualization Growth can resume.	90%
PPR4	Restoration Cycle	Expanded conception	7	ADAPT reformulates the Transition Cycle as a six-phase Restoration Cycle – consisting of Recognition, Resurrecting, Confronting, Re-experiencing, Re-integrating, and Resuming.	85%
PPR5	Collective Growth	Substantial agreement	1	Both agree that Growth can occur not only with Individuals, but also with Groups of people.	95%

---

[21] Wilber differentiates between the two forms of Growth, not by explicitly naming them, but by assigning them to different sections of his studies. In *Integral Psychology*, for example, Restoration Growth is addressed on pp. 91-110 and Table 1A – while a Program for Actualization Growth (primarily) is outlined on pp. 113-14 (although at this point still called 'integral therapy').

ADAPT & WILBER COMPARED

Letter/Number	Parameter	Type of ADAPT modification	Mod #	ADAPT Modification of Wilber	Confidence in ADAPT position
PPR5	Collective Growth	Rendering explicit	2	ADAPT makes explicit that both Vertical Growth and Horizontal Growth can occur not only with Individuals, but also with Groups of people.	90%
PPR5	Collective Growth	Expanded conception	7	ADAPT expands the Processes of Collective Growth to include not just Cultures, but Groups of all sizes and composition – couples, teams, ethnic groups, etc. (P2b)	90%
PPR5	Collective Growth	Rendering explicit	2	ADAPT makes explicit that Collective Growth can take place through the same mechanisms as Individual Growth (PPR1-4, 6-9).	80%
PPR5a	Collective Growth	Differentiation	6	ADAPT differentiates between Static Groups that don't grow or change, and Evolving Groups that do.	90%
PPR5b	Generation Cycle	Added Concept	11	ADAPT introduces an additional mechanism for growth at the Cultural level, the Generation Cycle.	70%
PPR5b	Generation Cycle	Restatement of concept	5	ADAPT restates Strauss & Howe's Generation Cycle as four phases: Prophetic, Reactive, Civic, and Bureaucratic.	70%
PPR5b	Generation Cycle	Added conception	11	ADAPT observes that a small number of great people typify, influence, and dominate each Generation.	70%
PPR5b	Generation Cycle	Restatement of concept	5	ADAPT restates Strauss & Howe's contention that five American Generation Cycles that have occurred since the European discovery of America.	65%
PPR5b	Generation Cycle	Differentiation	6	ADAPT differentiates between the shorter-term Generation Cycle from the very long-term Cultural Evolution (DD1+2b), which takes place over eons of time.	70%
PPR6	Horizontal Growth	Differentiation	6	ADAPT makes explicit the differentiation between General Processes pertaining to Vertical Growth (PPR1-5) and those pertaining to Horizontal Growth (PPR6). [Wilber's *Horizontal Translation*]	90%
PPR6	Horizontal Growth	Substantial agreement	1	ADAPT and Wilber agree that Horizontal Growth is Growth that takes place within a Stage.	95%
PPR6	Horizontal Growth	Substantial agreement	1	ADAPT and Wilber agree that Stages are generally periods when we extend related activities and skills we already know how to do.	95%
PPR6	Horizontal Growth	Elevated role	10	ADAPT elevates Horizontal Growth to a status comparable to Vertical Growth. [Wilber diminishes the role of Horizontal Growth, calling it 'moving furniture around' on a particular floor of a building.]	95%
PPR6 a-c	Horizontal Growth	Differentiation	6	ADAPT differentiates Horizontal Growth into 3 forms – Improvement & Translation, Equivalence, and Improvement Within Types.	85%
PPR6a	Horizontal: Improvement & Translation	Differentiation	6	ADAPT differentiates Improvement & Translation into its two aspects – Improving our abilities and Translating our competence to other related abilities.	90%
PPR6b	Horizontal: Equivalence	Substantial agreement	1	ADAPT and Wilber agree that both Gender and Enneagram Types are examples of true Horizontal Equivalence. That is, different Types go through the same Stages, but in different Styles.[22]	85%
PPR6b	Horizontal: Equivalence	Substantial agreement	1	ADAPT and Wilber agree that Enneagram Types do not grow Vertically, from one Type to the next.	90%

---

[22] As Wilber points out (*IP* 53-4), the Enneagram Types are examples of true Horizontal Equivalence – since each of the nine Roles exist on the same hierarchical level.

ADAPT & Wilber Compared

Letter/Number	Parameter	Type of ADAPT modification	Mod #	ADAPT Modification of Wilber	Confidence in ADAPT position
PPR7	Perspective Growth	Rendering explicit	2	ADAPT makes explicit that we can grow by broadening the Perspectives from which we view and orchestrate our lives.	90%
PPR7 a-b	Persp. Growth: Fundamental & Inclusiveness	Differentiation	6	ADAPT differentiates Perspective Growth into Fundamental Perspectives and Inclusiveness.	90%
PPR7 a-b	Persp. Growth: Fundamental & Inclusiveness	Expanded conception	7	ADAPT observes that Perspective Growth enables us to assume Multiple Identities (P6a-b) – either by Shifting or Broadening our Identity.	85%
PPR7a	Perspectives: Fundamental	Rendering explicit	2	ADAPT makes explicit that we can grow by broadening our viewpoint, interests, and actions to incorporate all four Fundamental Perspectives (P6a, D5a).	85%
PPR7b	Perspectives: Inclusiveness	Rendering explicit	2	ADAPT makes explicit that we can grow by broadening those with whom we Identify and empathize to include different Gender Types, different Ethnic Types, or other forms of Diversity (P6b).	85%
PPR8	Evolution & Involution	Rendering explicit	2	ADAPT makes explicit that Evolution & Involution are the twin Processes by which Directional Growth takes place.	90%
PPR8	Evolution & Involution	Substantial agreement	1	Both differentiate between the Ascending Direction of Evolution and the Descending Direction of Involution (D6a).	90%
PPR8 a-c	Evolution & Involution	Added conception	11	ADAPT identifies three manifestations of Evolution & Involution: Transcend & Include, Life Trajectories, and Gender Types.	80%
PPR8a	Ev & Inv: Transcend & Include	Restated conception	5	ADAPT restates the Transition and Restoration Cycles (PPR1, 4) as a three-phase Transcend & Include Cycle (PPR8a): Evolution, Disconnection, and Involution.	85%
PPR8b	Ev & Inv: Trajectories	Expanded conception	7	ADAPT identifies Life Trajectories as a form of Evolution & Involution, played out over the course of a lifetime (D6b).	85%
PPR8c	Ev & Inv: Gender Types	Expanded conception	7	ADAPT identifies the Equivalence of Male and Female Gender Types as manifestations of Evolution and Involution, respectively.	90%
PPR9	Awakening	Substantial agreement, differing term	1	Both agree that, whereas normal Actualization Growth (PPR4) is the Process of changing from one Stage to the next ('Growing Up'), spiritual Transcendence (PPR9) is the Process of Awakening to a truth that is unchanging and eternal ('Waking Up').	85%
PPR9	Awakening	Expanded conception	7	ADAPT observes that Droids (IN2) are those who remain in a coma-like sleep, while Creatives are engaged in a process of Awakening (PPR9).	85%
PR	**SPECIFIC PROCESSES**[23]			**Totals: 9, 8, 7, 2**	
PR	Specific Processes	Rendering explicit	2	ADAPT makes explicit that the Specific Processes are all the specialized Techniques and Methods that move us along particular Stages, Realms, and Arenas of the Growth Continuum.	95%

---

[23] Wilber's conception of the Specific Processes has evolved over the years. His first extensive recommendations of Growth techniques occurs at ends of each chapter in *No Boundary* (1979). In *Integral Psychology* (2000) he divides his recommendations between Restoration Processes, for people with serious pathologies – and Actualization Processes, for basically healthy people seeking to evolve [our terms]. In *Integral Spirituality* (2006) he advocates an expanded array of Processes under the title Integral Life Practice (ILP). Wilber's most complete application of Processes is found in the very valuable *Integral Life Practice* (2008), by Wilber, Patten, et al.

ADAPT & WILBER COMPARED

Letter/Number	Parameter	Type of ADAPT modification	Mod #	ADAPT Modification of Wilber	Confidence in ADAPT position
PR	Specific Processes	Expanded conception	7	ADAPT describes Specific Processes as methods of Personal and Cultural Evolution – originally invented to pass along specific forms of wisdom and expertise from one Generation to the next.	95%
PR	Specific Processes	Elevation of function	10	ADAPT identifies Parenting and Child Rearing (PF1) as the original source of the Specific Processes.	90%
PR	Specific Processes	Expanded conception	7	ADAPT observes that Specific Processes numerous, because they are primarily invented -- whereas General Processes are few in number, because they are primarily innate.	80%
PR	Specific Processes	Modified Methodology	8	Wilber derives his Specific Processes primarily from the psychological and spiritual literature and prevailing therapeutic practice. ADAPT adds to these, derivations from professional and personal experience in teaching, counseling, and child rearing.	90%
PR	Specific Processes	Expanded conception	7	ADAPT observes that many Specific Processes originate in the learning experiences of Everyday Life (D3a).	90%
PR 1-35	Specific Processes	Consolidation of Methods	3	ADAPT collects the many Methods and Techniques into 35 Specific Processes. [Wilber's *Integral Life Practice* (*ILP*) covers about half the 35 Specific Processes.]	90%
PR 1-35	Specific Processes	Consolidation of Methods	3	ADAPT categorizes the Specific Processes into 7 Themes of emphasis.	90%
PR 1-35	Spec. Processes: All Themes	Added Processes	11	ADAPT adds several Processes and Modalities to each of the seven Themes. [See tan textboxes in each of the seven PF sections for comparisons to Wilber.]	90%
PF	PATHFINDERS			Totals: 47, 23, 21, 8	
PF	Pathfinders	Substantial agreement, differing term	1	Both agree on the need for external assistance to Implement the growth process.	95%
PF	Pathfinders	Differentiation	6	ADAPT differentiates between two modes of implementing the growth process – Guidance & Orchestration.	95%
PF	Pathfinders: Guidance	Rendering explicit	2	ADAPT makes explicit that Guidance is the process of choosing and directing our activities through all the alternatives life offers us.	95%
PF	Pathfinders: Orchestration	Rendering explicit	2	ADAPT makes explicit that Orchestration is the process of weaving together, coordinating, and unifying all the Dimensions, Participants, and Processes, and Pathfinders that comprise the growth process.	95%
PF	Pathfinders	Consolidation of concept	3	ADAPT identifies 12 modes of Guidance & Orchestration, called Pathfinders.	95%
PF	Pathfinders	Consolidation of concept	3	ADAPT differentiates the 12 Pathfinders into three categories – Collective & Societal, Individual & Personal, and Internal.	90%
PF1-4	Pathfinders: Collective & Societal	Rendering explicit	2	ADAPT makes explicit that we receive Collective Guidance & Orchestration in the growth process from the Groups and Societies we grow up in.	95%
PF1	Pathfinders: Parents	Elevation in importance	10	ADAPT emphasizes the key role of Parents as the original, the most influential, and (ideally) most beneficial Guides of our growth Journey.	95%

ADAPT & WILBER COMPARED

Letter/Number	Parameter	Type of ADAPT modification	Mod #	ADAPT Modification of Wilber	Confidence in ADAPT position
PF1	Pathfinders: Parents	Expanded conception	7	ADAPT observes that Parents have five advantages over all other forms of Pathfinder: Understanding, Opportunity, Authority, Identification, and Motivation.	95%
PF2	Pathfinders: Society & Culture	Rendering explicit	2	ADAPT makes explicit that Society & Culture has a major role in guiding & orchestrating our lives.	95%
PF2	Pathfinders: Society & Culture	Rendering explicit	2	ADAPT observes that Society & Culture is uniquely positioned to influence our Growth: By providing a set of role models, a series of lessons on living life, a process of behavioral reinforcement, and a ready-made system of values to conduct our activities by.	95%
PF3	Pathfinders: Holistic Growth Situations	Added conception	11	As an important Pathfinder, ADAPT adds the Holistic Growth Situation -- a cluster of experiences that offers many diverse opportunities for growth in a single integrated activity.	95%
PF3	Pathfinders: Holistic Growth Situations	Differentiation	6	ADAPT identifies seven major Holistic Growth Situations: Child-raising, family gardening, building projects, theater productions, team sports, group backpacking, the workplace.	95%
PF4	Pathfinders: Authorities	Rendering explicit	2	ADAPT makes explicit that Guidance & Orchestration is provided by Authorities -- people with exceptional knowledge and wisdom whose work sheds light on and contributes to our growth.	95%
PF4	Pathfinders: Authorities	Differentiation	6	ADAPT identifies 12 different types of Authorities: From self-help gurus and politicians to philosophers and spiritual leaders.	95%
PF5-10	Pathfinders: Personal & Individual	Rendering explicit	2	ADAPT makes explicit that we receive Personal Guidance & Orchestration from Guides who we choose ourselves, or who work with us personally.	95%
PF5	Pathfinders: Long-term Partner	Rendering explicit	2	ADAPT makes explicit that we receive important Guidance & Orchestration from a Long-Term Partner -- a special person we choose to share our journey through life.	95%
PF5	Pathfinders: Long-term Partner	Expanded conception	7	ADAPT identifies three key features of a good Long-Term Partnership: Understanding, Trust, Commitment.	95%
PF6 a-d	Pathfinders: Counselor, Coach, Therapist	Rendering explicit	2	ADAPT makes explicit that Counselors, Coaches, and Therapists are a major form of Personal Guidance & Orchestration.	95%
PF6 a-d	Pathfinders: Counselor, Coach, Therapist	Differentiation	6	ADAPT differentiates between four types of Growth Professional: Counselor, Life Coach, Specialty Counselor, and Therapist.	95%
PF6a	Pathfinders: Counselor	Rendering explicit	2	ADAPT makes explicit that a Counselor is a Growth Practitioner specially trained to implement some aspect of Actualization Growth (PPR3) for people with Challenges (D7a).	95%
PF6b	Pathfinders: Life Coach	Rendering explicit	2	ADAPT makes explicit that a Life Coach is a Growth Practitioner specially trained to implement Growth in the 12 Arenas of Life Passages (D4a)	95%
PF6c	Pathfinders: Specialty Counselor	Rendering explicit	2	ADAPT makes explicit that a Specialty Counselor is a Growth Practitioner who provides assistance and implements Growth in a specific Arena of Life Passages (D4a)	95%
PF6bb	Pathfinders: Specialty Counselor	Differentiation	6	ADAPT differentiates among seven types of Specialty Counselor: Education, Career, Finances, Health, Relationships, Sexuality.	95%
PF6c	Pathfinders: Therapist	Rendering explicit	2	ADAPT makes explicit that a Therapist is a Growth Practitioner who is specially trained to implement Restoration Growth (PPR4) for people with Impasses (D7b).	95%

ADAPT & WILBER COMPARED

Letter/ Number	Parameter	Type of ADAPT modification	Mod #	ADAPT Modification of Wilber	Confidence in ADAPT position
PFa, d	Pathfinders: Growth Professionals	Shift in emphasis	9	ADAPT gives greater emphasis to non-traditional, Humanistic Growth Professionals who combine intuitive, experiential, body-aware therapies (PR29-33) -- techniques that go beyond traditional verbal exploration.	95%
PF7	Pathfinders: Spiritual Guide	Rendering explicit	2	ADAPT makes explicit that a trustworthy Spiritual Guide, with no pretensions to infallibility or godhood, is important for maintaining a consistent and diligent spiritual practice.	95%
PF7	Pathfinders: Spiritual Guide	Substantial agreement	1	Both agree that there are several types of Spiritual Guide -- including spiritual master, teacher, rabbi, and pastor.	95%
PF7	Pathfinders: Spiritual Guide	Substantial agreement	1	Both agree that there are several types of Spiritual Practices (PR33) -- including meditation, prayer, yoga, Tantra, Qi Gong, etc.	95%
PF8	Pathfinders: Mentors	Rendering explicit	2	ADAPT makes explicit that growth may also be implemented by Mentors – people who impart knowledge from their particular field of expertise, but also impart the processes of Growth that underlie that field.	95%
PF8	Pathfinders: Mentors	Differentiation	6	ADAPT identifies ten types of Mentors: Teachers, professors, creative artists, specialty counselors, social workers, natural medicine practitioners, doctors, social activists, motivational speakers, and managers & bosses.	95%
PF9	Pathfinders: Growth Center	Rendering explicit	2	ADAPT makes explicit the nature of the Growth Center -- a Holistic Growth Situation where people gather together with the explicit intent of cultivating a particular aspect of growth.	95%
PF9	Pathfinders: Growth Center	Rendering explicit	2	ADAPT makes explicit that a Growth Center is particularly effective at guiding growth, since it controls and orchestrates every aspect of the growth environment – thus directing each activity toward the desired form of development.	95%
PF9	Pathfinders: Growth Center	Differentiation	6	ADAPT identifies six main types of Growth Center: Monastery or Meditation Center, Liberal Arts College or University, Health Retreat, Creative Grade School, Intentional Community, and Human Potential Growth Center.	95%
PF9f	Pathfinders: Human Potential Growth Center	Broadened emphasis	4	In *Integral Spirituality*, Wilber extols the offerings of his own Growth Center, Integral Institute. ADAPT emphasizes the unique features and benefits of many established Growth Centers, such as Esalen Institute.	95%
PF10	Pathfinders: Integral Life Guide	Substantial agreement	1	Both agree that the highest form of Counseling & Therapy is Integral – combining all pertinent Growth Parameters.	95%
PF10	Pathfinders: Integral Life Guide	Broadened emphasis	4	ADAPT broadens the scope of Integral to incorporate all the Domains and Sectors of ADAPT -- thereby broadening the range of expertise and resources needed for assistance.	95%
PF10	Pathfinders: Integral Life Guide	Added conception	11	ADAPT identifies Integral Life Guide as the ideal professional to incorporate all the Domains and Sectors of ADAPT.	95%
PF10	Pathfinders: Integral Life Guide	Shift in emphasis	9	ADAPT emphasizes that the Integral Life Guide may be proficient in some areas, but able to refer clients for assistance in other areas.	95%
PF11-12	Pathfinders: Internal	Rendering explicit	2	ADAPT makes explicit that we can receive Internal Guidance & Orchestration in the growth process through Guidance we provide within ourselves, or develop internally.	95%
PF11	Pathfinders: Internal Navigator	Rendering explicit	2	ADAPT renders explicit the paramount importance of the Internal Navigator -- the Guide we form within ourselves by internalizing and integrating all the Guidance we receive from outside sources.	95%

Page 84. WILBER APPENDICES

ADAPT & WILBER COMPARED

Letter/ Number	Parameter	Type of ADAPT modification	Mod #	ADAPT Modification of Wilber	Confidence in ADAPT position
PF11	Pathfinders: Internal Navigator	Expanded conception	7	ADAPT broadens the scope of Growth experiences to incorporate all the Domains and Sectors of ADAPT -- thereby broadening the range of expertise and wisdom that must be assimilated by the Internal Navigator.	95%
PF11	Pathfinders: Internal Navigator	Expanded conception	7	ADAPT observes that the Internal Navigator enables us to become progressively more independent, more self-sufficient, more self-regulating, more autonomous, more mature.	95%
PF11	Pathfinders: Internal Navigator	Expanded conception	7	ADAPT observes that the Internal Navigator enables us to form an Internal Compass that leads us intuitively to the right decisions – decisions that orient our life in the right direction.	95%
PF12	Pathfinders: Providence	Rendering explicit	2	ADAPT makes explicit that Providence is the Guidance & Orchestration we receive from the Divine Presence (P7).	70%
PF12	Pathfinders: Providence	Differing conception	12	ADAPT views Providence as an objective, External Reality (upper-right), as well as a subjective, Internal Experience (upper-left).	65%
PF12	Pathfinders: Providence	Differing conception	12	ADAPT offers five common arguments for the existence of Providence.	70%
S	**SYSTEMS**			**Totals: 18, 16, 10, 5**	
S	Systems	Rendering explicit	2	ADAPT makes explicit that Growth occurs through the mechanism of the System.	95%
S	Systems	Expanded conception	7	To elucidate the concept of the System, ADAPT describes Systems of Civilization, Systems of Transportation, and Calvin's cartoon Systems.	95%
S	Systems	Consolidation of concepts	3	ADAPT consolidates the various mechanisms of Growth into a single concept called Systems of Growth.	90%
S	Systems	Added conception	11	ADAPT defines the System of Growth: The set of Dimensions, Participants, Processes, and Pathfinders that function together to move us along the Growth Continuum.	90%
S	Systems	Differentiation	6	ADAPT differentiates Systems into 8 types: Individual, Collective, Actualization, Restoration, Horizontal, Perspective, Evolution/ Involution, and Spiritual.	85%
S	Systems: Study	Modified Methodology	8	ADAPT defines the procedure for the study of Systems – consisting of eight Study Programs of selected readings.	90%
S1-8	Systems: ADAPT	Expanded conception	7	ADAPT shows how the whole ADAPT Model can be viewed as one grand System.	90%
S1-8	Systems: Life Journey	Expanded conception	7	ADAPT shows how the symbolic version of the ADAPT Model can be viewed as one grand System: the Life Journey Archetype.	90%
S1 thru 8	Systems	Added conception	11	ADAPT shows how each of the eight Systems of Growth is a mechanism that combines certain Dimensions, Participants, Processes, and Pathfinders.	90%
S1	Systems: Individual	Rendering explicit	2	ADAPT makes explicit that Individual Growth of the Self System (P1) by means of the Transition Cycle (PPR1) is a fundamental System of Growth.	90%
S2	Systems: Collective	Expanded conception	7	ADAPT expands Wilber's implicit System of Cultural Development (DD1+2b) to include Groups of all sizes, from Couples to Cultures (P2b).	90%

ADAPT & WILBER COMPARED

Letter/Number	Parameter	Type of ADAPT modification	Mod #	ADAPT Modification of Wilber	Confidence in ADAPT position
S2	Systems: Collective	Added conception	11	In addition to the normal Processes of Individual Growth, ADAPT proposes a System that incorporates Group-specific Collective Processes like the Generation Cycle (PPR5b).	70%
S3	Systems: Actualization	Expanded conception	7	ADAPT expands Wilber's implicit System of Actualization Growth (PPR3), facilitated by a Counselor and/or a Growth Center, by incorporating an Actualization Cycle (PPR3a).	90%
S4	Systems: Restoration	Expanded conception	7	ADAPT expands Wilber's implicit System of Restoration Growth (PPR4), facilitated by a Therapist, by incorporating a Shadow Cycle (PPR2a) and a Restoration Cycle (PPR4a).	90%
S5	Systems: Horizontal	Expanded conception	7	ADAPT expands Wilber's conception of Horizontal Growth (PPR6) into a System that incorporates 2 modes: Improvement & Translation and Equivalence.	85%
S6	Systems: Perspectives	Expanded conception	7	ADAPT expands Wilber's conception of Perspectives [PPR7, Wilber's *Quadrants*] into a System that incorporates two modes: Fundamental Perspectives and Inclusiveness.	80%
S7	Systems: Evolution/ Involution	Expanded conception	7	ADAPT expands Wilber's conception of Evolution & Involution (PPR8) into a System that incorporates two modes: Transcend & Include, and Life Trajectories	75%
S8	Systems: Spiritual	Expanded conception	7	ADAPT expands Wilber's conception of States of Awakening (PPR9), into a System that incorporates two Participants: the Core Self and the Witness (P7a-b).	70%
CL	**CONCLUSION**			**Totals: 9, 7, 7, 3**	
CL	Conclusion	Rendering explicit	2	ADAPT renders explicit that Awareness of the potential for Growth is the first step in growing.	90%
CL	Conclusion	Rendering explicit	2	ADAPT renders explicit that one of the best ways to enhance Awareness is to review the features of this book.	90%
CL	Conclusion	Revised methodology	8	ADAPT proposes two Methods of reviewing the features of this book in a focused manner: Follow the Thread and ADAPT Gallery.	95%
CL	Conclusion: Thread	Revised methodology	8	ADAPT defines Follow the Thread as following a single feature through the entire book.	95%
CL	Conclusion: Thread	Differentiation	6	ADAPT differentiates 15 Threads that can be followed to review any of 15 features.	95%
CL	Conclusion: Thread	Expanded conception	7	ADAPT observes that the Threads function to enhance one's Internal Navigator (PF11).	95%
CL	Conclusion: Thread	Expanded conception	7	ADAPT observes that the insights from the Threads may be 'forgotten' once the Internal Navigator is created – so that the Navigator can function intuitively and spontaneously.	95%
CL	Conclusion: Gallery	Revised methodology	8	ADAPT defines the Gallery as a set of entertaining cartoons and graphics, illustrating important concepts of the book.	95%
CL	Conclusion: Gallery	Expanded conception	7	ADAPT observes that transforming concepts into entertainment is one of the most effective ways to affix those concepts in one's mind.	95%
Appx A	**WILBER APPENDICES**			**Totals: 62, 47, 34, 19**	
A-C	Appendices	Differentiation	6	ADAPT differentiates seven ways the Appendices enhance the Main Text	95%

ADAPT & WILBER COMPARED

Letter/Number	Parameter	Type of ADAPT modification	Mod #	ADAPT Modification of Wilber	Confidence in ADAPT position
A1a-b	Wilber Diagrams	Differentiation	6	ADAPT differentiates in these diagrams between Wilber's AQAL and IOS Models.	95%
A1b	Wilber IOS Diagram	Consolidation of features	3	ADAPT consolidates the entire Wilber IOS Model of Systems, Domains, and Sectors into one comprehensive Circle Diagram.	95%
A1c	ADAPT Diagram	Consolidation of features	3	ADAPT consolidates the entire ADAPT Model of Systems, Domains, and Sectors into one comprehensive Circle Diagram.	95%
A2	ADAPT & Wilber	Substantial agreement	1	Both agree that Integral Theory is an investigation of the correspondences between all Developmental Systems, in all fields, from all four Perspectives.	95%
A2	ADAPT & Wilber	Added conception	11	From a more personal perspective, ADAPT views Integral Theory as an investigation of the structures, sequences, and systems that make human life significant and rewarding.	90%
A2	ADAPT & Wilber	Alternative methodologies	8	Wilber's positions are largely derived from the psychological literature, the perennial traditions, and descriptions of therapeutic practice. ADAPT adds to these further derivations from professional and personal experience -- including counseling clients, teaching school, the study of symbolic literature, extensive experience in personal growth, and raising children.[24]	90%
A2a	AQAL & IOS	Agreement	1	ADAPT and Wilber agree that the AQAL Parameters are Quadrants and Levels -- with Lines, States, Self, and/or Types often added in the extended version.	95%
A2a	AQAL & IOS	Differentiation	6	ADAPT differentiates between Wilber's more limited AQAL Model and his complete Integral Operating System (IOS) Model of Human Development.[25]	95%
A2b-d	AQAL & IOS	Consolidation of parameters	3	ADAPT collects all the Parameters of Wilber's IOS into one, more comprehensive Developmental Model.	95%
A2b	AQAL & IOS	Differentiation	6	ADAPT differentiates the Parameters of Wilber's IOS Model into four major Domains – Dimensions, Participants, Processes, and Pathfinders.	95%
A2c	AQAL & IOS	Expanded conception	7	ADAPT observes that Wilber's AQAL consists of 4 Dimensions and 2 Participants.	95%
A2d	AQAL & IOS	Expanded conception	7	ADAPT observes that Wilber's IOS consists of over two dozen Dimensions, Participants, Processes, and Pathfinders.	95%
A2e	ADAPT	Consolidation of features	3	ADAPT formulates the five Domains (incl. Systems) as a new Integral Model called ADAPT: All Dimensions, All Participants, All Processes, all Pathfinders, Together.	95%
A2f	ADAPT	Reorganization of concepts	5	ADAPT substantially fine-tunes Wilber's IOS – by revising and expanding the number and character of Parameters that define Human Development.	90%
A2g	ADAPT	Reorganization of concepts	5	ADAPT formulates the complete ADAPT Model -- consisting of 8 Dimensions, 7 Participants, 9 General Processes, 35 Specific Processes, 12 Pathfinders, and 8 Systems.	90%

---

[24] For details, see Biographical Background in Appendix.

[25] Wilber uses the term *Integral Operating System* to describe the AQAL Model, as applied to Human Development. ADAPT uses the term to cover all Wilber's Parameters applied to Human Development.

ADAPT & Wilber Compared

Letter/Number	Parameter	Type of ADAPT modification	Mod #	ADAPT Modification of Wilber	Confidence in ADAPT position
A2h	ADAPT	Added conception	11	As the fifth Domain of ADAPT, ADAPT adds Systems – the mechanisms by which the other four Domains are combined and coordinated.	95%
A2i	ADAPT	Methodology	8	ADAPT depicts the Systems as a set of concentric circles, divided into section representing the four Domains.	95%
A2j	ADAPT	Methodology	8	ADAPT fills in the sectors to depict the entire ADAPT Model as one, grand Circle Diagram.	90%
A2k	ADAPT	Elevation of validity	10	ADAPT performs point-by-point comparisons between Wilber's positions and those of ADAPT, to reveal Wilber positions most in need of reconsideration.	85%
A2l	Life Journey	Added conception	11	ADAPT reveals the parallels between the conceptual ADAPT Model and the symbolic Life Journey Archetype – both for Domains and for Sectors.	90%
A2l	Life Journey	Elevation of validity	10	ADAPT uses the Life Journey Archetype to demonstrate that the ADAPT Model is not just one theory among many, but the universal model that people have used since the dawn of time to describe the progressions of human life.	85%
A2l	Life Journey	Enhanced methodology	8	ADAPT uses the Life Journey both to illustrate important points and as an analytical source for further insights.	90%
A2m	ADAPT: Revelations	Elevation of role	10	ADAPT transforms the ADAPT Model from intellectual exercise to personal revelation – revealing the Model's applicability to real life.	90%
A2m	ADAPT: Revelations	Elevation of role	10	ADAPT is raised in significance to a detailed blueprint on how to live a life that is richly satisfying and rewarding.	90%
A2n	ADAPT: Applications	Expanded conception	7	ADAPT broadens the applicability of ADAPT to include a wide variety of occupations and fields of study (IN1a).	90%
A7a	Developmental Sequences: External & Internal	Added conception	11	ADAPT distinguishes between Developmental Sequences that are External and those that are Internal.	90%
A7a	Developmental Sequences: External & Internal	Rendering explicit	2	ADAPT renders explicit that External Sequences follow the tangible, observable externals of the human biological cycle – and are therefore relatively predictable and inevitable.	95%
A7a	Developmental Sequences: External & Internal	Expanded conception	7	ADAPT observes that External Sequences are characteristic of the Life Passages Realm and Arenas.	95%
A7a	Developmental Sequences: External & Internal	Rendering explicit	2	ADAPT characterizes the Internal Developmental Sequences as neither predictable or inevitable – with each person following a pace of their own.	90%
A7a	Developmental Sequences: External & Internal	Expanded conception	7	ADAPT observes that Internal Sequences are characteristic of the Realms of Psyche, Body, and Spirit.	90%

ADAPT & Wilber Compared

Letter/Number	Parameter	Type of ADAPT modification	Mod #	ADAPT Modification of Wilber	Confidence in ADAPT position
A7b	Fundamental Developmental Sequence	Rendering explicit, differing term	2	ADAPT makes explicit the all-inclusive series of Internal Stages & Transitions that is implicit in Wilber's Tables (especially Correlative Structures, the vertical coordinate displayed on each page).[26] ADAPT calls this the Wilber's Fundamental Developmental Sequence (FDS).	80%
A7b	Fundamental Developmental Sequence	Rendering explicit	2	ADAPT makes explicit: The FDS subsumes all other, more abbreviated Developmental Sequences – and therefore allows Wilber to make direct correspondence between the Developmental Models of many different Authorities.	80%
A7b	Fundamental Developmental Sequence	Rendering explicit	2	ADAPT makes explicit: That these Correspondences among Developmental Models are the foundation for Wilber's 'Theory of Everything.'	90%
A7c	Fundamental Developmental Sequence	Rendering explicit	2	ADAPT observes that Stages from different researchers can be shown to match by assigning them to the proper Steps of the FDS.	80%
A7d	Fundamental Developmental Sequence	Consolidation of Parameters	3	For clarity and simplicity, ADAPT consolidates Wilber's 38 FDS Steps into colored bands – consisting of 12 Clusters, and in turn into 7 central Zones. [Wilber's Functional Groupings]	80%
A7d	Chakras	Rendering explicit	2	ADAPT makes explicit that this consolidation of Steps into Clusters, and Clusters into Zones, represents Wilber's Western conception of the Chakras.	70%
A7d	Chakras	Rendering explicit	2	ADAPT observes that this consolidation approximates Wilber's own conception of the Chakras, but is not identical to it.	80%
A7d	Chakras	Expanded conception	7	ADAPT describes one version of the Eastern Chakras as energy phenomena manifested simultaneously in the three Internal Realms of Psyche, Body, and Spirit. (See D3b-d)	60%
A7d	Chakras	Expanded conception	7	ADAPT observes that the two versions of the Chakras dictate two forms of Growth for Body, Psyche, and Spirit – one successive, the other simultaneous (A7f).	80%
A7e	Chakras	Revised methodology	8	ADAPT demonstrates that the simplified Chakra version of the FDS clarifies correlations among researchers (A7C).	75%
A7f	Succession & Accumulation	Added conception	11	ADAPT differentiates between two very different forms of growth – Succession and Accumulation	90%
A7f	Succession Growth	Substantial Agreement	1	Both agree that Succession Growth is ladder-like – with Growth progressing from one distinct Step to the next.	90%
A7f	Succession Growth	Expanded conception	7	ADAPT characterizes Succession Growth as occurring primarily in the Realm and Arenas of Life Passages – as well as in certain Arenas of the Psyche (Cognitive).	90%
A7f	Accumulation Growth	Added conception	11	ADAPT describes Accumulation Growth as a tree-like – with Growth occurring simultaneously and reciprocally in roots (Body), trunk (Life), branches (Psyche), and buds (Spirit).	90%
A7f	Accumulation Growth	Expanded conception	7	ADAPT characterizes Accumulation Growth as occurring in most Realms of the Psyche, the Body, and the Spirit.	75%

---

[26] In the authors' study *Arrays of Light,* note the left-hand column of all Wilber's Tables. Note in particular Table 1A, the Fundamental Developmental Sequence – which we have transcribed directly from the left-hand reference column of Wilber's Tables, adding a definition of each Step that corresponds (to the best of our understanding) to Wilber's intent. See also the Fundamental Developmental Sequence section, page 5, of the Introduction to those Tables.

ADAPT & WILBER COMPARED

Letter/ Number	Parameter	Type of ADAPT modification	Mod #	ADAPT Modification of Wilber	Confidence in ADAPT position
A7g	Models of Self	Added conception	11	ADAPT differentiates between the Layered Model of Self (Archeology) and the Retrofit Model of the of Self (Architecture). [27]	90%
A7g	Models of Self	Substantial agreement	1	Both agree that the Archeology Model consists of one Layer of Self stacked on another.	90%
A7g	Models of Self	Added conception	11	ADAPT observes that with the Architecture Model, the Self is like an old building retrofitted with new functionality.	85%
A7g	Models of Self	Added conception	11	ADAPT observes that the Self is both Archeology and Architecture.	85%
A7h	Modes of Treatment	Added conception	11	ADAPT distinguishes between Archeology and Architecture as modes of Actualization Growth (PPR3).[28]	90%
A7h	Modes of Treatment	Added conception	11	ADAPT distinguishes between Archeology and Architecture as modes of Restoration Growth (PPR4).	90%
A8a-c	Dev Sequences: Arenas	Expanded conception	7	ADAPT observes that, for every Realm (D3a-d) with a Developmental Sequence, there is a set of Arenas (D4a-d) with comparable Developmental Sequences.	90%
A8a	Dev Sequences: Life Passage Arenas	Expanded conception	7	ADAPT outlines Developmental Sequences for the 12 Arenas of Life Passages.	90%
A8b	Dev Sequences: Psyche Passage Arenas	Expanded conception	7	ADAPT outlines Developmental Sequences for the nine Arenas of Psyche Passages.	80%
A8c	Dev Sequences: Spirit Passage Arenas	Expanded conception	7	ADAPT outlines Developmental Sequences for the nine Arenas of Spirit Passages.	70%
A9a	Actualization Growth	Substantial agreement, differing terms	1	ADAPT & Wilber agree that the Methodologies of Integral Life Practice (ILP) are important and valuable Specific Processes (PR).	95%
A9a	Actualization Growth	Expanded conception	7	ADAPT approximately doubles the number of Specific Processes offered in Integral Life Practice.	90%
A9b	Restoration Growth	Substantial agreement	1	ADAPT and Wilber agree that Pathologies at different Stages of Development require different Modes of Treatment.	90%
A9b	Restoration Growth	Substantial agreement	1	ADAPT and Wilber substantially agree on what Modes of Treatment are appropriate at different Stages of Development.	90%
A9c	Actualization Growth	Added conception	11	ADAPT adds to ILP another conception of Actualization Growth: Anodea Judith's Balancing the Chakras.	80%
A9c	Actualization Growth	Added conception	11	ADAPT adds the Healing Strategies & Balanced Characteristics from Anodea Judith's Balancing the Chakras.	80%

---

[27] Wilber portrays our interior architecture as an '**Archeology**' -- where the Realms of Body, Psyche, and Spirit are stacked on one another, like layers of an archeological dig. (See for example: *IP, The Archeology of Spirit*, pp. 89-114.)

[28] The distinction between Archeology and Architecture affects the whole strategy of Personal Growth or therapeutic treatment. With a **Layered Model** (Wilber's) the Realms of Body, Mind, and Spirit are dealt with *sequentially* – because they succeed one another on the developmental ladder. With a **Retrofit Model**, all three Realms are addressed *simultaneously* at every Stage of Development -- because they are structurally inseparable.

ADAPT & Wilber Compared

Letter/Number	Parameter	Type of ADAPT modification	Mod #	ADAPT Modification of Wilber	Confidence in ADAPT position
Appx B1-3	**CAMPBELL APPENDICES**			Totals: 30, 22, 17, 12	
B1	Archetypes	Substantial agreement	1	ADAPT and Wilber agree that Archetypes and Myths originated as an archaic Stage of Cultural Development.	90%
B1	Archetypes	Added conception	11	ADAPT views Archetypes and Myths as also a language for describing the progressions through all Stages of Development (D1).	90%
B1	Archetypes	Added conception	11	ADAPT views Archetypes and Myths as also a subtle language for describing, apprehending, accessing, and evoking the Transcendent States (D8).	80%
B1	Hero's Journey	Substantial agreement	1	Both agree that the Hero's Journey is a pattern of symbolic narrative featuring the trials and triumphs of a central heroic character.	95%
B1	Hero's Journey	Substantial agreement	1	Both agree that the Hero's Journey is an important and valid method of analyzing myths and legends.	90%
B1	Hero's Journey	Expanded conception	7	ADAPT expands the conception of the Hero's Journey to include: A means of interpreting movies and literature, a means of analyzing myth and legend, a means of interpreting one's own trials and triumphs, Campbell's own public persona, etc.	90%
B1	Life Journey	Differentiation	6	ADAPT identifies the Campbell's Hero's Journey as a special case of the Life Journey.	90%
B1	Life Journey	Expanded conception	7	ADAPT identifies the archetypal Life Journey as one of the Spirit Arenas (D4d4).	80%
B1	Life Journey	Expanded conception	7	ADAPT observes that the innumerable, small Hero's Journeys of our childhood are just a rehearsal for the great Life Journey we will take.	90%
B1a	Hero's Journey	Substantial agreement	1	Both substantially agree that Campbell's own persona is that of a Hero in popular culture.	90%
B1b	Hero's Journey	Substantial agreement	1	Both substantially agree that the Hero's Journey is useful tool for interpreting prominent themes in pop culture.	95%
B1b	Hero's Journey	Substantial agreement	1	Both substantially agree that many icons of popular culture, like *Star Wars* and *The Wizard of Oz*, are manifestations of the Hero's Journey.	95%
B1c	Hero's Journey	Substantial agreement	1	ADAPT and Wilber substantially agree as to the number and content of the 17 Steps in Campbell's Hero's Journey.	95%
B1d	Hero's Journey	Differentiation	6	ADAPT differentiates among 5 types of Hero's Journeys: Realistic or Symbolic, combined with Individual or Cultural, or all four together.	90%
B1e	Hero's Journey	Expanded conception	7	ADAPT applies the Hero's Journey to many examples classic literature and movies.	90%
B1f	Hero's Journey	Expanded conception	7	ADAPT applies the Hero's Journey to personal growth – the Inner Hero's Journey.	90%
B1f	Hero's Journey	Differentiation	6	ADAPT differentiates the Inner Hero's Journey into three levels breadth and significance: Micro, Macro, and Mega.	90%
B1f	Hero's Journey	Expanded conception	7	ADAPT applies the three levels of Inner Hero's Journey to nine different areas of life -- education, relationships, career, etc.	90%
B1g	Hero's Journey	Expanded conception	7	ADAPT identifies the 14 Steps of the Inner Hero's Journey.	90%

ADAPT & WILBER COMPARED

Letter/Number	Parameter	Type of ADAPT modification	Mod #	ADAPT Modification of Wilber	Confidence in ADAPT position
B1g	Hero's Journey	Expanded conception	7	ADAPT applies the 14 Steps of the Inner Micro-Journey.	90%
B1h	Archetypal Characters	Substantial agreement	1	Both agree the myths, legends, and classic literature are populated with archetypal stock characters that occur time and again	95%
B1h	Archetypal Characters	Differentiation	6	ADAPT differentiates Archetypal Characters into eight Types.	85%
B1h	Archetypal Characters	Expanded conception	7	ADAPT applies the eight Archetypal Character Types to two examples of classic, mythic literature.	90%
B2	Life Journey	Alternative methodology	8	By reverse engineering, ADAPT derives Campbell's Hero's Journey from the ADAPT Model.	85%
B2a	Life Journey	Expanded conception	7	ADAPT derives the symbolic Domains of the Life Journey Archetype from the conceptual Domains of ADAPT.	95%
B2b	Life Journey	Expanded conception	7	ADAPT derives the symbolic Sectors of the Life Journey Archetype from the conceptual Sectors of ADAPT.	90%
B2c	Hero's Journey	Reorganization of concept	5	To allow meaningful comparisons, ADAPT rearranges the Steps of Campbell's Hero's Journey to match the various Domains and Sectors of ADAPT.	80%
B2c	Hero's Journey	Elevation of status	10	ADAPT reinterprets the Hero's Journey as an extensive (though incomplete) version of ADAPT.	90%
B3b	Homer's *The Odyssey*	Expanded conception	7	ADAPT applies ADAPT Model to Homer's *The Odyssey*, resulting in additional features for the Model.	90%
B3b	Homer's *The Odyssey*	Expanded conception	7	ADAPT applies Life Journey Archetype to Homer's *The Odyssey*, resulting in additional features for the Archetype.	90%

THE INTERNAL DEVELOPMENTAL SEQUENCE...

Can be an Ascending Spiral...

Or a Great Tree... Or both.

The two Symbols represent the two forms of Internal Development: Succession Growth (Spiral) and Accumulation Growth (Tree). (see Appx A7f)

Appendix A7.
The Internal Developmental Sequence:
How Wilber's FDS Became ADAPT's IDS

External Developmental Sequences. For the External Realm of Life Passages (D3a), and for the External Arenas such as Relationships and Career & Calling (D4b-d, Appx. A8a), the Developmental Sequence is determined primarily by our biological Life Cycle. That is, we all go through the Stages of Infancy, Toddlerhood, Childhood, Adolescence, etc. – and in the course of those Stages, we develop in our Relationships, in our Education, in our Career, etc. These are our **External Developmental Sequences**.

Internal Developmental Sequences. On the other hand, how do we describe the Developmental Sequence for the Internal Realms of Psyche, Body, and Spirit? Clearly, we grow from Stage to Stage – but that Growth is not necessarily linked to the Life Cycle. We all know of child prodigies whose thinking capacities are far more advanced than most adults. We also know of mentally retarded adults whose thinking capacities will never surpass those of a typical six-year-old. These phenomena require another sort of Developmental Sequence altogether – an **Internal Developmental Sequence**.

Wilber's Internal Developmental Sequence Ken Wilber addressed these issues by propounding a comprehensive Sequence for Internal Development – a Sequence that applies to all three Internal Realms (D3b-d), and to all Arenas within those three Realms (D4b-d). We call that conception Wilber's **Fundamental Developmental Sequence**, or **FDS**. The FDS enables us to correlate any Developmental Sequence with any other, and therefore to see all Developmental Sequences as one. The underlying unity of all Sequences of Development is what Wilber means by **Integral**. It is the basis for his **Theory of Everything**.

The Chakras: A Condensation of Wilber's FDS. Wilber's FDS is far too complex and cumbersome for general use. Therefore, we have stripped the FDS down to its essentials – the seven basic Internal Stages or Phases we refer to as the **Chakras**. Throughout this book, we have used the Chakras as an approximation of the FDS for depicting any Internal Developmental Sequence. In this section, we show how an Internal Developmental Sequence based on the Chakras may be derived from the FDS – and explore other conclusions that result from that derivation. On the facing page, we outline the points we will be covering.

The Internal Developmental Sequence is particularly complex, abstruse, and esoteric. This topic is currently under development and subject to revision. Comments and suggestions from readers are welcome.

The Internal Developmental Sequence (Appx A7) describes the Stages (D1) and Transitions (D2) of Actualization Growth (PPR3), in the Realms of Psyche, Body, and Spirit (D3b-d) – as well as in their corresponding Arenas (D4b-d). For further details, see: The Developmental Sequence (esp. D1+2b-c.) and the complete set of Arenas for Psyche and Spirit (Appx A8b-c).

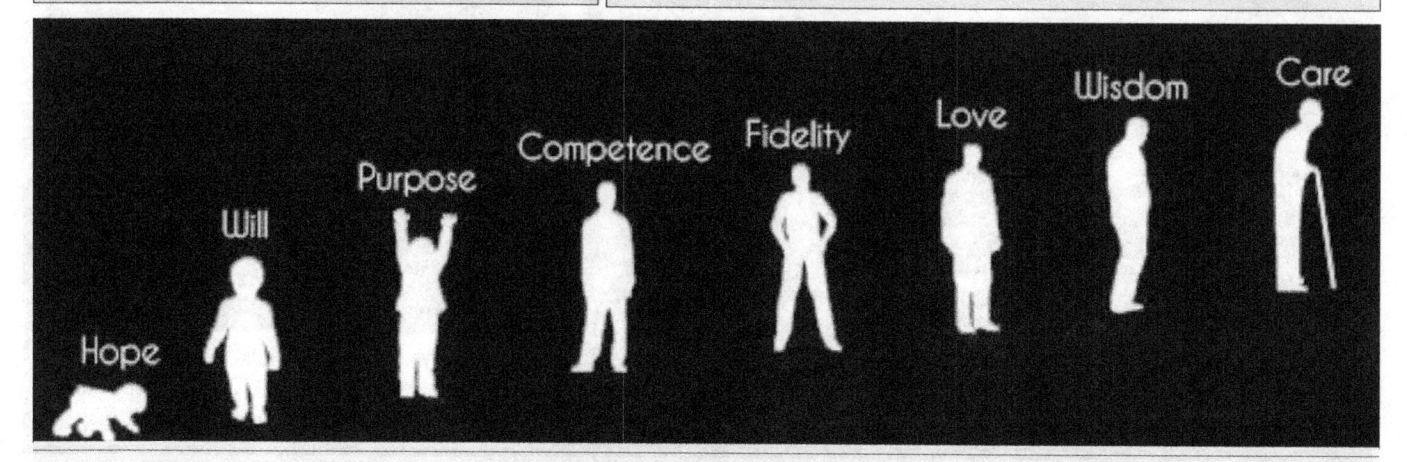

Hope · Will · Purpose · Competence · Fidelity · Love · Wisdom · Care

Internal Developmental Sequence
The internal qualities of our character and personality develop over the course of a lifetime.

THE INTERNAL DEVELOPMENTAL SEQUENCE:
How It Is Derived, What It Tells Us

The Internal Developmental Sequence (IDS) describes the Developmental Stages & Transitions for the Internal Realms of Psyche, Body, and Spirit (D3b-d). This concept is crucial for tracing how Growth that takes place in these Realms and in their corresponding Arenas (D4b-d). In the sections that follow, we describe the most comprehensive of all IDS's: Ken Wilber's 38-Step **Fundamental Developmental Sequence**, or **FDS**. We show how the FDS can be simplified to form the seven-Stage Sequence called the **Chakras**. Then we show how this Internal Developmental Sequence of the Chakras can be applied to two contrasting Models of Self and two corresponding Modes of Treatment.

- **A7a. External & Internal Developmental Sequences.** Developmental Sequences (D1+2) are of two basic types -- External and Internal. External: Sequences like Physical Development and Life Passages that occur in the externals of people's lives. Internal: Sequences in the Realms of Psyche, Body, and Spirit that occur on people's insides. (page 96)

- **A7b. Wilber's Fundamental Developmental Sequence.** The most comprehensive Developmental Sequence for Internal Passages is Ken Wilber's Fundamental Developmental Sequence (FDS) – an overarching progression of 38 Steps that incorporates all possible Stages of Internal Development in their proper order. (page 97)

- **A7c. Correlations Among Researchers: Self & Ego.** The FDS is important because: It enables us to compare and correlate Developmental Sequences for any form of Human Development in the Realms of Psyche, Body, or Spirit. For instance, the Stages propounded by four researchers in the Arena of Self & Ego correlate fully with one another, when positioned according to the FDS. (page 100)

- **A7d. The Chakras: A Simplified FDS.** The FDS is too complex and cumbersome for general use. Therefore, we consolidate Wilber's 38 Steps into the seven Phases – Phases commonly known as the Chakras. We then distinguish between two versions of the Chakras – the Chakras of Eastern philosophy, and the similar but not identical set of Chakras propounded by Ken Wilber. (page 102)

- **A7e. Correlations Among Researchers: Chakra Version.** When the Developmental Systems of the same four researchers (A7c) are presented using the simplified Sequence of the Chakras, they show even more how clearly how the Stages from the four Researchers correlate with one another. (page 106)

- **A7f. Succession vs. Accumulation.** A particular Developmental Sequence may take one of two forms -- Succession Growth or Accumulation Growth. In Succession Growth (like Life Passages and Psyche Passages), we progress sequentially from one Stage to the next. In Accumulation Growth (like Body and Spirit Passages), each new Stage is <u>added</u> to the last, as an additional mode of functionality. Because of these two forms, the Chakras can sometimes appear as Stages of Development (Succession) and sometimes as regions of the Body or sets of characteristics (Accumulation). (page 108)

- **A7g-h. Two Models of Self, Two Modes of Treatment.** The form that Growth takes (A7f) will determine the appropriate Model of Self (A7g) and Mode of Treatment (A7h). Succession Growth produces a Layered Model of the Self – where problems are resolved exploring our inner Archeology. Accumulation Growth produces a Retrofit Model of Self – where problems are resolved by renovating our internal Architecture. (page 110)

A7a. External & Internal Passages of Growth

EXTERNAL DEVELOPMENTAL SEQUENCES

In the earlier sections of this book, we concentrated primarily on Developmental Sequences that pertain to the externals of people's lives – especially the Life Passages Sequence (D1, D2, D1+2), the Relationships Sequence (DD1+2aa), and the Career & Calling Sequence (D4ab). These **External Developmental Sequences** trace the Development of the tangible, observable externals of people's lives. They describe familiar, predictable, and often inevitable Stages that are governed by the human biological life cycle. That is, everyone on earth goes through the external Stages of Gestation, Infancy, Toddlerhood, Childhood, Adolescence, etc. – because that is our nature as human beings.

INTERNAL DEVELOPMENTAL SEQUENCES

However, we may also go through a series of **Internal Passages** – Stages and Transitions that pertain to the Realms of our Psyche, Body, and Spirit (D3b-d). Unlike External Sequences, Internal Sequences are by no means inevitable. All of us grow in physical maturity from child to adult (external) – but we do not necessarily grow in emotional or spiritual maturity over that same period (internal). We all know of precocious children who think and behave like adults even at an early age. We also know of immature adults who never grow up, and continue to behave like spoiled, self-centered brats even in their later years. (For further details, see D1+2b-c.)

External Developmental Sequences. The Developmental Sequence for Life Passages includes all the Stages & Transitions of the biological Life Cycle between Infancy and Old Age.

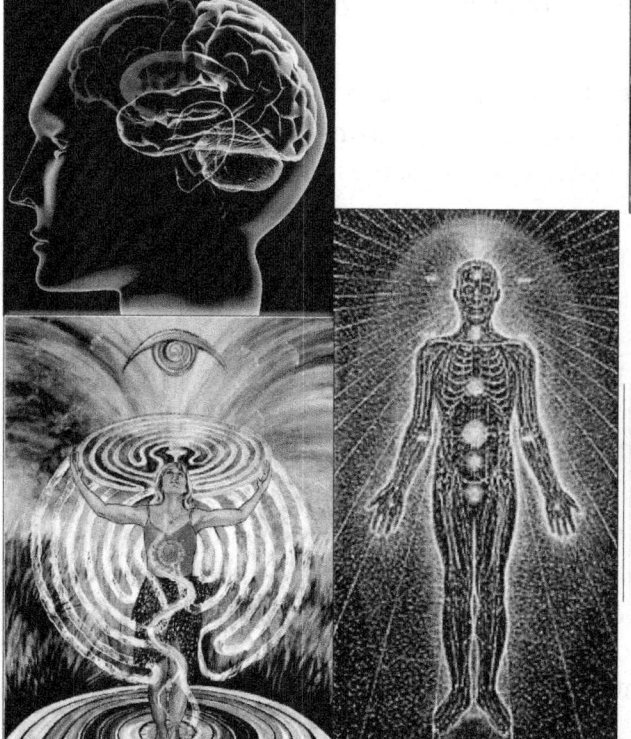

Internal Developmental Sequences. The internal Developmental Sequences describe all the Growth that's occurring on the inside in the Realms of Psyche, Body, and Spirit.

External & Internal Passages: Wilber concentrates on Internal Passages of *Transformation*.

A7b. Wilber's Fundamental Developmental Sequence

The External Developmental Sequence can be described by a series of Stages and Transitions familiar to us all – Conception, Gestation, Birth, Infancy, etc. But how can we describe the Stages and Transitions of Internal Development – Stages that clearly take place, but are far less obvious and familiar? A viable answer is provided by Ken Wilber's Fundamental Developmental Sequence.

The **Fundamental Developmental Sequence** (FDS) is perhaps Ken Wilber's most significant contribution to human thought. Wilber surveyed over 200 Developmental Systems to determine what Stages and Transitions they all had in common. These Systems were drawn from scientists, scholars, psychologists, philosophers, and mystics from both ancient and modern times – Authorities who had each propounded Sequences of Human Development in their own particular field of expertise. In order to correlate and combine the Stages from these Sequences, Wilber devised an overarching progression we call the Fundamental Developmental Sequence. That Sequence accounts for all the Stages in all these systems, puts those Stages in their proper order, and shows how all those Systems relate to one another. In that way, Wilber combines all individual and particular developmental systems into one grand system – a system he characterizes as his Theory of Everything.

Ken Wilber's Fundamental Developmental Sequence (slightly abbreviated and modified) is shown on the following two facing pages. It consists of 27 Stages and States, separated by 11 Transitions – 38 Steps in all.

The Ultimate Developmental Sequence.
"Ken Wilber's Fundamental Developmental Sequence is an effort to incorporate all Developmental Sequences from all researchers into a one, grand Sequence that encompasses them all. That's what makes it a Theory of Everything."

Experiencing Your Internal Evolution

Consider Ken Wilber's FDS on the following two facing pages. The left column is the Step Number. The second column lists the Stages and States Wilber has identified. The third column describes those Stages and States in greater detail. *** Beginning at the bottom of the right-hand page, focus on that third column and scan upward. Do not be concerned with understanding every detail of these concepts. You are merely attempting to experience what feels like to evolve internally. *** Imagine yourself as a being that is evolving through all these Stages of Development – first inert matter, then a living entity, then an organism with the capacity to respond to stimuli, then a dawning awareness of identity, then a capacity for primitive thought, then a capacity of logical thought and generalization, and so forth. ***
Meditate for perhaps half a minute upon each state of being. Let your imagination flow without restraint. *** Then portray the major steps through some form of artistic expression – with colored markers on large sheets of butcher paper, for example.

[Disregard Columns 4 & 5 for now. These columns will be filled in under Chakras (Appx A7d, page 102).]

[Read table from bottom of facing page to top of this page.]

A7b. Wilber's Fundamental Developmental Sequence (FDS)

#	FDS Steps & Stages (Wilber)	FDS Step Descriptions		
38	[Beyond consciousness/ Divine]	[Beyond consciousness]		
37	- transition -	[Relinquishment of consciousness]		
36	Non-dual: Late	Constant consciousness		
35	Non-dual: Middle	Spirit and World Process		
34	**Non-dual**: Early	Non-dual mysticism – union of form and formless		
33	- transition -	Merging of consciousness with Creator		
32	Causal: Late	Cessation – union with the source of all manifest realms		
31	**Causal** (formless): Early	Formless mysticism – awareness of the source of consciousness		
30	- transition -	Emergent consciousness of the holy essence of the Creator		
29	Subtle: Late	Union with creator of gross realm		
28	**Subtle** (archetype): Early	Deity mysticism – awareness of divine source of creation		
27	- transition -	Departure from the material realm. Emergent consciousness of the Creator		
26	Psychic: Late	Union with the world process		
25	**Psychic** (vision): Early	Nature mysticism – awareness of divine embodied in the material		
24	- transition -	Emergent consciousness of supernatural realm beyond the material		
23	Vision/Logic: Late	Integrated perspectives: Holistic, unified, integral thinking		
22	Vision/Logic: Middle	Interacting perspectives: Dialectical, comparative thinking		
21	**Vision/Logic**: Early	Multiple perspectives: Relative, pluralistic, contextual thinking		
20	- transition -	Emergence from mechanistic to fluid, multi-dimensional thinking		
19	Formal: Late	Broad, complex abstract and logical thinking		
18	**Formal**: Early	Small, simple abstract and logical thinking		
17	- transition -	Emergence from myth and superstition to generalized, abstract logical thinking		
16	Rule/role: Late	Large, complex social structures – elaborate rules and roles		
15	**Rule/role**: Early	Small, simple social structures – basic rules and roles		

Increasing Advancement & Maturity →

Wilber's Fundamental Developmental Sequence (cont.)

Increasing Advancement & Maturity ↑

#	FDS Steps & Stages (Wilber)	FDS Step Descriptions
14	*- transition -*	*Emergence of God-centered social structures (rules and roles) and concrete, literal thinking*
13	**Concept**	Capacity to derive abstract principles from related experiences
12	**Endocept**	Grasping or apprehending the internal, hidden characteristics of an object
11	**Symbol** *- transition -*	Capacity to use signs, characters, objects to represent something else *Emergence of the individual identity*
10	**Image**	Capacity to visualize or otherwise experience something not present
9	**Impulse/ emotion**	Capacity to experience self-centered urges, drives, desires
8	*- transition -*	*Emergence of capacity to respond*
7	**Exocept**	Apprehending the external appearance of an object
6	**Perception**	Capacity to receive information from environment through sense organs
5	**Sensation**	Capacity to feel undifferentiated stimulation of sense organs *Emergence of life*
4	Matter: Molecular, polymer	Atoms bonded into molecules
3	Matter: Atomic	Discrete atoms
2	**Matter**: Subatomic *- transition -*	Subatomic particles [*Creation event: Matter created from energy and/ or void*]
1	[Before matter/ Void]	[Before creation. Before matter came into existence]

[Read table from bottom of this page to top of facing page.]

Fundamental Developmental Sequence (A7b): Wilber's set of *Correlative Structures* -- the left-hand column of Wilber's Tables from *Integral Psychology*. Correlations among researchers (A7c, A7e): Wilber's *Integral*, the Integration of all Developmental Systems into one master System.

There is no need to understand each term of Wilber's FDS (A7b), or of the Developmental Systems propounded by other researchers (A7c, A7e). Just get a feel for the overall flow of development. For details on the FDS and all its subsidiary systems, refer to the authors' study *Arrays of Light* (IntegralWorld.net).

A7c. Correlations Among Researchers: Self & Ego

The Fundamental Developmental Sequence is important, because it outlines the complete range of developmental Steps for any Internal Developmental Sequence. Thus, it enables us to compare and correlate the Developmental Sequences for any form of Internal Development in the Realms of Psyche, Body, or Spirit. (D3b-d)

For instance, in the table below, four prominent academic researchers in the Arena of Ego Development (D4b4, Appx 8b4) have each propounded their own set of Stages and Transitions – but none of them quite correspond. However, when their Stages are placed in the proper positions of the FDS, they all dovetail beautifully – forming a single, combined picture of Ego Development that is far more nuanced and complete than any one researcher alone.

[Read table from bottom of facing page to top of this page.]

DEVELOPMENT IN THE ARENA OF SELF AND EGO

	Investigator Line of Inquiry >> **Stage of Development**	Harry Stack Sullivan (1892-1949) Self-integration	Clare Graves (1914-86) Ego Types	Jane Loevinger (1918-2008) Ego Stages	Robert Kegan (~1940-) Stages of Development
38	[Beyond consciousness/ Divine]				
37	- transition -				
36	Non-dual: Late				
35	Non-dual: Middle				
34	**Non-dual**: Early				
33	- transition -				
32	Causal: Late				
31	**Causal** (formless): Early				
30	- transition -				
29	Subtle: Late				
28	**Subtle** (archetype): Early				
27	- transition -				
26	Psychic: Late				
25	**Psychic** (vision): Early				
24	- transition -				
23	Vision/ logic: Late				
22	Vision/logic: Middle	7. Relativity-integration		Integrated	5. Post-formal inter-individual
21	**Vision/ logic**: Early	6. Self-consistency	7. Systemic (integrated)	Autonomous	
20	- transition -	5. Continuity		Individualistic	
19	Formal: Late		6. Relativistic/ individualistic	Conscientious	4. Formal-institutional
18	**Formal**: Early	4. Early individuation	5. Multiplistic	Conscientious-conformist	
17	- transition -				3. Interpersonal
16	Rule/role: Late	Rules-conformist		Conformist	
15	**Rule/role**: Early		4. Socio-centric		
14	- transition -	Rules-'cons'		Self-protective	2. Imperial

DEVELOPMENT IN THE ARENA OF SELF AND EGO

Investigator Line of Inquiry >> Stage of Development	Harry Stack Sullivan (1892-1949) __Self-integration__	Clare Graves (1914-86) __Ego Types__	Jane Loevinger (1918-2008) __Ego Stages__	Robert Kegan (~1940-) __Stages of Development__
13 Concept	3. Power			
12 Endocept		3. Egocentric		
11 Symbol - transition -	2. Manipulative-demanding		Impulsive	1. Impulsive
10 Image				
9 Impulse/ emotion		2. Magical-animistic	Symbiotic	
8 - transition -	1. Differentiation of self & nonself			
7 Exocept				
6 Perception		1. Autistic	Autistic	0. Incorporative
5 Sensation			Presocial	
4 Matter: Molecular, polymer				
3 Matter: Atomic				
2 - transition -				
1 [Before matter/ Void]				

[Read table from bottom of this page to top of facing page.]

The Evolving Self. This famous book by Harvard educator Robert Kegan brought the Stages of Human Development into the mainstream.

Developmental Systems from Several Researchers

Consider the table on these two facing pages. Do not be concerned with understanding these terms in detail. *** The table depicts the Developmental Systems for the Psyche Arena of Self & Ego, as propounded by four prominent psychology researchers. Select one band of Steps to explore further: The purple Vision Logic band, for example, Steps 21-23. *** The Stages these researchers propose show some similarities – but notice how often they differ, both in content and in placement. Two of the Stages proposed by Sullivan and Loevinger fall in the Vision Logic band, Steps 21-22. Only one Stage proposed by Graves and Kegan falls in the Vision Logic band – but Graves is Step 21, while Kegan is Step 22. *** As time permits, choose another band of Steps, and make similar comparisons. *** Now notice also: Although many Stages proposed by these researchers fail to correspond with one another, they all correspond to some stage of Wilber's Fundamental Developmental Sequence. *** These correspondences demonstrate the underlying unity among researchers – that they all are contributing to a fuller understanding of a single fundamental model. This underlying unity of focus is what Ken Wilber means by Integral.

A7d. The Chakras – A Simplified FDS

Although very illuminating, Wilber's Fundamental Developmental Sequence is far too complex and cumbersome for general use. For that reason, we sought a simplified and abbreviated version of the FDS – a version that would be easier to apply, yet would retain the essential developmental flow of the original FDS. We found that simplified version in the concept of the **Chakras**.

FROM FDS TO CHAKRAS. Wilber himself shows us how the FDS can be simplified to form the seven Chakras. To trace this derivation, turn to the table of Wilber's FDS on the next two facing pages (page 104) – this time focusing on the two right-hand columns, where two versions of the Chakras have been filled in.

WESTERN CHAKRAS. In Column 4, we have used bands of color to collect Wilber's 38 Steps into **12 Developmental Clusters** – 12 groups of related Steps, separated by 11 Transitions. (Wilber calls these Clusters **Functional Groupings**.) The top five Clusters are all Transcendent States, so they may be combined into one -- the Crown Chakra. The bottom Cluster refers to the Stage before life has been created, so it can be omitted from the sequence. The result is a series of seven Developmental Clusters -- fundamental Stages of Internal Development we call the **Western Chakras**.

WILBER'S CHAKRAS. Wilber's conception of the Chakras differs somewhat from these Clusters. In Column 4, we overlay Wilber's own formulation and placement of the Chakras (numbered items) on the bands of color. Wilber's Chakras are thus a particular version of the Western Chakras.

EASTERN CHAKRAS. In Column 5, we show the traditional **Eastern Chakras**, as Wilber has placed them within his FDS. As you will notice, these Eastern Chakras differ slightly from both the Western and the Wilber versions of the Chakras.

Thus, there are actually three basic versions of the Chakras -- all tracing a similar pattern of Internal Development. As we show on the facing page, this book employs a combination of all three.

> There is no need to understand each term of Wilber's FDS or of the two versions of the Chakras. Just get a feel for the overall flow of development. For details on the FDS and all its subsidiary systems, refer to the authors' study *Arrays of Light* (IntegralWorld.net).

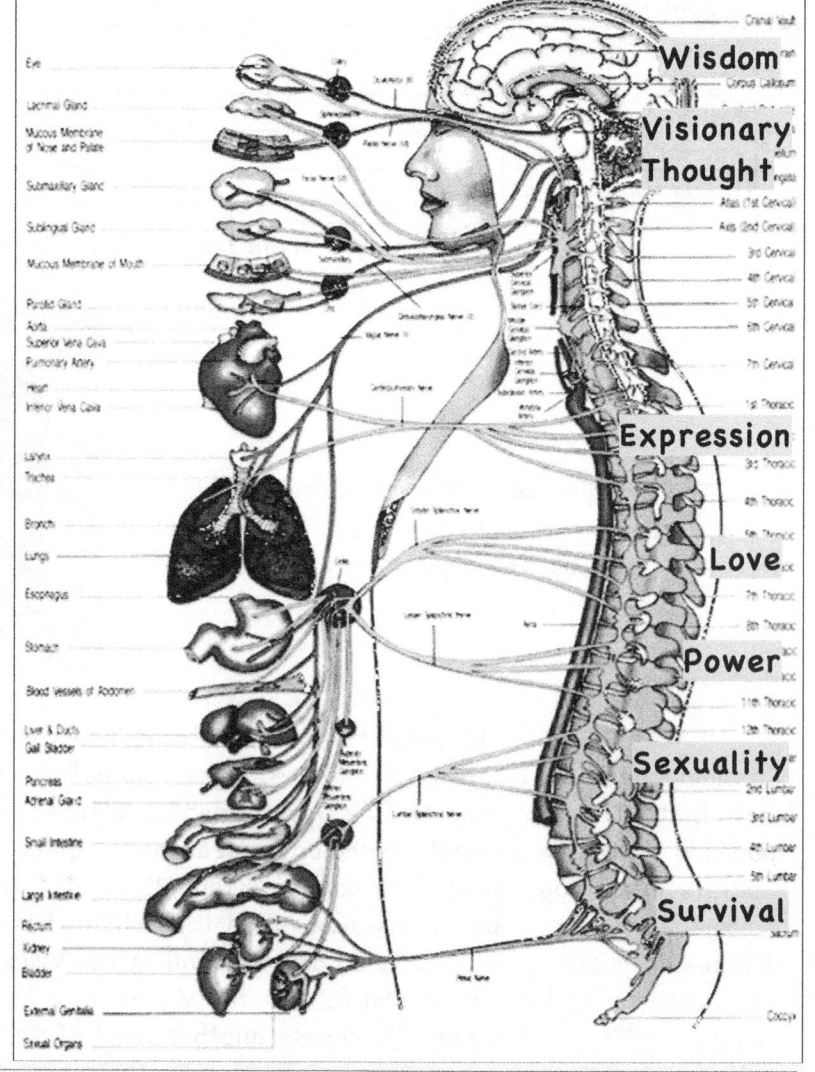

Bodily Chakras: West & East. "According to Western thinking, my spine is divided into seven regions. Those regions are associated with seven nerve plexes. Each nerve plexus influences the functioning of certain internal organs. According to Eastern thinking, each of those regions, plexes, and organs affect me simultaneously in the Realms of Psyche, Body, and Spirit."

THE CHAKRAS – WEST AND EAST

Columns 4 and 5 of the FDS Table depict the two major versions of the Chakras – Western and Eastern:

Chakras – Western Perspective. From a Western perspective, the Chakras are merely a consolidation, condensation, or simplification of the Fundamental Developmental Sequence into its seven basic Clusters. Each of these Clusters is what Wilber calls a Functional Grouping – a set of psychological Stages that are functionally similar.

Chakras – Eastern Perspective. From an Eastern perspective, the Chakras are an integration of the three Internal Realms of Body, Psyche, and Spirit. The Chakras may (for instance) be viewed as energy phenomena that manifest themselves simultaneously in all three internal Realms and within all seven Levels:

- **Psyche.** As experienced by the Psyche, the Chakras are seven Stages of mental and emotional Development.
- **Internal Body.** As experienced by the Body, the Chakras are seven areas of physical aliveness -- located in ascending bodily regions (spinal vertebrae, nerve plexes, and associated internal organs) from the base of the spine to the crown of the head.
- **Spirit.** As experienced by the Spirit, the Chakras are seven portals through which universal cosmic energy flows into our being.

Chakras – Western vs. Eastern. From a developmental perspective, there is a fundamental distinction between the Western and Eastern conception of the Chakras. From a Western perspective, we grow successively -- by ascending the Chakras from Body, to Psyche, to Spirit. By contrast, from an Eastern perspective, we grow simultaneously – by actualizing our potential in the Realms of Psyche, Body, and Spirit at each Stage of Development. (As we shall see in sections A7f-h, these two conceptions result in radically different Models of Self, Modes of Growth, and procedures of psychological Treatment.)

The Eastern and Western conceptions are both correct in their own sphere. Therefore, in this book, we will employ the version of the Chakras that is appropriate for a given situation. When considering the Realms of Everyday Life and the Psyche (D3a-b), we will generally use the Western conception. When exploring the Realms of Body and Spirit (D3c-d), we will generally employ the Eastern conception.

Chakras, Eastern Perspective.
"When I do yoga, each pose activates and enlivens a particular Chakra. I feel that enlivenment simultaneously in all three Internal Realms – in my Body, in my Psyche, and in my Spirit."

Chakras: Wilber's *Chakras, Seven Ages of a Person, Functional Groupings.*

The Chakras derive from Wilber's FDS (Appx A7b). The Chakras will serve as an abbreviated and simplified Developmental Sequence for the Internal Realms of Psyche, Body, and Spirit (D3b-d).

Opinions differ widely as the nature, content, and validity of the Chakras. Here, we merely present three ways the Chakras are commonly conceived.

[Read table from bottom of facing page to top of this page.]

A7d. Wilber's Fundamental Developmental Sequence + Chakras

#	FDS Steps & Stages (Wilber)	FDS Step Descriptions	Chakras (Wilber)	Chakras (Eastern/ New Age)
38	[Beyond consciousness/ Divine]	[Beyond consciousness]		**7. WISDOM** (crown of head)
37	- transition -	[Relinquishment of consciousness]		
36	Non-dual: Late	Constant consciousness		
35	Non-dual: Middle	Spirit and World Process		
34	**Non-dual**: Early	Non-dual mysticism – union of form and formless	(Release of all Chakras in the Real)	
33	- transition -	Merging of consciousness with Creator		
32	Causal: Late	Cessation – union with the source of all manifest realms		
31	**Causal** (formless): Early	Formless mysticism – awareness of the source of consciousness		
30	- transition -	Emergent consciousness of the holy essence of the Creator	(Higher Chakras to cessation)	
29	Subtle: Late	Union with creator of gross realm		
28	**Subtle** (archetype): Early	Deity mysticism – awareness of divine source of creation		
27	- transition -	Departure from the material realm. Emergent consciousness of the Creator	7. Sahasrara: Transcendental consciousness: light	
26	Psychic: Late	Union with the world process		
25	**Psychic** (vision): Early	Nature mysticism – awareness of divine embodied in the material		
24	- transition -	Emergent consciousness of supernatural realm beyond the material	6. Psychic mind: vision (Ajna)	
23	Vision/Logic: Late	Integrated perspectives: Holistic, unified, integral thinking		**6. VISIONARY THOUGHT** (brow, third eye)
22	Vision/Logic: Middle	Interacting perspectives: Dialectical, comparative thinking		
21	**Vision/Logic**: Early	Multiple perspectives: Relative, pluralistic, contextual thinking		
20	- transition -	Emergence from mechanistic to fluid, multi-dimensional thinking	5. Verbal-rational mind	
19	Formal: Late	Broad, complex abstract and logical thinking		**5. EXPRESSION** (throat)
18	**Formal**: Early	Small, simple abstract and logical thinking		
17	- transition -	Emergence from myth and superstition to generalized, abstract logical thinking	4. Community-mind: love	
16	Rule/role: Late	Large, complex social structures – elaborate rules and roles		**4. LOVE** (heart)
15	**Rule/role**: Early	Small, simple social structures – basic rules and roles		

Increasing Advancement & Maturity →

A7. The Internal Developmental Sequence. Page 105

A7d. Wilber's Fundamental Developmental Sequence + Chakras

Increasing Advancement & Maturity ↑

#	FDS Steps & Stages (Wilber)	FDS Step Descriptions	Chakras (Wilber)	Chakras (Eastern/ New Age)
14	- transition -	*Emergence of God-centered social structures (rules and roles) and concrete, literal thinking*		
13	**Concept**	Capacity to derive abstract principles from related experiences	3. Intentional-mind: power	**3. POWER** (solar plexus)
12	**Endocept**	Grasping or apprehending the internal, hidden characteristics of an object		
11	**Symbol** - transition -	Capacity to use signs, characters, objects to represent something else *Emergence of the individual identity*		
10	**Image**	Capacity to visualize or otherwise experience something not present		**2. SEXUALITY** (genitals)
9	**Impulse/ emotion**	Capacity to experience self-centered urges, drives, desires	2. Emotional-sexual	
8	- transition -	*Emergence of capacity to respond*		
7	**Exocept**	Apprehending the external appearance of an object		**1. SURVIVAL** (floor of pelvis)
6	**Perception**	Capacity to receive information from environment through sense organs		
5	**Sensation**	Capacity to feel undifferentiated stimulation of sense organs *Emergence of life*		
4	**Matter**: Molecular, polymer	Atoms bonded into molecules		
3	**Matter**: Atomic	Discrete atoms	1. Material	
2	**Matter**: Subatomic - transition -	Subatomic particles *[Creation event: Matter created from energy and/ or void]*		
1	**[Before matter/ Void]**	*[Before creation. Before matter came into existence]*		

[Read table from bottom of this page to top of facing page.]

Experiencing Your Chakra Evolution

Consider again Ken Wilber's Fundamental Developmental Sequence, shown on this page with the Eastern and Western versions of the Chakras. *** Beginning at the bottom of the right-hand page, focus on the two right-hand columns, and scan upward. Do not be concerned with understanding every detail of these concepts. You are merely attempting to experience what it feels to evolve internally. *** Imagine yourself as a being that is evolving through all these Chakras of Development. First, you are concerned only with basic Survival needs – food, shelter, defense, etc. Then you add your Sexual and Emotional drives. Then you add Will, Volition, and Power. Then you add Awareness, Concern, and Love for others. And so forth. *** Meditate for a minute or more upon each state of being. Let your imagination flow without restraint. *** Then portray the major steps through some form of artistic expression – with colored markers on large sheets of butcher paper, for example.

[Columns 2 & 3 were explored under Wilber's Fundamental Developmental Sequence (Appx A7b).]

A7e. Correlations Among Researchers: Chakra Version

Now that we have a simplified version of the FDS based on the Chakras, let's apply that Model to four psychology researchers we previously compared. Here, we present the same data that appeared on page 100, but with the Stages telescoped down to the seven Chakras. With these changes, the Stages here are substantially simplified, but they still retain a significant degree of accuracy and specificity.

[Read table from bottom of facing page to top of this page.]

DEVELOPMENT IN THE ARENA OF SELF AND EGO [Chakras]

#	Researchers>> Chakras (Eastern/ New Age)	Ken Wilber (1949-) Chakras (Western/ Wilber)	Harry S. Sullivan (1892-1949) Self-integration	Clare Graves (1914-86) Ego Types	Jane Loevinger (1918-2008) Ego Stages	Robert Kegan (1946-) Stages of Development
38						
37						
36		(Release of all Chakras in the Real)				
35						
34						
33						
32						
31						
30		(Higher Chakras to cessation)				
29						
28						
27	**7. WISDOM** (crown of head)	7. Sahasrara: Transcendental consciousness: light				
26						
25						
24		6. Psychic mind: vision (Ajna)				
23	**6. VISIONARY THOUGHT** (brow, third eye)		7. Relativity-integration 6. Self-consistency	7. Systemic (integrated)	Integrated Autonomous	5. Post-formal inter-individual
22						
21						
20		5. Verbal-rational mind	5. Continuity		Individualistic	
19	**5. EXPRESSION** (throat)		4. Early individuation	6. Relativistic/ individualistic 5. Multiplistic	Conscientious Conscientious-conformist	4. Formal-institutional
18						
17		4. Community-mind: love				3. Interpersonal
16	**4. LOVE** (heart)		Rules-conformist	4. Socio-centric	Conformist	
15						
14			Rules-'cons'		Self-protective	2. Imperial
13	**3. POWER** (solar plexus)	3. Intentional-mind: power	3. Power	3. Egocentric		
12						

A7. The Internal Developmental Sequence. Page 107

	DEVELOPMENT IN THE ARENA OF SELF AND EGO [Chakras]					
	Researchers>>	**Ken Wilber** (1949-)	**Harry S. Sullivan** (1892-1949)	**Clare Graves** (1914-86)	**Jane Loevinger** (1918-2008)	**Robert Kegan** (1946-)
#	**Chakras** (Eastern/ New Age)	**Chakras** (Western/ Wilber)	**Self-integration**	**Ego Types**	**Ego Stages**	**Stages of Development**
11			2. Manipulative-demanding		Impulsive	1. Impulsive
10	2. SEXUALITY (genitals)	2. Emotional-sexual		2. Magical-animistic	Symbiotic	
9						
8			1. Differentiation of self & nonself			
7	1. SURVIVAL (floor of pelvis)	1. Material		1. Autistic	Autistic Presocial	0. Incorporative
6						
5						
4						
3						

[Read table from bottom of this page to top of facing page.]

Simplified Model. The seven Chakras are a Model that simplifies and streamlines Wilber's FDS – yet retains its essential outlines and major features.

The Internal Development Sequence – Full and Simplified Versions

For the Stages of Development for the four researchers, compare the simplified version on these two facing pages with the full version shown on page 100. Select one band of Steps for comparison: The purple Visionary Thought band ('Vision Logic') you explored previously, for example. *** Note that the Stages that were previously in similar positions now appear at the identical level. Instead of three sub-stages for Vision Logic, we now have one consolidated Stage of Visionary Thought. *** Note how much easier the simplified table reads, and how much more directly it conveys the flow of Growth from one Stage to the next. *** Throughout this book, tables depicting various Sequences of internal Development will use the Chakras as approximations for the Internal Stages.

> In our Life Journey, SUCCESSION GROWTH is like traveling from island to island: When we sail to a new island, we leave the old island behind. Succession Growth might also be characterized as an upward spiral, a rocket-like trajectory, a ladder-like climb, or the successive floors of a high-rise building.

A7f. Two Forms of Growth: Succession & Accumulation

For a given Developmental Sequence, our Growth may take one of two forms – either Succession or Accumulation. Each form of Growth creates a particular Model of Self, necessitates a particular form of Actualization or Treatment, and applies to particular Realms and Arenas. Because our Growth can take these two forms, the Chakras can sometimes appear as a Developmental Sequence (Succession) and sometimes as regions the Body or sets of characteristics (Accumulation).

SUCCESSION GROWTH

In **Succession Growth**, we transition from one Stage to the next -- each time leaving the previous Stage behind. Succession Growth applies primarily to the Realms of Life Passages and sometimes Psyche Passages (D3a-b). For example, in Life Passages we progress from Infant, to Toddler, to School Child, to Teenager, etc. – at each Stage looking back on the previous Stage as one we have outgrown. Likewise, in the Cognitive Arena (according to Piaget, D4b6), we grow in our thinking abilities from Sensorimotor, to Pre-conceptual, to Intuitive Conceptual, to Concrete Operational, etc. – at each level leaving behind our previous mode of thinking as immature or obsolete.

Succession Growth: Wilber's *Ladder*, *Levels*, *Layers*, *Spiral*, or *Floors* of a high-rise building.

Succession Growth occurs primarily in the Realms and Arenas of Everyday Life and sometimes the Psyche (D3a-b, D4a-b). Additional Developmental Sequences for those Arenas are shown in Appx A8a-b. Succession Growth implies an Archeology Model of Self and corresponding Mode of Treatment (Appx A7g-h).

Succession Growth. "Succession Growth is like steps of a ladder. Each time I climb to a new Step, I leave the previous Step behind."

Your Succession Growth

Refer back to your Explorations in Section D1, Stages. *** Scan through the Developmental Sequence of Life Passages (D1). For the first few of those Stages, recall again some episode or event that typified that Stage of your life. *** As an Infant, you might imagine yourself sucking on a bottle. As a Toddler, you might recall attempting your first steps. And so forth. *** After each such recollection, recall also how at that point you felt about the previous Stage. Did you feel much different from the person you previously had been? Had you outgrown your Old Self? This Growth from Stage to Stage, each time leaving the previous Stage behind, is **Succession Growth**. *** In what other situations of your life do you experience Succession Growth?

A7. The Internal Developmental Sequence. Page 109

> ACCUMULATION GROWTH is like building a Castle: Each new wall or battlement is an addition to the floors or pediments that were built before. Accumulation Growth might also be characterized as a Great Tree, where all parts grow interdependently and in unison.

ACCUMULATION GROWTH

In **Accumulation Growth**, we transition from one Stage to the next by building on the previous Stage and adding to it. Accumulation Growth applies primarily to the Realms of Body Passages, sometimes Psyche Passages, and sometimes Spirit Passages (D3c-d). For instance, in Body Passages, we do not grow a skeletal system, then reproductive, then digestive, then circulatory, etc. Rather, we start with a complete body, and continue to grow out every part of it simultaneously. Likewise, in Psyche Passages, we begin with the full range of Affect & Emotions (D4b3) – but then shape and refine those Emotions as our life progresses. Similarly, in Spirit Passages, devout Christians generally don't work their way through Heavenly Virtues (D4d7) -- beginning with Fortitude and Temperance, and later progressing up to Hope and Faith. Rather, they generally embrace all seven Virtues, and to attempt improve in all seven simultaneously. Even if they concentrate on one Virtue at a time, they do not outgrow the previous Virtues they have acquired, but add to them.

Accumulation Growth. "Accumulation Growth is like the growth of a Great Tree. With each new period of development, I build on the Growth that's already taken place. I extend my roots, expand my trunk, and spread my branches – with each part of the structure sustaining and supporting every other."

Accumulation Growth: Wilber *Not mentioned*.

Accumulation Growth occurs primarily in the Realms and Arenas of the Body, sometimes the Psyche, and sometimes the Spirit (D3b-d, D4b-d). Additional developmental Sequences for these Arenas are shown in Appx A8b-c. Accumulation Growth implies an Architecture Model of Self and corresponding Mode of Treatment (Appx A7g-h).

Your Accumulation Growth

Again, refer back to your Explorations in Section D1, Stages. This time, visualize what your body looked like at each Stage – and how it felt from the inside. *** As an Infant, feel your big head, your sensitive lips, your eager fingers grasping for the bottle. As a Toddler, feel your thumping heartbeat, your trembling legs, your bulging eyes as you first attempt to rise up off all fours. *** At each of these Stages, did you still have the same body parts? How did they grow and develop as you matured? How did they <u>feel</u> different at each Stage? *** This expansion and extension of existing characteristics is **Accumulation Growth**. *** In what other situations of your life do you experience Accumulation Growth?

Page 110. Wilber Appendices

A7g. Two Models of Self: Layered and Retrofit

For a given Developmental Sequence, our Growth may take one of two forms – either Succession Growth or Accumulation Growth (A7f). The two forms of Growth result in two radically different Models of Self (A7g). These two contrasting Models are explored on these two facing pages.

THE ARCHEOLOGY MODEL OF SELF (Layered, Stacked)

Succession Growth implies a **Layered** or **Stacked Model of Self,** because each Stage of Growth is layered or stacked on the last. In our memories, the experiences of Infancy are overlaid with the experiences of Toddlerhood, which are overlaid with the experiences from Young Childhood, and so forth. Using Wilber's metaphor of the archeological dig, we call this the **Archeology Model of Self**.

Archeology. "According to the Archeology Model of Self, the past Stages of our Development are deposited in our Subconscious like layers of an archeological dig."

Layered, Stacked, Archeology Model: Wilber's *Archeology. Ladder, Levels, Layers, Spiral, Floors* of a high-rise building. Retrofit, Multi-Function, Architecture Model: Wilber *Not mentioned.*

As with Succession Growth (Appx 7f), the Archeology Model pertains primarily to the Realms and Arenas of Everyday Life and sometimes the Psyche (D3a-b, D4a-b). As with Accumulation Growth (Appx 7f), the Architecture Model pertains primarily to the Realms and Arenas of the Body, sometimes the Psyche, and sometimes the Spirit (D3b-d, D4b-d).

THE ARCHITECTURE MODEL OF SELF (Retrofit, Multi-function)

Accumulation Growth implies a **Retrofit** or **Multi-Function Model of Self**, because each Stage of Growth is added to the existing structure as an additional level of functionality. According to this view, the Self is much like an old building that has been retrofitted – first with indoor plumbing, later with electricity and lighting, then with telephone, and finally with internet. Using the metaphor of structure renovation, we characterize this as the **Architecture Model**,

ARCHEOLOGY VS. ARCHITECTURE

From one perspective, the evolution of the Internal Realms is an example of the Archeology Model. That is, as human beings evolved from lower animals, to primates, to *homo sapiens*, the Internal Realms of Self were developed sequentially – first Body, then Psyche, then Spirit.

However, from another perspective, the development of the Internal Realms is also an example of the Architecture Model. In the course of evolution, each new Realm was added to human nature as an additional capacity of functioning. That is, the seven Chakral regions – originally only physical – took on psychological and then spiritual functions as humans evolved. From this perspective, every stage of our past evolution is still evident in our present structure. Thus, **the Self is both Archeology and Architecture**.

Architecture. "According to the Architecture Model, the Self is like an old building where new forms of functionality have been added to the existing structure. We renovate an old structure by improving the foundation, the frame, the plumbing, the wiring. Then we add phone, cable, the internet, and maybe a security system."

A7h. Two Modes of Treatment: Archeology & Architecture

The distinction between Archeology and Architecture affects the whole strategy for Personal Growth and therapeutic Treatment. With the **Archeology Model**, the Realms of Body, Mind, and Spirit are dealt with *sequentially* – because they follow one another on the developmental ladder. With the **Architecture Model**, all three Realms are addressed *simultaneously* at every Stage of Development -- because they are structurally inseparable. Both Modes can be effective in the right situation, as shown on these two facing pages.

ARCHEOLOGY MODEL

The Archeology Model of Self dictates an archeological Mode of Treatment:

Restoration Growth (PPR4). We can apply the Archeology Model to our problems. If we wish to resolve a Neurosis, we may use Talk Therapy to 'dig back' in our memory to 'uncover buried layers' of past Development -- layers where some painful Trauma occurred that caused the original Impasse (PPR2, D7b).

Actualization Growth (PPR3). Likewise, we can use the Archeology Model to Actualize our Potential. We can apply for a very special job that will take us to a new Level in the Arena of Career & Calling (D4a2). When we land that job, we will be giving up the job of our past, and moving on to the career of our future.

Archeology. "With my analyst's help, I've been digging back through past layers of memory. I've finally struck a painful layer of Trauma – the place where many of my fears and misconceptions about intimacy began."

Your Mode of Treatment: Archeology

Refer back to some Impasse your explored under Impediments (D7b) or Restoration Growth (PPR4). (If you can't think of any, imagine some Impasse a person like you <u>might</u> experience.) *** How did you endeavor to deal with that Impasse? *** In a past-oriented way? Through Introspection (PR30) – where you plumbed your memory for experiences that lead up to this Impasse? Through Talk Therapy (PR31) -- where you explored the origins of this Impasse in your early relations with your mother? *** Modes of Resolution where you delve into the <u>past</u> employ the **Archeology Model** of Treatment. *** For what issues does the past-oriented Archeology Model work better for you?

ARCHITECTURE MODEL

The Architecture Model of Self dictates an architectural Mode of Treatment:

Restoration Growth (PPR4). We can apply the Architecture Model to resolve our problems. We can use Reichian Therapy, Rolfing, and other Body Therapies to resurrect problems that are locked in our present Body Armor. When we heal the present Structure, we will at the same time be healing the past Trauma.

Actualization Growth (PPR3). Likewise, we can use the Architecture Model to Actualize our Potential. We may enliven our bodies by practicing some form of yoga, tai chi, or Tantra. Or we may engage in some present-oriented healing practice, like chiropractic or acupuncture. With any such practices, we simultaneously raise our functioning at all seven Chakras, and in all three Internal Realms – Body, Psyche, and Spirit.

Architecture. "When Trish and I practice Tantra, we feel a surge of Kundalini Energy from the base of our spine to the crown of our head. When this happens, we experience all seven Chakras in each of three ways -- through physical arousal, emotional bonding, and spiritual communion."

As with Succession Growth (Appx 7f), the Archeology Mode of Treatment pertains primarily to the Realms and Arenas of Everyday Life and sometimes the Psyche (D3a-b, D4a-b). As with Accumulation Growth (Appx 7f), the Architecture Mode of Treatment pertains primarily to the Realms and Arenas of the Body, sometimes the Psyche, and sometimes the Spirit (D3b-d, D4b-d).

Archeology Mode of Treatment: Implicit in Wilber's *Pathologies & Treatments*. Architecture Model: Implicit in the many present-oriented Modalities of Wilber's *Integral Transformative Practice*.

Your Mode of Treatment: Architecture

Continue to explore the Impasse you addressed in part 1 (or another one of your choice). *** Did you also endeavor to deal with that Impasse in some present-oriented way? Did you use massage, or Rolfing, or Reichian Therapy (PR29) to unlock your present Body Armor that resulted from some past Trauma? Did you use Spiritual Practices like yoga, tai chi, or meditation (PR33) to dissolve your present preconceptions that had their origin in the past? Did you use Psycho-Biologic Techniques (PR32) to resolve present bio-chemical Blocks that have kept you locked in your past? *** Modes of Resolution where you address the present effects of past experiences employ the **Architecture Model** of Self. *** In what life situations is the present-oriented Architecture Model more effective for you?

Appendix A8.
THE PROGRESSIONS OF HUMAN DEVELOPMENT:
Developmental Sequences -- Arenas of Life Passages, Psyche, Spirit

Developmental Sequences (D1+2) occur within each Realm (D3a-d) of Growth, and within each Arena (D4a-d) of those Realms. The tables on the following pages provide one example of a Developmental Sequence for each of the Arenas in the Realms of Life Passages, Psyche, and Spirit. **In all these Arenas, we find that our Growth Trajectory is deeply grounded, influenced, and inspired by our early childhood experiences in that Arena.**

Sequences for the Arenas in three of the four Realms will be found in this section. The fourth is in the Main Text:

- **Appendix A8a. Arenas Of Life Passages.** (p. 115)
- **Appendix A8b. Arenas of the Psyche.** (p. 129)
- **Appendix A8d. Arenas of the Spirit.** (p. 132)
- **D4c. Arenas of The Body.** Tables for four Body Arenas are displayed in section D4c.

> These Sequences are not intended to be academically rigorous – but merely to give the reader a general sense of how Development might progress within a given Arena.

> The Arenas are the specific areas of activity where our Growth (and our life) actually takes place. In this Appendix, we present Developmental Sequences for all the Arenas of Life Passages, Psyche, and Spirit (D4a, b, d) -- including those covered in the Main Text. The Internal Developmental Sequence (for Psyche, Spirit) was derived in Appendix A7.

The Arenas of Life Passages (1)

Consider the tables of the 12 Life Passages Arenas on the following pages. Choose one of those tables to explore in detail. (You have already explored Career & Calling [D4a2] and Relationships & Marriage [DD1+2a], so choose some other one.) *** Let's suppose you choose Emotions & Personal Growth (p. 123). Without being too analytical, scan through this Developmental Sequence from bottom to top. Get a general, intuitive sense of the Growth that can take place in each Stage. *** Now concentrate on your present Stage of Development -- Middle Adulthood, for example. Ask yourself questions like these: As a Middle Adult, how do your actual Emotions compare to what your read in the table? Are you in a rut? Does your stable career and home life dictate your emotional states? Is your range of expression, openness, and spontaneity relatively static? *** Now shift your attention to Personal Growth: Describe the most important Growth activities you currently engage in: Club tennis team, yoga, couples therapy, adventure vacations, etc. Give yourself lots of latitude; any activity that stimulates your Growth as a person qualifies. *** Do these activities produce significant changes in your personality or self-concept? Do they merely help you maintain the Growth you have already achieved? Are they nothing more than diversions that keep you busy?

The Arenas of Life Passages (2)

Next, direct your explorations to your previous Stage of Development – Young Adulthood, for example. Ask yourself similar questions. *** Make comparisons between the two Stages of Development: How about your state of mind? Are you now more balanced and serene? More bored and dissatisfied? *** Think of one specific activity that might challenge your composure: A long wait for a table at a crowded restaurant, for example. As a Middle Adult, how would you now handle such a situation? How would you have handled it as a Young Adult? *** Compare your current Growth activities to those you engaged in as a Young Adult: Are they more staid and predictable? More selective and comfortable? *** Based on the table, in what ways are you a typical Middle Adult? In what ways were you a typical of a Young Adult? In what ways have you been a maverick, a rebel, against the grain? *** Now choose your next future Stage: Mature Adulthood, for example. In your imagination, what is your Emotional Life like? What Growth activities are you engaging in? How have you changed as a person? *** In another Session, choose another Arena to explore, and ask yourself similar questions. *** Continue to engage in similar Explorations, until you have investigated all the Life Passage Arenas you have a special interest in.

A8a. Arenas of Life Passages

Life Passages (D3a) are the external Phases of accomplishment or achievement that occur as we progress through the biological Life Cycle. The tables on the following pages display Developmental Sequences for the Realm of Life Passages, and for each of the 12 Arenas within that Realm (D4a). The Life Passage tables are as follows:

| DEVELOPMENTAL SEQUENCES: LIFE PASSAGES ||
ARENAS	PAGE
Life Passages (Realm)	116
1. Education & Skills-building	117
2. Career & Calling	118
3. Finances & Investments	119
4. Health & Well-being	120
5. Recreation & Enjoyment	121
6. Nature & Environment	122
7. Emotions & Personal Growth	123
8. Religion & Spirituality	124
9. Relationships & Marriage	125
10. Sensuality & Sexuality	126
11. Family & Children	127
12. Friendships & Community	128

The Arenas of Life. Each of the 12 Arenas of Life Passages has its own set of Developmental Stages and Transitions.

These tables pertain to the Developmental Sequence of Stages (D1) and Transitions (D2), in the Realm of Life Passages (D3a), in the Process of Actualization Growth (PPR3). The tables derive from the authors' own research and experience.

The reader need not be concerned to understand every detail of these Life Passage tables. Just get a general sense of the progression from lower to higher Stages in each of these Arenas.

A8-A. LIFE PASSAGES DEVELOPMENTAL SEQUENCE

Life Passages are the external phases of accomplishment or achievement that occur as we progress through the biological Life Cycle. The general Developmental Sequence for Life Passages is shown below. The Developmental Sequences for the 12 specific Arenas of Life Passages (D4a) are shown on subsequent pages.

[Read from bottom to top.]

Step	Stages/ Transitions	Age of Ascendance	Characteristics
27	Legacy	After death	The genetic, cultural, psychological, & material endowments we pass on to succeeding generations.
26	Death		Physical functioning stops.
25	Senescence	90-100+	Diminished capacities of body and mind.
24	Debility or Illness		Significant physical or mental setback.
23	Elderhood	75-90	Communicating experience and wisdom to next generation.
22	Passing-the-Baton		Recognition of mortality. Shift of attention to next generation.
21	Mature Adulthood	60-75	Endeavors based on significance, internal identity.
20	Mid-Life Passage		Breakdown of externally-validated identity. Shift to internally-validated identity. From success to significance.
19	Middle Adulthood	40-60	Expanding upon life achievements to their maximum potential. Stability of stature and position.
18	Making-the-Grade		Peak of external life achievements, success.
17	Young Adulthood	21-40	Striving for external life achievements: Relationship, family, home, career.
16	Nudged from the Nest		Completing school. Finding long-term career, long-term partner.
15	[college]	18-22	Established independent identity, while supported by home.
14	Adolescence [high school]	13-18	Formation of independent identity, while living at home.
13	Coming-of-Age		First adolescent traits – physical, psychological.
12	[upper grades]	9-12	Later grade schooling. Established in society outside of home.
11	Middle Childhood [primary grades]	6-8	Early schooling. First enrollment in society outside the home.
10	Entering School		First days at school.
9	Young Childhood	3-6	Partial independence within home environment.
8	Onset of Terrible 2s		First actions independent of (or contrary to) mother.
7	Toddler	1.5-3	Early efforts at self-sufficiency and self-support.
6	Crawling/ Walking		First mobility and self-sufficiency.
5	Infancy	0-1.5	Total sustenance and bonding outside the womb.
4	Birth		Emergence from the womb.
3	Gestation	Before birth	Total sustenance and support within the womb.
2	Conception		Sperm meets egg.
1	Heritage	Before conception	The genetic, cultural, psychological, & material endowments we inherit.

A8a. Developmental Sequences: Life Passages. Page 117

A8-a1. Dev Sequence: EDUCATION & SKILLS-BUILDING

In the Education & Skills-Building Arena, we obtain the education and training we need to achieve our life goals. This table demonstrates that our Education & Skills-Building Trajectory is grounded, influenced, and inspired by our earliest childhood learning and education experiences – a family respect for education, favorite nursery rhymes, picture books on daddy's lap, a bright aquarium, intense classroom spelling bees, etc.

[Read from bottom to top.]

Step	Stages/Transitions	Age of Ascendance	Typical Situations, Typical Issues
27	Legacy	After death	**Wisdom & knowledge for future generations.** The effect of your wisdom on those who live after – children, family, associates, adherents. Distribution mechanism for accumulated wisdom.
26	*Death*		
25	Senescence	90-100+	**Diminished mental capacities, energy, focus.** Shifting mental strengths – to big picture, long perspective. Techniques for maintaining and exercising mental capacities
24	*Debility or Illness*		
23	Elderhood	75-90	**Passing on knowledge & wisdom to others. Protégés, apprentices, mentoring.** Stepping into role of educational authority. Creating receptive minds for your communication. Casting life lessons in a permanent form that lives after you.
22	*Passing-the-Baton*		
21	Mature Adulthood	60-75	**Evaluation of rewards and satisfaction of chosen educational path. Integrating personal calling with education.** Changing priorities. Revisiting neglected or undiscovered personal interests. Return to school to change life direction.
20	*Mid-Life Passage*		
19	Middle Adulthood	40-60	**Advanced career training. Educational enrichment.** Honing skills for advanced career challenges. Use of new-found leisure time for educational exploration.
18	*Making-the-Grade*		
17	Young Adulthood	21-40	**Applied, results-oriented learning. On-the-job training.** Applicability of formal learning to career requirements. Applying processes of learning to career advancement. Maintaining enrichment needs.
16	*Nudged from the Nest*		
15	Adolescence [college]	18-22	**Advanced schooling: Peak learning skills & study habits. Assimilating adult knowledge.** Theoretical vs. practical in learning environment. Rapid progression in knowledge. Team learning, cooperative learning. Models of educated persons from media and outside world.
14	Adolescence [high school]	13-18	**Advanced schooling: Accelerated learning skills. Intro to adult knowledge. Refined study habits.** Enrichment vs. abstraction in learning environment. Incremental progression in skills; rapid in knowledge. Team learning, peer teaching, competitive learning. Models of educated persons from media and outside world.
13	*Coming-of-Age*		
12	Middle Childhood [upper grades]	9-12	**Formal schooling: Established learning skills. Advancing knowledge. Consistent study habits.** Degree of enrichment in learning environment. Consistent progression in skills and knowledge. Group learning, peer teaching. Teacher and parents as models of educated persons.
11	Middle Childhood [primary grades]	6-8	**Formal schooling: Basic skills in formal learning environment. Early study habits.** Enriched classroom learning environment. Consistent progression in basic learning skills. Group learning. Teacher and parents as models of educated persons.
10	*Entering School*		
9	Young Childhood	3-6	**Parent-initiated informal education – vocabulary, reading, numbers, nature.** Frequency, consistency, competence, engagement, and enjoyment in education opportunities.
8	*Onset of Terrible 2s*		
7	Toddler	1.5-3	**Father joins mother as educator – observing, pointing-out, learning language.** Level of father's involvement, shared verbalized experiences, balance of learning and fun.
6	*Crawling/Walking*		
5	Infancy	0-1.5	**Early education by mother – fingers/toes, counting, nursery rhymes.** Consistency and competence of mother's efforts. Combinations of enjoyment and edification.
4	*Birth*		
3	Gestation	Before birth	**First education of the nature of life.** How comfortable, reliable, or nourishing life will be.
2	*Conception*		
1	Heritage	Before conception	**Typical family and ancestral education.** Traditions and expectations of literacy, advanced education.

A8-a2. Developmental Sequence: CAREER & CALLING

In the Career & Calling Arena, we discover what work we are meant for, how to succeed in it, and how to adjust to changing work conditions. This table demonstrates that our Career & Calling Trajectory is grounded, influenced, and inspired by their earliest childhood career- and work-related experiences – the jobs and careers of our parents, household chore assignments, schoolwork study habits, gardening jobs around the neighborhood, etc.

[Read from bottom to top.]

Step	Stages/Transitions	Age of Ascendance	Typical Situations, Typical Issues
27	Legacy	After death	**Career/ calling accomplishments provide standard for future generations.** Material accomplishments vs. contributions of greater significance. Conveying decision-making capacities to those choosing future careers.
26	*Death*		
25	Senescence	90-100+	**Living off fruits of career.** Availability of successors to provide support. Adequate accumulation of assets. Support from other career veterans.
24	*Debility or Illness*		
23	Elderhood	75-90	**Passing on career skills/ wisdom to others.** Family succession. Availability of protégés or apprentices. Capacity to translate one's own experience to those following. Lasting consequences of career/ calling choices.
22	*Passing-the-Baton*		
21	Mature Adulthood	60-75	**Evaluation of rewards and satisfaction of chosen career path.** Evaluating and integrating career & calling. Adequacy of original career choice. Changing priorities. Exploration of alternative career paths. Return to school to change careers.
20	*Mid-Life Passage*		
19	Middle Adulthood	40-60	**Developing career to full proficiency and earning power. Career vs. calling issue on back burner.** Adequacy and satisfaction of career path chosen. Time allocation between career & home. Level of prominence and success achieved.
18	*Making-the-Grade*		
17	Young Adulthood	21-40	**First career-oriented jobs. First training for specific jobs. First major career/ calling decisions.** Adequacy of career track chosen. Satisfactory performance evaluations and progressions on early career path. Awareness and implementation of career vs. calling.
16	*Nudged from the Nest*		
15	Adolescence [college]	18-22	**Internships. Introductory jobs pertaining to ultimate career.** Seeking ultimate work that offers challenge, material rewards, satisfaction. Working with mentors, supervisors, bosses.
14	Adolescence [high school]	13-18	**First outside jobs. First specific work skills. Introduction of career/ calling issue.** Level of challenge, remuneration, success in outside work. Levels of aptitude & progression in basic and work-related academic skills.
13	*Coming-of-Age*		
12	Middle Childhood [upper grades]	9-12	**Formal schooling: Advancing skills preparation for work. Increasing home responsibilities.** Consistent progression in advancing skills. Improving work habits. Consistent socialization. Teaching profession modeled. Work expectations and benefits shown in home.
11	Middle Childhood [primary grades]	6-8	**Formal schooling: Basic skills preparation for work. Home chores.** Consistent progression in basic skills. Introduction to work habits & socialization. Teaching as work modeled. Work expectations introduced in home.
10	*Entering School*		
9	Young Childhood	3-6	**Introduction of gender-specific occupations.** Awareness and emulation of working parent/s. Imitation and playing at adult work. Work models from parents & media.
8	*Onset of Terrible 2s*		
7	Toddler	1.5-3	**First participation in maternal work.** Participation and imitation of maternal work.
6	*Crawling/ Walking*		
5	Infancy	0-1.5	**Observing and experiencing mother's work patterns.** Reliability and competence of maternal efforts.
4	*Birth*		
3	Gestation	Before birth	**First work of staying alive.** Regularity and adequacy of sustenance.
2	*Conception*		
1	Heritage	Before conception	**Typical family and ancestral careers.** Family career expectations & opportunities.

A8a. Developmental Sequences: Life Passages. Page 119

A8-a3. Dev Sequence: FINANCES & INVESTMENTS

In the Finances & Investments Arena, we build and maintain the financial resources we need to live comfortably and to achieve our life goals. This table demonstrates that our Financial Trajectory is grounded, influenced, and inspired by our earliest childhood experiences with money, resources, and exchange – the material comforts of infancy, a weekly allowance from household chores, neighborhood cleanup jobs, our first bank account, a monthly paycheck from waiting tables, saving up to buy our first car, etc.

[Read from bottom to top.]

Step	Stages/ Transitions	Age of Ascendance	Typical Situations, Typical Issues
27	Legacy	After death	**Passing financial assets and their benefits to future generations.** Creating an endowment that will serve as safety net and as source for worthy projects, without sapping the ambition and initiative of the recipients.
26	*Death*		
25	Senescence	90-100+	**Preserving financial wealth for next generation.** Maintaining ease and comfort without massive depletion of assets through medical costs or fraud. Delegating financial decisions to reliable counselor.
24	*Debility or Illness*		
23	Elderhood	75-90	**Passing financial wealth & wisdom to next generation.** Estate plan to avoid government confiscation. Enjoying ease and security of ample assets. Teaching money management to children/recipients. Long-term, multi-generational perspective.
22	*Passing-the-Baton*		
21	Mature Adulthood	60-75	**Significance takes center-stage. Financial concerns and investments operate automatically in background.** Shift from material to emotional and spiritual gratification. Expenditures for new direction in life: Education, travel, new hobbies, a new relationship.
20	*Mid-Life Passage*		
19	Middle Adulthood	40-60	**Income and asset accumulation approaches maximum.** Partnership earnings far exceed current needs. Attention shifts from income-production to asset preservation. Budgeting and investing becomes routine and automatic. Expenditures for new-found leisure and enrichment activities.
18	*Making-the-Grade*		
17	Young Adulthood	21-40	**Income steady and increasing. Partnership pools earnings. Assets begin to accumulate.** Levels and reliability of remuneration. Financial incentives for performance. Introductory budgeting, investing. Income depletion from growing family, one earner. Teaching children about money.
16	*Nudged from the Nest*		
15	Adolescence [college]	18-22	**Intensive study as primary work:** College education as investment for future income stream. **Immediate income:** Outside job, small business, work study. Correlation of higher skills to higher rewards. Role models for income-earners and wealth users.
14	Adolescence [high school]	13-18	**Steady outside job:** Restaurant, clerk. **Small business:** car detailing, window washing. **Continuing home responsibilities.** Accumulation of savings for major purchase: Car, college ed. Weighing effort expended to financial benefit. Parents as financial advisors.
13	*Coming-of-Age*		
12	Middle Childhood [upper grades]	9-12	**Allowance, in exchange for advanced chores. Progressive payment for chores:** Laundry, cooking, dishes. **Paid outside jobs:** Gardening, paper route. Accumulation of savings for larger purchase. Weighing work involved to reward produced. Parents as income-producers.
11	Middle Childhood [primary grades]	6-8	**Allowance, in exchange for basic chores.** Rewards and payment for chores: Cleanup, trash, pet. Accumulation of savings for small purchases. Weighing effort against benefit. Parents as material providers.
10	*Entering School*		
9	Young Childhood	3-6	**Father introduces concepts of earning, exchange, reciprocity.** Tasks in exchange for rewards. Money as medium of exchange. The power of money to satisfy desires.
8	*Onset of Terrible 2s*		
7	Toddler	1.5-3	**Father joins mother in providing resources. First steps toward self-sufficiency.** Taking chances. Encouragement for progress. Apprehension about risks. Over- or under-protectiveness.
6	*Crawling/ Walking*		
5	Infancy	0-1.5	**Total dependence on mother's resources. Unconditional flow of support.** Quality of maternal care: Health, nourishment, emotional state, living environment. Responsiveness to needs.
4	*Birth*		
3	Gestation	Before birth	**Union with mother's internal resources.** Quality of mother's resources: Health, nourishment, physical comfort, mood chemistry, toxicity.
2	*Conception*		
1	Heritage	Before conception	**Material inheritance from ancestors.** Amount, liquidity, and accessibility of ancestral assets.

A8-a4. Dev Sequence: HEALTH & WELL-BEING

In the Health & Well-Being Arena, we maintain, enhance, and restore our health, vitality, and wellbeing. This table demonstrates that our continuing Health & Well-Being is affected by how we take care of ourselves at each Stage of Development – our genetic predisposition for diabetes or heart disease, the absence of drugs or alcohol in the pregnant mother, our responses to colic or teething, how we deal with mumps or measles, etc.

[Read from bottom to top.]

Step	Stages/ Transitions	Age of Ascendance	Typical Situations, Typical Issues
27	Legacy	After death	**Health Legacy.** Health habits passed on to descendants. DNA legacy, uncontaminated by toxins.
26	*Death*		
25	Senescence	90-100+	**Senescence wellbeing.** Alzheimer's, dementia, incontinence, malnutrition, bed sores.
24	*Debility or Illness*		
23	Elderhood	75-90	**Elderhood wellbeing.** Osteoporosis, arthritis, bronchitis. Loneliness, depression, sleep disorders, memory loss. Vision, hearing. Safe walking, driving. Parkinson's, pneumonia.
22	*Passing-the-Baton*		
21	Mature Adulthood	60-75	**Mature Adult wellbeing.** Diabetes, heart disease, cancer, arthritis, ulcers. Eye disorders, cataracts. Hearing.
20	*Mid-Life Passage*		
19	Middle Adulthood	40-60	**Middle Adult wellbeing.** Blood pressure, constipation, migraines, tooth loss, hormone deficiency, potency.
18	*Making-the-Grade*		
17	Young Adulthood	21-40	**Young Adult wellbeing.** Pregnancy, childbirth. Accidents, violence, obesity, alcohol, smoking, drugs. Hepatitis, chronic fatigue, sexually-transmitted diseases, HIV, mental distress.
16	*Nudged from the Nest*		
15	[college]	18-22	**Adolescent wellbeing.** Acne, menstrual, anxiety, eating disorders, allergies, asthma. Risk-taking behaviors, sports injuries, auto accidents. Smoking, alcohol, drug abuse, unwanted pregnancy, anxiety, depression.
14	Adolescence [high school]	13-18	
13	*Coming-of-Age*		
12	[upper grades]	9-12	**Elementary Grades wellbeing.** Communicable childhood diseases: Measles, mumps, chicken pox, whooping cough. Colds, flu, infections, bumps & scrapes. Vision & hearing problems, headaches, ADD, tooth cavities,
11	Middle Childhood [primary grades]	6-8	
10	*Entering School*		
9	Young Childhood	3-6	**Pre-School Child wellbeing.** Bed-wetting, thumb-sucking, constipation, restlessness.
8	*Onset of Terrible 2s*		
7	Toddler	1.5-3	**Toddler wellbeing.** Potty training, teething, tantrums, bumps & bruises, burns.
6	*Crawling/ Walking*		
5	Infancy	0-1.5	**Infant wellbeing.** Trauma of childbirth, colic, rashes, diarrhea, lactose intolerance, sleeping thru night. Warmth, cleanliness, seclusion.
4	*Birth*		

A8-a5. Developmental Sequence: RECREATION & ENJOYMENT

In the Recreation & Enjoyment Arena, we savor life to the fullest and take pleasure in everything we do. This table demonstrates that our capacity for Recreation & Enjoyment is grounded, influenced, and inspired by our earliest childhood experiences with pleasure and fun – soothing music in the womb, making faces with baby, slapstick pratfalls with a toddler, outings to beach and zoo with youngsters, limiting canned entertainment like TV and movies, etc. As with Sexuality & Sensuality (#10), the roots of this Arena are in one's capacity for pleasure.

[Read from bottom to top.]

Step	Stages/ Transitions	Age of Ascendance	Typical Situations, Typical Issues
27	Legacy	After death	**Legacy of pleasure.** Depolarizing pleasure & purpose – so that future generations see both as essential in complete human being.
26	*Death*		
25	Senescence	90-100+	**Senescent pleasure.** Comfortable, secure financial & material support. Appealing, pleasure-giving, low-stress home environments. Comfortable, pleasurable activities. Supportive, personalized friendships & care. Wholesome, harmonious, soothing entertainment.
24	*Debility or Illness*		
23	Elderhood	75-90	**Elderhood pleasure.** Comfortable, secure financial & material support. Appealing, pleasure-giving work & home environments. Activities that continue to satisfy needs for relevance & significance. Supportive, cooperative friendships & relationships. Couple- and friend-centered fun & entertainment.
22	*Passing-the-Baton*		
21	Mature Adulthood	60-75	**Mature Adult pleasure.** Comfortable, secure financial & material support. Appealing, pleasure-giving work & home environments. Occupations, activities, recreation, entertainment, relationships -- all satisfy renewed needs for relevance & significance.
20	*Mid-Life Passage*		
19	Middle Adulthood	40-60	**Middle Adult pleasure.** Comfortable, secure financial & material support. Appealing, pleasure-giving work & home environments. Home & work occupations that satisfy both practical and experiential needs. Supportive, cooperative friendships & relationships. Couple- and family-centered fun & entertainment: Shows, museums, beach, mountains. Wholesome, uplifting entertainment: Movies, TV, music, arts.
18	*Making-the-Grade*		
17	Young Adulthood	21-40	**Young Adult pleasure.** Supportive, low-stress transition to self-support. Appealing work and home environments. Occupation that satisfies both abstract and experiential needs. Supportive, cooperative friendships & relationships. Couple- and family-centered fun: Shows, museums, beach, mountains. Passionate sex within committed relationship. Wholesome, uplifting entertainment: Movies, TV, music.
16	*Nudged from the Nest*		
15	[college]	18-22	**Adolescent pleasure.** Enriched school environment: Drama, art, music. Balance of experiential and abstract learning. Self-paced lessons, self-directed curriculum, supportive classroom environment. Wholesome relationships: Cooperation, support, non-violent, deemphasized sex. Wholesome school and social event fun, with protective boundaries. Appropriate camaraderie & hugging. Outings: Museum, park, beach, countryside. Movies, TV, music with limited disturbing elements: Violence, sex, dysfunctional relationships, discordant sounds.
14	Adolescence [high school]	13-18	
13	*Coming-of-Age*		
12	[upper grades]	9-12	**Older Child pleasure.** Supportive, low-stress transition to school. Enriched, sensory school environment. Balance of experiential and abstract learning. Low-stress, self-paced lessons. Unrestricted classroom & playground fun, with protective boundaries. Appropriate touching & hugging. Outings: Museum, park, zoo, farms. Movies & TV without disturbing elements: Violence, sex, dysfunctional relationships.
11	Middle Childhood [primary grades]	6-8	
10	*Entering School*		
9	Young Childhood	3-6	**Young Child pleasure.** Hugging, cuddling, carrying. Grooming, bathing. Comfortable, fun clothes. Fun activities: Park, beach, zoo.
8	*Onset of Terrible 2s*		
7	Toddler	1.5-3	**Toddler pleasure.** Protected environment, safety net for risks. Hugging, cuddling, touching, carrying, bathing. Slapstick humor, pratfalls.
6	*Crawling/ Walking*		
5	Infancy	0-1.5	**Infant pleasure.** Home- or water-birth, secure & protected environment. Touching, hugging, massage, bathing. Making faces, pets.
4	*Birth*		
3	Gestation	Before birth	**Comfort & pleasure within the womb.** Nutrition, stress, toxins. Soothing environment, music, voice, massage.
2	*Conception*		
1	Heritage	Before conception	**Familial attitudes toward pleasure.** Religion-, moral-, ethnic- based attitudes toward pleasure and self-indulgence.

A8-a6. Developmental Sequence: NATURE & ENVIRONMENT

In the Arena of Nature & Environment, we enjoy the beauty and harmony of Nature. Based on that experience, we create Living Environments and engage in activities that are natural, harmonious, and authentic. This table demonstrates that our appreciation for Nature & Environment is grounded, influenced, and inspired by our earliest childhood experiences with nature and natural things – a tradition of family outdoor activities, a toxin-free womb environment, a child's unfettered freedom to explore his surroundings, outings to the aquarium or beach, family vacations in the mountains, etc. This Arena bears similarities to Recreation & Enjoyment (#5).

[Read from bottom to top.]

Step	Stages/ Transitions	Age of Ascendance	Typical Situations, Typical Issues
27	Legacy	After death	**Legacy of nature & the natural.** Passing along to future generations a love of natural. An appreciation of natural activities, relationships, & living situations.
26	*Death*		
25	Senescence	90-100+	**Senescent environments.** Comfortable, secure financial & material support. Appealing, natural home environments. Comfortable, pleasurable, low-stress nature activities: garden, park. Supportive, personalized care with minimum medical paraphernalia. Live, natural, interactive entertainment.
24	*Debility or Illness*		
23	Elderhood	75-90	**Elderhood environments.** Comfortable, secure material circumstances. Appealing, natural home & recreational environments. Nature-centered and natural recreation: Spontaneous, intuitive activities that satisfy needs for relevance & significance. Supportive, cooperative friendships with natural expressions of feeling. Natural fun & entertainment.
22	*Passing-the-Baton*		
21	Mature Adulthood	60-75	**Mature Adult environments.** Comfortable, secure material circumstances: Facilitates personal satisfaction over material needs. Appealing, pleasure-giving work & home environments. Occupations & retirement activities that nourish natural processes of body & soul. Nature-centered and natural recreation: Return to nature as source of authenticity and grounding in basic needs. Activities & entertainment support new, emerging self.
20	*Mid-Life Passage*		
19	Middle Adulthood	40-60	**Middle Adult environments.** Comfortable, secure, low-anxiety financial & material circumstances. Appealing, pleasure-giving work & home environments. Occupation continues to include experiential, interpersonal component. Nature-centered and natural recreation: Live shows, group dinners, beach, mountains. Natural flow of emotional expression. Wholesome, natural entertainment: Movies, TV, music, arts.
18	*Making-the-Grade*		
17	Young Adulthood	21-40	**Young Adult environments.** Natural, appealing work & home environments. Occupation that includes experiential, interpersonal activities. Nature-centered couple & family fun: Live shows, zoo, beach, mountains. Unrestrained expressions of affection, with appropriate boundaries. Limited pre-packaged entertainment: Movies, TV, music.
16	*Nudged from the Nest*		
15	[college]	18-22	**Adolescent environments.** School environment emphasizing natural expression: Drama, art, music. Experiential, self-paced, self-directed curriculum. Supportive, wholesome, natural classroom environment, relationships. Natural outdoor activities: Museums, beach, countryside. Minimized TV, movies, video games, pop music.
14	Adolescence [high school]	13-18	
13	*Coming-of-Age*		
12	[upper grades]	9-12	**Older Child environments.** Enriched, sensory, experiential school environment. Learning arises from natural curiosity at natural, individual pace. Unrestrained body movement, vocal expression in classroom & playground fun, Appropriate natural expressions of affection. Outings: Museum, park, zoo, farms.
11	Middle Childhood [primary grades]	6-8	
10	*Entering School*		
9	Young Childhood	3-6	**Young Child environments.** Limitations on artificial entertainment: TV, movies, IPOD. Unfettered exploration of surroundings. Outdoor play. Outings to natural places: Park, beach, zoo. Natural, unrestrained contact & affection.
8	*Onset of Terrible 2s*		
7	Toddler	1.5-3	**Toddler environments.** Unfettered exploration of surroundings –no crib, playpen, harness. Outdoor play: back yard, garden, park. Natural, unrestrained affection & contact.
6	*Crawling/ Walking*		
5	Infancy	0-1.5	**Infant environment.** Natural bedding, plants, sunlight, colors. Natural rhythms of sleeping, feeding. Natural childbirth in home environment. Breast-feeding.
4	*Birth*		
3	Gestation	Before birth	**Natural conditions within the womb.** Natural uterine environment, free of drugs, alcohol, nicotine, other contaminents..
2	*Conception*		
1	Heritage	Before conception	**Cultural & familial attitudes toward nature and the outdoors.** Traditions of appreciating nature & enjoying the outdoors. Valuing natural activities & environments.

A8-a7. Developmental Sequence: EMOTIONS & PERSONAL GROWTH

In the Emotions & Personal Growth Arena, we open up to our feelings and emotions, and actualize our full potential as human beings. This table demonstrates that a our capacity for emotional expression and our commitment to ongoing Personal Growth is grounded, influenced, and inspired by our earliest Growth experiences – the nurturing from our mother, the guidance and encouragement from our father, success in our first efforts to walk and talk, a sympathetic preschool teacher, etc. (This Arena pertains to the <u>external</u> activities of cultivating Emotions and encouraging one's Personal Growth. This contrasts to the <u>internal</u> processes by which our Affect & Emotions develop in Psyche Passages, Arena #3.)

[Read from bottom to top.]

Step	Stages/ Transitions	Age of Ascendance	Typical Situations, Typical Issues
27	Legacy	After death	**Growth perspective passed on to descendants.** Passing along a legacy and tradition of wisdom, experience, emotional clarity, commitment to Growth Continuum.
26	*Death*		
25	Senescence	90-100+	**Remaining intact.** Retaining conscious presence, perceptive awareness, & emotional expressiveness, despite debilities. Increasing awareness of world to come.
24	*Debility or Illness*		
23	Elderhood	75-90	**Growth & expression gives back.** Contributions to the growth & emotional fluidity of others – thru personal influence, organizational structures, writings & other communications media.
22	*Passing-the-Baton*		
21	Mature Adulthood	60-75	**Growth & expression rejuvenate.** Mid-life wakeup shakes the status quo. Renewed search for career, relationship, activities that offer new opportunities for growth. Shift from exterior to interior growth.
20	*Mid-Life Passage*		
19	Middle Adulthood	40-60	**Stabilized levels of personal growth & emotional expression.** Career functions as pre-established growth program. Shift from change to maintenance: the rut. Joint growth with partner, or increasing separation. Established growth programs beyond home & work environments. Maintenance of existing range of expression, openness, spontaneity.
18	*Making-the-Grade*		
17	Young Adulthood	21-40	**First independently-initiated program for growth & change. Narrowed opportunities for emotional expression.** Career decisions as enrollment in pre-established growth programs. Joint growth with partner. First search for alternative growth programs, modes of expression, beyond those offered by birth family or school.
16	*Nudged from the Nest*		
15	[college]	18-22	**Advanced program for growth & change. Advanced laboratory for emotions.** Differentiation and tracking within school's program of mental & character growth. Designation of those destined for maximum growth. Capacity to retain openness, expressiveness, authenticity amid complex social currents.
14	Adolescence [high school]	13-18	
13	*Coming-of-Age*		
12	[upper grades]	9-12	**Formalized program for growth & change. Laboratory for emotions.** Capacity to participate & succeed in school's program of mental & character growth. Capacity to retain openness & expressiveness amid social pressures.
11	Middle Childhood [primary grades]	6-8	
10	*Entering School*		
9	Young Childhood	3-6	**Focused support for growth & change.** Shift from comfort to accomplishment. Rewards for achievement. Balance of unconditional and conditional love.
8	*Onset of Terrible 2s*		
7	Toddler	1.5-3	**First efforts at self-initiated change.** Moves toward independence. Emotional risk-taking. Over-protectiveness or inattention. Father's increasing participation.
6	*Crawling/ Walking*		
5	Infancy	0-1.5	**Emotional connection with mother.** Quality and availability of attention & interaction. Mother's neglect, unresponsiveness, overprotection. Father's involvement. Unconditional love.
4	*Birth*		
3	Gestation	Before birth	**Emotional expressiveness of pregnant mother.** Body chemistry and physical stance of excessively rigid or overly emotional mother. Emotions as soothing or threatening.
2	*Conception*		
1	Heritage	Before conception	**Attitudes toward emotions of extended family & ancestors.** Prevalence of open expression. History of personal growth and change – incl. risks, dangers, consequences.

A8-a8. Developmental Sequence: RELIGION & SPIRITUALITY

In the Arena of Religion & Spirituality, we expand our capacity for spiritual experience and raise our consciousness of a Higher Power. This table demonstrates that a our capacity for spiritual Growth is grounded, influenced, and inspired by our earliest spiritual experiences – ancestral patterns of religious observance, our intuitive sense of a personal Creator, spiritual serenity in the mother, sessions of family worship, the lessons of Sunday school or catechism, school and peer group pressures against religion, etc. (This Arena pertains to the external activities of religious observance and spiritual practice. This contrasts to the internal processes by which our spiritual life develops in Spirit Passages (D3d) and the Spirit Arenas (D4d). (This topic is highly speculative and controversial. Readers should feel to substitute their own views on Spiritual Growth.)

[Read from bottom to top.]

Step	Stages/Transitions	Age of Ascendance	Typical Situations, Typical Issues
27	Legacy	After death	**Religious & spiritual insights & perspectives passed on to descendants.** Legacy & tradition: Wisdom, spiritual clarity, commitment to Divine Presence as core of existence.
26	*Death*		
25	Senescence	90-100+	**Moving toward spiritual plane.** Diminishing involvement in the material world. Increasing immersion in world to come.
24	*Debility or Illness*		
23	Elderhood	75-90	**Shift from Enlightenment toward Compassion.** Blessings received increasingly returned to the world – alleviating human suffering, raising aspirations, grooming disciples.
22	*Passing-the-Baton*		
21	Mature Adulthood	60-75	**Rejuvenated religion & spirituality.** Mid-life wakeup renews hunger for cosmic significance. Renewed search for career, relationship, leisure activities in tune with ultimate truths. Shift from exterior observance to interior immersion.
20	*Mid-Life Passage*		
19	Middle Adulthood	40-60	**Established program for religion & spirituality.** Religious programs chosen as Young Adult continue. Partners may remain close thru joint participation, or separate spiritually & emotionally. Spiritual practices become routine, detached from significance, required.
18	*Making-the-Grade*		
17	Young Adulthood	21-40	**First independently initiated program for religion & spirituality. Broadened opportunities for religious choice.** Search for alternative religious programs, beyond those offered by birth family or childhood religious institutions. Spiritual & ideological influences on career choice. Joint religious participation with partner.
16	*Nudged from the Nest*		
15	[college]	18-22	**Advanced program of religious observances, spiritual practices.** Formal adolescent program for advanced doctrine, practices. Assembles, socializes, conforms with or departs from other initiates. Testing boundaries of faith: Questioning doctrine, exploring consequences of prohibited behaviors.
14	Adolescence [high school]	13-18	
13	*Coming-of-Age*		
12	[upper grades]	9-12	**Formalized program of religious observances, spiritual practices.** Child attends formal children's program at church, synagogue, mosque. Learns basic doctrine, practices. Assembles, socializes, conforms with other young initiates.
11	Middle Childhood [primary grades]	6-8	
10	*Entering School*		
9	Young Childhood	3-6	**Family religious observances.** Family unified through shared home- and family-centered religious observances. Young child absorbs the ambience, if not the content.
8	*Onset of Terrible 2s*		
7	Toddler	1.5-3	**Father as medium: Experiencing balance of conditional and unconditional love from Divine Presence.** Establishing expectations for spiritual progress, growth, improvement, enlightenment.
6	*Crawling/Walking*		
5	Infancy	0-1.5	**Mother as medium: Experiencing unconditional love from Divine Presence.** Sense of being protected and cared-for at cosmic level.
4	*Birth*		
3	Gestation	Before birth	**Spiritual serenity of pregnant mother.** Influence of spiritual convictions and practices on body chemistry, emotional stability, physical fluidity. Primordial sense of being formed by personal Creator.
2	*Conception*		
1	Heritage	Before conception	**Family, ancestral, & ethnic traditions of religious observance & spiritual practice.** Consequences of religious conformity or apostasy.

A8-a9. Developmental Sequence: RELATIONSHIPS & MARRIAGE

In the Arena of Relationships & Marriage, we build intimate relationships that are happy, stable, mutually supportive, and lasting. In the process, we find the right lifetime partner. This table demonstrates that our Relationships Trajectory is grounded, influenced, and inspired by our earliest interpersonal experiences – ancestral marriages and familial connections, a mother's breast-feeding during infancy, a father's guidance and encouragement in early childhood, best friends in the classroom and conflicts on the playground, the strength and intimacy of our parents' own marriage, etc. This Arena is closely related to Family & Children (#11).

[Read from bottom to top.]

Step	Stages/Transitions	Age of Ascendance	Typical Situations, Typical Issues
27	**Legacy**	After death	**Influence on descendants.** Continuing bonds down thru the centuries. Passing along a lifetime of wisdom and experience. Adding to family and cultural traditions.
26	*Death*		
25	**Senescence**	90-100+	**Loss of partner.** Facing, mourning, & recovering from loss of loved one's presence, whether thru death or diminished capacities.
24	*Debility or Illness*		
23	**Elderhood**	75-90	**Partners support and assist.** Supporting one another both physically & psychologically with compassion and trust.
22	*Passing-the-Baton*		
21	**Mature Adulthood**	60-75	**Relationship rejuvenates.** Surviving & resolving storms of mutual mid-life passage. Restoring passion & intimacy, starting afresh.
20	*Mid-Life Passage*		
19	**Middle Adulthood**	40-60	**Relationship stabilizes.** Continuing commitment & shared growth, despite emerging differences. Remaining close while maintaining individuality, growing separately. Resolving differences & conflicts maturely, constructively.
18	*Making-the-Grade*		
17	**Young Adulthood**	21-40	**Long-term partnership. Formally-committed relationship. Marriage.** Finding & building solid, authentic, long-term or lifelong relationship based on meaningful shared values & goals.
16	*Nudged from the Nest*		
15	[college]	18-22	**Committed partnerships.** Serious relationships predominate. Discovering desired qualities in long-term partner.
14	**Adolescence** [high school]	13-18	**Temporary partnerships.** Experimentation and experiencing casual & serious relationships. Playing the field.
13	*Coming-of-Age*		
12	[upper grades]	9-12	**Fast friends, social groups.** Solidifying, deepening friendships. First romantic infatuations.
11	**Middle Childhood** [primary grades]	6-8	**Friends, schoolmates.** Relationships in society take precedence. Building friendships. Adjusting to others, acculturation. Rules of interpersonal behavior.
10	*Entering School*		
9	**Young Childhood**	3-6	**Bonding with father.** Degree and quality of father's attentiveness. Detachment, domination, abuse.
8	*Onset of Terrible 2s*		
7	**Toddler**	1.5-3	**Semi-independence from mother.** Over-protectiveness or inattention. Initial bonding with father.
6	*Crawling/ Walking*		
5	**Infancy**	0-1.5	**Bonding with mother.** Quality and availability of attention. Maternal neglect, unresponsiveness.
4	*Birth*		
3	**Gestation**	Before birth	**Union with mother.** Uterine environment: Nourishment, body chemistry, toxicity, responsiveness, moods, expressions of care.
2	*Conception*		
1	**Heritage**	Before conception	**Influence of ancestors.** Genetic endowments. Heritage of family traditions – cultural, religious, behavioral, anecdotal. Family dynasty, lineage. Patterns of connection, privilege, distinction, abuse.

A8-a10. Developmental Sequence: SENSUALITY & SEXUALITY

In the Arena of Sensuality & Sexuality, we enjoy the world around us as a pleasure-filled, sensory experience. As part of that experience, we share a sexual relationship with a beloved partner that is intimate, meaningful, and satisfying. This table demonstrates that a our capacity for sensual & sexual expression is grounded, influenced, and inspired by our earliest sensory experiences – cultural & familial attitudes toward sex, the sensory experiences of the womb, hugging and tussling with mommy and daddy, playground games like tag and dodge-ball that energize and enliven our whole bodies, etc. (This Arena pertains to the <u>external</u> experiences and activities of Sensuality & Sexuality. This contrasts to the <u>internal</u> processes by which our Sexuality develops in Psyche Passages, Arena #2. As with Recreation & Enjoyment (#5), the roots of this Arena are in our capacity for pleasure.)

[Read from bottom to top.]

Step	Stages/ Transitions	Age of Ascendance	Typical Situations, Typical Issues
27	**Legacy**	After death	**Attitudes & perspectives passed on to descendants.** Legacy of sensual & sexual openness, appropriate expression, focused sublimation.
26	*Death*		
25	**Senescence**	90-100+	**Senescent sensuality.** Retaining sensual & sensory awareness and pleasure, despite debilities. Increasing sensory experience of world to come.
24	*Debility or Illness*		
23	**Elderhood**	75-90	**Elderhood sensuality & sexuality.** Maintaining sensuality & sexuality within committed relationship. Supporting sensual expression in others – thru personal influence, organizational structures, writings & other communications media.
22	*Passing-the-Baton*		
21	**Mature Adulthood**	60-75	**Sensuality & sexuality rejuvenates.** Mid-life wakeup shakes the status quo. Reviving sexuality within committed relationship. Renewed search for activities & relationships that offer opportunities for sexual/sensual expression. Shift from external proving or conquest to internal fulfillment & satisfaction.
20	*Mid-Life Passage*		
19	**Middle Adulthood**	40-60	**Stabilized levels of sexual & sensual expression.** Fulfilling sensuality & sexuality within committed relationship. Joint sensual & sexual growth with partner, or increasing separation. Shift to perfunctory, routine sex: the rut.
18	*Making-the-Grade*		
17	**Young Adulthood**	21-40	**Sensuality & sexuality in service of primary relationship.** Long-term relationship solidified & strengthened thru exclusive sexual relationship. Mutual trust enables dissolution of defenses, fuller sensual experiences. Childbirth as culmination of shared sexual experience. Energies previously directed to sexual liaisons now sublimated toward career accomplishments.
16	*Nudged from the Nest*		
15	[college]	18-22	**Adolescent sensuality & sexuality.** Interest in & attraction to opposite sex. Maintaining healthy, wholesome sensual & sexual pleasure, within heightened social pressures. Appropriate sensual & sexual expression. Differentiation between feeling & acting out. Defenses against corruption and degradation of healthy sensuality.
14	**Adolescence** [high school]	13-18	
13	*Coming-of-Age*		
12	[upper grades]	9-12	**School-age sensuality.** Maintaining openness to sensory & sensual pleasure, within context of social pressures. Sexual differences, first infatuations & experimentations. Appropriate touching & hugging. Defenses against playground corruptions of healthy sensuality.
11	**Middle Childhood** [primary grades]	6-8	
10	*Entering School*		
9	**Young Childhood**	3-6	**Pre-school sensuality.** Availability of intimate & sensual contact, even while exploring independence. Shift from sensory experience to accomplishment. Hugging, cuddling, carrying, tussling. Grooming, bathing.
8	*Onset of Terrible 2s*		
7	**Toddler**	1.5-3	**Toddler sensuality.** Active, full-body, unrestrained movement. Exhilaration of risk-taking. Hugging, cuddling, carrying. Grooming, bathing. Over-protectiveness or inattention. Father's increasing sensual contact.
6	*Crawling/ Walking*		
5	**Infancy**	0-1.5	**Sensory relationship with mother.** Attention, interaction. Neglect, unresponsiveness, overprotection. Touching, hugging, massage, bathing.
4	*Birth*		
3	**Gestation**	Before birth	**Sensory experience within the womb.** Nutrition, moods, stress, toxins. Pleasurable environment: Warmth, comfort, music, voice, massage.
2	*Conception*		
1	**Heritage**	Before conception	**Ancestral, cultural, familial attitudes.** Sexual repression, sensual deprivation. Prevailing morality & codes of behavior.

A8-a11. Developmental Sequence: FAMILY & CHILDREN

In the Arena of Family & Children, we birth and raise Children who are happy, healthy, and well-adjusted – in the context of a Family that is close, caring, and supportive. This table demonstrates that our attitudes toward Family & Children are grounded, influenced, and inspired by our earliest childhood and family experiences – traditions of family ties & loyalties, intimate family bonds with mommy & daddy, the fellowship and support of our siblings, grade school teachers as our first surrogate parents, competitions with surrogate siblings on the playground, etc. This Arena is closely related to Relationships & Marriage (#9.)

[Read from bottom to top.]

Step	Stages/ Transitions	Age of Ascendance	Typical Situations, Typical Issues
27	Legacy	After death	**Influence on descendants.** Continuing traditions of strong, resilient family -- centrality of children & child-rearing. Preserve legacy thru: Recollections, photos, memorabilia of quintessential family experiences.
26	*Death*		
25	Senescence	90-100+	**Support of family.** Parent becomes the child. Comfort & support thru bonds of family. In-home care vs. elder warehousing.
24	*Debility or Illness*		
23	Elderhood	75-90	**Multi-generational family.** Extending family ties to children's children, extended family. Promoting the benefits of family – thru personal relationship, family traditions, books & other communications media.
22	*Passing-the-Baton*		
21	Mature Adulthood	60-75	**Family reaches fruition.** Children form their own families. Empty nest: return to couple status. Attention redirected toward couplehood; storms of mutual mid-life passage. Relationships with grandchildren: Friending & mentoring vs. indulging & spoiling.
20	*Mid-Life Passage*		
19	Middle Adulthood	40-60	**Family stabilizes.** Maintenance of chosen family structure, routines of child-rearing. Navigating changes in temperament & roles as children mature. Cooperation or conflicts between mother's & father's influence. Siblings as surrogate parents for younger children. Capacity to allow & encourage children's independence & capacity to excel.
18	*Making-the-Grade*		
17	Young Adulthood	21-40	**First self-initiated family.** Rediscovering family experiences and values of early childhood in establishing one's own family. Emulating models of ideal relationships & families. Exploring alternative family structures, child-rearing techniques.
16	*Nudged from the Nest*		
15	[college]	18-22	**School as family in flux.** Teachers & classmates diminish as surrogate parents and siblings. Subject-oriented vs. home-oriented classrooms. Competitive, undermining siblings. Defensive shells of conformity, rebellion, defiance. Circles of friends increasingly essential as familial subgroups. Values of school society ascendant over home family. Shift toward caring, support, cooperation as adolescence approaches adulthood.
14	Adolescence [high school]	13-18	
13	*Coming-of-Age*		
12	[upper grades]	9-12	**School as family.** Teacher & classmates as surrogate parent and siblings. Supportive vs. undermining relationships. Family mentality supported or assaulted: Defense, withdrawal. Circles of friends as familial subgroups. Weighing values of home family vs. school family.
11	Middle Childhood [primary grades]	6-8	
10	*Entering School*		
9	Young Childhood	3-6	**Home recognized as family.** Recognition of nuclear family unit: Mother, father, siblings, close relations. Esprit de corps: Identification as family member. Differentiation of roles: Whole greater than parts.
8	*Onset of Terrible 2s*		
7	Toddler	1.5-3	**Flexibility of family boundaries.** Toleration & support for exploration, risk-taking. Over-protectiveness, inattention. Increased prominence of father in family circle. Care & attention from older siblings.
6	*Crawling/ Walking*		
5	Infancy	0-1.5	**Bonding with mother.** Extension of most fundamental family relationship. Strength & character of maternal bonds. Maternal neglect, unresponsiveness.
4	*Birth*		
3	Gestation	Before birth	**Union with mother.** The most fundamental family relationship. Nature & character of family conveyed thru: Nourishment, responsiveness, moods, toxicity, expressions of care.
2	*Conception*		
1	Heritage	Before conception	**Familial, ancestral, & cultural influences.** Inherited traditions of family ties, loyalties, obligations. Family unity as a core principle, fundamental building block of culture.

A8-a12. Developmental Sequence: FRIENDSHIPS & COMMUNITY

In the Arena of Friendships & Community, we develop deep, lasting Friendships with kindred spirits. Through a network of such friendships, we contribute to the strength and vigor of our Communities. This table demonstrates that our relationships with Friends & Community is grounded, influenced, and inspired by our earliest interpersonal and community experiences – the community traditions we inherit from our ancestors, our first prototype community of parents & siblings, our friendships on the playground, the communities of our first classrooms, etc. This Arena is closely related to Family & Children (#11).

[Read from bottom to top.]

Step	Stages/Transitions	Age of Ascendance	Typical Situations, Typical Issues
27	Legacy	After death	**Community of succeeding generations.** Tradition of care, concern, involvement embedded in structure of extended community. Legacy preserved thru: Local written & oral histories, photos, museum, traditional events.
26	*Death*		
25	Senescence	90-100+	**Support of friends & community.** Diminished capacities. Comfort & support thru bonds of community & friendships. In-community care vs. elder communities: Personal vs. institutional attention.
24	*Debility or Illness*		
23	Elderhood	75-90	**Community responsibility.** Supporting, contributing to, enhancing local community. Community service, infrastructure projects, government. Long-term community planning perspective.
22	*Passing-the-Baton*		
21	Mature Adulthood	60-75	**Community in ascendance over family.** Return to couple status redirects parents toward peer friendships, community involvement. Mid-life passage motivates search for alternative friendships, communities, interest groups. Family community broadens to include children's spouses, grandchildren.
20	*Mid-Life Passage*		
19	Middle Adulthood	40-60	**Community stabilizes, expands.** Maintenance of chosen community locale, school environment. Strengthening ties & habitual social routines within established community relationship. Differing participation by husband, wife, children; differing sources of community involvement. Flexibility in adapting family structure to community expectations.
18	*Making-the-Grade*		
17	Young Adulthood	21-40	**First self-initiated community.** Attention focused on primary relationship & family: Prior friendships diminish, community participation shrinks. Shift to children's school and school parents as primary community. Shared experience of child-rearing. Exploring alternative school communities. Conscious choice of locale to settle in.
16	*Nudged from the Nest*		
15	[college]	18-22	**Community identity in flux.** Values of school community ascendant over home. Shift from community-oriented to subject-oriented classrooms. Community as battleground: Pressure, strife. Conformity, rebellion, defiance. Circles of friends as havens of safety. Shift toward caring, support, cooperation as adolescence approaches adulthood.
14	Adolescence [high school]	13-18	
13	*Coming-of-Age*		
12	[upper grades]	9-12	**School: Intro to larger community.** First friendships, circles of friends. Supportive vs. undermining relationships. First community involvement: Classroom, playground. Competing values of home community vs. school community.
11	Middle Childhood [primary grades]	6-8	
10	*Entering School*		
9	Young Childhood	3-6	**Home recognized as fundamental community.** Nuclear family as prototype community. Esprit de corps: Identification as family member. Differentiation of community roles: Parents, siblings, relations.
8	*Onset of Terrible 2s*		
7	Toddler	1.5-3	**Flexibility of community boundaries.** Community as safety net for exploration, risk-taking. Over-protectiveness, inattention. Increased prominence of father & siblings in community circle.
6	*Crawling/Walking*		
5	Infancy	0-1.5	**Bonding with mother.** Continuation of most fundamental friendship and most mutually-committed community. Strength & character of maternal bonds. Maternal neglect, unresponsiveness.
4	*Birth*		
3	Gestation	Before birth	**Union with mother.** The most fundamental friendship. Character of friendship & community connections conveyed thru: Maternal nourishment, responsiveness, moods, toxicity, expressions of care.
2	*Conception*		
1	Heritage	Before conception	**Familial, ancestral, & cultural influences.** Inherited traditions of mutual responsibilities, supportive friendships, strong community ties.

A8b. Arenas of the Psyche

Psyche Passages are the internal Phases of mental Maturation that occur as we progress through the Stages of psychological development. The two tables on the following pages display examples of Developmental Sequences for each of the nine Arenas of Psyche Passages. The nine Psyche Arenas are as follows:

DEVELOPMENTAL SEQUENCES: PSYCHE PASSAGES	
ARENAS	PAGE
1. Basic Needs	130
2. Sexuality	130
3. Affect & Emotions	130
4. Self & Ego	130
5. Leadership	131
6. Cognition	131
7. Art, Aesthetics, & Creativity	131
8. Ethics & Morals	131
9. Worldviews	131

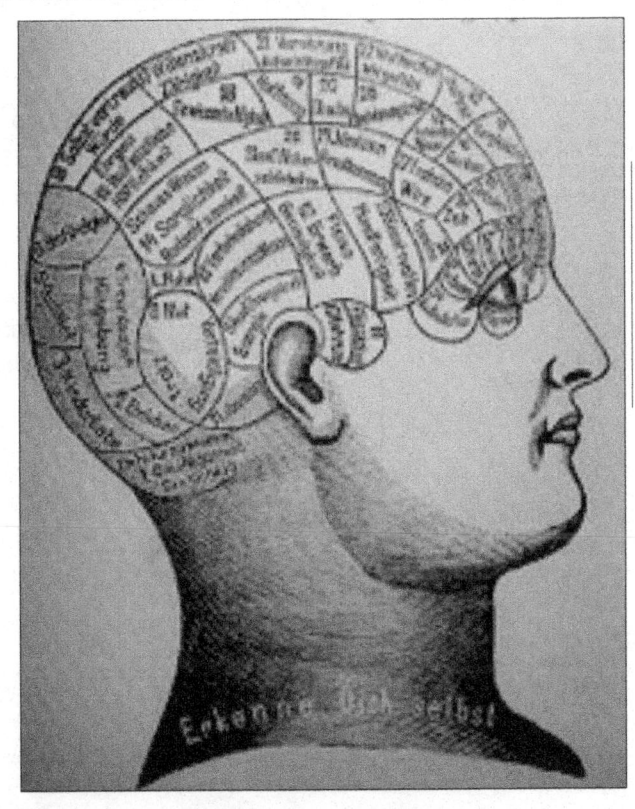

Arenas of the Psyche. Each of the nine Arenas of the Psyche has its own set of Internal Developmental Stages.

The reader need not be concerned to understand every detail of these Psyche Passage tables. Just get a general sense of the progression from lower to higher Stages in each of these Arenas.

These tables pertain to the Developmental Sequence of Stages (D1) and Transitions (D2), in the Realm and Arenas of Psyche Passages (D3b, D4b), for the Process of Actualization Growth (PPR3). The tables are consolidations of Tables from Ken Wilber's Integral Psychology, where the 38 Steps of Wilber's Fundamental Developmental Sequence (FDS) are telescoped into the seven Stages of the Chakras (Appx A7). For a more complete set of Wilber's Psyche tables, including all Steps of his Fundamental Developmental Sequence, refer to the authors' companion study, *Arrays of Light*.

A8b. Wilber's Arenas Of The Psyche: 1-4

ARENA. Line >> (Investigator) >> **Chakras**	FUND. NEEDS Needs (Maslow)	SEXUALITY Erotic Relationships (Fortune)	EMOTIONS Affect (Wilber)	SELF/EGO Psycho-Social Dev (Erikson)
7. WISDOM Understanding, knowing, transcendence, peace	Self-Transcendence	Pure Spirit Concrete spirit	One Taste Bodhisatvic compassion Infinite freedom-release Saintly commitment Love-bliss Ananda, ecstacy Compassion All-species love Awe, rapture	Immortality vs Extinction
- transition -				
6. VISIONARY THOUGHT Clairvoyance, imagination, psychic experiences, inspiration	Self-Actualization	Abstract Mental	World-centric altruism All-human love Compassion	Integrity vs Despair Generativity vs Stagnation
- transition -			Global justice, care	
5. EXPRESSION Communication, creative expression, synthesis of ideas into symbols/ words	Self-Esteem		Universal affect	Intimacy vs Isolation Individual Identity vs Role Confusion
- transition -			Belongingness	
4. LOVE Relationships, emotions, affinity, compassion, self-acceptance	Care Belongingness	Concrete Mental	Joy, depression, hate Love	Group Identity vs Alienation Industry vs Inferiority
- transition -			Wishing, liking, safety	
3. POWER Will, purpose, autonomy, identity, self-esteem	Security Safety		Anxiety, anger	Initiative vs Guilt-Anxiety
- transition -			Satisfaction	
2. SEXUALITY Urges, desire, passion, pleasure, feelings		Emotional	Tension, fear, rage	Autonomy vs Shame-Doubt
- transition -	Beginning of Safety		Pleasure-pain	
1. SURVIVAL Grounding, security, stability, trust, vitality physical health	Physiological	Instinctual Physical	Touch, temperature	Trust vs Mistrust

A8b. WILBER'S ARENAS OF THE PSYCHE: 5-9

Chakra	LEADERSHIP Action/Inquiry (Torbert)	COGNITION Cognitive Stages (Piaget)	ART, CREATIVITY Art (Wilber)	ETHICS Moral Judgment (Kohlberg)	WORLDVIEWS Worldviews (Wilber)
7			ARCHETYPAL Thangka, bhakti expressivist SYMBOLIST Psychic perceptual Fantastic realist	Universal spiritual	Non–Dual Causal Subtle Psychic
				POST-CONVENTIONAL	Developmentalism as World Process
6	Ironist Existential	Polyvalent Logic	APERSPECTIVAL Cubist, abstract	Universal ethical	Cross-paradigmatic, dialectical Integrates multiple contexts, paradigmatic Multiple contexts/ histories
			Impressionistic	Prior rights/ social contract	Pluralistic systems, dynamic
5	Achiever Technician	Formal Operational	PERSPECTIVAL Conceptual, formal Naturalistic, empirical-representational	Transition POST-CONVENTIONAL Law & order	Static systems/ contexts Static universal formalism
	Diplomat			Approval of others CONVENTIONAL	Demythologizing, formalizing
	Opportunist	Concrete Operational	MYTHOLOGICAL-LITERAL Concrete religious art, icons	Naïve hedonism	Rationalization of mythic structures. Locus of magic power is deified Other
				Punishment/ Obedience	Concrete-literal myths
3		Intuitive Conceptual	MAGICAL IMAGERY Cave art, dream imagery, surrealist		Ego omnipotence transferred to gods. Omnipotence of ego challenged, security
	Impulsive			Magic wish	Ego is locus of magic power
2		Pre-Conceptual	EMOTIONAL-EXPRESSIVIST Feeling-expression	PRE-CONVENTIONAL	Egocentric, word magic, narcissistic. Self-object
					Subject-object fusions
1		Sensorimotor	SENSORIMOTOR Initial aesthetic impact		Hallucinatory wish-fulfillment. Undifferentiated, pleromatic

A8c. Arenas of the Spirit

Spirit Passages are the internal Phases or Modes of spiritual Enlightenment that occur as we experience higher States of Consciousness (D8), awaken to the Divine Presence (P7), or open ourselves to the leadings of Providence (PF12). The tables on the following pages display examples of Developmental Sequences for each of nine Arenas of Spirit Passages (4d). The nine Spirit Arenas are as follows:

CHAKRA SEQUENCES: SPIRIT PASSAGES	
ARENAS	**PAGE**
1. Spectrum of Consciousness	133
2. Transcendent Stages & States	134
3. Deities & Heroes	135
4. Archetypal Journeys	136
5. Prophetic Revelations	137
6. Rituals & Practices	138
7. Virtues & Gifts	139
8. Scripture & Holy Writ	140
9. Cultural Stages of Worship	141

Deities & Heroes. The pantheon of Greek Gods is a sub-Arena in the Realm of the Spirit that corresponds to seven Levels of Internal Spiritual Development.

These tables pertain to the Chakral levels (Appx A7d), in the Realm and Arenas of Spirit Passages (D3d, D4d), for the Process of Awakening (PPR9). The first two of these Sequences are consolidations of Tables from Ken Wilber's *Integral Psychology*, where the 38 Steps of Wilber's Fundamental Developmental Sequence (FDS) are telescoped into the seven Levels of the Chakras (Appx A7). The remaining seven tables are derived from Wilber, Campbell, Anodea Judith, the authors' own research and experience, and others. For a more complete set of Wilber's Spirit tables, including all Steps of his Fundamental Developmental Sequence, refer to the authors' companion study, *Arrays of Light*.

The Spirit Arenas are especially speculative and controversial. This topic is currently under development and subject to revision. Comments and suggestions from readers are welcome. *** The reader need not be concerned to understand every detail of these Spirit tables. Just get a general sense of the progression from lower to higher Stages & States in each of these Arenas.

A8c1. Arenas of the Spirit: SPECTRUM OF CONSCIOUSNESS

Wilber's Spectrum of Consciousness displays the full range of human awareness – beginning with base material needs and culminating in the Transcendent States. Investigators include mystics, philosophers, psychologists, academics, and the originators of ancient spiritual systems.

[Read from bottom to top.]

Line of Inquiry >> (Investigator) >> **CHAKRAS**	Levels of Consciousness (Plotinus. ~200 AD)	Levels of Consciousness (Aurobindo. ~1900)	Anthroposophy (Steiner. ~1900)	Levels of Consciousness (Grof. ~1970)
7. WISDOM (Understanding, consciousness, bliss. Crown of head.)	Absolute One Nous World soul	Satchitananda Supermind Overmind Intuitive mind Illumined mind	Spirit-man Spirit-life Spirit-self	8. Unitary 7. Transcendent
- transition -				
6. VISIONARY THOUGHT (Imagination, intuition, clairvoyance. Brow, 3rd eye.)	Creative reason	Higher mind (systems)	Consciousness soul	6. Authentic
- transition -				
5. EXPRESSION (Communication, creativity, symbolization. Throat.)	Logical faculty	Logical mind (reasoning)	Rational soul	5. Achievement/ affiliative
- transition -				
4. LOVE (Compassion, peace. Heart.)		Concrete mind		4. Conformist
- transition -	Opinions			
3. POWER (Will, assertiveness, self-esteem. Solar plexus.)	Concepts	Lower mind	Sensation-soul	3. Egocentric
- transition -				
2. SEXUALITY (Emotions, pleasure, procreation. Genitals.)	Images Pleasure/ pain	Vital-emotional	Astral body (emotion)	2. Naïve
- transition -				
1. SURVIVAL (Grounding, security, stability. Floor of pelvis.)	Perception Sensation Matter	Perception Sensation Physical	Etheric body Physical body	1. Reactive Pre-, peri-, neo-natal (possible transcendent)

A8c2. Arenas of the Spirit: TRANSCENDENT STAGES & STATES

Wilber's Stages & States sometimes display the full range of human awareness – but concentrate primarily on the Transcendent States. Investigators include mystics, philosophers, psychologists, academics, and the originators of ancient spiritual systems.

[Read from bottom to top.]

Line of Inquiry >> (Investigator) >> **CHAKRAS**	**Yoga Sutras** (Patanjali. ~200 BC)	**Stages of Interior Life** (Teresa/Avila. ~1550)	**Christian Mysticism** (Underhill. ~1920)	**Levels of Consciousness** (Grof. ~1970)
7. WISDOM (Understanding, consciousness, bliss. Crown of head.)	Raincloud Cessation (nirohd) Oneness of buddhi Shining forth Luminosity Subtle perception One-pointedness	7. Spiritual marriage 6. Cessation (formless) Luminosity 5. Prayer of union (ego dies, soul emerges) Early visions 4. Prayer of recollection	Union Dark night Divine ignorance (cessation) Divine love (contemplation) Luminosity Recollection (archetypal) Lateral expansion of consciousness Union with stream of life	Ultimate Supracosmic void Universal mind Deity, luminosity Archetypal Extra-human identifications. Astral-psychic
- transition -				
6. VISIONARY THOUGHT (Imagination, intuition, clairvoyance. Brow, 3rd eye.)	Recollection (dhyana)		Contemplative illumination	Death-rebirth Existential
- transition -				
5. EXPRESSION (Communication, creativity, symbolization. Throat.)	Cleansing, restraint (pranayana)	3. Exemplary life 2. Practice, prayer 1. Humility		
- transition -				
4. LOVE (Compassion, peace. Heart.)				
- transition -			Conceptual faith & beliefs	
3. POWER (Will, assertiveness, self-esteem. Solar plexus.)				Condensed experience (COEX) Freudian
- transition -				Psychodynamic
2. SEXUALITY (Emotions, pleasure, procreation. Genitals.)				
- transition -				Aesthetic
1. SURVIVAL (Grounding, security, stability. Floor of pelvis.)				Somatic

A8c3. Arenas of the Spirit: NON-CHRISTIAN DEITIES & HEROES

From an energy perspective, the pantheons of ancient gods and heroes may be viewed as symbolic representations of the seven forms of power emanating from the seven Chakras. Alternatively, they can be seen as seven modes by which one may experience the Divine Presence.

[Read from bottom to top.]

CHAKRAS	Hero Types (Campbell)	Greek Deities (Judith, Bolen)	Norse Gods (Judith, Martin)	Hindu Deities (Judith, Martin)	Seven Samurai (Kurusawa)	Seven Dwarfs (Disney) [really!]
7	Saint	Zeus (ruler). Hera (co-ruler)	Odin (ruler, wisdom) Heimdall (rainbow bridge)	Brahma (original creator of universe) Shiva (male principle) Gayatri (glorious light)	Kambei (noble leader)	Happy
6	World Redeemer	Athena (wisdom, reason)	Skadi (justice, vengeance)	Durga (moral order) Saraswati (learning, wisdom)	Katsushiro (idealistic coming-of-age)	Doc
5	Emperor/ Tyrant	Apollo (music, healing) Hermes (messenger)	Loki (trickster, fire)	Rama (ideal hero) Krishna (ideal incarnation)	Gorobei (doesn't live up to name)	Sneezy
4	Lover	Aphrodite (love) Hestia (hearth, family)	Freya (love, beauty, battle)	Vishnu (preserves universe) Hanuman (loyal supporter) Gauri (purity)	Shichiroji (loyal supporter)	Bashful
3	Warrior	Ares (war) Poseidon (sea, natural forces)	Thor (thunder, battle) Tyr (war, law)	Kartikeya (war) Ganesha (success)	Kyuzo (master swordsman)	Grumpy
2	Childhood of Hero	Demeter (agriculture) Dionysus (wine, passion)	Freyr (fertility, success) Baldur (death, rebirth)	Lakshmi (prosperity)	Kikuchiyo (buffoon)	Dopey
1	Primordial	Gaia (Earth) Hades (underworld)	Frigga (mother of all) Hel (the dead)	Shakti (female principle)	Heihachi (woodcutter, sword school)	Sleepy

A8c4. Arenas of the Spirit: ARCHETYPAL JOURNEYS

From a Chakra perspective, the Archetypal Journey may be viewed symbolically as a series of passages – beginning in the corrupt material world and culminating in Spiritual Enlightenment, or a progressive encounter with the Divine Presence. (For Archetypal Journeys, see also Campbell Appendices B.)

[Read from bottom to top.]

Line of Inquiry >> (Investigator) >> **CHAKRAS**	**Hero With Thousand Faces** (Campbell)	**The Odyssey** (Homer)	**Pilgrim's Progress** (Bunyan)	**Seven Storey Mountain** (Merton)
7. WISDOM (Understanding, consciousness, bliss. Crown of head.)	Home restored 6. Ultimate Boon	13. Ithaca [restored harmonious society] 12. Phaecians [ideal society]	15. Celestial City 14. Beulah Land 13. Delectable Mountains	10. Sweet Sun of Liberty [monastery]
- transition -			12. River of Death	8. True North
6. VISIONARY THOUGHT (Imagination, intuition, clairvoyance. Brow, 3rd eye.)	5. Apotheosis [union of male/ female]	11. Calypso's Island, 10. Cattle of the Sun, 9. Scylla & Charybdis 8. Sirens [final impediments, achieving clarity]	11. Giant Despair, Doubting Castle 10. Faithful [sacrificed] Shadow of Death 8. Battle with Apollyon [final impediments]	7. Magnetic North 5. With a Great Price [character of God]
- transition -				
5. EXPRESSION (Communication, creativity, symbolization. Throat.)		7. Hades [pronouncements of the dead]	7. House Beautiful [Christian congregation] 6. House of Interpreter [Christian Faith]	9. Sleeping Volcano [writing, teaching]
- transition -			5. Good Will [presence of Christ]	6. Waters of Confusion [commitment]
4. LOVE (Compassion, peace. Heart.)	3. Meeting with Goddess [mother/goddess]	6. Circe [false love] 5. Laestrygonians [false hospitality]	4. Wicket Gate, Evangelist, Shining Light [guiding love]	4. Children in the Marketplace [Columbia, Van Doren]
- transition -		4. Aeolus [winds]		
3. POWER (Will, assertiveness, self-esteem. Solar plexus.)	5. Atonement with Father	3. Cyclops [brute force]	3. Worldly Wiseman, The Law, Mt. Sinai [legalism]	3. Harrowing of Hell [prep school]
- transition -				
2. SEXUALITY (Emotions, pleasure, procreation. Genitals.)	4. Woman as Temptress	2. Lotus Eaters [sensual pleasure]	9. Vanity Fair [material pleasures] 2. Slough of Despond [emotional indulgence]	2. Lady of the Museum [France]
- transition -				
1. SURVIVAL (Grounding, security, stability. Floor of pelvis.)	2. Road of Trials 1. Belly of Whale Crossing First Threshold, Call to Adventure, Home	1. Troy [survival in material world]	1. City of Destruction [Godless material reality]	1. The Prisoner's Base [origins]

A8c5. Arenas of the Spirit: PROPHETIC CHRISTIAN REVELATIONS

From a Chakra perspective, the sets of seven apocalyptic events in the Bible's *Book of Relations* may be viewed as symbolic depictions of the release of Kundalini energy – the surge of creative or destructive power that is unleashed as the seven Chakras are progressively unblocked on the final Day of Judgment.

[Read from bottom to top.]

Line of Inquiry >> (Investigator) >> **CHAKRAS**	**Seven Churches** [Rev. 2-3] (Martin)	**Seven Seals/ Book of Life** [Rev. 6-8] (Martin)	**Seven Trumpets** [Rev. 8-11] (Martin)	**Seven Plagues** [Rev. 16] (Martin)
7. WISDOM (Understanding, consciousness, bliss. Crown of head.)	2. Smyrna (rich despite afflictions, crown of life)	7. Opens Seven Trumpets	7. Third woe. Return of Christ. Dead are judged. Temple opened, ark of covenant revealed.	7. Worldwide earthquake and huge hailstones destroy cities and nations. Every mountain leveled.
- transition -				
6. VISIONARY THOUGHT (Imagination, intuition, clairvoyance. Brow, 3rd eye.)	1. Ephesus (persevered, forgot first love, eat of tree of life)	6. Great Tribulation	6. Second woe. Floodwaters of 4 rivers released. Horsemen spread plague from mouths.	6. Euphrates dries up. To enable enemy armies to approach Israel for Battle of Armageddon.
- transition -				
5. EXPRESSION (Communication, creativity, symbolization. Throat.)	3. Pergamos (did not renounce, sacrilege, hidden manna)	5. Martyrs (persecution)	5. First woe. Opening of the smoking abyss. Locusts torment any man without the seal of God.	5. Beast's kingdom plunged into abyss. Sinners still unrepentant
- transition -				
4. LOVE (Compassion, peace. Heart.)	6. Philadelphia (kept word, endured patiently, pillar in temple of God)	1. White horse (conqueror, false messiah)	4. Sun, moon, and stars turn dark.	4. Intense sun scorches unrepentant sinners with fire.
- transition -				
3. POWER (Will, assertiveness, self-esteem. Solar plexus.)	7. Laodicea (rich, lukewarm, sit with Jesus on throne)	2. Red horse (war)	3. Wormwood star falls to Earth. Rivers and springs poisoned.	3. Rivers and springs become blood.
- transition -				
2. SEXUALITY (Emotions, pleasure, procreation. Genitals.)	4. Thyatira (sacrilege, sexual immorality, false prophetess, power over nations)	3. Black horse (vengeance, famine)	2. Burning mountain plunges into sea. Sea turned to blood	2. Sea turns to blood, all dead.
- transition -				
1. SURVIVAL (Grounding, security, stability. Floor of pelvis.)	5. Sardis (dead, wake up, clothed in white garments)	4. Pale horse (death)	1. Hail, fire, blood. Earth burned.	1. Sores on worshipers with Mark of the Beast.

A8c6. Arenas of the Spirit: CHRISTIAN RITUALS & PRACTICES

From a Chakra perspective, religious Rituals and Practices represent various ways the seven Chakras can be prepared to attain Enlightenment, to receive the Holy Spirit, or to live a virtuous life.
[Read from bottom to top.]

Line of Inquiry >> (Investigator) >> CHAKRAS	Days of Creation (Gen. 1-2) (Martin)	Feast Days (Lev. 23) (Martin)	Works of Mercy (Martin)	Sacraments (Myss)	Monastic Life (Martin)
7. WISDOM (Understanding, consciousness, bliss. Crown of head.)	Sabbath (rest)	Tabernacles (Celebration of deliverance: New heaven, new earth)	Bury the dead	Unction	Visitations, angels, Holy Spirit
- transition -					
6. VISIONARY THOUGHT (Imagination, intuition, clairvoyance. Brow, 3rd eye.)	Land animals, mankind	Atonement (High priest sits on mercy seat: Sinners spared by Grace)	Minister to prisoners	Ordination	Contemplation, revelation, prophecy
- transition -					
5. EXPRESSION (Communication, creativity, symbolization. Throat.)	Sea life, birds	Trumpets (Sacrificial ram substituted for Isaac: Call to Last Judgment)	Visit the sick.	Confession	Song, chant, silence
- transition -					
4. LOVE (Compassion, peace. Heart.)	Sun, moon, stars	Pentecost (final harvest: Apostles receive Holy Spirit)	Shelter to strangers	Marriage	Worship, prayer, seclusion. Neighbor as thyself.
- transition -					
3. POWER (Will, assertiveness, self-esteem. Solar plexus.)	Land and sea, plant life	First fruits (first harvest: Resurrection)	Cloth the naked	Confirmation	Meekness, humility. Renunciation of earthly possessions.
- transition -					
2. SEXUALITY (Emotions, pleasure, procreation. Genitals.)	Firmament (waters above, below)	Unleavened bread (sustenance for journey: Last supper)	Drink to the thirsty	Communion	Mortification of flesh, abstinence
- transition -					
1. SURVIVAL (Grounding, security, stability. Floor of pelvis.)	Light (day, night)	Passover (spared from death: Christ's return to Jerusalem)	Feed the hungry	Baptism	Material self-sufficiency. Grow own food. Fasting.

A8c7. Arenas of the Spirit: CHRISTIAN VIRTUES & GIFTS

From a Chakra perspective, religious Virtues and Gifts show how a virtuous, exemplary life (or the contrary) may be manifested through each of the seven Chakras.

[Read from bottom to top.]

Line of Inquiry >> (Investigator) >> CHAKRAS	Deadly Sins	Contrary Virtues (Martin)	Heavenly Virtues	Full Armor of God (Eph. 6:11-17) (Martin)	Gifts of Holy Spirit (1 Cor. 12:1-11) (Martin)
7. WISDOM (Understanding, consciousness, bliss. Crown of head.)	Pride	Humility	Faith	5. Helmet of Salvation (Word of God)	1. Wisdom
6. VISIONARY THOUGHT (Imagination, intuition, clairvoyance. Brow, 3rd eye.)	Sloth	Diligence	Hope	4. Shield of Faith	2. Knowledge 6. Prophecy
5. EXPRESSION (Communication, creativity, symbolization. Throat.)	Anger	Patience	Prudence	6. Sword of the Spirit	8. Tongues 9. Interpretation of Tongues
4. LOVE (Compassion, peace. Heart.)	Envy	Kindness	Charity	3. Gospel of Peace (feet)	3. Faith
3. POWER (Will, assertiveness, self-esteem. Solar plexus.)	Greed	Liberality	Justice	2. Breastplate of Righteousness	5. Miracles
2. SEXUALITY (Emotions, pleasure, procreation. Genitals.)	Lust	Chastity	Temperance		7. Discerning of Spirits
1. SURVIVAL (Grounding, security, stability. Floor of pelvis.)	Gluttony	Abstinence	Fortitude	1. Belt of Truth	4. Healing

A8c8. Arenas of the Spirit: CHRISTIAN SCRIPTURE -- FOUNDATIONAL PASSAGES

From a Chakra perspective, Foundational Passages of Scripture or Holy Writ represent essential wisdom, positive example, or key events that are addressed in turn to each of the seven Chakras.
[Read from bottom to top.]

Chakra	Life of Christ (Martin)	Passion of Christ (14 Stations of the Cross) (Martin)	Ten Commandments (Martin)	23rd Psalm (Martin)	Lord's Prayer [Matt. 6:9-13] (Martin)
7	Ascension. Sitting at right hand of the Father. Last judgment. New Jerusalem.	[16. Ascension into heaven.]	1. No other gods.	16. Surely goodness and mercy shall follow me. 17. All the days of my life. 19. Forever and ever.	2. Who art in Heaven. 7. As it is in Heaven. 18. And the Glory. 19. Forever and ever.
6	Prophecies of coming Messiah. Annunciations by angels: Zechariah, Elizabeth, Mary, Joseph. Road to Emmaus. End times.	2. Acceptance of the cross. 6. Assistance lifting cross	2. No graven images.	5. He restoreth my soul. 6. He leadeth me in the paths of righteous. 14. Thou anointest my head with oil.	4. Thy Kingdom come. 13. For Thine is the Kingdom.
5	Sermon on the Mount. Addressing the multitudes. Healing by word alone.	1. Condemned to death by Pilate.	3. Not take Lord's name in vain. 9. Not bear false witness.	7. For His Name's sake. 20. Amen.	3. Hallowed be Thy Name. 20. Amen.
4	Nativity. Compassion for poor, lame, insane. Only begotten Son.	4. Encounter with Mother Mary. 6. Veronica wipes face. 8. Meets women of Jerusalem.	4. Keep the Sabbath. 5. Honor father and mother.	1. The Lord is my shepherd. 10. For Thou art with me. 18. And I shall dwell in the house of the Lord.	1. Our Father. 10. And forgive us our debts. 11. As we forgive our debtors.
3	Disciples. Growing ministry. Driving out moneychangers.	5. Simon the Cyrene helps carry cross. 10. Stripped of garments. 13. Taken down from the cross. [15. Resurrection from death.]	8. Not steal.	11. Thy rod and thy staff, they comfort me.	5. Thy Will be done. 14. And the power.
2	Virgin birth. Temptation in the wilderness. Mary Magdalene.	3, 7, 9. Three falls.	7. Not commit adultery. 10. Not covet.	9. I fear no evil. 13. In the presence of mine enemies.	12. And lead us not into temptation. 13. But deliver us from evil.
1	Loaves & fishes. Dematerializing escapes. Healing. Raising of Lazarus. Campfire by the beach.	11. Crucifixion, nailed to the cross. 12. Dies on the cross. 14. Laid in the tomb.	6. Not kill.	2. I shall not want. 3. He maketh me to lie down in green pastures. 4. He leadeth me beside still waters. 8. Yea, though I walk through the Valley of the Shadow of Death. 12. Thou preparest a table before me. 15. My cup runneth over.	6. On earth. 8. Give us this day. 9. Our daily bread.

A8c9. Arenas of the Spirit: CULTURAL STAGES OF WORSHIP

Components of the Cultural Stages of Worship: a) Objects of Worship: The entities the Culture values or reveres most; b) Administrators of Worship: The individuals or systems in charge; c) Accessories of Worship: The objects or implements by which Worship is enacted; d) Worldviews: The foundational perspectives upon which the Worship are built.

[Read from bottom to top.]

Chakra	Spiral Dynamics Stage (Beck, Cowan)	Objects of Worship (Beck, Martin)	Administrators of Worship (Beck, Martin)	Accessories for Worship (Beck, Martin)	Worldviews (Wilber)
7	**Coral: Next awakening?**	Divine Presence, Holy Spirit, Enlightenment	Saints, realized beings, guiding lights	Altar, meditation room, prayer flags	Non–Dual / Causal / Subtle / Psychic
					Developmentalism as World Process
6	**Turquoise: GlobalView.** Broad synthesis/ renewal, holistic/ experiential **Yellow: FlexFlow.** Qualities/ responsibilities of being, systematic integrative	Organism / System	Systems theorists	Information network	Cross-paradigmatic, dialectical / Integrates multiple contexts, paradigmatic / Multiple contexts/ histories
	Green: HumanBond. Community, harmony, equality. Relativistic/ sociocentric	Community, humanity, social structures, Gaia	Ecologists, communal conscience reps	Nature gear, communal kitchen	Pluralistic systems, dynamic
5	**Orange: StriveDrive.** Success, autonomy, materialistic/ achiever	Success, money, celebrities, superstars	Communications media	Posh neighborhood, cars, tech gear, perks	Static systems/ contexts / Static universal formalism
					Demythologizing, formalizing
	Blue: TruthForce. Stability, purpose, absolutist/ saintly	Dominant social god, ideology	Prophets, priests, teachers	Scripture, commandments, codes, duties, constitutions, treaties, law, traditions, honor	Rationalization of mythic structures / Locus of magic power is deified Other
					Concrete-literal myths
3	**Red: PowerGods.** Power, action, egocentric/ exploitive	Gods, heroes, strongmen, conquests, Big Me	Priests, commanders	Myths, enhanced weapons, war games, prizes, spoils, horses, vehicles	Ego omnipotence transferred to gods / Omnipotence of ego challenged, security
					Ego is locus of magic power
2	**Purple: KinSpirits.** Safety, security, animistic/ tribalistic	Animistic spirits, ancestors, natural phenomena	Shamans, medicine men, magicians, elders	Enchantment, rituals	Egocentric, word magic, narcissistic / Self-object
					Subject-object fusions
1	**Beige: SurvivalSense.** Stay alive, automatic/ instinctive	Instincts, drives, biological needs	Necessity	Weapons, body parts	Hallucinatory wish-fulfillment / Undifferentiated, pleromatic

Appendix A9.
The Processes of Ken Wilber & Anodea Judith

This section outlines the programs for Actualization Growth (PPR3) and Restoration Growth (PPR4) offered by Ken Wilber and Anodea Judith. The practical techniques and methods shown here are roughly comparable to the 35 Specific Processes of the ADAPT Model (PR1-35). The three programs are as follows:

- **A9a. Integral Life Practice: Wilber's Specific Processes.** The nine Modules and approximately 62 Methods of Wilber's Integral Life Practice (ILP) constitute Wilber's Personal Growth program for relatively healthy people (PPR3). (this page)
- **A9b. Wilber's Pathologies & Treatments.** The Pathologies & Treatments specific to each of seven Stages of Psyche Passages (D3b) represent Wilber's therapeutic program for people with entrenched 'problems' (PPR4). (p. 145)
- **A9c. Anodea Judith's Balancing the Chakras.** In Anodea Judith's Bioenergetic Model of Personal Growth, health is attained by striking a balance between excess rigidity and excess flaccidity at each level of the Chakras. (p. 146)

Each of these will be discussed in turn.

A9a. Integral Life Practice: Wilber's Specific Processes

Ken Wilber's version of the Specific Processes (PR1-35) is presented in the Modules and Methodologies of **Wilber's Integral Life Practice (ILP)**. These two tables display the nine Modules of ILP, including their attendant Methodologies (from *Integral Spirituality* (2006), p. 203).

The four Core Modules (foundational) are shown on the first table, with five Auxiliary Modules (supplementary) shown on the second table. An Asterisk (*) indicates methodologies Wilber designates as 'Gold Star.' In [#brackets], we indicate which of ADAPT's 35 Processes (PR1-35) correspond most closely to a particular ILP Methodology. For an explanation of the terminology of these tables, and for a description of how these Methodologies can be applied, see Patten, *Integral Life Practice* (2008).

The ILP Tables on the following two facing pages show which of ADAPT's Specific Processes are well-covered by Wilber's Integral Life Practice, and which are limited or missing. As you peruse the tables, note that **the ILP Methodologies cover less than half of the 35 Specific Processes included in the ADAPT Model.** In the authors' view, the ILP Program – while excellent and very helpful -- fails to cover a substantial number of Processes that are extremely important for Growth.

Wilber's Comprehensive Growth Program. Integral Life Practice (ILP) is a comprehensive, self-directed Growth Program that incorporates all four Perspectives (D5a): Internal/ Individual, External/Individual, Internal/ Collective, and External/ Collective.

In the Specific Processes section of the Main Text (PR1-35), we showed all the methods and techniques by which Growth is implemented, according to the ADAPT Model. In this Appendix, we show the comparable methods offered by Ken Wilber and Anodea Judith. The Modules of Wilber's Integral Life Practice (Appx A9a) are Specific Processes that primarily implement Actualization Growth (PPR3). Wilber's Pathologies & Treatments (Appx A9b) are primarily Conscious Development Processes (PR29-33) that implement Restoration Growth (PPR4). Judith's Balancing the Chakras (Appx A9c) are alternative Specific Processes that primarily implement Actualization Growth (PPR3).

INTEGRAL LIFE PRACTICE
Core Modules

Body (Physical, Subtle, Causal)	Mind (Framework, View)	Spirit (Meditation, Prayer)	Shadow (Therapia)
Weight-lifting (P) [#8]	Reading & Study [#19, 21]	Zen [#33]	Gestalt Therapy [#31]
Aerobics (P) [#8]	Belief system [#19, 35]	Centering Prayer [#33]	Cognitive Therapy [#31, 21]
F.I.T. (P, S) * [?]	Integral (AQAL) Framework [#19, 35]	Big Mind Meditation * [#33]	3-2-1 Process [#31]
Diet – Atkins [#2] Ornish, The Zone (P)	Mental Training [#21]	Kabbalah [#33]	Dreamwork [#30, 31, 17]
ILP Diet (P) * [#2]	Taking Multiple Perspectives [#19, 21, PPR7]	Compassionate Exchange * [#3, 6]	Interpersonal [#31, 5, 6]
T'ai Chi Ch'uan (S) [#29, 33, 8]	Any worldview or meaning system that works for you [#35, 19]	Transcendental Meditation [#33]	Psychoanalysis [#31, 30]
Qi Gong (S) [#29. 33, 8]		Integral Inquiry * [#35, 33, 19, 21]	Art & Music Therapy [#28]
Yoga (P, S) [#29, 33, 8]		The 1-2-3 of God * [#33]	
3-Body Workout (P, S, C) [#29, 33, 8]			

Opening Up. "With **Integral Life Practice**, we expand our Consciousness and connect with Kindred Spirits."

* Asterisk = Wilber's Gold Star practices.
P, S, C = Wilber terms *Physical, Subtle, Causal*.
#Numbers in [brackets] = Equivalent Specific Process in ADAPT Model. Correspondences to ADAPT are only approximate.

INTEGRAL LIFE PRACTICE
Auxiliary Modules

Ethics	Sex	Work	Emotions	Relationships
Codes of Conduct [# 13, 15, 19, 33]	Tantra [# 33, 29, 7, 4, 5, 11]	Right Livelihood [# 11, 13, 14, 15, 9, 33]	Transforming Emotions * [# 31, 33, 30]	Integral Relationships * [#4, 5, 31]
Professional Ethics [# 13, 15, 19, 33]	Integral Sexual Yoga * [#33, 29, 7, 4, 5, 11]	Professional Training [#11, 9, 12, 22]	Emotional Intelligence Training [#31, 30]	Integral Parenting * [#4, 5, 13, 15]
Social & Ecological Activism [#13, 14, 15, 16, 9]	Kama Sutra [#29, 33, 7, 4, 5, 11]	Money Management [#13, 22]	Bhakti Yoga (Devotional Practices) [#33, 31]	Communication Skills [#31, 24, 4]
Self-Discipline [#12, 11, 13]	Kundalini Yoga [#33, 29, 7, 4, 5, 11]	Work as a Mode of ILP * [#9, 11, 13]	Emotional Mindfulness Practice [#33, 31, 30, 7]	Couples Therapy [#31, 24, 5, 13]
Integral Ethics * [#13, 15, 21, 33]	Sexual Transformative Practice [#33, 29, 4, 5, 11]	Kama Yoga [#13, 15, 21, 33]	Tonglen (Compassionate Exchange Meditation) [#33, 5]	Relational Spiritual Practice [#33, 5]
Sportsmanship [#13, 15, 33, 8, 11]		Community Service & Volunteering [#11, 13, 15]	Creative Expression & Art [#28, 24]	Right Association (Sangha) [#33, 5, 13, 15]
Vows & oaths [#13, 19, 33]		Work as Transformation [#9, 13, 14]		Conscious Marriage [#5, 6, 31, 13]

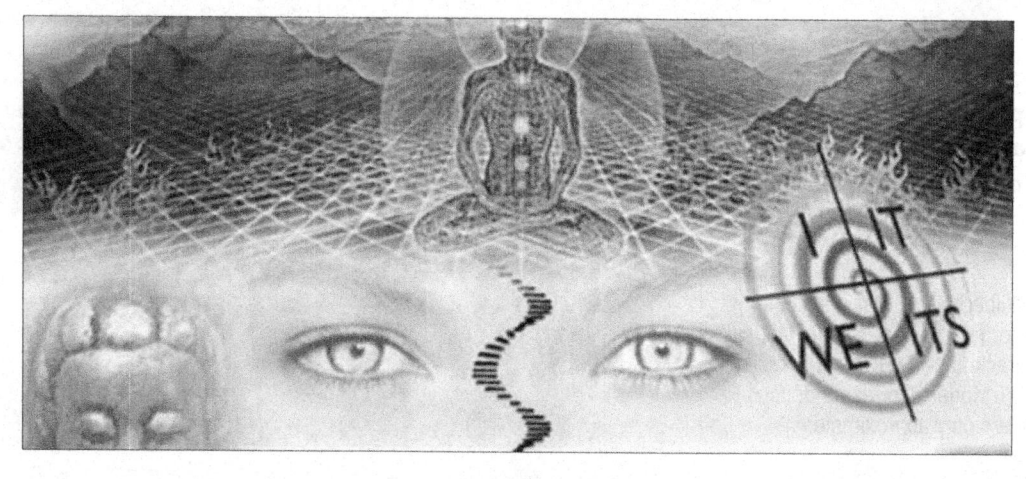

Appendix A9b. KEN WILBER'S PATHOLOGIES & TREATMENTS
At Various Stages of Psyche Passages

A traumatic episode or situation can occur at any Stage of Development – resulting in an Impasse or Pathology characteristic of that Stage. By recognizing the Stage where problems originated, a therapist can apply the appropriate Treatment. This table displays in consolidated form the potential Pathologies and appropriate Treatments for each Chakra-related Stage of Development, as outlined in Wilber's *Integral Psychology*. (Table A1, *IP*, p. 197)

[Read from bottom to top.]

Stage (Chakras)	Central Focus	Normal Development	Pathology	Treatment
7. WISDOM (crown of head)	Understanding, knowing, transcendence, peace	Transpersonal domain comes into focus	**Psychic, Subtle, Causal, & Non-dual Pathologies**	Paths of the Shamans, Saints, Sages, & Siddhas
- transition -				
6. VISIONARY THOUGHT (brow, third eye)	Clairvoyance, imagination, psychic experiences, inspiration	Shift to universal existential principles: life/death, authenticity, self-actualization, global awareness, bodymind integration.	**Existential Pathologies.** Inauthenticity, deadening.	Existential therapy
- transition -				
5. EXPRESSION (throat)	Communication, creative expression, synthesis of ideas into symbols/ words	Self-reflexive ego emerges, shift from conformist to individualist.	**Identity crisis.** Role confusion. Shift to self-derived universal principles	Introspection
- transition -				
4. LOVE (heart)	Relationships, emotions, affinity, compassion, self-acceptance	Shift to roles and rules of society. Prescriptive morality. Often displayed in traits of mythic gods.	**Script pathology.** False, misleading scripts, stories, myths	Script analysis
- transition -				
3. POWER (solar plexus)	Will, purpose, autonomy, identity, self-esteem	Conceptual mind emerges, differentiates from emotional body.	**Neurosis.** Repressions of emotional self. Fusion with emotional self.	**Uncovering.** Relaxing repression barrier, uncovering & recontacting shadow self, reintegrating into psyche.
- transition -				
2. SEXUALITY (genitals)	Urges, desire, passion, pleasure, feelings	Identity switches from fusion with material body to identity with emotional-feeling body.	**Borderline psychosis.** Self/object fusion, projection	**Structure-building.** Build self's boundaries, strengthen ego.
- transition -				
1. SURVIVAL (floor of pelvis)	Grounding, security, stability, trust, vitality physical health	Differentiates body from environment.	**Psychosis.** Hallucination. Delusional Projection. Can't tell where body ends, world begins. Can't tell fantasy from reality.	**Medication/ Pacification**

For an Exploration of this table, see Shadow Self (P4).

A9c. Anodea Judith's Balancing the Chakras

The ADAPT and Wilber Models of Restoration Growth (PPR4) endeavor to dissolve Impediments in the form of Impasses or Blocks (D7b), so that normal Actualization Growth (PPR3) can resume. Both these approaches employ a model of Self based on Succession Growth (Appx A7f).

However, from a somatic or Bioenergetic point of view (PR29), psychological dysfunction can result from regions of the anatomy that are too rigid (Blocks) – as well as bodily regions that are too flaccid or unformed (Vacuums). In Anodea Judith's Bioenergetic Model, these areas of dysfunction are **Imbalances** of the Chakras. The **Blocks** are regions where energy flow is deficient. The **Vacuums** are regions where energy flow is excessive. Health is attained by dissolving those Blocks and filling those Vacuums – a Process which Judith calls as **Balancing the Chakras**. This approach employs a model of Self based on Accumulation Growth (Appx A7f also).

The table on these two facing pages is derived from Judith's *Eastern Body, Western Mind*. It outlines the major factors to be considered in a therapeutic program of this type -- as follows:

- **Col. 2.** **Traumas & Abuses.** The original situations or episodes that caused the dysfunction.
- **Col. 3.** **Deficiencies & Distortions.** Conditions resulting from blocked, inadequate, or inconsistent energy flow.
- **Col. 4.** **Excesses.** Conditions resulting from excessive or unrestrained energy flow.
- **Col. 5.** **Healing Strategies.** Processes for balancing and healing these Deficiencies and Excesses.
- **Col. 6.** **Balanced Characteristics.** Characteristics of healthy people whose Chakras are in proper balance.

Judith's Restoration Growth: BALANCING THE CHAKRAS
[Read from bottom of facing page to top of this page.]

Chakra	Traumas & Abuses	Deficiencies & Distortions	Excesses	Healing Strategies	Balanced Characteristics
7	Forced religiosity, blind obedience, spiritual abuse. Spiritual cynicism or skepticism, invalidation of beliefs. Misinformation, withheld information, deception, lies. Education that thwarts curiosity.	Rigid belief systems. Opaqueness, obtuseness, apathy. Lower chakra dominance: materialism, greed, domination of others. No dream recall. Learning difficulties.	Grandeur, spiritual addiction. Detachment, confusion, dissociation from body. Delusions, hallucinations, nightmares.	Reestablish spiritual, emotional, physical connections. Spiritual discipline, meditation. Therapy: Examine belief systems, develop inner witness.	Spiritual connection. Broad understanding, mastery, wisdom. Access to dreams. Intelligent, thoughtful, aware.
6	Stultifying education. Cognitive dissonance. Invalidation of insights. Ugly or frightening environment.	Difficulty foreseeing future, imagining alternatives, visualizing. Polarized viewpoint, indecisiveness, denial of reality. Insensitivity, indifference. Can't remember dreams. Poor vision, memory.	Over-intellectualization. Obsessions. Poor concentration. Self-deception, pride.	Visual stimulation. Create visual art: Drawing, coloring, vision painting. Therapy: art therapy, memory work, dream work, hypnosis, guided visualizations, regression to past lives. Meditation.	Capacity to perceive, analyze, assimilate. Capacity to think symbolically, visualize. Perceptive, imaginative, intuitive. Open-minded, able to question. Good memory.

Judith's Restoration Growth: BALANCING THE CHAKRAS
[Read from bottom of this page to top of facing page.]

Chakra	Traumas & Abuses	Deficiencies & Distortions	Excesses	Healing Strategies	Balanced Characteristics
5	Lies, mixed messages, secrets (threats for telling). Criticism, verbal abuse, yelling. Repressive parents. Alcohol, chemical dependency.	Introversion, shyness. Weak voice, fear of speaking, difficulty putting feelings into words. Tone deaf, poor rhythm.	Opinionated, dominating voice, talking as a defense, interruptions. Inability to listen, poor auditory comprehension. Gossiping, hypocrisy, self-deception.	Loosen neck and shoulders. Release voice: Singing, chanting, toning. Storytelling, journaling, letter writing, automatic writing. Non-goal-oriented activity. The practice of silence. Therapy: Communication skills, inner child communications.	Clear communication, resonant voice. Good listener. Good rhythm, sense of timing. Lives creatively
4	Loveless, cold environment. Conditional love, enmeshment. Shaming, constant criticism. Abandonment, rejection, betrayal. Death of loved one, grief. Departure of loved one, divorce. Sexual or physical abuse, abuses to lower chakras.	Fear of intimacy, relationships. Antisocial, withdrawn, cold, lack of empathy. Lonely, isolated, depressed, grief. Critical, judgmental, intolerant. Anticipatory rejection. Narcissism.	Demanding, clinging, jealous. Over-sacrificing, codependent, poor boundaries.	Breathing exercises, pranayama. Arms: reaching out, taking in. Journaling, self-discovery, inner child, self-acceptance. Therapy: Animus/ anima integration, relationship assumptions, co-dependency, release of grief, forgiveness.	Compassionate, loving, empathetic. Self-assured, self-loving. Altruistic, peaceful, balanced. Strong immune system.
3	Authoritarianism, domination, fear of punishment. Blaming, shaming, guilt. Emotional manipulation, enmeshment. Physical abuse, dangerous environment, volatile situations. Age- inappropriate responsibilities (parentified child).	Passive, ineffectual, indecisive, unreliable. Weak will, easily manipulated. Poor self-discipline, follow-through. Low self-esteem. Victim mentality, blaming others. Low energy. Attraction to stimulants.	Aggressive, domineering, controlling, arrogant, stubborn. Need to be right, have the last word. Power-hungry, ambitious (type-A), competitive, possessive. Manipulative, deceitful. Temper tantrums, violent outbursts, hyperactivity. Attraction to sedatives.	Grounding and emotional contact. Deep relaxation, stress control. Vigorous exercise (running, aerobics, martial arts, sit-ups). Risk-taking. Therapy: Build ego strength, release anger, deal with shame, strengthen will, encourage autonomy.	Responsible, reliable. Balanced, effective will. Confidence, sense of personal power, ability to meet challenges. Balanced self-esteem, ego strength. Self-regulation, self-discipline. Warm personality.
2	Sexual, emotional abuse. Neglect, coldness, rejection. Denial of child's feeling states, lack of mirroring. Emotional manipulation, enmeshment. Physical restriction, crib, playpen. Religious, moral severity. Alcoholic families.	Sexual dysfunction (impotence, frigidity, fear of sex). Guilt, shame. Denial/ lack of pleasure, passion, excitement. Rigid body, attitudes, poor rhythm. Excess boundaries, fear of change.	Sexual or pleasure addictions, seductiveness. Excess emotions (hysteria, bipolar, crisis junkies). Obsessive desires, attachments. Emotional dependency. Poor boundaries, invasion of others.	Movement therapy. Sensate intelligence. Healthy pleasures. Appropriate emotional release/ containment. Inner child work. Boundary work. Addiction programs, 12-Step.	Ability to experience pleasure. Emotional intelligence. Graceful movement. Spontaneity, playfulness, humor. Ability to change. Clear boundaries.
1	Birth trauma. Malnourishment, feeding difficulties. Poor physical bonding with mother. Physical abuse/ violence. Physical neglect. Abandonment. Illness, surgery.	Fear, insecurity, instability, anxiety, restlessness. Disconnection from body. underweight. Poor focus or discipline, disorganization. Poor boundaries. Financial difficulties.	Intransigence, stolidity, rigidity, plodding. Sluggish, lazy, tired. Obesity, overeating, addiction. Hoarding, greed, material fixation. Rigid boundaries, obsession with security, fear of change.	Reconnect with body. Physical activity (aerobics, weights, running, dance). Touch, massage. Bioenergetic grounding. Hatha yoga. Explore earliest relationship with mother. Reclaim right to be here.	Good health, vitality. Trust in world, feeling safe, secure. Well-grounded, comfortable in body, stable. Ability to relax, be still. Prosperity, right livelihood.

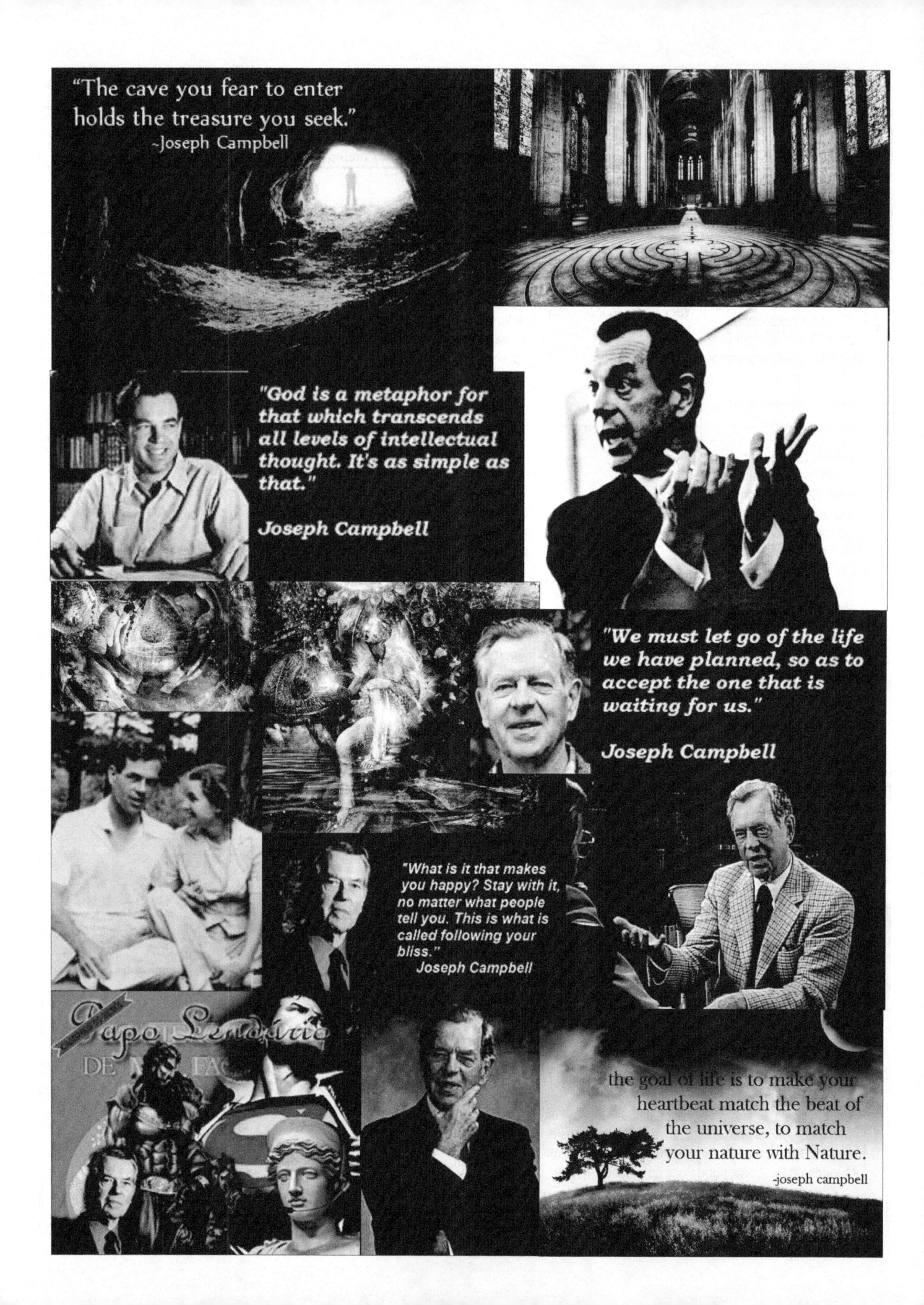

"The cave you fear to enter holds the treasure you seek."
~Joseph Campbell

"God is a metaphor for that which transcends all levels of intellectual thought. It's as simple as that."

Joseph Campbell

"We must let go of the life we have planned, so as to accept the one that is waiting for us."

Joseph Campbell

"What is it that makes you happy? Stay with it, no matter what people tell you. This is what is called following your bliss."
Joseph Campbell

the goal of life is to make your heartbeat match the beat of the universe, to match your nature with Nature.
-joseph campbell

B1-3. Campbell Appendices. Page 149

CAMPBELL APPENDICES

How the Life Journey Archetype derives from, illuminates, and extends the Hero's Journey 'Monomyth' of scholar and mythologist Joseph Campbell.

B1. Joseph Campbell's Hero's Journey

Eight ways Campbell's Hero's Journey manifests itself in myth, literature, the media, and one's own inner life. (page 150)

B2. Beyond Joseph Campbell:
How the Hero's Journey Became the Life Journey

The Life Journey Archetype, one of the twin foundations of this book. How it was derived from the Hero's Journey of Joseph Campbell, and other sources. (page 172)

B3. Parallels to Homer's The Odyssey

The premier example of the Life Journey Archetype. An outline of the many parallels between the ADAPT Model and that greatest and most complete of all mythic Life Journeys, *The Odyssey* by Homer. Includes a synopsis of epic itself. (page 184)

OUR NURSERY RHYME JOURNEYS

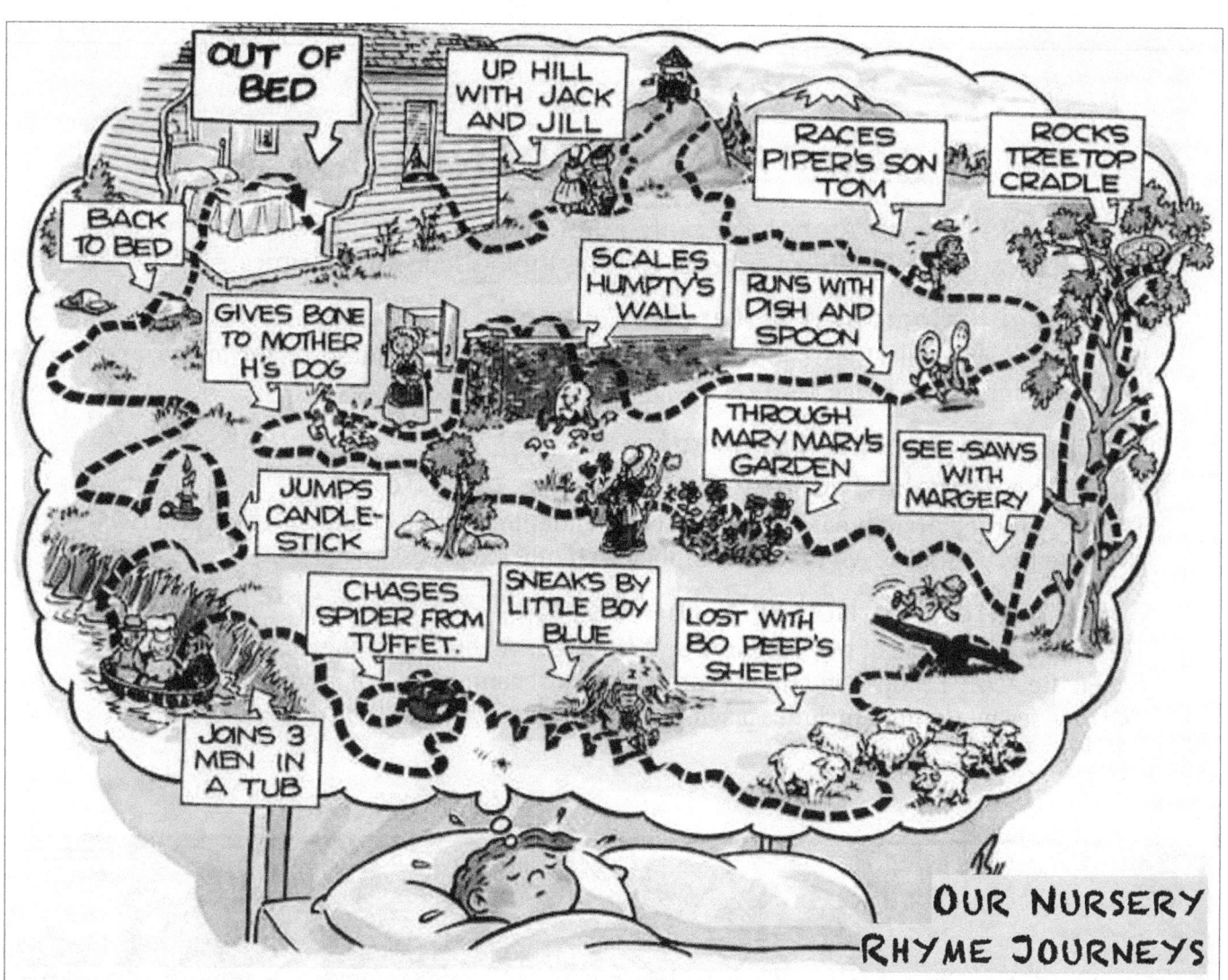

OUR FAIRY TALE JOURNEYS

Our Hero's Journey (p. 150)

Our Life Journey (p. 172)

Creating Our Own Human Odyssey
The innumerable, small **Hero's Journeys** of our childhood
are just a rehearsal for the great **Life Journey** we will take.

Appendix B1.
The Hero's Journey:
How Joseph Campbell's Archetypal Journey Manifests itself in Human Culture

Of all Spirit Arenas (D4d), perhaps the most comprehensive, compelling, and profound is **The Archetypal Life Journey**. In its various forms, the Life Journey addresses multiple levels of human society and multiple regions of the human interior. Because of its depth and comprehensiveness, each variation of the Life Journey was the Integral Theory of its day. This section explores a very special version of the Life Journey called The Hero's Journey.

The Hero's Journey is what scholar Joseph Campbell calls the **Mono-Myth** -- a pattern of symbolic narrative that appears again and again in many diverse cultures. Variations on this pattern appear in drama, novels, film, storytelling, myth, religious ritual, and psychological development. This Monomyth describes the epic adventures of the Archetypal Character known as **The Hero** -- a person who goes out and achieves great deeds on behalf of his group, tribe, or civilization. The pattern of the Hero's Journey can take any of several similar formulations. However, in the typical case, the Hero ventures forth from the Ordinary World of Everyday Reality; enters into some Enchanted World of supernatural wonder; encounters fabulous forces; overcomes ordeals and trials; wins some great victory; and returns home with the power to bestow some wondrous Treasure on humankind.

The Hero's Journey

On the following pages, we explore the Hero's Journey from eight perspectives:

B1a. The Campbell Persona (page 153)
Joseph Campbell's own Persona as a Hero of pop culture.

B1b. The Hero's Journey: Pop Culture (page 154)
Two of the most fully-developed Hero's Journeys in popular culture: The Star Wars saga and the Land of Oz. Plus, a cartoon panorama that depicts famous characters from movies at each of 13 Stages of the Hero's Journey.

B1c. The Hero's Journey: Campbell Version (page 156)
Joseph Campbell's original 17-Step Hero's Journey from *Hero With a Thousand Faces*.

B1d. Hero's Journeys: The Five Types (page 158)
The five types of Hero's Journey. The five combinations of story elements that are either individual or collective, either realistic or symbolic, or composite of all four.

B1e. The Hero's Journey: Literature & Movies (page 160)
The various elements of the Hero's Journey – as they appear in classic books and films.

B1f. Your Inner Hero's Journeys: Their Scope (page 162)
Our own Inner Hero's Journeys: The three levels of scope at which they manifest themselves.

B1g. Your Inner Micro-Journey: Its Steps (page 164)
Our personal Hero's Journey, as described by Disney screenwriter Chris Vogler. How the Hero's Journey applies to the trials and triumphs of our own lives.

B1h. Archetypal Characters of the Hero's Journey (page 166)
The eight stock characters that populate the Archetypal Hero's Journey.

B1. The Hero's Journey . Page 153

B1a. The Campbell Persona

Joseph Campbell himself became a culture hero of sorts by popularizing the concept of the Hero's Journey.

Hero With a Thousand Faces. Campbell's 1949 best-selling classic won numerous awards and honors – and served as a major influence on generations of creative scholars and artists.

Campbell at Esalen. Beginning in 1965, Campbell made annual pilgrimages to lead workshops at California's Esalen Institute. Campbell described Esalen as his 'paradise on the Pacific Coast.'

The Power of Myth. Campbell became world-famous for his 1988 PBS series with Bill Moyers – filmed at George Lucas's Skywalker Ranch. As Newsweek Magazine noted, 'Campbell has become one of the rarest of intellectuals in American life: a serious thinker who has been embraced by the popular culture.'

Hero's Journey: Wilber *same term*. In *Up From Eden* (1981), Wilber uses Campbell as his primary source for the Mythic Stage of Cultural Development. *** Archetypal Journeys: Wilber views myths of all sorts as products of the Archaic Stages in the Evolution of Human Consciousness. However, in the authors' view, although myths originated at an archaic Stage, they describe a full range of Stages in a manner that is still pertinent today.

In Appendix B1, we describe Joseph Campbell's concept of the Hero's Journey – showing the various ways it manifests itself in Human Culture. In Appendix B2, we show how the Hero's Journey evolves to become the Life Journey Archetype -- the overarching metaphor of this book. In Appendix B3, we show how each element of the Archetypal Journey may be found in the preeminent heroic epic, Homer's *The Odyssey*. The Archetypal Journey is an Arena in the Realm of Spirit (D4d).

Page 154. CAMPBELL APPENDICES

B1b. The Hero's Journey: Myth & Legend

The World of Star Wars. "The Star Wars Saga is probably the most fully developed Archetypal Journey of modern times."

The World of Oz. "Frank Baum's *Wizard of Oz* (with its many sequels) was probably the most fully populated Archetypal World of the early 20th Century."

The various Steps of the Hero's Journey depicted in the cartoon montage on the facing page will be discussed at length in Appx B1c.

Hero's Journeys of Myth & Legend

Consider the cartoon Hero's Journey on the facing page. Read through the panels clockwise from the upper-left. *** What Heroes from movies, epics, legends, or myths are depicted there? What activities are each of them engaged in? Where do those episodes occur in that particular Hero's story? *** Now choose one Hero to explore in detail: Luke Skywalker, for example. *** Ask yourself questions like these: Which step in Luke's Hero's Journey is depicted in the cartoon? At what points in the story does Luke encounter Darth Vader? How does Luke's relationship with Darth Vader change over time? In what ways does an Atonement take place? *** Now move on to another character you are familiar with, and ask similar questions. As time permits, continue through the cartoon, exploring the part each character plays in the Hero's Journey. *** Which characters represent the most typical Heroes? Which characters depart most from the Hero stereotype?

B1. The Hero's Journey . Page 155

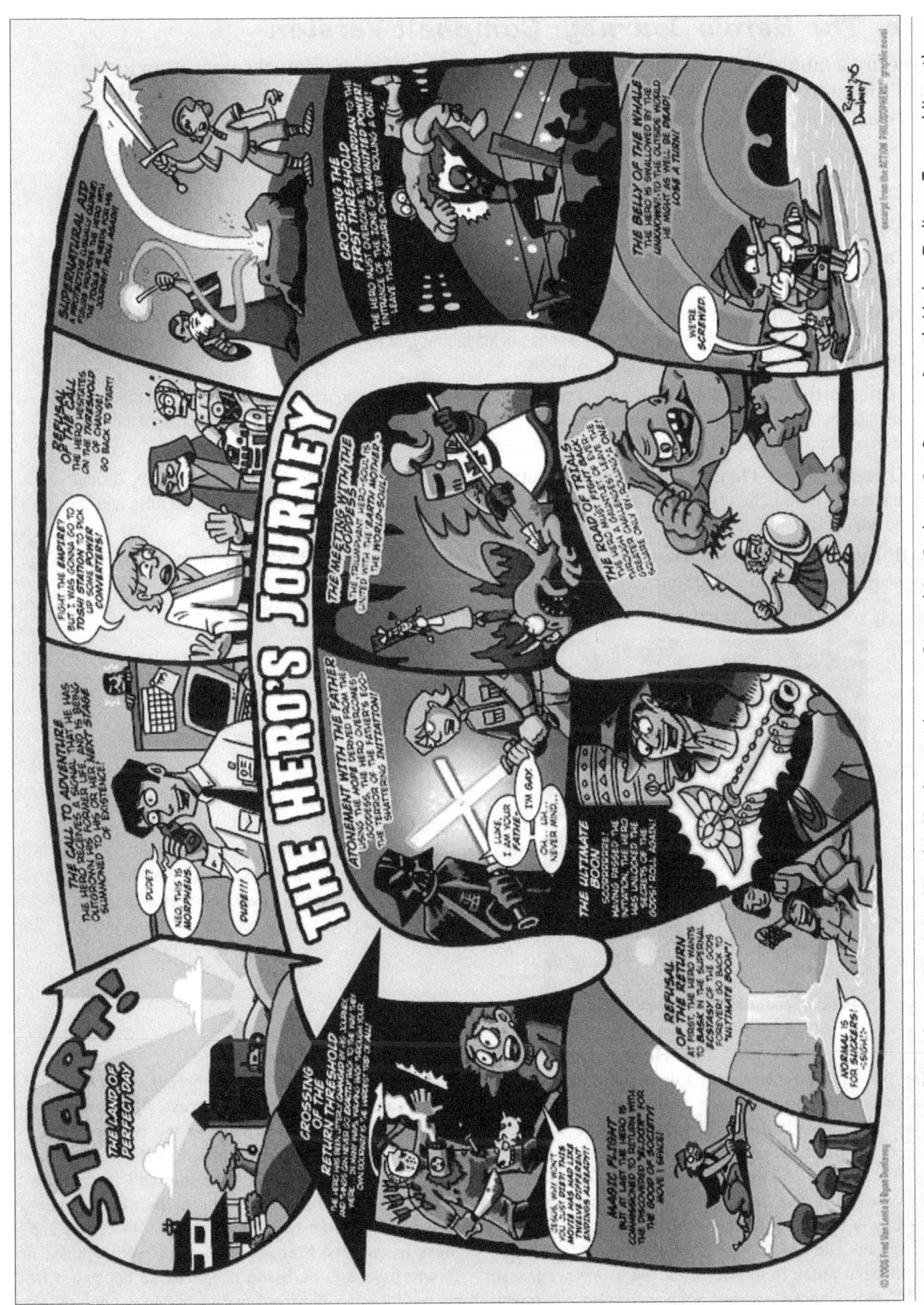

The Hero's Journey. "Morpheus, Obi-Wan Kenobi, Merlin, Spiderman, Pinocchio, Cyclops, St. George, Darth Vader, Indiana Jones, Hiawatha, Aladdin, even Jason from Friday 13th: They're all characters in the Great Monomyth that describes the Seeker's Journey through Life."

Page 156. CAMPBELL APPENDICES

B1c. The Hero's Journey: Campbell Version

There are a number of variations on the Hero's Journey. But the original comes from Joseph Campbell's masterwork, *Hero With a Thousand Faces*. Here is Campbell's classic 17-Stage Hero's Journey (with assistance from Wikipedia):

THE HERO'S JOURNEY

DEPARTURE

1. **Call to Adventure.** The Hero begins in a mundane situation of normality from which some information is received that acts as a call to head off into the unknown.

2. **Refusal of Call.** Often when the call is given, the future Hero first refuses to heed it. This may be from a sense of duty or obligation, fear, insecurity, a sense of inadequacy, or any of a range of reasons that work to hold the person in his or her current circumstances.

3. **Supernatural Aid.** Once the Hero has committed to the quest, consciously or unconsciously, his guide and magical helper appears, or becomes known. More often than not, this supernatural mentor will present the hero with one or more talismans or artifacts that will aid them later in their quest.

4. **Crossing First Threshold.** The point where the Hero actually crosses into the field of adventure, leaving the known limits of his or her world and venturing into an unknown and dangerous realm where the rules and limits are not known.

5. **Belly of Whale.** The final separation from the Hero's known world and self. By entering this stage, the Hero shows willingness to undergo an initial metamorphosis.

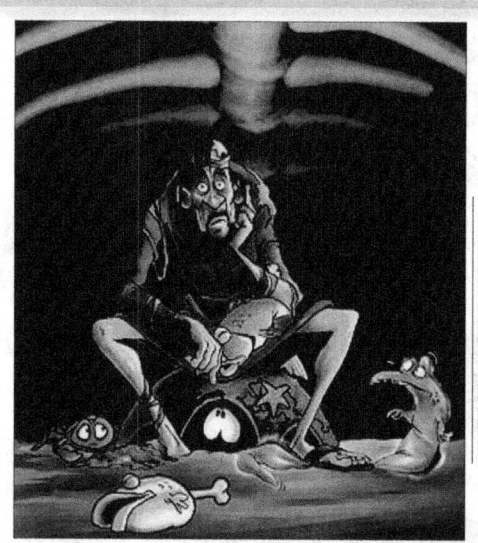

Belly of the Whale. "While the prophet Jonah is trapped in the Belly of the Whale, he must consider two hard truths: The Lord's commandment that he travel to Nineveh to save the people from their sins, and his own cowardice in attempting to evade the Lord's command."

The Hero's Journey of Joseph Campbell

Consider the table of Campbell's Hero's Journey shown on these two facing pages. Scan through the 17 Steps. Don't be concerned to understand every detail. Just get a general sense of the Hero's progress. *** Now choose one Step to explore in detail: The Belly of the Whale, for example. *** Match this Step to the corresponding cartoon on the previous page, and ask yourself questions like these: How does the description in the table compare to the cartoon of Pinocchio on the previous page? What does the description in the table add to the cartoon? What does the depiction in the cartoon add to the table? *** Pinocchio is literally in the Belly of the Whale — but is he there figuratively as well? How is Pinocchio separated from his known world? How is he separated from his Old Self? How is he showing increased willingness to undergo Metamorphosis? *** What kinds of change will take place in Pinocchio as the story progresses? In what ways is he being prepared to become a Real Boy? *** Now choose another Step in the Hero's Journey, match it to the cartoon on the previous page, & ask yourself similar questions. Continue through all the Steps of the Hero's Journey that especially interest you.

THE HERO'S JOURNEY (cont.)

INITIATION

6. **Road of Trials.** A series of tests, tasks, or ordeals that the Hero must undergo to begin the transformation. Often the person fails one or more of these tests, which often occur in threes or sevens.

7. **Meeting with Goddess.** The point when the Hero experiences a love that has the power and significance of the all-powerful, all-encompassing, unconditional love that a fortunate infant may experience with his or her mother. This is a very important step in the process and is often represented by the person finding the other person that he or she loves most completely.

8. **Woman as Temptress.** The Hero faces temptations that may lead him to abandon or stray from his quest. Often of a physical or pleasurable nature, but not necessarily represented by a woman. Woman is a symbol for the physical or material temptations of life, since the hero-knight was often tempted by lust from his spiritual journey.

9. **Atonement with Father.** The Hero must confront and be initiated by whatever holds the ultimate power in his or her life. In many myths and stories this is the father, or a father figure who has life and death power. This is the center point of the journey. All the previous steps have been moving into this place, all that follow will move out from it. Although this step is most frequently symbolized by an encounter with a male entity, it does not have to be a male -- just someone or thing with incredible power.

10. **Apotheosis.** The final separation from the Hero's known world and self. By entering this stage, the person shows willingness to undergo the ultimate metamorphosis.

11. **Ultimate Boon.** The achievement of the goal of the quest. It is what the Hero went on the journey to get. All the previous steps serve to prepare and purify the person for this step, since in many myths the boon is something transcendent -- like the elixir of life itself, or a plant that supplies immortality, or the holy grail.

RETURN

12. **Refusal of Return.** Having found bliss and enlightenment in the other world, the Hero may not want to return to the ordinary world to bestow the boon onto his fellow man.

13. **Magic Flight.** Sometimes the Hero must escape with the boon, if it is something that the gods have been jealously guarding. It can be just as adventurous and dangerous returning from the journey as it was to go into it.

14. **Rescue From Without.** Just as the Hero may need guides and assistants to set out on the quest, oftentimes he (or she) must have powerful guides and rescuers to bring him back to everyday life, especially if the he has been wounded or weakened by the experience.

15. **Crossing Return Threshold.** The trick in returning is to retain the wisdom gained on the quest, to integrate that wisdom into normal human life, and then discover how to share the wisdom with the rest of the world.

16. **Master of Two Worlds.** Often represented by a transcendental Hero like Jesus or Gautama Buddha. For a human Hero, it may mean achieving a balance between the material and spiritual -- becoming comfortable and competent in both the inner and outer worlds.

17. **Freedom to Live.** Mastery leads to freedom – often freedom from the fear of death, which in turn is the freedom to live without restraint. This is sometimes characterized as living in the moment, neither preoccupied by the future nor obsessed by the past.

The Hero's Journey (B1c) is an abbreviated version of the Life Journey Archetype (as explained in Appx B2). The Hero's Journey is populated by Archetypal Characters (B1h), whose adventures recur again and again in literature and movies (B1e). These stories can be of five types (B1d) – as determined by their degree of symbolism and cultural significance. In the ADAPT Model, the Life Journey Archetype is an Arena in Spirit Passages (D4d).

B1d. Hero's Journeys: The Five Types

Hero's Journeys occur with great frequency in literature and movies. These Hero's Journeys can be of various types. Some are more realistic, some more symbolic. Some focus more on the individual Hero, some more on the Culture he represents. Some of the greatest Hero's Journeys are Integral: They combine all four elements in relatively equal proportions. The table on the facing page shows some representative examples of each of the five types of Hero's Journey.

Individual/ Realistic. *The African Queen* is primarily a realistic narrative of an unlikely romance between two strong individuals – set in the context of a treacherous journey down a leech-infested river during World War I, culminating in the sinking of a menacing German gunboat.

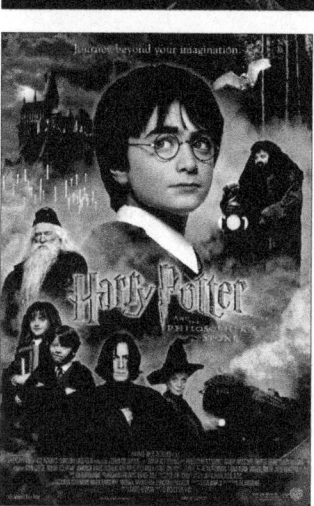

Cultural/ Realistic. Although focused upon the love affair between Scarlett O'Hara and Rhett Butler, *Gone With the Wind* is fundamentally a realistic saga about the demise of the Culture of the Old South.

Individual/ Symbolic. *Harry Potter* is primarily the story of one boy's initiation into a symbolic world of fantasy and magic.

Hero's Journeys: The Five Types

Consider the five types of Hero's Journeys shown on the facing page. Without being too analytical, get a general sense of how the five types differ from one another. *** Now choose one Hero's Journey you are familiar with to explore in detail: *Huck Finn*, for example. *** Ask yourself questions like these: What makes *Huck Finn* the story of an individual? Although primarily individual, what elements of the story reflect on Huck's Culture as a whole – the 19th Century America of Mark Twain? *** What makes the story of *Huck Finn* realistic? Although primarily realistic, what elements of the story ascend into the realm of symbolism and myth? In what ways is Huck's Journey down the river a kind of Odyssey? What might the River itself symbolize? *** Choose a Hero's Journey of another type, and ask yourself similar questions. As time permits, continue through all five types, asking yourself similar questions. *** Do you agree with the table as to how each story is categorized? What other category might each story fall into? *** What other stories can you think of that might fall into these categories? *** In what types of stories is the Hero's Journey most difficult to detect? Where is it most obvious? *** Are most (or all) stories you encounter in books and movies some version of the Hero's Journey? Can you name any that are not?

THE HERO'S JOURNEY: FIVE TYPES

A particular Hero's Journey in literature or movies can focus primarily on an Individual, or on the Culture. It can also be primarily Realistic, or Symbolic. Or it can be all of the above: Integral. Putting these factors together, we find that Hero's Journeys can be of five different types. Here are some familiar books and films for each type:

- **Individual / Realistic.** Robinson Crusoe, Great Expectations, Huck Finn, Mutiny on the Bounty, Seven Storey Mountain (Merton). African Queen, High Noon, North By Northwest, Third Man, Big Sleep, True Grit, North to Alaska.

- **Cultural / Realistic.** Life of Moses, Aeneid, Canterbury Tales, Robin Hood, Don Quixote, Hiawatha, Les Miserables, Moby Dick. Ben Hur, Gone With the Wind, Grapes of Wrath, Casablanca, 1984, From Here to Eternity, Quiet Man, On the Road, Rebel Without Cause, American Graffiti, MASH, The Sting, Easy Rider.

- **Individual / Symbolic.** Book of Jonah, Pilgrim's Progress, Faust, Alice in Wonderland. Snow White, Pinocchio, Peter Pan, Wizard of Oz, Indiana Jones, Harry Potter.

- **Cultural / Symbolic.** Morte d'Arthur, Gulliver's Travels, Paradise Lost, Brave New World. King Kong, Watership Down, 2001 Space Odyssey, Close Encounters, The Matrix.

- **Integral.** The Odyssey, Siddhartha, Life of Christ, Divine Comedy, King Lear, The Tempest. Wonderful Life, My Fair Lady, Star Wars, Lord of Rings, Chronicles of Narnia.

Cultural/ Symbolic. *King Arthur* is primarily the story of the fellowship of valiant men – the Knights of the Round Table. Together, they engage in fantastical challenges and ordeals – on a symbolic quest for honor, virtue, and the Holy Grail.

Integral. *The Odyssey* is the story of both Odysseus the Hero, and of Ithaca, the culture that Odysseus restores. That restoration is set in a realistic world of conflict and battle, but is accomplished by Odysseus' immersion into the world of Enchanted Islands, where Odysseus' character is tested and refined.

Page 160. Campbell Appendices

B1e. The Hero's Journey: Literature & Movies

There are innumerable examples of the Hero's Journey to be found in stories, folk tales, legend, and myths. Many of the most compelling of these have been translated into novels, epic poems, dramatic plays, and movies. On the facing page, we show how various episodes from literature and movies fall into the recurrent Steps of the Hero's Journey.

A Very Merry Un-Birthday. "If *Alice in Wonderland* is a Hero's Journey, what Step is the Tea Party?"

Hero's Journeys in Books & Movies

Consider the table of Hero's Journey on the facing page. Without being too analytical, scan through each of Step from bottom to top. Get a general, intuitive sense of what each Step consists of, and how the particular stories might apply. *** Now choose one Step to explore in detail: the Culminating Ordeal, for example. *** Ask yourself questions like these: What is the Culminating Ordeal for Odysseus? For Jesus? For Dorothy? For Alice? For Skywalker, Frodo, the Pevensie children (*Narnia*)? *** Focusing on just one of these Heroes, what is the Road of Trials that precedes the Ordeal? How do the Trials prepare our Heroes for their Ordeal? *** What is the Ultimate Boon their Ordeal leads to? How is this Treasure bestowed upon the Ordinary World they return to? *** As time permits, choose another Hero in another Step of the Hero's Journey, and ask yourself similar questions. *** In certain stories, what Steps are especially emphasized? What other Steps are minimized or omitted? What Steps are presented out of order? *** Does a departure from the formula make the story more surprising, more engaging, less sentimental? *** At what age would you have preferred stories that stick to the formula? At what age did you begin preferring stories that differed widely from the formula? How far can a story stray from the formula before it becomes uncomfortable, unsettling, distasteful? *** Does this Exploration add to your understanding and enjoyment? Does it illuminate the story and reveal hidden levels? *** Be careful not to over-analyze. Pursue this line of inquiry only so long as it adds to the magic.

THE HERO'S JOURNEY: Literature & Movies
[Read from bottom to top.]

ORDINARY WORLD, TRANSFORMED

16-17. RETURN WITH THE ELIXIR. Odysseus: Reunited with Penelope, restored harmony to Ithaca. Jesus: Sits at right-hand of Father, still dwells on Earth as Holy Spirit. Dorothy: Reunion and renewed appreciation for family. Narnia: Restored harmony.

TRANSITION BACK TO ORDINARY WORLD

13-14. MAGIC FLIGHT/RESCUE FROM WITHOUT. Odysseus: Athena aids escape from Calypso's Island. Moses: Pillar of Fire guiding escape from Egypt. Jesus: Final ascension into heaven. Dorothy: Magical return by ruby slippers.

12, 15. REFUSAL OF RETURN, CROSSING RETURN THRESHOLD. Odysseus: Trapped in Cave of Calypso, finally gives up immortality of a demi-god. Jesus: Gethsemane, then accepts will of God. Peter Pan: Refuses to return. Dorothy: Balloon return fails.

ENCHANTED WORLD

6b. CULMINATING ORDEAL. Odysseus: Returns to Ithaca to battle suitors. Jesus: The crucifixion. Dorothy: Battles Wicked Witch. Skywalker: Blows up Death Star. Rings, Narnia: Culminating battles.

10. APOTHEOSIS. Odysseus: Guidance from dead Mother, Achilles. Jesus: Resurrection after death. Dorothy: Apparition of Auntie Em. Neo: Loses sight, gains knowledge. Kenobi: Becomes part of Force itself.

9. ATONEMENT WITH FATHER. Telemachus: Reunites with Odysseus. Jesus: Recognizes identity with God. Dorothy: Meets Wizard. Skywalker: Meets Darth Vader.

8. WOMAN AS TEMPTRESS. Odysseus: Circe, Calypso. Samson: Delilah. David: Bathsheba. Jesus: Temptations in wilderness. Han Solo: Claims reward money, abandons rebels. Potter: Tempted by Mirror of Eristed.

7. LOVE INTEREST. Odysseus: Penelope. Potter: Mother's pure love. Peter Pan: Wendy. Skywalker: Leia. Neo: Trinity.

6a. ROAD OF TRIALS. Odysseus: Enchanted Islands. Jesus: Week of the Passion. Dorothy: Dangers on Yellow Brick Road. Rings: Galdalf lost fighting Balrog. Kenobi: Killed by Darth Vader.

TRANSITION TO THE ENCHANTED WORLD

5. BELLY OF WHALE. Odysseus: Journey to Underworld. Jonah: Belly of whale. Skywalker: Sucked into enemy space fortress. Potter: Enters Forbidden Forest.

4. CROSSING FIRST THRESHOLD. Jesus: Water into wine. Skywalker: Leaves Tatooine. Potter: Defeats troll. Frodo: Sam feeling separated from home.

3. MENTOR. Athena: Guidance for Odysseus. Dorothy's good witch Glinda: Ruby slippers. Kenobi: Gives light saber. Dumbledore: Gives Cloak of Invisibility. Frodo: Given armor, sword, Phial of Galadriel.

2. REFUSAL OF CALL. Lot's wife: Looks back. Skywalker: Refuses to help, finds home destroyed. Frodo: Offers ring to Gandalf.

1. CALL TO ADVENTURE. Odysseus: Blown off-course by Aeolus winds. Dorothy: Cyclone. Neo: Phone call from Morpheus. Skywalker: Message for Kenobi. Potter: Accepted into Hogwarts. Frodo: Gandalf arrives.

ORDINARY WORLD

0. THE ORDINARY WORLD. Odyssey: Trouble back home in Ithaca. Lot: Trouble in Sodom. Dorothy in drab Kansas: 'Over the Rainbow.'

B1f. Your Inner Hero's Journeys: Their Scope

The Hero's Journey is far more than a technique for analyzing myths and legends. It is a lens we can use to reveal the meaning, purpose, and significance of key moments in our life. For those of us who are Seekers or Cultural Creatives (IN2), each of those key moments constitute an **Inner Hero's Journey** – a personal Hero's Journey that elevates and enlivens every aspect of our existence. These Inner Journeys can function on at least three levels of duration, scope, and significance:

- **The Micro-Journey.** Every Challenge we face in daily life can be viewed as a small Hero's Journey – whether it be summoning up the courage for our first date, or preparing for our first major job interview, or closing our biggest deal. (In the language of this book, the Micro-Journey is a single Transition Cycle (PPR1) from one Stage (D1) to the next.)

- **The Macro-Journey.** The major events of our life can likewise be viewed as Hero's Journeys – especially where they entail some unexpected Challenge, some ultimate Test of our resources. In Hugh's case, for example, a whole series of tumultuous events was unleashed when Hugh was diagnosed at age 24 with terminal cancer (later miraculously cured). Later in life, the authors were plunged into another turbulent journey, when pregnant Kaye's water broke prematurely, and Baby Olivia was delivered barely alive after a gestation of just 24 weeks. (In the language of this book, the Macro-Journey is the Developmental Sequence (D1+2) for a whole series of Transition Cycles (PPR3) within a given phase or Arena of life.)

- **The Mega-Journey.** All these life events – the first dates, the first jobs, the cancer, the premature birth – all these can be viewed as parts of one vast Hero's Journey that encompasses the entirety of our lives. Although not as neat and tidy as a novel or a movie, our Life Journey is replete with Calls to Adventure, Dark Nights of the Soul, a Road of Trials, and perhaps a few Culminating Battles. (In the language of this book, the Mega-Journey can be viewed as the Human Odyssey itself – a whole set of Growth processes that move us along the various Dimensions of the Growth Continuum (D6b, PPR8b).)

On the facing page, we show further examples of personal Hero's Journeys – Journeys in all three ranges of experience, and for each of nine Arenas of life.

Micro-Journey. "I crammed for the test, finally mastered the material, and then got a great grade. That whole process was like a small Hero's Journey."

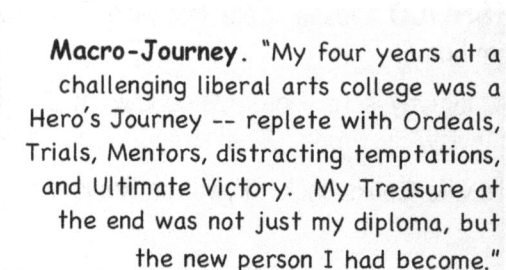

Macro-Journey. "My four years at a challenging liberal arts college was a Hero's Journey -- replete with Ordeals, Trials, Mentors, distracting temptations, and Ultimate Victory. My Treasure at the end was not just my diploma, but the new person I had become."

Mega-Journey. "My fun-filled experiences with books at an early age were a Call to Adventure that have led to a lifelong Journey of discovery and learning."

YOUR INNER HERO'S JOURNEYS

Many people view the events of their lives as nothing more than a series of random and relatively insignificant activities they happen to participate in. However, those same events can often be viewed as episodes of a personal Hero's Journey – key moments of life that are infused with significance, purpose, and meaning. Depending on their duration, scope, and impact, these important moments may take the form of Micro-, Macro-, or Mega-Journeys -- as shown in the table below.

Situation	Micro-Journey	Macro-Journey	Mega-Journey
Education	My first day at Salmon Creek School.	The years from kindergarten through 8th grade I spent at Salmon Creek School.	My lifelong love of learning.
Relationships	My first date with Sarah.	The summer Sarah and I drove across country.	My lifelong marriage to Sarah.
Career	My auspicious job interview with the firm I eventually decided to go with.	The process of mounting a defense in my most important case.	The span of my entire law career -- defending those who were unjustly accused.
Health	The night when I was rushed to the hospital for an emergency operation.	My prolonged battle against a debilitating disease.	My lifelong dedication to trusting the body's capacity to heal itself.
Nature	Our weekend outing at the beach with the family.	Our extended backpack trip to the High Sierra backcountry.	Our lifetime engagement with the restorative powers of Nature.
Travel	Our Sunday outing to visit the zoo and the amusement park.	Our year living and studying abroad in Florence, Italy.	Our ever-increasing appreciation of people and places throughout the world.
Creativity	Making an impromptu sketch of an interesting scene.	Completing an ambitious landscape painting with oils on a large canvas.	Compiling a significant body of artistic work over the course of a lifetime.
Nutrition	Joining with other family members to create a very special family feast.	Creating a dietary plan for the school's lunch program.	Our lifelong dedication to natural, whole foods grown locally.
Social Activism	Integrating a restaurant lunch counter in a backward Southern town.	My summer Civil Rights campaign in the Deep South, registering citizens to vote.	The course of race relations over the span of American history.

> The Hero's Journey can have significance at both the Symbolic Level (B1b-e, h) and at the Psychological Level (B1f-g). The psychological Hero's Journey consists of an abbreviated number of Steps (B1g) –and can be of three varieties (B1e), depending upon it scope and duration.

B1g. Your Inner Micro-Journey: Its Steps

Our Inner Hero's Journey follows much the same pattern as the narrative Hero's Journey of myth and legend – replete with a Call to Adventure, a Road of Trials, a Culminating Ordeal, and a return with some Treasure of the heart. The Inner Micro-Journey traces out the Hero's Journey pattern for a single personal Challenge – a pattern the corresponds to the Transition Cycle described in the Processes section of this book (PPR1). The Steps of a typical Micro-Journey are outlined on the facing page.

Bridge to Adventure. As with the Transition Cycle (PPR1), the Micro-Journey can be our Bridge from one Stage to the next.

Micro-Journey. "My first date was a small Hero's Journey – complete with Call to Adventure, Road of Trials, and Culminating Ordeal. Although the relationship never went anywhere, I brought home a Treasure of experience and self-awareness."

Your Inner Hero's Journeys: Micro-, Macro-, and Mega- [Exploration for previous page]

Consider the table of Hero's Journeys on the preceding page (p. 163). This table describes Hero's Journeys of varying breadth and significance in nine Arenas of life activity. *** Without getting too analytical, scan through the table – getting a general, intuitive sense of the differences between Micro-, Macro-, and Mega-Journeys. Select one Arena to explore in detail: Travel, for example. *** Ask yourself questions like these: Regarding Micro-Journeys, what brief outing or adventure has been especially enjoyable for you? Did it transport you from your Ordinary World of obligations and chores to a Special World of spontaneous fun and excitement? Was there a Road of Trials to get you there?

Was there an Ultimate Boon you received from the experience? Was there some Treasure you brought back to your Ordinary World that made life more worthwhile? *** Now think of an especially enjoyable or illuminating Travel experience that was long enough and deep enough to qualify as a Macro-Journey. Ask yourself similar questions. *** Next, think of a Travel experience (or unified series of Travel experiences) that encompassed a significant portion of your life. Ask yourself similar questions about his Mega-Journey. *** In what fundamental ways are the three types of Journeys different? Which type do you prefer? Which is most feasible in your life? Do your Micro-Journeys expand to become Macro-Journeys, which in turn lead to a Mega-Journey? *** Do your experiences with actual Travel in some way parallel your symbolic Travel of the Growth Continuum. Have you made your Life Journey the greatest and most all-consuming Travel experience of them all?

YOUR INNER HERO'S JOURNEY: The Micro-Journey
[Read from bottom to top.]

ORDINARY WORLD, TRANSFORMED

17-18. RETURN WITH THE ELIXIR ('Master of Two Worlds, Freedom to Live'). Living out your transformed Self in daily life.

TRANSITION BACK TO ORDINARY WORLD (Campbell's 'Return')

14-15. THE RESURRECTION ('Magic Flight. Rescue From Without'). One final, Major Test of your resolve. Solidifies your commitment to change.

13, 16. THE ROAD BACK ('Refusal of Return. Crossing Return Threshold'). Dedication to applying your new insights and abilities in your everyday life.

ENCHANTED WORLD (Internal Realms of Body, Psyche, Spirit [D3b-d]. Campbell's 'Initiation.')

12. THE REWARD ('Ultimate Boon'). Surmounting your Major Challenge, achieving your goal.

7b. CULMINATING ORDEAL. Meeting Major Challenge or big change with the trepidation of life or death.

10-11. APPROACH ('Atonement with Father. Apotheosis'). Alignment with Fundamental Values. Preparing through newfound abilities and friends for your Major Challenge.

8-9. ALLIES & ENEMIES. ('Meeting with Goddess. Woman as Temptress'). Experimenting with new friends and identifying opponents. Distinguishing positive from negative influences.

7a. ROAD OF TRIALS. Taking on new Challenges.

TRANSITION TO THE ENCHANTED WORLD (Campbell's 'Departure')

6. BELLY OF WHALE. Overcoming Fear.

5. CROSSING FIRST THRESHOLD. Initial Commitment to change.

4. MENTOR ('Supernatural Aid'). Seeking Guidance and Support.

3. REFUSAL OF CALL. Fear of the unknown. Resistance to Change.

2. CALL TO ADVENTURE. Increased awareness of your Need for Change.

ORDINARY WORLD (External Realm of Everyday Life [D3a])

1. THE ORDINARY WORLD. Limited awareness of problem.

Your Inner Micro-Journey

Consider the table of your Inner Hero's Journey above. This sequence of 12 steps is simpler and less academic than Campbell's 17-step version -- because it was created by Disney screenwriter Chris Vogler as a template for movie scripts. *** Without being too analytical, scan through the Steps from bottom to top. *** Now refer back to the table of Hero's Journeys from the previous Exploration (page 163). Select another Arena of life activity to explore further: The Micro-Journey of your first date (Relationships), for example. *** If you are a male, ask yourself questions like these: Who was she? What prompted you to ask her out? How did you prepare yourself to ask her? How did she respond? Where did you take her? How did the two of you get along? What went right, or wrong? Did the date lead to a Relationship? *** Once you have reconstructed the details of this date, switch your attention back to the table above. How do the various moments of your date correspond to Steps of your Inner Hero's Journey? Which Steps were emphasized? Which are missing? Did this first experience with dating eventually lead to some Epic Relationship of long duration? Did your Micro-Journey become a Mega-Journey?

Page 166. CAMPBELL APPENDICES

B1h. Archetypal Characters of the Hero's Journey

According to psychologist Carl Jung, **Archetypal Characters** are the stock character Types (P3g) that occur with regularity in the mythic stories from our Collective Unconscious (D4d). These Archetypes are important for analyzing and interpreting stories and myths. However, they are even more important as windows to our own Souls. That is, each Archetype represents an aspect of our Identity – a psychological entity that participates in our own personal Journey of Life. Through Archetypes, we project our interior qualities in external form – thereby enabling us to recognize who we are, understand why we act as we do, and anticipate where our life is taking us.

According to Christopher Vogler, the Disney screenwriter known for bringing the Hero's Journey framework to the movies, there are eight major Archetypes. Those eight Archetypes are outlined on next two facing pages (p. 168) – using characters from *The Odyssey* and *The Wizard of Oz* as examples.

Archetypal Action Figures. Because Archetypal Characters are universal, they make the perfect toys. Children of every background can recognize them, and relate to the stories they are part of.

> Archetypal Characters are Personality Types (P3g) – characters that recur with regularity in the stories of our Life Journey (B1c, e).

B1. The Hero's Journey . Page 167

Mentor and Shadow. In *The Wizard of Oz*, the Good Witch and the Wicked Witch are countervailing Archetypes that grapple for control of Dorothy's destiny.

Your Archetypal Characters (1)

Consider the table of Archetypal Characters on the following two facing pages. Without getting too analytical, scan through the eight Archetypes. Get an intuitive feel for how they apply in stories like *The Wizard of Oz* or *The Odyssey*. *** Now select one Archetype to explore in detail: The Mentor, for example. *** Ask yourself questions like these: In what ways was Glinda the Good Witch a Mentor to Dorothy in *The Wizard of Oz*? When did she appear? What advice or directions did she give? What magical powers did she possess? What gifts or talismans did she present? *** How well did Dorothy fare when Glinda (or Glinda's influence) was present? What difficulties arose when Glinda was absent? *** Ask yourself similar questions about the Mentors in Homer's *The Odyssey* – the goddess Athena, the old counselor whose name is Mentor. *** What other stories do you know where some sort of Mentor provides guidance and support for the Hero? Who is the Mentor in *Star Wars*, or *Lord of the Rings*? In an inner city film, like *Stand By Me*? In any sports movie, like *Hoosiers*? In a battle film like *Dirty Dozen*? *** What do all these Mentors have in common? How do they differ? *** In what cases do Mentors fail to help, or abandon the Hero? Where do we find deceptive or false Mentors? *** Now consider your own life. Who have been your Mentors at key times in your life? How have they influenced key decisions? How have they provided support for major challenges? Where have they mislead you, or let you down? *** Who do you serve as a Mentor to? In what ways are you a good Mentor? In what ways do you not feel up to the task? How could you become a better Mentor?

Page 168. Campbell Appendices

Archetypal Characters of the Hero's Journey

Archetype	Odyssey	Wizard of Oz
Hero. The central figure of the story. Willing to sacrifice his own needs on behalf of others. The Ego's search for identity & wholeness.	**Odysseus**, the Everyman who undergoes trials of purification in preparation for the ultimate battle.	**Dorothy**, a girl trying to find meaning in the humdrum of everyday life.
Mentor. The Hero's Guide or guiding principles. The figure who aids or trains the Hero – who teaches, or protects, gives him essential gifts, or imparts divine wisdom. Often speaks with the voice of God, or of departed parent or ancestor.	Wise **Mentor**, who counsels Telemachus on dealing with the suitors. **Athena**, the goddess who watches over Odysseus and gives help when all seems lost. The **Kings of Pylos and Sparta**, who counsel Telemachus on finding his long lost father. The prophet **Tiresias**, to whom Odysseus comes for advice in the Underworld.	**Glinda** the Good Witch, who directs Dorothy to the Yellow Brick Road. **Auntie Em**, whose goodness is a beacon to Dorothy in times of distress.
Threshold Guardian. The force that stands in the way at important turning points. Jealous enemy, dangerous henchman, professional gatekeeper -- often placed to keep the unworthy from entering. Can often be overcome, bypassed, or turned into allies. One's own fears and doubts -- inner demons that hold one back from Growth and progress.	The **Cyclops**, who rolls the stone over the mouth of the cave to trap Odysseus and his men. The demigoddess **Calypso**, who holds Odysseus captive in her cave. The god **Poseidon**, whose winds blow Odysseus off-course, just as he is about to reach home. **Odysseus** himself, who bars the door of the Great Hall, so that no suitor can escape the slaughter.	The Sentry or **Gatekeeper**, who guards the gate to the Emerald City. The **Flying Monkeys**, who defend the approach to the Wicked Witch's castle.
Herald. Figure who conveys important information -- including important changes, new challenges, a message from the gods. Can be a real person, a dream figure, a new idea, an event.	The omens of **Grappling Birds** in the sky, foretelling the eventual destruction of the suitors. The god **Hermes**, who delivers Zeus's order for Odysseus' release from the Cave of Calypso.	The crotchety **Miss Gulch**, who comes to complain that Toto is trouble – and who heralds Dorothy's ultimate adversary, the Wicked Witch. The **Tornado** that sweeps Dorothy out of her ordinary life.

Archetypes in Story and Myth. *The Odyssey* and *The Wizard of Oz* are two very different stories. Yet their characters are Archetypes who serve almost identical functions.

Archetype	Odyssey	Wizard of Oz
Shapeshifter. Figure that challenges Hero's view of stable or predictable reality. Creatures who change shape or attitude. People (or our perceptions of them) who keep changing – the changeable love interest, ambiguous or duplicitous people.	The demigod **Proteus**, who changes shape to escape Menelaus, who is trying to discover which god he must propitiate to get strong winds for his sail home. **Odysseus** himself, who plays different roles as part of his stratagems of trickery. **Odysseus' foolish crew**, who are turned into pigs by the demigoddess Circe.	The transformation of reality through the magic of the **Tornado**. The **Scarecrow**, **Tin Man**, and **Cowardly Lion**, who all hope to be transformed by the magic of the Wizard. The **Wicked Witch**, who appears menacingly out of nothing, and finally is reduced to slime by a bucket of water.
Shadow. Villain, enemy, vengeful god, dangerous monster. The dark side of the Hero -- the repressed possibilities, his potential for evil. Repressed grief, anger, frustration or creativity that is dangerous if it doesn't have an outlet.	**Antinous** and the other evil **Suitors**, attempting to displace Odysseus in his kingdom and his marriage bed. The god **Poseidon**, who wreaks vengeance on Odysseus for insulting him and injuring his son Cyclops. The sun god **Helios** who punishes Odysseus' crew by destroying his ship and all hands.	The **Wicked Witch**, from whom Dorothy must obtain the broom, before the Wizard will aid her in getting home. The black-and-white **Kansas Shadows** of the major characters of Oz – the three hired hands, Professor Marvel, Miss Gulch.
Ally. Figure who travels with or stands by the Hero, helping him through change. Companion, partner, sidekick, buddy, girlfriend, conscience, comic relief -- who accompanies, advises, and defends the Hero through the transitions of life. The unexpressed or underused parts of the personality that can be brought into action when needed.	Odysseus' faithful wife **Penelope**, who holds the fort during the long years while he is gone. Odysseus' loyal son **Telemachus**, who joins him in the slaughter of the suitors. The noble **Phaecians**, who nurse Odysseus back to health, and provide him a way home. **Eurycleia**, the loyal nurse, who recognizes Odysseus for his scar.	Dorothy's three companions in adventure – the **Scarecrow**, the **Tin Man**, and the **Cowardly Lion**. Her dog **Toto**, who Dorothy risks a tornado to save, and for whom she eventually sacrifices a ride home in the Wizard's balloon.
Trickster. Figure who makes mischief, rocks the boat, upsets the status quo, mocks pretensions of Hero or villain, misleads people to achieve his own ends. Our own mischievous subconscious, urging us to approach reality in a new way.	**Odysseus** himself, whose Gift Horse overcame the Trojans through trickery. Who used trickery to escape the Cyclops, uses seduction to escape Circe, etc. Who finally enters his own palace as a beggar, so he can entrap the suitors in their own treachery.	The **Wizard of Oz**, whose magic is total fakery – yet who successfully tricks Dorothy into killing his enemy, the Wicked Witch.

Your Archetypal Characters (2)

Consider the Archetypes described on these two facing pages. Now choose a favorite Hero's Journey from movies or literature to explore further (see Appx B1d): Robin Hood, for example. *** Once you recall the story, ask yourself questions like these: What Archetype is Robin Hood? How about Little John, Friar Tuck, Will Scarlett? What about the Sheriff of Nottingham, or King John? How about Maid Marian, or the long-absent King Richard the Lionheart? *** How does each character conform to, and differ from, the stereotype? What personal touches are added to make a character more than a formula? Which characters break through their Archetypes and change over time? *** How do the various Archetypes of the story relate to each other? How do they each function to move the story forward? *** In what ways do the Archetypes make this story universal and timeless? *** As time permits, choose another story, and ask yourself similar questions.

A UNICORN? ...

OR A DRAGON?

The inner Sanctum of Our Labyrinth. When we travel to the core of our being, what will we find? A peaceful Unicorn? Or a raging Dragon?

OUR HERO'S JOURNEY (p. 150)

OUR LIFE JOURNEY (p. 172)

Into the Enchanted World. In our **Hero's Journey**, we enter the Enchanted World to face our Dragons. In our **Life Journey**, we explore the entire Enchanted World -- including our Dragons.

Appendix B2.
BEYOND JOSEPH CAMPBELL:
How the Hero's Journey Became the Life Journey

In *Beyond Ken Wilber* (Appx A2), we described how our ADAPT Model evolved from Ken Wilber's AQAL and Integral Operating System (IOS). There, we found that Wilber's IOS is actually a very extensive (though incomplete) version of our own ADAPT Model.

In a similar manner, we now describe how our Life Journey Archetype evolved from Joseph Campbell's *Hero's Journey*. Here, we find that Campbell's Hero's Journey is actually a very extensive (though incomplete) version of our own Life Journey Archetype.

The derivation of the Life Journey Archetype takes place in three steps. These steps occur in reverse – because we begin with the ADAPT Model we have already derived, and work backwards. In each of the three steps, we begin with abstract concepts and discover their symbolic equivalents:

- ✻ **B2a. From ADAPT to Life Journey: Domains.** If our conceptual ADAPT Model consists of five major Domains, what are the symbolic or archetypal equivalents for those Domains? (p. 173)
- ✻ **B2b. From ADAPT to Life Journey: Sectors.** If our ADAPT Model contains seven or more Sectors within each Domain, what are the symbolic or archetypal equivalents for each of those Sectors? (p. 174)
- ✻ **B2c. From Life Journey to Hero's Journey.** If the Life Journey Archetype consists of five Domains and numerous Sectors within each Domain, which of those Domains and Sectors correspond to Steps in Campbell's Hero's Journey? (p. 180)

As we identify the many parallels between the Hero's Journey and the Life Journey Archetype, it becomes clear that **Campbell's Hero's Journey is actually a very extensive (though incomplete) version of our Life Journey Archetype.**

The Hero's Journey. Campbell's Hero's Journey is an abbreviated version of a much more extended epic story – the Life Journey Archetype.

In Appendix B2, we derive Campbell's Hero's Journey (B1c) from the ADAPT Model in three steps: B2a) Convert the Domains of ADAPT from conceptual to symbolic. B2b) Convert the Sectors of ADAPT conceptual to symbolic. B2c) Simplify the Life Journey Archetype down to the Hero's Journey. In our original process of derivation, we compared ADAPT to a classic mythic journey, *The Odyssey* by Homer -- noting the remarkable number of parallels between the two. (See Appx C3b for details.) *** The derivations in B2b and B2c are the same as those in *Beyond Ken Wilber* (Appx A2I).

B2a. From ADAPT to Life Journey: Domains

As our ADAPT Model of Human Development evolved from Ken Wilber's AQAL and IOS, we made a surprising discovery: The ADAPT Model shows some remarkable parallels to the fundamental Archetype of Human Development – the **Life Journey**, or **Human Odyssey**. For instance, if we conceive of the Life Journey as a sea voyage comparable to Homer's *The Odyssey*, the five Domains of ADAPT become the major components of that Voyage:

- **Dimensions > Map**
  The Dimensions answer the question 'Where does the Growth take place?'. So the Dimensions are the **Map** of Life's Journey.

- **Participants > Voyagers**
  The Participants answer the question 'Who does the Growing?'. So the Participants are the crew, passengers, and other **Voyagers** on that Journey.

- **Processes > Ships**
  The Processes answer the question 'What means are used to facilitate the Growth?'. So the Processes are the **Ships** and other modes of conveyance that carry us on that Voyage.

- **Pathfinders > Navigator/Captain**
  The Pathfinders answer the question 'With whose assistance is the Growth brought about?'. So the Pathfinders are the **Navigator** and **Captain**, who guide our Ships and orchestrate our Journey.

- **Systems > Shipping System**
  The Systems answer the question 'How do the various factors work together to produce Growth?'. So the Systems are the **Shipping System** (docks, warehouses, shipyards, port officials, administrative personnel, etc.) that provides the coordination and support necessary to make such Voyages possible.

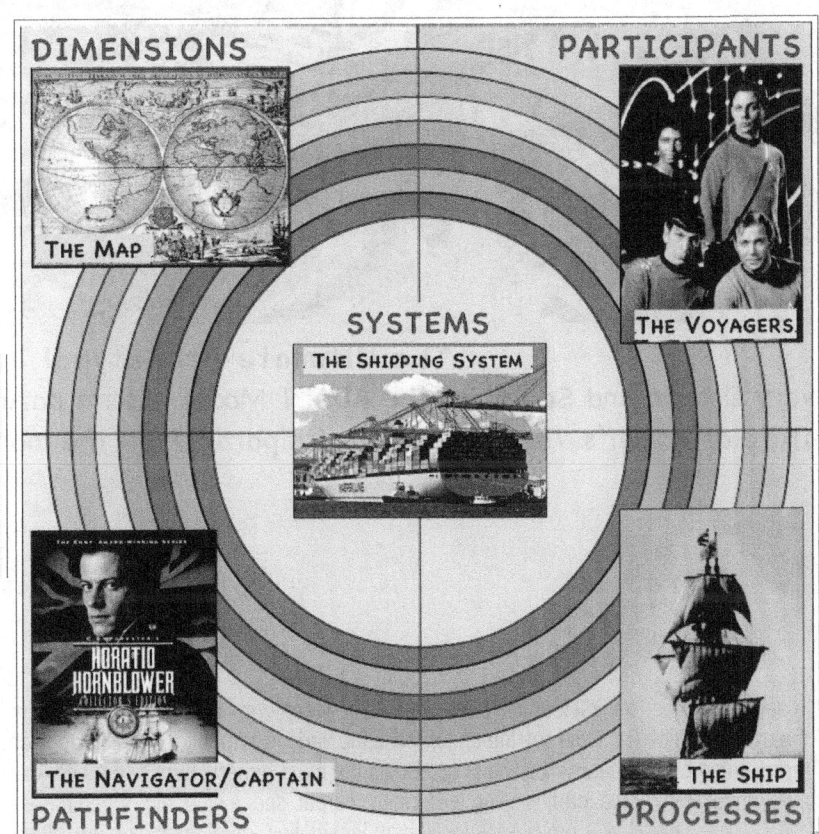

The Life Journey. The five Domains of the ADAPT Model correspond very precisely to the five components of the Life Journey Archetype.

Map: Wilber *same term*. Voyagers, Ships, Navigator/Captain, Shipping System: Not mentioned.

Page 174. CAMPBELL APPENDICES

B2b. From ADAPT to Life Journey: Sectors

Once we had discovered the symbolic equivalents of the five Domains, we then expanded the Life Journey Archetype to encompass all the Sectors of ADAPT. Using Homer's *The Odyssey* as our primary mythic example, we asked: 'For each Sector of ADAPT, what is the symbolic or archetypal equivalent?' When we did so, we discovered a remarkably exact set of correspondences between the conceptual and the symbolic versions of ADAPT. Examples of these correspondences are shown on the facing page. A depiction of all the Life Journey Domains and Sectors is shown on the four facing pages, beginning page 176.

The Ultimate Archetypal Journey

Every Domain and Sector of the ADAPT Model has its parallel in Homer's *The Odyssey*. Each feature of Homer's *The Odyssey* has its parallels in the more general Life Journey Archetype.*

> The complete set of Parallels between ADAPT and the Life Journey is displayed in the Overview section (OV1-2). Parallels to Homer's *The Odyssey* are outlined in Appx B3b.

*In actual practice, we first identified the parallels between our ADAPT Model and Homer's *The Odyssey* (Appx B3). Then, we generalized the symbolism of *The Odyssey* the encompass the various symbolic forms of the Archetype. For instance, the Processes (PPR/PR) are represented by Odysseus's Sailing Ship. But in the more general form of the Life Journey Archetype, the Processes can be any mode of conveyance: Raft, horse, cart, running feet, magic carpet, space ship, etc. Even more generally, the Processes can be any means by which our Hero's progress is facilitated: Incantation, ritual, magic potion, clever strategem, miraculous weapon, etc.

FROM ABSTRACTIONS TO ARCHETYPES

For each conceptual Parameter of ADAPT, we asked: 'What is the symbolic or archetypal equivalent?' Here are a few of our answers:

- **Dimensions > Map**
  If the Dimensions represent the Map of our Life Journey, then the Stages (D1) are the Islands or Ports of Call we encounter in the course of our Voyage. Likewise, the Transitions (D2) are the treacherous Open Seas between one Port of Call and the next…

- **Participants > Voyagers**
  If the Participants represent the Voyagers of our Life Journey, then the Self System (P1) is the Hero of our adventure. Likewise, the Individual Selves (P2a) are the Individual characters on our Voyage (the Captain, the Sidekick, the Faithful Wife, the Villain, etc.) – while the Collective Selves (P2b) are the Group characters in our drama (the Crew, the Townsfolk, the Invading Army, etc.)…

- **Processes > Ships**
  If the Processes represent the Ships of our Life Journey, then the Transition Cycle (PR1) is the means by which these Ships travel from one Port of Call to the next. Likewise, the Shadow Cycle (PR2) represents the mishaps that cause these Ships to diverge from their course, or founder in the deep…

- **Pathfinders > Navigator/Captain**
  If the Pathfinders represent the Navigator and Captain that provide Guidance and Orchestration for our Life Journey, then the Society & Culture (PF2) is the influence members of the Ship's Crew have on the voyage. Likewise, the Mentor (PF8) is the Guiding Spirit that appears in time of need…

- **Systems > Shipping System**
  If the Systems are the Shipping System that supports and facilitates our Journey, then the specific Systems are the combinations of docks, warehouses, shipyards, port officials, and administrative personnel that make such Voyages possible…

A complete outline of the Domains and Parameters for the Life Journey Archetype is displayed on the next two facing pages.

The Power of Symbol. "If the Earth is an ice cream cone, then Global Warming is the hot day that causes the Earth to melt into a sticky mess." Symbols convey nuances and associations far beyond what the concept alone can tell us.

Page 176. Campbell Appendices

DIMENSIONS

HUMAN GROWTH. The Journey we take across the turbulent seas and exotic lands of life.
D1-8. GROWTH CONTINUUM. The Map of our Life Journey. *** **DIMENSIONS.** The Coordinates of that Map.
D1. STAGES. The Islands or Way Stations we visit in the course of our Journey -- our Stopovers or Ports of Call.
D2. TRANSITIONS. The Open Seas and Routes of Passage our Ship will take between one port of call and the next.
D1+2. DEVELOPMENTAL SEQUENCE. Our entire Life Journey until our Ship reaches its final destination.
D3. REALMS. The four regions where our Life Journey takes place – Everyday Life, Enchantment, Ordeals, Heavens.
D4. ARENAS. The various Areas of Activity at every Port of Call – waterfront, downtown, residential area, countryside.
D5. PERSPECTIVES. The four Points of View from which our story can be told. *** **PATHS.** The four Directions of Journey.
D6. DIRECTIONS. The two Vertical Paths our Journey can take – upward to the Heavens, or downward to the Underworld.
D7. IMPEDIMENTS. The two major Obstacles between us and our destination – Challenges & Impasses.
D8. TRANSCENDENT STATES. The supremely Illuminating Moments when we commune with the gods.

B2. How the Hero's Journey Became the Life Journey. Page 177

PARTICIPANTS

P1-8. PARTICIPANTS. The crew, passengers, and other VOYAGERS who take part in our Life Journey.

P1. SELF SYSTEM. Our HERO -- the CENTRAL CHARACTER, the adventurer who triumphs over challenges and hardships.

P2. INDIVIDUAL SELF. INDIVIDUAL CHARACTERS – Hero, Sidekick, Mentor, Spiritual Guide, Main Villain.
*** COLLECTIVE SELF. GROUP CHARACTERS – the Ship's Crew, Townsfolk, Invading Army, Gang of Villains.

P3. PERSONALITY TYPES. The stereotyped 'CHARACTERS' we find aboard Ship – the Forceful Leader, Dutiful Helper, Jovial Carouser, Reclusive Thinker, Cooperative Mate, Free Spirit, Jokester, Voice Of Prophecy, Slouch.

P4. SHADOW SELF. The MISFIT or TROUBLEMAKER, who disrupts things and causes the Journey to go wrong -- the Grumbler, Slacker, Rebel, Plotter, Saboteur, Mutineer, Stowaway.

P5. FUNCTIONAL CONSTITUENTS. The various members of the SHIP'S CREW, characterized by their FUNCTION aboard ship – the Captain, Navigator, Helmsman, Surgeon, Cook, Carpenter, Midshipman, Mate.

P6. MULTIPLE IDENTITIES. The fluid, changing, SHAPE-SHIFTING IDENTITIES -- when our Hero assumes a disguise, when a character turns into an animal, when a god appears in human form.

P7. DIVINE PRESENCE. The SPIRITUAL ENTITY who orchestrates the Hero's World. ***** Core Self.** The FAMILIAR SPIRIT – takes a personal interest in the Hero's life. ***** Witness.** The PERVASIVE SPIRIT -- presides over the Hero's World from afar.

Page 178. Campbell Appendices

GENERAL PROCESSES

PPR1-9. PROCESSES. The SAILING SHIPS, and other MEANS OF CONVEYANCE, that carry us along the channels, trade routes, and open seas of our Growth. *** **General Processes.** The MEANS OF PROPULSION that can power any Ship – Sails, Oars, Animal Power, Steam Engine, Diesel. *** **Specific Processes.** The specific KINDS OF SHIPS – from rowboats to ocean liners.

PPR1. TRANSITION CYCLE. The Process by which we travel from ONE ISLAND TO THE NEXT – embarking, sailing, arriving at port.

PPR2. SHADOW CYCLE. When our NORMAL PASSAGE from one port to the next GOES AWRY – adverse winds, storms, a mutiny.

PPR3. ACTUALIZATION GROWTH. The NORMAL PROGRESS OF OUR VOYAGE – from one Island to the next, then the next, etc.

PPR4. RESTORATION GROWTH. GETTING BACK ON TRACK after our Ship has been blown off course.

PPR5. COLLECTIVE GROWTH. The challenges and adventures that all the Voyagers SHARE TOGETHER.

PPR6. HORIZONTAL GROWTH. The explorations that take us to VARIOUS PARTS OF THE ISLAND -- waterfront, shops, pubs.

PPR7. PERSPECTIVE GROWTH. Our story is told from MULTIPLE PERSPECTIVES -- thereby giving increased clarity and depth. *** **Inclusiveness.** A VARIETY OF CHARACTERS are presented sympathetically -- so that we can feel affinities with them all.

PPR8. EVOLUTION & INVOLUTION. Symbolically, the GREAT TREE that grows Upward & Outwards, but also Downward & Inwards. *** **Transcend & Include.** That same Tree adding new RINGS OF GROWTH to the Original Tree at its core.

PPR9. SPIRITUAL GROWTH. The WISDOM our Hero receives from a HIGHER BEING -- during a dream, vision, visitation.

B2. How the Hero's Journey Became the Life Journey. Page 179

PATHFINDERS

PF1-8. PATHFINDERS. The means by which our Voyage is Guided and Orchestrated. **Guidance.** Directing our Ship –the task of the Navigator. **Orchestration.** Arranging and Coordinating our Voyage -- the responsibility of the Captain.

PF1. PARENTS & FAMILY. The voices of our Hero's Origins. The reverberations of his Troubled Past.

PF2. SOCIETY & CULTURE. The influence exerted by any Society our Hero encounters in the course of his adventures.

PF3. HOLISTIC GROWTH SITUATION. Any Self-Contained Living Environment where our Hero pauses or dwells.

PF4. AUTHORITIES. Heroes and Legends from times past. Sacred Writings and Ancient Sayings that hold important truths.

PF5. LONG-TERM PARTNER. The Faithfulness or Treachery and Deceit of the person on whom our Hero most relies.

PF6. COUNSELOR OR THERAPIST. Anyone with Special Gifts that enable our Hero overcome Challenges or Impasses.

PF7. SPIRITUAL GUIDE. Anyone who connects our Hero with the Spirit World, or aids our Hero with supernatural insights.

PF8. MENTORS. People other than Parents, Counselors, or Spiritual Guides who Aid Our Hero in the course of his travels.

PF9. GROWTH CENTER. The Harmonious Kingdoms or Bewitching Kingdoms where our Hero pauses or dwells.

PF10. INTEGRAL LIFE GUIDE. The Wise Counselor who possesses an intimate knowledge of our Hero's four Worlds.

PF11. INTERNAL NAVIGATOR. Our Hero's Character, once he has absorbed the lessons from his many Ordeals & Trials.

PF12. PROVIDENCE. The continuing presence and influence of some Divine Being in our Hero's life. The Great Loom of Fate.

Page 180. CAMPBELL APPENDICES

B2c. From Life Journey to Hero's Journey

Once we had derived the symbolic Domains and Sectors of the Life Journey Archetype, we then applied that Model to Joseph Campbell's Hero's Journey. We asked ourselves, 'For each of the Steps in the Hero's Journey, what is the Domain and Sector it corresponds to?' Depending on how his Steps are interpreted, we found that Campbell's Hero's Journey may include at least part of over 30 Sectors and sub-Sectors (*see footnote facing page) drawn from the Life Journey Archetype – as follows:

- ✪ **Seven Dimensions** (max). Stages, Transitions, Developmental Sequence (Individual & Collective), Realms, Arenas, Trajectories, Challenges/ Impasses, and States.
- ✪ **Six Participants** (max). Self System, Individual & Collective Selves, Types, Shadow Self, Shifting Identity, Core Self/ Divine Presence.
- ✪ **Eight General Processes** (max). Transition & Shadow Cycles, Actualization & Restoration Growth, Collective Growth, Perspective Growth, Evolution & Involution, and Awakening.
- ✪ **Twelve Pathfinders** (max). Parents, Society & Culture, Holistic Growth Situations, Authorities, Long-term Partner, Counselor, Spiritual Guide, Mentor, Growth Center, Integral Life Guide, Internal Navigator, Providence.

For our derivation, we first reconfigured the Hero's Journey in our Life Journey format (p. 181). Then we compared the Hero's Journey to our Life Journey Archetype (p. 182) to locate all the parallels.

The Hero's Journey
* Seven Dimensions (max)
* Six Participants (max)
* Eight General Processes (max)
* Twelve Pathfinders (max)

Life Journey Archetype
* Eight Dimensions
* Seven Participants
* Nine General Processes
* Twelve Pathfinders

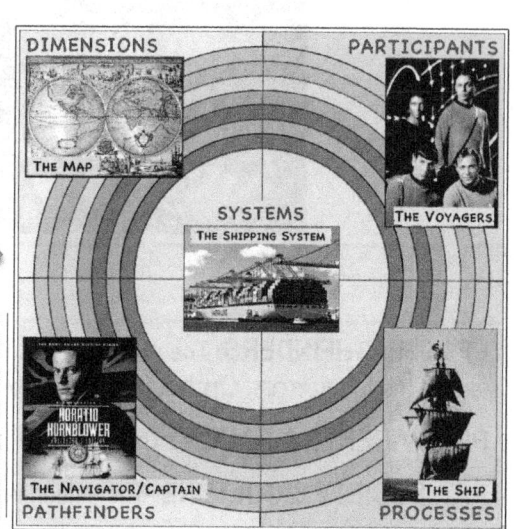

ADAPT and the Hero's Journey (1)

Consider the ADAPT version of the Hero's Journey shown on the next two facing pages (p. 180). Without becoming too analytical, scan over the table from bottom to top, refreshing your recollection of the Steps in Campbell's sequence. *** Now notice the ways Campbell's sequence is enhanced to highlight parallels to the Life Journey Archetype. *** First, direct your attention to the Steps with colored background and **black type**. These are the **Stages** (D1) in our Hero's Journey. Choose one to examine more closely: What makes it a Stage? *** Next, direct your attention to the Steps with colored background and **blue type**. These are the **Participants** and **Pathfinders** (P and PF) in our Hero's Journey. Choose one to examine more closely: What makes it a Participant or a Pathfinder? *** Next, direct your attention to the Steps with **grey background**. These are the **Transitions** (D2) of our Hero's Journey – especially the major Transitions between the Ordinary World and the Enchanted World. Choose one to examine more closely: What makes it a Transition?

B2. How the Hero's Journey Became the Life Journey. Page 181

THE HERO'S JOURNEY RECONFIGURED

In order to make meaningful comparisons, we reconfigured the Hero's Journey to conform to the format we used for the Life Journey Archetype. The results of these changes are shown on the next two facing pages.

- **Reverse the Order.** We flipped the order of Campbell's sequence, so it can be read from bottom to top – thus emphasizing the developmental nature of the sequence.

- **Change the Names.** We changed the names of certain Steps to make them more familiar and less esoteric.

- **Separate Stages from Transitions.** We separated the Steps that are Stages (D1: in color) from those that are Transitions (D2: in grey).

- **Distinguish Stages from Pathfinders.** We distinguished true Stages (Dl) from Pathfinders (PF) -- by using **blue type** for the Pathfinders.

- **Consolidate Steps.** We consolidated pairs of Steps where they represented twin aspects of the same phenomenon. 'Meeting with the Goddess' and 'Woman as Temptress' are consolidated because they represent true and false desire. 'Refusing the Return' and 'Crossing the Return Threshold' are consolidated because two sides of the Hero's ambivalence about leaving the Enchanted World.

- **Add the Ordinary World.** We added a Step at the beginning called Ordinary World – to provide the Hero with a launching place for his adventure, and to balance with the transformed Ordinary World our Hero returns to at the end of his Journey.

- **Link Trials & Ordeals.** We linked together the three sections of 'Road of Trials,' 'Culminating Ordeal,' and 'Ultimate Boon' to indicate that together they form one continuous Developmental Sequence (D1+2) – the primary locus where Growth takes place.

- **Identify Realms.** We renamed Campbell's middle section he calls 'Initiation' as the 'Enchanted World' – and identify that World as the Internal Realms of Psyche, Body, and Spirit (D3b-d). Likewise, we renamed Campbell's beginning and ending sections of 'Departure' and 'Return' as the 'Ordinary World' – and identify that World as the External Realm of Everyday Life (D3a).

- **Correspondences to ADAPT.** Perhaps most importantly, we indicated in [BOLD BRACKETS, SMALL CAPS] which Parameter of ADAPT corresponds to a given step in the Hero's Journey.

This reconfiguration of the Hero's Journey on this page is rather detailed and technical. The reader should merely be aware that we reorganized parts of the Hero's Journey to make meaningful comparisons possible. *** The analysis of the many correspondences between the Hero's Journey and the Life Journey Archetype (next two facing pages) is also somewhat detailed and technical. The reader needs merely to check out a few to be satisfied that such parallels exist.

*Footnote from facing page. The Hero's Journey is not nearly as complete as it might appear at first glance. As the table on the next page shows, each of Campbell's Steps is capable of several possible interpretations. It is only by summing up all those interpretations that we arrive at the 30+ Sectors and sub-Sectors encompassed by Campbell's Hero's Journey.

*Footnote for next two facing pages. In this table, the corresponding Parameters of ADAPT are shown in [BOLD BRACKETS, SMALL CAPS]. Where Campbell's steps are ambiguous, or open to multiple interpretations, more than one Parameter is given.

Page 182. Campbell Appendices

Life Journey to Hero's Journey: Correspondences

When Joseph Campbell's Hero's Journey is reconfigured in accordance with the ADAPT format, it turns out that every step of the Hero's Journey corresponds to a particular Domain and Sector of ADAPT. For example, Campbell's Call to Adventure (#1) is the Challenge (D7a) that initiates the Transition (D2) from the Ordinary World (D3a) to the Enchanted World (D3b-d). Likewise, the Road of Trials (#6a) is a series of Challenges (D7a), which together form a Developmental Sequence (D1+2). As this table demonstrates, **Campbell's Hero's Journey is actually a very extensive (though incomplete) version of our ADAPT Model, in its symbolic form.**

Culminating Ordeal (Step 6b). What makes Pinocchio's deliverance from Monstro the Whale his Culminating Ordeal? What was the Culminating Ordeal in The Wizard of Oz? In The Odyssey? What Culminating Ordeals have you faced in your own life?

ADAPT and the Hero's Journey (2)

Direct your attention to the Steps that are included in the <u>same</u> band of color. These are different aspects of the same Stage, Transition, or Participant. Choose one such combination to examine more closely: How are these elements linked? *** Why does Meeting with the Goddess belong with Woman As Temptress? Why does Magic Flight belong with Rescue From Without? Why do Road of Trials, Culminating Ordeal, and Ultimate Boon all belong together? *** Next, direct your attention to the <u>braided lines</u> that separate the Ordinary World from the Enchanted World. These lines separate the External Realm of Everyday Life (D3a) from the Internal Realms of Psyche, Body, and Spirit (D3b-d). *** Choose one Step from each to examine more closely: What makes it part of the Internal Realm? Of the External Realms? *** Finally, direct your attention to the items in [BOLD BRACKETS, SMALL CAPS]. These are the specific Parameters of ADAPT that correspond to a given Step in the Hero's Journey. *** Ask yourself questions like these: What makes the Call to Adventure a Transition? What makes the Belly of the Whale a Shadow Self? What makes the Culminating Ordeal a Restoration Cycle? Are there any Steps you might categorize differently? *** What other parallels do you see between the Hero's Journey and the Life Journey Archetype? In what ways (if any) do the two versions of life's journey seem different?

THE HERO'S JOURNEY: ADAPT Parallels
[read from bottom of facing page to top of this page]

ORDINARY WORLD [REALM OF EVERYDAY LIFE: D3a; TRANSFORMED SOCIETY & CULTURE: PF2]

16-17. MASTER OF TWO WORLDS, FREEDOM TO LIVE ('Return with the Elixir '). Hero returns home (or continues Journey), bearing some element of the Treasure that has the power to transform the world, as the Hero has been transformed. [Collective Developmental Sequence: DD1+2; TRAJECTORIES: D6b; CORE SELF: P7a; TRANSITION CYCLE: PPR1; Collective Growth: PPR5; Perspective Growth: PPR7; Evolution & Involution: PPR8b; Awakening: PPR9; Internal Navigator: PF11]

TRANSITION BACK TO ORDINARY WORLD (Campbell's 'Return')

13-14. MAGIC FLIGHT/RESCUE FROM WITHOUT. Escape from the Enchanted World to bring Treasure back to Ordinary World – often with Supernatural Assistance. [TRANSITION: D2; Spiritual Guide: PF7; PROVIDENCE: PF12]

12, 15. REFUSAL OF RETURN, CROSSING RETURN THRESHOLD. Having found bliss or enlightenment in Enchanted World, Hero may first choose not to return to Ordinary World, then accept it. [FAILED/ SUCCESSFUL TRANSITION: D2]

THE HERO'S JOURNEY: ADAPT Parallels (cont.)
[read from bottom of this page to top of facing page]

ENCHANTED WORLD (Campbell's 'Initiation.') [REALMS OF PSYCHE, BODY, SPIRIT: D3b-d]

11. ULTIMATE BOON (Reward for 'Culminating Ordeal'). Hero achieves the goal of his quest – the Treasure, often something Supernatural or Transcendent. [DEVELOPMENTAL SEQUENCE: D1+2, IMPASSE: D7b; RESTORATION CYCLE: PPR4]

6b. CULMINATING ORDEAL (Climax of 'Road of Trials'). After preparation on the Road of Trials, Hero faces the Ultimate Trial – the battle for the Treasure itself. Original conflicts or polarities are finally resolved. [DEVELOPMENTAL SEQUENCE: D1+2, IMPASSE: D7b; RESTORATION CYCLE: PPR4; GROWTH CENTER: PF9]

10. APOTHEOSIS. Revered person who has died reappears in spirit to provide assistance for the Ordeal. (Hero receives Divine Blessing to assure victory.) [TRANSCENDENT STATE: D8; DIVINE PRESENCE: P7; SPIRITUAL GUIDE: PF7; AWAKENING: PPR9; PROVIDENCE: PF12]

9. ATONEMENT WITH FATHER. Hero confronts, and is initiated by, Father – or whatever holds Ultimate Power in his life. (Hero proved worthy to face ultimate Ordeal.) [TYPE: P3; SHADOW SELF: P4; FATHER: PF1; AUTHORITY: PF4]

8. WOMAN AS TEMPTRESS. Hero tempted by sexual lust, or by other physical and material Temptations of Life. (False and misleading incentives and Inspirations.) [TYPE: P3; SHADOW SELF: P4; SHIFTING IDENTITY: P6A; FALSE MOTHER: PF1; FALSE PARTNER: PF5]

7. MEETING WITH GODDESS ('Love Interest'). Hero's encounter with all-powerful, all-encompassing, unconditional love – often mother or sweetheart. (Incentive and Inspiration to face Trials.) [TYPE: P3; MOTHER: PF1; PARTNER: PF5]

6a. ROAD OF TRIALS. Hero undergoes tests, tasks, challenges – often with companions, sometimes failing in at least one. [DEVELOPMENTAL SEQUENCE: D1+2; ARENAS: D4; CHALLENGES: D7a; ACTUALIZATION GROWTH: PPR3; HOLISTIC GROWTH SITUATION: PF3]

TRANSITION TO ENCHANTED WORLD (Campbell's 'Departure')

5. BELLY OF WHALE. Hero undergoes dark night of the soul, death and rebirth. (Wrenching Transformation that prepares the Hero psychologically and spiritually to enter the Enchanted World.) [IMPASSE: D7b; SHADOW SELF: P4; RESTORATION CYCLE: PPR4]

4. CROSSING FIRST THRESHOLD. Hero commits to leaving the safe, familiar Ordinary World for the dangerous, mysterious Enchanted World. [TRANSITION: D2; SUCCESSFUL CHALLENGE: D7a]

3. SUPERNATURAL AID ('Mentor'). A seasoned traveler of the Enchanted World appears to give the Hero training, guidance, talismans, or advice that will help on the journey. (Support for entry into the Enchanted World.) [TYPE: P3; SHIFTING IDENTITY: P6a; AUTHORITY: PF4; COUNSELOR: PF6; SPIRITUAL GUIDE: PF7; MENTOR: PF8; INTEGRAL LIFE GUIDE: PF10]

2. REFUSAL OF CALL. Because of fear, duty, inadequacy, etc., Hero tries to turn away from the adventure. [FAILED TRANSITION: D2; FAILED CHALLENGE: D7a]

1. CALL TO ADVENTURE. Something shakes up the situation, external or within, so Hero must face the beginnings of change. [TRANSITION: D2; CHALLENGE: D7a]

ORDINARY WORLD [REALM OF EVERYDAY LIFE: D3a; SOCIETY & CULTURE: PF2]

0. THE ORDINARY WORLD. Mundane world of ordinary reality. Some kind of polarity in Hero's life is pulling in different directions and causing stress.

Appendix B3a.
HOMER'S *THE ODYSSEY*: SYNOPSIS

The Odyssey of Homer is widely recognized as the greatest literary metaphor for man's journey through life. Like many epics, *The Odyssey* represents the Integral vision of its time. Although circumstances and interpretations have changed dramatically, the basic Domains and Sectors of the Integral vision have not. Thus, *The Odyssey* contains a remarkably complete array of the same Dimensions, Participants, Processes, and Pathfinders found in ADAPT.

Beginning on page 188 (Appx B3b), we will trace the many parallels between ADAPT and *The Odyssey*. But to refresh your memory of *The Odyssey* before we begin those comparisons, we first present a brief synopsis of the story. Characters or situations that are referred to, or pertain to, our ADAPT Model are **bolded** or [bracketed].

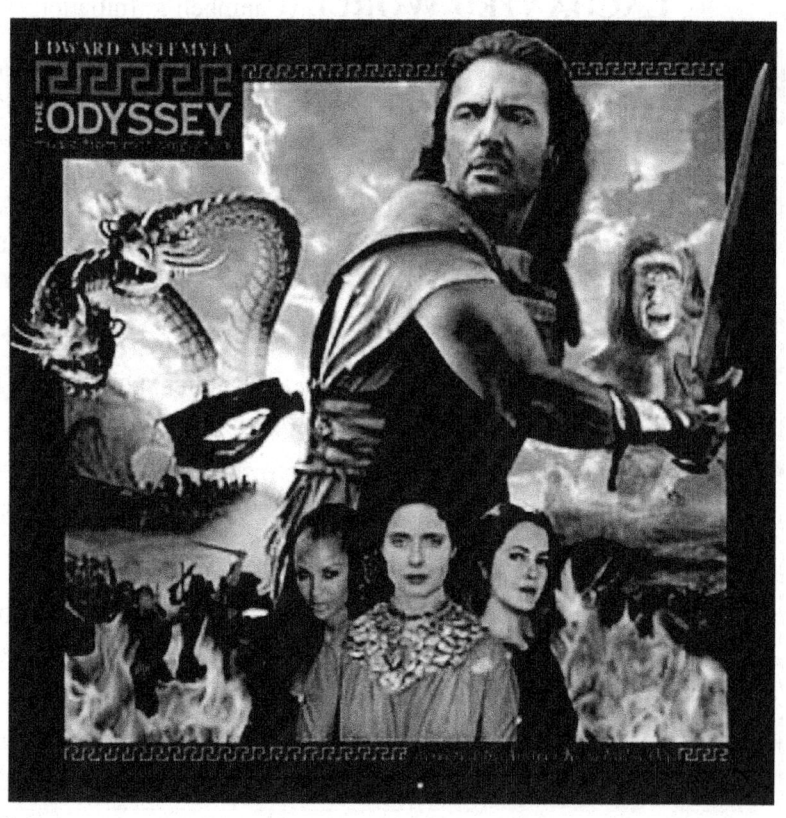

These parallels demonstrate that **the Life Journey Archetype (Appx B2) accounts for all the major features of a myth or epic – far more features than are described through Campbell's Hero's Journey (Appx B1).**

Explorations in *The Odyssey*

Even before your read Homer's *The Odyssey* (or reread it), read this synopsis – with a focus on its literary elements. *** In your initial reading of the synopsis, just pay attention to the story, and enjoy its narrative flow. What happened in Troy? What happens on the way back to Ithaca? What happens after Odysseus returns to Ithaca? *** Read through the synopsis a second time – this time with a focus on the Characters. Who are the main Characters? The supporting Characters? The supernatural Characters? The Groups of Characters? What are the Relationships between Characters? What part does each Character (or Group) play in the story? *** Read through the synopsis again – this time with a focus on the magical or supernatural elements. How do these affect the story? *** Continue in the same vein, until you have explored all the elements of the story you can think of. *** Now that you are well-prepared, read Homer's *The Odyssey* itself. We recommend a translation written in easily-accessible, engaging language: The Rouse version, for example. *** Where available, listen to an audio version of the same translation – such as the one read by a great interpreter, Nadia May. *** As you read, forget about all the Explorations and analyses you have just gone through. Immerse yourself in the story, and enjoy its flow of action. Allow any interpretations to arise spontaneously and intuitively as the story progresses.

The Odyssey, by Homer

After an **invocation to the Muse** of poetry, the epic begins *in medias res* ("in the middle of things"). **[ORDINARY WORLD: Life Passages:] Odysseus** has been gone from Ithaca for about 20 years—the first ten spent fighting the **Trojan War**, the last ten trying to **get home**. Meanwhile, Odysseus' wife, **Penelope**, tries to fend off a multitude of **Suitors** who have invaded the royal palace, seeking her hand in marriage (and a chance of ruling Ithaca), and indulging in great amounts of food and wine at the hosts' expense. **Telemachus**, son of Odysseus and Penelope, is just coming of age (he is approximately 21) and is at a loss as to what to do about the Suitors. Mother and son yearn for Odysseus' return.

The first four books deal with Telemachus' struggles at home. (In fact, Odysseus does not appear in the epic until Book 5.) **[Life Passages:]** A secondary plot in *The Odyssey* is **Telemachus' coming of age**, his own quest, which scholars sometimes refer to as the "Telemacheia." The goddess **Athena** appears to the young prince in disguise and advises him to gather an assembly of the island's leaders to protest the invasion of the Suitors. Soon after, he is to visit **King Nestor** of **Pylos** and **King Menelaus** of **Sparta**, old comrades of his father's, to gather from them any new of Odysseus. At the assembly, the two leading **Suitors**—the aggressive **Antinous** and the smooth-talking **Eurymachus**—confront the prince. They accuse Penelope of delaying too long in her choice of a new husband. Telemachus speaks well but accomplishes little at the **assembly** because the Suitors are from some of the strongest families in the area and are impatient with Penelope's delays. (Penelope has promised decide on a new husband once she has completed a **Weaving** for her father-in-law. However, she unravels at night any weaving she has completed during the day.)

As Telemachus secretly sets off for Pylos and Sparta, the Suitors plot to assassinate him. At Pylos, Telemachus learns little of his father but is encouraged to visit Sparta where King Menelaus reports that Odysseus is alive but held captive by the goddess nymph **Calypso**.

Homer leaves the story of Telemachus as the Suitors are about to ambush his ship on its return to Ithaca. **[ENCHANTED WORLD. Transition to Psyche Passages:]** At Athena's urging, the gods have decided to free Odysseus from Calypso. **Hermes**, the messenger god, delivers the order to Odysseus' captor. Odysseus has spent seven years with the goddess, sleeping with her at night and pining for his home and family during the day. **Calypso** is a beautiful, lustful nymph who wants to marry Odysseus and grant him immortality, but he longs for Penelope and Ithaca. Reluctantly, Calypso sends Odysseus on his way. **Poseidon**, the sea god, spots the wayfarer and, seeking revenge because Odysseus blinded Poseidon's son Cyclops, shipwrecks Odysseus on **Phaeacia**, which is ruled by **King Alcinous**. **[BORDERLINE ORDINARY WORLD]** The Phaeacians, civilized and hospitable people, welcome the stranger and encourage him to tell of his adventures.

Through Odysseus' narration, the reader goes back 10 years and hears his tale. Known as "The **Wanderings of Odysseus**," this section is the most famous of the epic. **[ORDINARY WORLD: Life Passages:]** At the end of the Trojan War, Odysseus and his men sail first to the land of the **Cicones**. The Greeks succeed in raiding the central city but linger too long and are routed by a reserve force. Hoping to sail directly home, the flotilla instead encounters a **severe storm**, brought on by Athena, that blows them far off course to the land of the **Lotus-eaters**. **[ENCHANTED WORLD. Psyche/ Body/ Spirit Passages:]** These are not hostile people, but eating the lotus plant removes memory and ambition; Odysseus is barely able to pull his men away and resume the journey. Curiosity compels Odysseus to explore the land of the **Cyclops**, a race of uncivilized, cannibalistic, one-eyed giants. One of them, Polyphemus (also known simply as "Cyclops"), traps Odysseus' scouting party in his cave. To escape, Odysseus blinds the one-eyed monster, incurring the wrath of the giant's father, **Poseidon**. Odysseus next visits the Island of **Aeolus**, the wind god. Initially, Aeolus is a friendly host. He captures all **adverse winds** and bags them for Odysseus, who is thus able to sail within sight of Ithaca. Unfortunately, Odysseus' **men** suspect that the bag holds treasure and open it while Odysseus sleeps. The troublesome winds blow the party back to Aeolus, who wants no more to do with them, speculating that they must be cursed by the gods. Their next hosts, the cannibalistic **Laestrygonians**, sink all the ships but Odysseus's in a surprise attack. The remaining Greeks reach Aeaea, home of the beautiful enchantress **Circe**, who turns several of the crew into **pigs**. With a potion from **Hermes**, Odysseus cleverly defeats Circe and becomes her lover. She lifts the spell from his men and aids in the group's eventual departure a year later, advising Odysseus that he must sail to the **Land of the Dead**. There, he receives various **Greek heroes** including a dolorous **Achilles**, a visit from his now-deceased **mother**, and important prophecies from the seer **Tiresias** – especially a warning not to eat the cattle the sungod, and an indication that he will triumph over the Suitors. Odysseus resumes his journey. Next, Odysseus survives the **Sirens** by having himself tied to the ship's mast while he listens to their tempting **Songs**. Next, Odysseus' ship passes between the boiling vortex of Carybdis and the cliffs of six-headed **Scylla**, where he loses six men to the monster. Odysseus and his crew arrive at the island of the **Sungod Helios**. Despite Tiresias' severe warnings, the men feast on the **cattle of the Sungod** during Odysseus' brief absence. **Zeus** is outraged and **destroys the ship** as the Greeks depart, killing all but Odysseus, who is washed ashore at **Calypso's Island**, where he stays until released seven years later.

[**BORDERLINE ORDINARY WORLD. Transition to Life Passages:**] The story of his adventures finished, Odysseus receives the admiration and gifts of the **Phaeacians** who follow their tradition of returning wayfaring strangers to their homelands by sailing him to Ithaca.

[**ORDINARY WORLD. Life Passages:**] Meanwhile, **Athena** helps Telemachus avoid the Suitors' ambush and arranges for him to meet his father at their pig farm not far from the palace. Reunited with his son and with the assistance of Athena and his faithful swineherd **Eumaeus**, Odysseus returns to his **home palace** disguised as a **beggar**. For the time, he resists striking back at the Suitors who insult and assault him. Penelope seems at least suspicious that he is her husband, but it is **Eurycleia**, a loyal nurse who cared for Odysseus when he was a child, who has no doubt of his identity as she discovers an old scar on his leg when she bathes him. Penelope arranges a contest, vowing to wed any man who can string the **Great Bow of Odysseus** and shoot an arrow through a dozen axes as he used to do. The Suitors all fail. Only the Old Beggar performs the feat, whereby he is dramatically revealed as Odysseus himself. With deft planning, Odysseus and Telemachus sequester the Suitors' weapons and bar the door of the banquet room, thereby preparing them for slaughter. Odysseus wreaks havoc with the Great Bow, and all the Suitors are wiped out. Odysseus and Penelope are reunited. Odysseus travel to his family's farm and reunite with his aging and ineffectual **father, Laertes**.

[**Integration of Psyche, Spirit, & Life Passages:**] Athena makes **peace** with the Suitors' vengeful friends and families, avoiding civil war. Social order and harmony has been restored to Odysseus' home and to the Kingdom of Ithaca.

Challenge: Odysseus in Cyclops's Cave. When Odysseus is trapped by the Cyclops, he masquerades his men as sheep, so Cyclops will let them pass out of the cave. No matter how difficult the Challenge (D7a), Odysseus is 'never at a loss.' (PPR3)

Impasse: Odysseus in Calypso's Cave. When Odysseus is enchanted by the sensual delights of Calypso, he is truly imprisoned (D7b) – and can only escape with the aid of his Guardian Angel, the goddess Athena. (PPR4)

Appendix B3b.
ADAPT AND HOMER'S *THE ODYSSEY*: PARALLELS

Homer's *The Odyssey* is perhaps the premier literary example of the Hero's Journey. However, *The Odyssey* was also especially important to the creation of this book -- because it was our bridge between our conceptual ADAPT Model and our symbolic Life Journey Archetype. To derive the Life Journey from ADAPT, we actually went through two steps:

ADAPT to *Odyssey*. We first asked: 'If the ADAPT Model consists of five Domains and several Sectors within each Domain, what are the symbolic or mythic equivalents to those features in Homer's *The Odyssey*?' Thus, the Stages of ADAPT are the Enchanted Islands of *The Odyssey*. The Transitions of ADAPT are the treacherous Open Seas between Islands in *The Odyssey*. The Developmental Sequence of ADAPT is Odysseus's Voyage from Island to Island, until he finally reaches his destination in Ithaca. And so forth.

***Odyssey* to Life Journey.** We then asked: 'If Homer's *The Odyssey* has a set of symbolic equivalents to the ADAPT Model, what is the more general Archetype of which *The Odyssey* is an example. Thus, the Island of The Odyssey becomes any location where our Hero pauses in his travels, and sets up a life. The Open Seas of The Odyssey become the turbulent risks and dangers our Hero must face on the way to his next Safe Haven. The Sea Voyage becomes any literal or figurative Travel Experience our Hero must take to reach his Ultimate Destination. And so forth.

In this section, we outline what we discovered in the first of these two steps: The many parallels between the ADAPT Model and Homer's *The Odyssey*.

The Odyssey as a Life Journey

Refer back to the Domains and Sectors of the Life Journey Archetype (Appx B2a-b). Explore the many parallels between this Archetype and the story of Odysseus. *** First, scan through the eight Dimensions. Select one Dimension for further exploration: Stages, for example. *** <u>Before you look at our answers</u>, ask yourself questions like these: What parts of Odysseus's Journey represents the Stages? If your answer is 'Islands,' what Islands does Odysseus visit on his way home? How do the various Islands differ? What tests of character are presented to Odysseus at each new Island? *** Select another Dimension, and ask similar questions. ***
Once you have explored all the Dimensions you care to, turn to the interpretations we ourselves have made on the following pages. Ask yourself questions like these: Where does our interpretation differ from yours? What have you (or we) left out? How could our interpretations (or yours) be improved upon? *** After you've finished with Dimensions, move on to Participants, then General Processes, then Pathfinders. In each case, select one or more Parameters, and ask yourself similar questions. Again, compare your interpretations to our own. ***
After you have finished all this analysis, forget what you've learned. Let all these interpretations to slip from your conscious mind. *** The next time you read through passages of *The Odyssey*, allow the meaning and significance of this great epic to rise up of its own accord. As you immerse yourself in this classic story, become your own Odysseus – facing and overcoming the Challenges that build your character -- finally returning, chastened and matured, to reclaim your true home.

Dimensions

D. Growth. Growth is the entire series of adventures Odysseus engages in throughout the course of *The Odyssey* – both in the Ordinary Worlds of Troy and Ithaca, as well as the Enchanted World of the Enchanted Islands.

D. The Growth Continuum. The Growth Continuum is a Map that outlines the entire set of islands, kingdoms, open seas, and subterranean depths that Odysseus visits in the course of his Journeys.

D. Dimensions. The Dimensions are the coordinates and other features of that Map of the Growth Continuum.

D1. Stages. The Stages are the Islands Odysseus chances upon in the course of his Journey. Here, he must outsmart the Cyclops, or extricate himself from the seductive wiles of Circe, before he can continue on his travels.

D2. Transitions. The Transitions are the treacherous seas Odysseus must cross to reach the next island. Here, his ship may be blown off course, be thrashed with storms by some wrathful god, be tempted by alluring but deadly Sirens, or be sent careening between two grim choices like the man-devouring Scylla and the roiling vortex of Charybdis.

D1+2. Developmental Sequence. The Developmental Sequence is the entire course of Odysseus' Journey. He must sail from one island to the next, encountering many harrowing dangers and tempting diversions, before he finally touches land in his home country.

D1+2b. Developmental Sequences – External & Internal. The External Developmental Sequences describes Odysseus' adventures in Everyday Reality – while still in Troy, or after returning to Ithaca. The Internal Developmental Sequences describes Odysseus' adventures in the Enchanted World – the magic islands, the underworld, the world of the gods (D3).

D1+2c. Developmental Sequences – The Chakras. The Chakras are the seven different types of Worlds Odysseus encounters – one focused on mere survival, another on sensual pleasure, another on brute power, another on false love, etc.

DD1+2. Developmental Sequences – Collective. The Collective Developmental Sequence is the Journey Odysseus and his crew share together. It is also the dynamics of Odysseus' Relationship with Penelope. On a broader scale, it is the upheavals of Odysseus' kingdom in Ithaca, and their subsequent resolution.

D3. Realms. The Realms are the four Worlds that Odysseus explores in the course of his adventures. His journey takes him from everyday reality of Troy (Life), through a series of Enchanted Islands (Psyche), down into the Underworld of the dead (Body), into contact with the divine world of the gods (Spirit), and then back to everyday, material reality of Ithaca (Life).

D4. Arenas. The Arenas are the various places of activity within the ports of call that Odysseus visits. In Ithaca, the Arenas are the special settings where each part of the story takes place -- the coastline, the countryside, the herdsman's hut, the public square, the palace, the banquet hall, the weapons room, the sleeping chamber.

D4d2. The Hero's Journey. The Hero's Journey is the Homer's archetypal story line, of which the story of Odysseus is a foremost example.

D5a. Perspectives. The Perspectives are the various points of view from which Homer tells his story – sometimes as an omniscient narrator, sometimes from a character like Odysseus or Telemachus, sometimes from the perspective of a god or of a denizen of the Underworld.

D5b. Paths. Odysseus' journey encompasses all four Paths. Sometimes, he travels individually, sometimes as part of a crew of intrepid sailors. Sometimes he travels through internal worlds (magic islands, dead spirits, gods) –sometimes through external worlds (the battlefields of Troy, his home in Ithaca).

D6. Polarities. The Polarities are represented by Odysseus and Penelope, Troy and Ithaca, Mount Olympus and the Underworld, men and swine

D6a. Directions. Odysseus ventures outward to explore islands of magic and enchantment, then inward to experience the cave of the Cyclops – upward to commune with the gods, then downward to plumb the depths of the Underworld.

D6b. Trajectories. Earlier in life, Odysseus travels outward -- to his *Iliad* of fame, glory, and conquest. Later in life, he travels inward – toward his *Odyssey* of loyalty, commitment, self-discovery, and home-coming.

D7. Impediments. The Impediments are all the factors that prevent Odysseus from returning home.

D7a. Limitations. Limitations are the temporary obstructions Odysseus must overcome or circumvent. They are the adverse winds that blow his ship off course, the conspiracies of his rebellious crew, the mind-numbing stupor of the Lotus Eaters, the huge stones thrown by angry Laestrygonian giants attempting to sink his ship, the enticing songs of the Sirens, and the treacherous channel between the blood-thirsty Scylla and the yawning vortex of Charybdis.

D7b. Impasses. For Odysseus, Impasses are the more permanent conditions that imprison or defeat him – sometimes requiring divine intervention. They are the captivity in the grisly cave of man-devouring Cyclops, the bewitching enchantments of Circe that turn his crew into animals, the soul-searing descent into the Underworld, the irresistible charms of Calypso's cave, the rage of the Sun God when his cattle are devoured, the storms of vengeful Poseidon that finally sink his ship and destroy his crew.

D8. Transcendent States. The Transcendent States are the visitations, edicts, and guidance Odysseus receives from Athena, from Hermes, from Poseidon, and from Zeus.

D8a. Romantic Fallacy. The Romantic Fallacy is reflected in the temptations offered by the Lotus Eaters, the enchantment of Circe's Cave, and the allurements of Calypso's Island – all 'tender traps,' where an apparent paradise diverts Odysseus from returning to his true home.

D8b. Inverse Romantic Fallacy. The Inverse Romantic Fallacy is reflected in Penelope's Suitors, who scoff at the power of the gods punish them for their ill behavior. It is also reflected in Odysseus' arrogant taunts at the Cyclops, which incite the offended Poseidon to take revenge.

Participants

P. Participants. The Participants are Odysseus and his crew. They are also the other characters in the story – Penelope, Telemachus, the Suitors, the demi-gods on the islands, the gods on Olympus.

P1a. Experienced Self. The Experienced Self is Odysseus in the midst of his adventures – the hero acting without self-conscious awareness.

P1b. Observed Self. The Observed Self is Odysseus in the banquet hall of the Phaecians – regaling the king with his adventures on the Enchanted Islands.

P2a. Individual Self. The Individual Selves are all the actors in the story whose character is delineated individually: Odysseus, his wife Penelope, his son Telemachus, the kings of Pylos and Sparta, the evil Suitor Antinous.

P2b. Collective Self. The Collective Selves are the actors in the story whose character is delineated only as a group: The impetuous crewmen of Odysseus' ship, the Ithaca townsfolk who react to controversy, the collection of other Suitors who carouse in the banquet hall.

P3. Types. Types are the actors in the story, as defined by their character type: Odysseus the fearless leader, Penelope the faithful wife, Telemachus the dutiful son, Mentor the trusted advisor, Antinous the evil schemer.

P3. Persona. The Personae are the various identities or guises a character may put on to convince, or trick, or mislead someone: The guise Athena puts on when giving advice to young Telemachus. The disguise of lowly Beggar that Odysseus wears to enter the palace before the final battle. At a more literal level, the Persona is the noble image Odysseus presents to portray himself to the Phaecians as a courageous hero. It is the convivial image Odysseus presents to the Cyclops to convince him to drink wine.

P3a. Gender Types. *The Odyssey* is built upon the archetypal Gender Types of Male and Female, in the form of Odysseus and Penelope. Both are going through a kind of Mid-Life Passage, but in uniquely male and female ways.

P3b. Enneagram Types. *The Odyssey* is filled with classic Enneagram Types: Odysseus the Achiever (#3), Penelope the Helper (#2), Telemachus the Loyalist (#6), Antinous the Challenger (#8), Circe the Individualist (#4), etc.

P3c. Birth-Order Types. Telemachus is a classic First Son – imbued with a drive to live up to his father, and carry on his tradition.

P3d. Ehnic Types. The strange peoples Odysseus encounters on his adventures – the Cicones, the Lotus Eaters, the Laestrygonians – are portrayed as ethnic groups with values and behaviors much different from the Greeks. By contrast, the courts of Pylos and Sparta encountered by Telemachus exemplify an ideal form of Greek culture.

P4. Shadow Self. The Shadow Self is any factor that causes the Journey to go wrong, or throws the society out of joint: The rapacious Suitors, who throw Odysseus's kingdom into turmoil. The jealous sailors, who unleash the bag of winds that blows Odysseus's ship off its intended course. Also, the bullying Cyclops, the vengeful Poseidon, the enticing Circe, the alluring Sirens, and the six-headed monsters of Scylla.

P5. Functional Constituents. Prominent character traits or Functional Constituents are often represented by the gods or demi-gods. Wise Athena represents (in part) the Rational, wrathful Poseidon the Volitional, seductive Circe the Creative, winged Hermes the Intersubjective, impulsive Cyclops the Instinctive, presiding Zeus the Integrative.

P6. Multiple Identities. In *The* Odyssey, Multiple Identities are the various ways characters shift or expand their Identity.

P6a. Shifting Identity. Odysseus himself is the great shape-shifter – the character who can assume whatever Identity is needed to prevail in a situation. In his disguise as an old beggar, he infiltrates the Ithacan court and prepares for the ultimate battle. Athena likewise appears as Mentor, and in numerous other disguises. Circe is an enchantress who shifts the Identities of others – by transforming the crew into their base animal nature. The ultimate shape-shifter is the demigod Proteus, referred to by Menelaus when Telemachus visits Sparta.

P6b. Broadening Identity. Broadening Identity is Odysseus' progress toward maturity. Over the course of his adventure, Odysseus broadens from pure self-interest, to concern for his crew, to concern for his wife and son, to concern for his kingdom, to concern for his relationship with the gods.

P7. Divine Presence. The Divine Presence is the pervasive presence of gods and demi-gods that inhabit or influence the world of mortals.

P7a. Core Self. For Odysseus, the Core Self is Odysseus' patron goddess -- the little voice that whispers in Odysseus' ear when he most needs guidance and support.

P7b. Witness. For Odysseus, the Witness is Zeus – the all-powerful deity who presides over both Mount Olympus and the mortal world below. The conduit of communication between those two worlds is Hermes – the god who transmits messages between Odysseus and Mount Olympus.

Processes

PR & PPR. Processes. The Processes are the sailing ships and other modes of transportation that carry Odysseus on his circuitous route from Troy to Ithaca.

PPR. GENERAL PROCESSES

PPR. General Processes. The General Processes are the various means of propulsion for those modes of transportation: Sail, oars, horse power, running and walking.

PPR1. Transition Cycle. The Transition Cycle is Odysseus' normal process of travel: Departing from one island, sailing the open seas, the establishing himself at the next island.

PPR2. Shadow Cycle. The Shadow Cycle occurs when Odysseus' normal progress from one island to the next goes awry: When he is imprisoned in the grisly cave of the Cyclops. When his ship is blown off-course when his crew unleashes the winds of Aeolus. When his men are transformed into pigs by the enchantress Circe. When his ship is wrecked after the crew eats the cattle of the sun god. When he is trapped in the cave of Calypso.

PPR3. Actualization Growth. Actualization Growth is the normal forward progress of Odysseus' journey – from one Enchanted Island to the next, as he gets closer and closer to his home destination.

PPR4. Restoration Growth. Restoration Growth is Odysseus' process of getting back on course after his progress has been diverted: His clever escape the cave of the Cyclops under the bellies of sheep. His seduction of Circe to convince her to relinquish her spell. The intervention by Athena that frees him from Calypso's cave. The dream-like voyage from the idyllic Phaecia back to the harsh reality of Ithaca. Restoration Growth is also Odysseus' descent into the lugubrious Land of the Dead to confront his own mortality -- followed by his reemergence at the surface with a renewed commitment to live.

PPR5. Collective Growth. Symbolically, Collective Growth is the series of voyages that Odysseus and his crew take together. It is the victory at Troy that the whole Greek army partakes in together. In a more literal sense, Collective Growth is the Restoration of the Kingdom of Ithaca – where the disruptions that originated with the Trojan War must be purged, before normal Actualization can resume. Ultimately, Collective Growth is the relinquishment of Ithaca's militant adventurism, in exchange for a peaceful pastoral society.

PPR5aa. Generation Cycle. The Generation Cycle is the progression of four Generations of men depicted in *The Odyssey*: The crafty Odysseus (Gen 3, Civic), harkens back to the heroes of old

(Gen 1, Prophetic), protects his ineffectual father (Gen 2, Reactive), and inspires his dutiful son (Gen 4, Bureaucratic).

PPR6. Horizontal Growth. Symbolically, Horizontal Growth is exploring various areas of a given location – the countryside of Ithaca, the palace grounds, the courtyard, the dining hall, the bedchamber. In a more literal sense, Horizontal Growth is the Growth that takes place in a character without leaving a given location.

PPR6a. Improvement & Translation. Improvement & Translation is the Growth in maturity and self-confidence that occurs for Telemachus in Pylos and Sparta, the Growth while remaining within the sphere of the Greek worlds. It is the Growth in constancy and commitment that occurs in Penelope in the course of defending herself against the siege of the Suitors.

PPR6a. Equivalence. Equivalence is the parallel Growth of Odysseus and Penelope – both going through a sort of Mid-Life, but each doing so in a Style that is typically Male and Female.

PPR7a. Perspective Growth: Fundamental Perspectives. [Discussed under D5a]

PPR7b. Perspective Growth: Inclusiveness. [Discussed under P6b]

PPR8a. Evolution & Involution: Transcend & Include. By traveling through the Enchanted Islands, Odysseus consorts with gods and demi-gods – thereby Transcending his mentality as a mere mortal. By consciously deciding to relinquish the immortality available to him on Calypso's Island, Odysseus returns home to share his new perspectives with family and country – thereby Including his previous Self in his present one.

PPR8b. Evolution & Involution: Life Trajectories. [Discussed under D6b]

PPR8c. Evolution & Involution: Gender Types. Odysseus as the prototypical Male takes the Outward Path of action and adventure. Penelope as the prototypical Female takes the Inward Path of domesticity and self-reflection.

PPR9. Spiritual Growth: Awakening. Symbolically, Odysseus sees through Athena's disguise as mentor to discover the real goddess underneath. Penelope sees through Odysseus' disguise as the Old Beggar to discover the savior/hero underneath. In a more literal sense, every time Odysseus awakens from sleep or dream, he sees the world with new clarity, or from a new perspective: When he awakens in Calypso's cave after the wreck of his ship and the destruction of his crew. When he awakens on the beach in Phaecia after Athena aids his escape from Calypso's cave. When he awakens on the beach in Ithaca, after his dream-voyage from Phaecia. From a deeper perspective, the messages Odysseus receives from the dead souls in the Underworld are a profound Awakening: Especially the lament of Achilles that he would rather be obscure and alive, rather than famous and dead.

PR. SPECIFIC PROCESSES

PR. Specific Processes. Symbolically, the Specific Processes are the specific kinds of transportation Odysseus uses to reach his destination. Odysseus' main vehicle is his trusty sailing ship. But other, more subtle 'vehicles' facilitate his journey: The prayers and offerings in the ideal kingdoms of Pylos, Sparta, and Phaecia that invoke the blessings of the gods. The clever stratagem that enables Odysseus to escape from Cyclops' cave. Hermes' miraculous potion that neutralizes Circe's charms. The ghoulish rituals that allow Odysseus to enter the World of the Dead. The cords that bind Odysseus to the mast, so he won't succumb to the Siren's beguiling call. The healing hospitality of the Phaecians that nurses Odysseus back to health after his shipwreck. The Great Bow that slaughters the rapacious Suitors. Athena's pact of peace that placates the gods and heals civil strife.

In the interest of space, we give examples from just one Specific Process in each of the seven categories:

PR1-6. Nurturing & Bonding (#3). Nurturing & Bond Processes are shown in the yearning of Odysseus and Penelope for each other, in the loyalty and teamwork of Odysseus and Telemachus as they dispatch the evil Suitors, in the tender bathing of Odysseus by his childhood nurse, Eurycleia.

PR7-10. Life Experience (#9). Life Experience Processes are shown in the visits by young Telemachus to the kingdoms of Pylos and Sparta to learn about harmonious societies. They are also shown in the final battle, where Telemachus learns from his father how to become a man.

PR11-17. Acculturation (#16). Acculturation Processes are shown in the many island societies Odysseus must become familiar with and adjust to: The enticing Lotus Eaters, the cannibalistic Laestrygonians, the brutal Cyclops, the seductiveness of Circe's Island, the dismal Land of the Dead.

PR18-23. Planning & Orchestration (#22). Planning & Orchestration Processes are shown in the complex strategy to trap the Suitors in the banquet hall for the final battle: Establishing their guilt in advance. Feeding their pride and vanity. Neutralizing their natural caution. Making the women and servants safe. Sequestering the weapons. Preparing the Great Bow. Barring the dining hall doors. Inciting alarm and panic to intensify the slaughter. Destroying without mercy.

PR24-28. Expressive Arts (#28). Expressive Arts Processes are shown in the entertainments presented to Telemachus and Odysseus on their visits to harmonious kingdoms. In Ithaca: The recitations by the Bard. In Pylos: The sacrificial ritual to Athena. In Sparta: The singers and dancers at the feast; the libation cup and weaving offered by Menelaus and Helen. In Phaecia: The multitude of mantles, tunics, cups, and swords given to Odysseus by various guests; the Olympian Games choreographed like a graceful dance.

PR29-33. Introspection & Self-Awareness (#30). Introspection & Self-Awareness Processes are shown in Odysseus' visit to the Underworld – when he must reflect on the brevity of life (his dead mother) and the fleeting pleasures of fame (Achilles). Symbolically, they are shown by occasions where Odysseus is visited by Athena – the personification of the inner workings of his mind.

PR34-35. Holistic Environments (#34). Holistic Environments Processes are shown in Telemachus' visits to Pylos and Sparta -- where he can contrast these harmonious societies to the turmoil that engulfs Ithaca. They are shown in Odysseus' visit to Phaecia, where our hero recollects what Ithaca must again become.

Pathfinders
SOCIETAL GUIDANCE

T. Guidance & Orchestration. For Odysseus, Guidance represents all the ways his ship is navigated and his adventure is guided. Orchestration represents the ways Odysseus himself (and his attendant goddess Athena) organizes and coordinates the various aspects of his voyage.

T1. Parents. Telemachus' character is shaped most by his devoted and concerned Parents, Odysseus and Penelope. Odysseus himself has a weak father (Laertes), and thus must learn male maturity through the experience of his adventures. The Suitors are unruly and lawless young men, who lack guidance because their fathers have been away fighting the Trojan War.

T2. Society & Culture. Telemachus' values and convictions are deeply influenced by the negative example of Ithaca and the positive examples of the harmonious kingdoms of Pylos and Sparta. Before returning to the turmoil of Ithaca, Odysseus is reminded by the idyllic Phaecia what a harmonious society should look like. Throughout Odysseus's voyage, the Ship's Crew represents a Society that influences Odysseus, and on whom he exerts influence.

T3. Holistic Growth Situation. For Odysseus, the whole journey through the Enchanted Islands serves as one great Holistic Growth Situation, whose challenges continuously work to improve his character. Although violent, the great battle with the Suitors is an ideal Holistic Growth Situation for Telemachus. Its success requires many different Growth skills directed toward a specific end. Throughout Odysseus's voyage, life aboard ship is a Holistic Growth Situation that encompasses every element of life in one small vessel.

T4. Authorities. For Odysseus, the Authorities are the gods and heroes from myths and legends. For Telemachus, the supreme Authority is Odysseus himself.

INDIVIDUAL GUIDANCE

T5. Long-Term Partner. For both Odysseus and Penelope, their devotion to their Long-Term Partner carries them through times of anguish and tribulation, when all seems hopeless.

T6. Counselor or Therapist. To decide upon the best course of action, Odysseus and Telemachus repeatedly draw upon the wisdom and experience of Counselors – especially wise Mentor and the dead prophet Tiresias.

T7. Spiritual Guide. When human prowess is not enough, Odysseus relies on the guidance and support of the goddess Athena. That goddess in turn serves as intercessor to the vengeful Poseidon and the all-powerful Zeus.

T8. Mentors. Aside from Counselors and Gods, Odysseus draws wisdom and guidance from other sources: From the king of harmonious Phaecia. From the swineherd Eumaeus, who warns Odysseus of the dangers he will face in Ithaca. From his nurse Eurycleia, who shields his identity from the Suitors. Odysseus' crew receives false counsel from their fellow crew members: When they seek to linger in the land of the Lotus Eaters. When they open the bag of adverse winds, hoping to find treasure. When they succumb to the seductive charms of Circe, and become swine. And finally, when they satiate their hunger on the cattle of the Sun God, thereby initiating their own destruction.

T9. Growth Centers. Much like modern-day Growth Centers, the harmonious kingdoms of Pylos, Sparta, and Phaecia offered a banquet of Growth opportunities – nourishing foods, entrancing entertainment, engaging competitions, valuable advice, and deep rest.

T10. Integral Life Guide. The goddess Athena is the ideal Integral Life Guide -- since she is omniscient, and since she involves herself in every aspect of Odysseus' progress. In a broader sense, the supreme god Zeus is the Integral Life Guide for the whole universe, since he is in charge of everything.

INTERNAL GUIDANCE

T11. Internal Navigator. Over the course of the story, Telemachus absorbs all forms of external Guidance. By the end, he is well on the way to becoming his own Internal Navigator. Odysseus begin the story with an Internal Navigator that is already strong – yet even he is blown off course until he humbles himself before the will of the gods. Odysseus is ready to perform the ritual sacrifice of the Suitors only after his own Internal Navigator has been purified through Ordeals & Trials.

T12. Providence. Throughout *The Odyssey*, Providence is almost always active – either directly, in the form of Athena or other gods, or indirectly in the form auguries and omens. When Odysseus is most in need, Athena directs Providence in his favor. Odysseus is left in despair only when Providence appears to desert him (as in the cave of Calypso), or when he defies the workings of Providence (as in his sacrilegious taunts at the Cyclops, that bring forth the wrath of Poseidon). Symbolically, the workings of Providence and Fate are represented by the Great Loom Penelope uses to weave Laertes' winding sheet – the strands of life, leading ultimately to the cloak of death.

Page 196. Wilber + Campbell Appendices

WILBER & CAMPBELL APPENDICES

How the ADAPT Model (from Wilber) and the Life Journey Archetype (from Campbell) combine to form a fully-rounded conception of Human Development. Plus additional general background information necessary to understand these concepts.

C1. Biographical Background
Biographical background and professional qualifications of the authors, Hugh and Kaye Martin. (page 197)

C2. Glossary of Terms and Concepts
Definitions of all the key terms and concepts of this book – along with the closest equivalent in Wilber's work. Serves also as an index: Contains references to key sections of the Main Text. (page 198)

C3. Reading System-by-System: The Study Programs
Detailed Lesson Plans for the study each of the eight Systems of Growth – showing what parts of this book should be read, and in what order. Also shows the portion of the ADAPT Circle Diagram (Appx A1c) that pertains to each System. (page 220)

C4. Resources for Personal Evolution
Annotated outline of important books, research studies, and other resources that explore the various facets of Wilber, Campbell, ADAPT, and the Life Journey. (page 264)

C5. Quick-Reference Guides
Outlines and thumbnail descriptions of every Domain and Sector of the ADAPT Model and the Life Journey Archetype. Plus a Circle Diagram for the ADAPT Model, showing the full model condensed into a single one-page diagram. (page 305)

Appendix C1.
HUGH AND KAYE MARTIN: BIOGRAPHICAL BACKGROUND

HUGH MARTIN is listed in Who's Who in America and Who's Who in the World. Mr. Martin received his degrees & credentials from Swarthmore College, University of Pennsylvania, & University of California, Berkeley -- with emphases in symbolic literature, early childhood education, & the physical sciences. Mr. Martin is the originator of AK Language Arts -- the first program to apply Integral Theory to full range of primary-grade language arts skills. Hugh has appeared on numerous talk shows, led seminars at many colleges and corporations, and spoken at many professional conferences. He is past president of the securities brokerage and investment advisory firm, Hugh Martin & Co.

AMALIA KAYE MARTIN ('Kaye') is an early-education specialist in the Sonoma County Public Schools, and a member of the Occidental, CA city council. Among other things, Kaye is a perceptive life coach, an instructor in nutrition and natural medicine, a certified natural foods chef, a dynamic community organizer, and a dedicated homemaker. She received her degrees and training from California State College Fullerton and Baumann College.

HUGH AND KAYE. Hugh and Kaye are best qualified as integral practitioners and theorists because they have lead integral lives. Both have richly diverse backgrounds in a multitude of fields:

- **PERSONAL TRANSFORMATION**: Esalen, Group Process, Gestalt, Reichian, Bioenergetics, Rolfing, yoga, various religious and spiritual traditions.
- **NATURAL MEDICINE AND HEALTH:** Homeopathy, chiropractic, acupuncture, organic nutrition, vibrational medicine. Terminal cancer survivor (Hugh). Expert practitioner in nutrition and natural medicine (Kaye)
- **ARTISTIC AND CREATIVE EXPRESSION:** Nature photographer, documentary videographer, poet, painter/sculptor (Hugh). Batik artist, home decorator (Kaye).
- **EDUCATION:** Ghetto schoolteacher, college literature instructor, financial seminar leader, early-reading curriculum developer (Hugh). Nutrition/natural medicine instructor, home-school network developer and coordinator (Kaye).
- **SOCIETAL CHANGE:** Civil rights, environmental issues, sustainability/ permaculture.
- **NATURAL AND CULTURAL ENVIRONMENTS:** Backpacking, mountain biking, exotic travel, international home exchange.
- **ACADEMICS:** Hugh -- Swarthmore College (B.A.), University of Pennsylvania (M.A.), Indiana University (doctoral), UC Berkeley (credential), Coaches Training Institute (CTI), member of Mensa. Kaye -- Cal State Northridge (B.A.), Baumann College (natural medicine), Coaches Training Institute (CTI).
- **MARRIAGE AND FAMILY.** Over thirty years of happy, passionate, and occasionally turbulent, marriage. Five highly-independent, multi-gifted kids with close family ties.

WHOLE LIFE COUNSELING. Hugh and Kaye are the founders and co-directors of the life planning and counseling firm, Whole Life Counseling. Whole Life Counseling is a comprehensive program for personal and professional growth, which empowers clients to achieve success and fulfillment in 12 key Arenas of life: Education, Career, Finances, Health, Recreation, Nature, Emotions, Spirituality, Relationships, Sexuality, Family, and Community. For more information on any personal or professional issues, please contact the authors at MartinHughCo@Gmail.com.

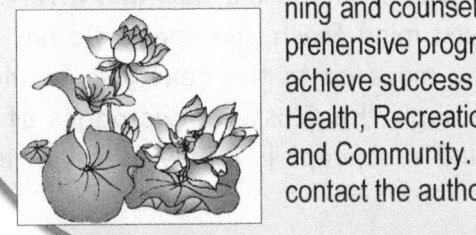

Appendix C2.
Glossary of Terms and Concepts

This Glossary displays all the key terms and concepts explored in this book. In Column 2, the term is defined. In Column 3, the primary sections where the term occurs in the text are indicated. In Column 4, the closest equivalent in Ken Wilber's AQAL or IOS is shown. Generally, in the main text, these key terms are <u>C</u>apitalized, and the first instance is **bolded.** .

The Terms of ADAPT

Treat this Glossary as a subject for study, just like any other section of this book. *** Scan over the first two facing pages. Select one item you feel most hazy, unclear, uncertain, or ambivalent about. Refer back to the indicated section of the main text, and review that item. *** Do the Exploration again, adding to the comments you have already made in your Journal. *** If the violet textbox refers to any other concepts, turn to those also, and note how the concepts are related. *** As you review, try to discover something new and interesting about the concept you had not noticed before. Keep you mind fresh and open. Do not allow this exercise to become a chore. *** As time permits, move on to the next two facing pages, and go through the same process. *** Continue through the Glossary two pages at a time. Just the process of deciding whether you understand a concept is a way of reviewing that concept.

Term/Concept	Definition	Primary occurrence	Wilber equivalent
Accomplishment & Achievement	The Growth that occurs in Everyday Life. (See Realm of Life Passages.)	D3a	
Accumulation	(See Growth, Accumulation.)	Appx A7f	
Actualization	The process of bringing Human Potentialities into actuality. Meeting Challenges to achieve Actualization Growth.	PPR3	Same
Actualization Cycle	The four-phase cycle by which Actualization can take place. Consists of Recognition, Engagement, Breakthrough, and Integration. (See Restoration Cycle.)	PPR3a	
Actualization Growth	The growth that occurs in basically healthy people, when they actualize qualities for which they have an innate Human Potential. (See Restoration Growth, Impediments, Actualization.)	PPR3	
Actualization Growth (System)	The System of Growth based upon the Process of Actualization Growth. (See Actualization Growth.)	S3, PPR3	
ADAP^{3}T	See ADAPT.	OV	AQAL, IOS
ADAPPPT	Acronym for: All Dimensions, All Participants, All Processes, All Pathfinders, Together (simplified to ADAPT). (See ADAPT. By contrast, see AQAL.)	OV	AQAL, IOS
ADAPT	The Model of Human Development upon which this book is based. Consists of five Domains: Dimensions, Participants, Processes, Pathfinders, Systems.	OV	AQAL, IOS
Adapt-ability	A fortunate coincidence: The acronym ADAPT corresponds to the Darwinian principle of Adapt-ation (qv).	OV1a	
Adapt-ation	The Darwinian principle whereby living things survive by 'adapting' to a changing environment. The psychological principle whereby people grow by 'adapting' to life Challenges (qv).	OV1a	Same
ADAPT, Ken Wilber's	The elements of Wilber's IOS, rearranged to correspond to the Domains and Sectors of the ADAPT Model. Used to demonstrate that the Wilber's IOS is actually a very extensive (though incomplete) version of ADAPT itself.	Appx A2-3	AQAL, IOS
Adulthood	In Life Passages, the six Stages of life after Childhood – from Young Adulthood to Legacy. In Transitions, the six Transitions after Childhood – from Nudged-from-the-Next to Death. (See Childhood.)	D1-2	Same
Adulthood, Earlier	In Life Passages, the first two Stages after Childhood – Young Adulthood and Middle Adulthood. In Transitions, the first two Transitions after Childhood – Nudged-from-the-Nest and Making-the-Grade. (See Adulthood, Later.)	D1-2	
Adulthood, Later	In Life Passages, the last four Stages of life – from Mature Adulthood to Legacy. In Transitions, the final four Transitions of life – from Mid-Life to Death. (See Adulthood, Earlier.)	D1-2	
Agape	Action through descent, compassion, love. The way women tend to engage in Transformation. (For males, see Agency, Eros. For females, see Communion.)	P3a	Same
Agency	Action through 'self-preservation.' The way men tend to engage in Translation. (For males, see Eros. For females, see Communion, Agape.)	P3a	Same
AQAL	Wilber's abbreviated acronym for: All Quadrants, All Levels, All Lines, All States, All Types. Also, shorthand for Wilber's entire system of thought. (See Integral Operating System.)	Appx A2	Same
AQAL-phobic	An approach to Integral Theory that is purported to have an inadequate respect or reverence for the opinions and dicta of Ken Wilber, especially his AQAL Model. (See Wilber-centric	Appx A4	

Term/Concept	Definition	Primary occurrence	Wilber equivalent
AQAL, Tyranny of	The authors' view that the AQAL Model has by now become an impediment to broad-ranging, original research on the nature of Human Development. (See AQAL.)	Appx A4-5	AQAL
Archeology	(See Self, Model of...)	A7g-h	same
Archetypal Characters	The Stock character Types that occur with regularity in most Life Journeys and other Archetypal stories. Believed by Jung to arise from our Collective Unconscious. (See Archetypes, Myths, Hero's Journey.)	P3g, Appx B1f	
Archetypes	Images, characters, and stories that arise from the Collective Unconscious – and therefore are believed to be innate and universal to the human species. (See Myths)	Appx B1	Same
Architecture	(See Self, Model of...)	Appx A7g-h	See Archeology.
Arena Growth	Growth within particular Arenas of one's life. Distance and speed of progression may differ from one Arena to another. (See Differential Growth.)	D4	Lines
Arenas	The spheres of action, the realms of experience, the themes of development, or the aspects of personal evolution within each Realm in which Growth takes place (See Lines, Studies, Issues.)	D4	Lines
Arenas, Body	The 4+ Arenas of the Body – from Nerve Plexes to Typical Maladies. (See Arena.)	D4c	
Arenas, Life	The 12+ Arenas of Everyday Life – from Education to Community. (See Arena.)	D4a	Translation
Arenas, Psyche	The 9+ Arenas of the Psyche – from Basic Needs to Worldview. (See Arena.)	D4b	Lines
Arenas, Spirit	The 9+ Arenas of the Spirit – from Spectrum of Consciousness to Cultural Stages of Worship. (See Arena.)	D4d	Lines
Assimilation	The process of incorporating experience into one's identity. For instance, the process of converting temporary States into permanent Traits. Symbolically, the Digestion or Metabolism that occurs within a Stage. (See Transition, Discovery.)	D1, PPR6b	Metabolism
Atrophy	The condition resulting from chronic failure to take advantage of Opportunities (qv). (See Blight.)	D7a	
Authorities	People of exceptional knowledge and wisdom -- often preserved through books, art forms, and other media -- whose work pertains to, sheds light on, or contributes to our growth.	PF4	
Awakening	Increased awareness, illumination, and revelation of a central unchanging truth.	PPR9, D8, P7, PF12	Waking Up
Blight	The condition of Atrophy or stunting that occurs, if Limitations (qv) are allowed to persist too long.	D7a	
Block	(See Impasse. Also see Medical Model vs. Guidance Model.)	D7b, PPR4	Same
Body	Combination of the Physical Body and the Internal Body (qv).	D3c, D4c	Same
Body Self	(See Body, Internal.)	D4c	same
Body-Oriented Growth Professions	All the practices of holistic health, wellbeing, psychotherapy, spirit, and Chakras that are directed toward some type of bodywork. (See Body; Mind-oriented Growth Practices.)	D4c, PR29	
Body, Experienced	(See Body, Internal.)	D3c, D4c	Felt Body
Body, Felt	(See Body, Internal.)	D3c, D4c	Same
Body, Internal	Our Experienced Body, Proprioceptive Body, or Felt Body. The body that we experience from the inside as we grow psychologically and spiritually. (By contrast, see Body, Physical.)	D3c, D4c	Felt Body
Body, Physical	Our overt, tangible, external Body – the Body that goes through the physical Stages of our biological Life Cycle. (By contrast, see Body, Internal.)	D3c, D4c	Same

Term/Concept	Definition	Primary occurrence	Wilber equivalent
Body, Proprioceptive	(See Body, Internal.)	D3c, D4c	Same
Bonding	Our affinity or connection to others. Important factor in the Transition Cycle (qv).	PPR1, PR1	Same
Breakthrough	Succeeding, winning, or prevailing. Mastering, surmounting, or otherwise resolving the challenge favorably. Phase Three of the Actualization Cycle (qv).	PPR3	Transformation
Bridge	A metaphor for Transition – crossing over from one Stage to the next. (See Transition.)	D2	
Campbell, Joseph	World-renowned scholar and mythologist, whose Hero's Journey is the basis for the Life Journey Archetype of this book. (See Wilber, Ken.)	Appx B1-2	Same
Chakra, Crown	The topmost or spiritual Chakra. (See Chakra.)	D1+2c, Appx A7d-e, D8, PPR9	
Chakras	(See Chakras, Eastern and Western.)	Appx A7d-e	same
Chakras, Balancing the	Attaining emotional health by dissolving Blocks (regions where energy flow is deficient) and filling Vacuums (regions where energy flow is excessive). See Chakra.	Appx A9c	
Chakras, Eastern	Energy phenomena that manifest themselves simultaneously in all three internal Realms of Body, Psyche, and Spirit. (See Chakras, Western.)	D1+2c, Appx A7d-e	Same
Chakras, Western	A consolidation, condensation, or simplification of the FDS (qv) into seven basic Stages.	D1+2c, Appx A7d-e	Same
Chakras, Wilber's	Wilber's special version of the Western Chakras that differs somewhat from the normal conception. (See Chakras, Eastern and Western.)	Appx A7d-e	Same
Challenges	Relatively benign Impediments, consisting of everyday obstacles faced by relatively healthy people. (See Impasses, Actualization Growth.)	D7a, PPR3	
Child-rearing	The activity of bringing children to maturity through Parenting -- a process of Guidance and Orchestration. (See Parents & Family.)	PF1	
Childhood	The first seven Stages of life – from Heritage to Adolescence. In Transitions, the first six Transitions of life – from Conception to Coming-of-Age. (See Adulthood.)	D1-2	Same
Childhood, Earlier	In Life Passages, the first five Stages of life – from Heritage to Young Childhood. In Transitions, the first four Transitions of life – from Conception to Terrible Two's. (See Childhood, Later.)	D1-2	
Childhood, Later	In Life Passages, the next two Stages after Earlier Childhood – Middle Childhood and Adolescence. In Transitions, the next two Transitions of life after Earlier Childhood – Entering School and Coming-of-Age. (See Childhood, Earlier.)	D1-2	
Childhood, Middle	The Stages of Childhood that include elementary school and middle school. (See Childhood.)	D1-2	
Circle Diagram	A diagram that displays the relationships among all the Domains, Systems, and major Sectors of the ADAPT Model. The four quadrants represent the four Domains; the eight concentric circles are the eight Systems; the items within each circle are the Sectors for that System; the items outside the circles pertain to all eight Systems. Comparable Diagram for Wilber's IOS.	Appx A1-2, Appx C5	Nest
Coach, Life	A Counselor who is trained to help people implement the 12 Arenas of Life Passages (qv). (See Counselor.)	PF6aa	
Collective	Characteristics pertaining to a Group of people. (See Self, Collective; Group.)	P2b	Cultural only
Collective Unconscious	The collection of deep understandings believed by Jung to be shared by an entire Culture. (See Self, Collective; Group.)	Appx B1	
Comic Stereotype	Eccentric behavior that is repeated again and again by comic characters in movies, TV, books, etc.	P3e	

Term/ Concept	Definition	Primary occurrence	Wilber equivalent
Communion	Action through 'self-adaptation.' The way women tend to engage in Translation. (For males, see Agency, Eros. For females, see Agape.)	P3a	Same
Comparisons	Matching the ADAPT and IOS Models point-for-point, to determine the degree of Divergence and level of Confidence in each case. (See Divergence, level of Confidence.)	Appx A2k, A6	
Confidence	The authors' degree of certainty as to the validity of the ADAPT position – ranging from 95% to 60%. Intended to highlight which ADAPT positions are the most viable (and vice versa). (See Divergence, Comparisons.)	Appx A2k, A6	
Confronting	Recognizing, accepting, facing, owning up to any deep-seated problems. Phase Three of the Restoration Cycle.	PPR4	
Consciousness	The capacity of human beings and other living things to have an awareness of their own interiors and of the world around them. (See Consciousness, Spectrum of.)	Appx A7b	Same
Consciousness, Spectrum of	The full range of potential levels of Consciousness (qv) -- from the simple awareness of the most primitive life forms to highest capabilities of evolved human beings.	Appx A7b, D4d	Same
Core Self	Our pure Identity, unaffected by material concerns, physical discomforts, or psychological obsessions and compulsions. (See Divine Presence, Imminent. For comparison, see Witness.)	P7a, D8, PPR9, PF12	I-I Self
Counselor	A Growth Practitioner specially trained to implement some aspect of Actualization Growth (qv) for people with Challenges (qv). (See Coach, Therapist.)	PF6a	Same
Counselor, Marriage & Family	A Counselor who specializes with Couples and Families. (See Counselor.)	PF6a	
Counselor, Specialty	A Counselor (qv) who specializes in a particular Arena or sub-Arena of Life Passages -- Education, Career, Finances, etc. (See Arena, Life Passages.)	PF6c, D4a	
Creative	(See Cultural Creative.)	IN2	
Cultural Creatives	People who seek various forms of Growth -- enlightenment, enlivenment, maturity, individuality, fulfillment, out-of-the-box thinking, the cutting edge, or realizing their human potential. Also known as Seekers, Self-Actualizers, Translucents, Enlightened Beings. (See Growth Mentality, Droids.)	IN2	
Culture	An extensive Group, as defined by its internal characteristics – shared customs, beliefs, attitudes, values, modes of artistic expression, etc. (See Society.)	DD1+2b, PR11-17, PPR5, P2b	Same
Culture, Dynamic	A culture that progresses along a Cultural Developmental Sequence. For certain periods and countries, includes much of Western Europe and its satellites. (See Culture, Dynamic.)	DD1+2b	Culture
Culture, Primitive	Cultures like the tribes of Amazonian natives, whose life revolves around the cycles of day, month, and season.	DD1+2b	
Culture, Static	A culture that goes through cycles of change, but does not progress along a Cultural Developmental Sequence. Traditional agrarian societies; primitive cultures; bureaucratic societies; tyrannies. (See Culture, Dynamic.)	DD1+2b	
Cycle	A mechanism consisting of several Phases whereby growth takes place.	PPR1-5, 8	
Detachment	In the Shadow Cycle, the process whereby a person distances himself from an unpleasant former Stage.	PPR2	
Development	See Development, Human.	IN1	Same
Development, Human	The changes, progression, or improvements that take place over the course a human's life span. Human Growth.	IN1	Same

C2. Glossary of Terms.

Term/ Concept	Definition	Primary occurrence	Wilber equivalent
Development, Personal	(See Growth, Personal.)	IN1a	Same
Development, Psychological	(See Growth, Psychological.)	D3b, D4b	Same
Development, Spiritual	(See Spiritual Growth.)	D3d, D4d	Same
Developmental Sequence	A growth sequence consisting of alternating Stages and Transitions. (See Fundamental Developmental Sequence.)	D1+2, Appx A7	Stream
Developmental Sequence, Collective	A Developmental Sequence for Groups of people – ranging from Couples to Cultures. (See Developmental Sequence, Individual.)	DD1+2	Cultural only
Developmental Sequence, External	A Developmental Sequence in the External Realm of Life Passages. (See Developmental Sequence, Internal.)	D3b-d, D1+2b, Appx A7d-e	Translation
Developmental Sequence, Fundamental	The complete series of alternating Stages and Transitions. Ken Wilber's FDS for Internal Passages consists of 38 distinct Steps.	Appx A7b, D1+2b	Correlative Structure
Developmental Sequence, Individual	A Developmental Sequence for Individual people. (See Developmental Sequence, Collective.)	D1+2	
Developmental Sequence, Internal	A Developmental Sequence in the Internal Realms of Psyche, Body, or Spirit Passages. (See Developmental Sequence, External.)	D3b-d, D1+2b, Appx A7	Correlative Structure
Developmental Sequence, Simplified	Wilber's Fundamental Developmental Sequence (qv), telescoped down to the seven Chakras. (See Developmental Sequence, Fundamental; Chakras.)	Appx A7d	Chakras
Differential Growth	The process of growing at differing rates in different Arenas or Realms – and being, as a result, more advanced in some areas than in others.	D3, D4	
Differentiation	The process by which the Self transcends a particular Stage -- by dis-identifying with it. Phase two of the Transition Cycle (qv).	PPR1	Same
Differentiation	The process of splitting a concept or category into distinct components.	Appx A6a	Same
Dimensions	The first Domain. The eight facets or types of Growth in the Growth Continuum.	D	Parameters
Directions	The contrary orientations or tracks our growth may take – either Ascending and outward, or Descending and inward. (See Directions, Ascending, Descending.)	D6, PPR8, S7	Height/ Depth. Evolution/ Involution
Directions, Ascending	The process of growth where we Evolve toward Achievement, Psychological Maturity, Aliveness, and Enlightenment. (See Directions, Descending.)	D6a, PPR8, S7	Evolution
Directions, Descending	The process of growth where we Involve toward Fulfillment, Authenticity, Grounding, and Compassion. (See Directions, Ascending.)	D6a, PPR8, S7	Involution
Disattachment	Failing to establish a solid bond or commitment to a new Stage – thereby remaining alienated, fragmented, rootless, homeless, in limbo. The opposite of Re-Identification (Phase 3 of Transition Cycle).	PPR1a	Same
Disconnection	The second phase of the Transcend & Include Cycle (qv) -- where a person Transcends, but does not Include. (See Detachment.)	PPR8a	

Term/Concept	Definition	Primary occurrence	Wilber equivalent
Discovery	Periods when we encounter new situations and insights we must assimilate during our next Stage of development. (See Transition, Transformation, Improvement & Translation.)	D2	Transformation
Dissociation	Avoiding, denying, repressing, or disowning the Observed Self. The opposite of Integration. Phase 4 of Shadow Cycle (qv).	PPR2a, PPR4	Same
Divergence	The way in which the ADAPT position on a given Parameter differs from Ken Wilber's. 12 levels, ranging from substantial agreement to markedly differing positions. Intended to highlight areas where Wilber's position may need re-examination and revision. (See Modification, Confidence, Comparisons.)	Appx A6a	
Divine Presence	The spiritual entity that pervades, orchestrates, governs, and presides over our lives. (See Core Self, Witness.)	P7, D8, PPR9, PF12	Spirit
Divine Presence, Eastern	From this perspective, the Divine Presence is Spirit – what one experiences when immersed in a Transcendent State. (See Divine Presence, Western.)	P7, D8, PPR9, PF12	Spirit
Divine Presence, Imminent	(See Core Self, Divine Presence, Transcendent.)	P7a, D8, PPR9, PF12	
Divine Presence, Transcendent	(See Witness, Divine Presence, Imminent.)	P7b, D8, PPR9, PF12	Spirit
Divine Presence, Western	From this perspective, the Immanent Presence is the Christ (or His surrogate, the Holy Spirit); the Transcendent Presence is God. (See Divine Presence, Eastern.)	P7, D8, PPR9, PF12	
Domain	Any of the five major components of growth – Dimensions, Processes, Participants, Pathfinders, and Systems. (See Sector, Parameter.)	OV1	Sphere, Parameter
Droids	Those who don't seek Growth of any sort. Also called: Zombies, Stepford Wives, Couch Potatoes, Flatlanders, Meatheads. (See Cultural Creatives, Growth Mentality.)	IN1	
Engagement	Meeting, facing, or confronting the challenge offered by a particular Growth Opportunity. Phase 2 of the Actualization Cycle (qv).	PPR3	
Enlightenment	The objective of Growth in the Realm of the Spirit (qv).	D3d	Same
Enlivenment	The objective of Growth in the Realm of the Body (qv).	D3c	
Enneagram	A system for categorizing ('typing') Personalities. (See Enneagram Type.)	P3b	Same
Enneagram Type, Contributing	An Enneagram Type that supports or assists the Dominant Type. (See Enneagram Type, Dominant.)	P3b	
Enneagram Type, Dominant	The primary or defining Enneagram Type of one's Personality. (See Enneagram Type, Contributing.)	P3b	Enneagram Type
Enneagram Types	The nine major personality clusters defined by the Enneagram. According to Riso & Hudson: Reformer, Helper, Achiever, Individualist, Investigator, Loyalist, Enthusiast, Challenger, and Peacemaker.	P3b	Same
Equivalence	The Growth that occurs as people with different Personality Types proceed through the Stages in Styles that are Horizontally Equivalent. (See Growth, Horizontal.)	PPR6b	Differing Voice
Equivalence, Horizontal	The differentiated characteristics of two individuals who are at the same Stage, but are of different Types.	PPR6b	Differing Voice
Eros	Action through ascent, creativity, lust. The way men tend to engage in Transformation. (For males, see Agency. For females, see Agape, Communion.)	P3a	Same

C2. Glossary of Terms. Page 205

Term/ Concept	Definition	Primary occurrence	Wilber equivalent
Essence	One's authentic nature or True Self, according to A.H. Almaas. (See Essence, Immature & Mature.)	PPR8	Pre- and Trans- (of Pre-/ Trans- Fallacy)
Essence, Immature	One's authentic nature or True Self, in an undeveloped state. The earliest Stages of our Life Trajectory (qv). (See Essence, Mature.)	PPR8	Pre- (of Pre-/ Trans- Fallacy)
Essence, Mature	One's authentic nature or True Self, in a fully-developed state. The later Stages of our Life Trajectory (qv). (See Essence, Immature.)	PPR8	Trans- (of Pre-/ Trans- Fallacy)
Ethics	The mental framework through which we determine what is good or bad, right or wrong. (See Morals.)	D4b8	same
Everyday Life	(See Life Passages, Realm of Everyday Life.)	D3a, D4a	
Evolution	The ascending arc of our life, where we evolve toward Achievement, Aliveness, Maturity, and Enlightenment. (See Involution; Life Trajectory.)	PPR8, D6	Same
Evolution & Involution	The twin Processes by which Directional Growth takes place. Three types: Transcend & Include, Life Trajectory, Gender Types (qv).	PPR8, D6	Same
Evolution & Involution (System)	The System of Growth based upon the Process of Evolution & Involution. (See Directions & Trajectories.)	S7	
Evolution, Cultural	The Developmental Sequence for Cultures. (See Developmental Sequence, Collective; Collective Growth; Spiral Dynamics.)	DD1+2b, PPR5	Same
Exploration	The process of illuminating a particular concept from this book through personal introspections of the reader's own observations and recollections. An exercise to elicit the reader's reflections, responses, and comments on a given concept in a written Journal.	PL3	
External	Characteristics pertaining to the outside of a person. (See External Body, External Developmental Sequence.)	D1+2b, D5, Appx A7a	Same
Family	People with whom we are related by blood (or who are bonded to us with similar intensity).	PF1, PR6	Same
Family, Extended	All other blood relations besides Parents, siblings, and children– grandparents and grandchildren, uncles and aunts, cousins, etc. (See Family, Immediate.)	PF1, PR6	
Family, Immediate	The Group consisting of Parents, siblings, and children. (See Family, Extended.)	PF1, PR6	
FDS	(See Developmental Sequence, Fundamental.)	Appx A7b, D1+2b	Correlative Structure
Fixation	Clinging to an old Stage. Failing to Differentiate; remaining fixated, fused, embedded, arrested. Impediment to Phase 2 of Transition Cycle (qv). (See Differentiation.)	PPR1-2, PPR4	Same
Functional Constituents	Fundamental components of the Self that enable it to function and grow. At least eleven components: Autonomic/ Instinctive, Programmed, Volition, Identity, Defense, Emotion, Intersubjectivity, Creativity, Rationality, Navigation, Assimilation/ Integration. (See Wilber's Functional Invariants.)	P5	Functional Invariants
Functional Invariants	Wilber's list of Functional Constituents. Ten elements: Identification, Will, Defense, Tension Regulation, Metabolism, Cognition, Aesthetics, Intersubjectivity, Navigation, and Integration. (See Functional Constituents.)	P5	Same
Fundamental Developmental Sequence	(See Developmental Sequence, Fundamental.)	Appx A7b, D1+2b	Correlative Structure
Generation	A biological period of life, normally about 20-25 years, between the time one is born and the time one first procreates.	PPR5b, P2b	Same

Term/Concept	Definition	Primary occurrence	Wilber equivalent
Generation Cycle	A four-phase cycle that occurs repeatedly in the growth of dynamic Cultures. The phases are: Prophetic, Reactive, Civic, Bureaucratic.	PPR5b	
Generation Growth	The form of Collective Growth that occurs from one Generation to the next, and from one Generation Cycle to the next.	PPR5b	
Generation, Reactive	The Generation that reacts against or detaches from the dominant influence of the Prophetic Generation. Phase 2 of the Generation Cycle.	PPR5b	
Generation, Bureaucratic	The Generation that institutionalizes and standardizes what once was the Prophetic Vision. Phase 4 of the Generation Cycle.	PPR5b	
Generation, Civic	The Generation that fills out and implements the vision of the Prophetic Generation. Phase 3 of the Generation Cycle.	PPR5b	
Generation, Prophetic	The Generation that conceives a new cultural vision and a new impetus for change. Phase 1 of the Generation Cycle.	PPR5b	
Generational Self	The aspect of Collective identity that participates in the Generation Cycle	P2b, PPR5b	
God	(See Divine Presence, Western and Transcendent.)	P7b, D4d	Same
Great Tree	(See Tree of Life.)	Appx A7f	
Gremlin	(See Sub-Personalities, Pernicious.)	P4, PPR2, D7b	Sub-personality
Group	A collection of people who form a Collective Self. At least 10 varieties: Couple, Family, Team, Workgroup, Community, Sub-culture, Ethnic Group, Nation, Generation, whole Societies & Cultures.	P2b, PPR5	Cultures only
Growing Up	The process of progressing from Stage to Stage. (By contrast, see Waking Up.)	PPR9, D8, P7, PF12	Same
Growth	Moving and progressing along the Growth Continuum. Actualizing any of the five Domains of the Growth Dynamic. Human Development.	IN1-3, D1+2	Same, Development
Growth Continuum	A composite of the various ways we can grow. A field of Growth consisting of the eight interwoven Dimensions.	D1-8	Morphogenetic Field
Growth Dynamic	Collective term for all five Domains of growth.	OV	
Growth Center	A Holistic Growth Situation where people of exceptional interests or abilities regarding a particular aspect of growth gather together for personal development. At least six varieties: Monastery, Liberal Arts College, Health Retreat, Creative Grade School, Intentional Community, Growth Center *per se*. (See Holistic Growth Situation.)	PF9, PF3	
Growth Mentality	The frame of mind that enables Cultural Creatives to grow so much more than Droids. (See Cultural Creatives.)	IN2	
Growth Professional	A Counselor, Coach, or Therapist who is specifically trained to help clients overcome emotional, relational, or situational difficulties. May also include various types of Mentors – such as Teachers, Artists, Doctors, etc.	PF6, 8, 10; D7; PPR3-4	
Growth, Accumulation	The form of Growth (like Body and Spirit Passages), where each new Stage is added to the last. Produces a Retrofit Model of Self (qv) – where problems are resolved by renovating our internal Architecture (qv). (See Growth, Succession.)	Appx A7f-g	
Growth, Actualization	(See Actualization Growth.)	PPR3, S3	
Growth, Collective	The Growth that occurs in Groups. (See Growth, Individual.)	PPR5, S2	

Term/ Concept	Definition	Primary occurrence	Wilber equivalent
Growth, Collective (System)	The System based upon the Process of Collective Growth. (See Growth, Collective.)	S2, PPR5	
Growth, Horizontal	Growth that occurs within a Stage. Three types: Improvement & Translation, Equivalence, Improvement Within Type. (See Growth, Vertical.)	PPR6	Translation
Growth, Horizontal (System)	The System of Growth based on the Process of Horizontal Growth. (See Growth, Horizontal.)	PPR6	
Growth, Human	See Development, Human. As compare with the term Human Development, conveys a more personal and experiential set of changes.	IN1	Same
Growth, Individual	Growth that occurs in Individuals. (See Growth, Collective.)	P2a, PPR1-4, 6-9	
Growth, Individual (System)	The System based upon the Process of Individual Growth. (See Growth, Individual.)	S1	
Growth, Personal	That aspect of Human Growth that pertains to Individuals, and in which the Individual develops a personal interest and becomes personally involved in the process. Personal Development.	IN1a	Same
Growth, Perspective	(See Perspective Growth.)	PPR7, S6, D5a	Quadrants
Growth, Psychological	Growth in the Realm of the Psyche and/or in one of the nine Arenas of the Psyche. Psychological Development..	D3b, D4b	Same
Growth, Restoration	(See Restoration Growth.)	PPR4, S4	Therapy
Growth, Spiritual	Growth in the Realm of the Spirit, and/or in one of the nine Arenas of the Spirit. Spiritual Development.	D3d, D4d	Same
Growth, Spiritual (System)	The System of Growth based upon the Process of Awakening. (See Growth, Spiritual.)	S8, PPR9, D3d, D4d	
Growth, Succession	The form of Growth (like Life Passages and Psyche Passages), where we progress sequentially from one Stage to the next. Produces a Layered Model of the Self (qv) – where problems are resolved through a form of inner Archeology (qv). (See Growth, Accumulation.)	Appx A7f-g	Ladder
Growth, Vertical	Growth or progression upwards from one Stage to the next. (See Growth, Horizontal.)	PPR1-5	Transformation
Guidance	The process of choosing and directing our activities through all the alternatives offered in the Life Journey. (Combines with Orchestration (qv).)	PF1-12	Integration
Guidance Model	An approach to growth for so-called 'normal' people, where growth is described as 'experiences,' 'explorations,' or 'navigation' in 'human potential,' 'self-actualization,' or 'personal evolution.' Actualization Growth, Wellness Model. (By contrast, see Medical Model.)	PPR3	
Guidance, Collective & Societal	The Guidance in the Growth process we receive from the society and culture we grow up in. (See Guidance, Individual & Personal.)	PF1-4	
Guidance, Individual & Personal	The Guidance in the growth process we receive from Guides who we choose ourselves, and who work with us personally. (See Guidance, Collective & Societal.)	PF5-10	
Guidance, Internal	The Guidance we provide for ourselves. After absorbing and internalizing the modes of Guidance, we become progressively more independent, more self-sufficient, more self-regulating, more autonomous, more mature. (See Internal Navigator.)	PF11-12	

Term/Concept	Definition	Primary occurrence	Wilber equivalent
Guide	Any person (or an instructive life situation) that assists in implementing the Guidance process. One who helps knit together and integrate the various Domains and Sectors of growth. (See: Counselor or Therapist; Spiritual Guide; Integral Life Guide.)	PF6, 7, 10	Therapist
Hang-up	See Impasse. (Also see Medical Model vs. Guidance Model.)	D7b, PPR2, PPR4	Pathology
Heritage	The genetic, cultural, psychological, & material endowments we inherit. (See Developmental Sequence, Life Passages.)	D1a, Appx A8a	
Hero	The central Archetypal Character in the Hero's Journey – the champion who goes out, faces trials and ordeals, and achieves great deeds on behalf of his group, tribe, or civilization. (See Hero's Journey, Life Journey.)	Appx B1-3	Same
Hero With a Thousand Faces	Joseph Campbell's landmark study on myth and symbol. The Hero figure (qv) who recurs in many guises throughout innumerable myths and legends.	OV, Appx B1-2	Same
Hero's Journey	A pattern of narrative featuring the Hero that appears again and again in many diverse cultures. (See Life Journey, Hero.)	Appx B1-3	Same
Hero's Journey, Campbell Version	Joseph Campbell's original 17-step version of the Hero's Journey, as described in his *Hero With a Thousand Faces* (qv). (See Hero's Journey.)	Appx B1c	
Hero's Journey, Inner	The Hero's Journey that engages our own personal life. At least three levels of breadth and significance: Micro-, Macro-, Mega- (q.v.).	Appx B1e	
Hero's Journey, Macro-	A personal Hero's Journey derived from some major event of one's life – especially where it entails some unexpected Challenge, some Test of our ultimate resources. (See Hero's Journey, Micro- and Mega-.)	Appx B1e	
Hero's Journey, Mega-	A personal Hero's Journey consisting a set of major events from our entire life. (See Hero's Journey, Micro- and Macro-.)	Appx B1e	
Hero's Journey, Micro-	A personal Hero's Journey consisting of the ordinary Challenges we face in Everyday Life. (See Hero's Journey, Macro- and Mega-.)	Appx B1e	
Hero's Journey, Scope	The three levels of duration, scope, and significance within which our personal Hero's Journeys can take place. (See Hero's Journeys -- Micro, Macro, Mega.)	Appx B1f	
Hero's Journey, Types	The five types of Hero's Journey, based upon participant and context. The four combinations of Individual/ Cultural and Realistic/ Symbolic – plus the Integral type that combines all four.	Appx B1d	
Holistic Growth Situation	A cluster of experiences that offers many opportunities for growth in a single integrated activity. Includes: Child-raising, gardening, building, theater, sports, backpacking, workplace. (See Growth Center.)	PF3, PF9	
Holy Spirit	In Christian theology, the aspect of Jesus Christ that remains after He himself physically departs. (See Divine Presence, Western and Immanent.)	P7, PF12	
Human Development	(See Development, Human.)	IN1	Same
Human Development, Breadth	How Human Development manifests itself in various fields of human endeavor, both individual and cultural. (See Human Development, Depth, Meaning.)	IN1a	
Human Development, Depth	How Human Development manifests itself in various Domains of human endeavor -- Dimensions, Participants, Processes, and Pathfinders. (See Human Development, Breadth, Meaning.)	IN1b	

Term/Concept	Definition	Primary occurrence	Wilber equivalent
Human Development, Meaning	How Human Development manifests itself in the significance and purpose human endeavor. (See Meaning of Life. See Human Development, Breadth, Depth.)	IN1c	
Human Odyssey	The entire adventure of Human Growth -- in both its conceptual form (ADAPT) and its symbolic form (the Life Journey Archetype).	Preface, OV	
Human Potential	Our potential qualities and capabilities as human beings, when we engage in Actualization Growth (qv). Actualizing Maslow's Hierarchy of Needs. (See Arenas of the Psyche.)	PPR3, D7a, S3	Same
Human Potential Growth	(See Actualization Growth, Challenges.)	PPR3, D7a, S3	
Human Potential Model	(See Guidance Model.)	PPR3, D7a, S3	
I-self	(See Self, Experienced. By contrast, see Me-Self.)	P1a	Same, Proximate Self
Identification	A powerful feeling of affinity or common identity with some person, group, or aspect of Self. Phases 1 and 3 of the Transition Cycle (qv).	PPR1	Same
Identity	The set of characteristics that we associate with our Self (qv).	P1-2	Same
Identity, Broadening	Situations where we can grow by becoming more Inclusive as to who or what we Identify or Empathize with. (Compare to: Identity, Shifting.)	P6b, PPR7b	Inclusiveness
Identity, Fundamental	The Identity we favor based on the Perspective & Path (qv) we choose.	P6a, D5, PPR7a	Quadrants
Identity, Multiple	Situations where healthy Individuals can assume more than one Identity – either by Shifting or by Broadening their Identity. (See Identity.)	P6, PPR7, D5	
Identity, Shifting	The Identity we assume as we view our life from any of four Fundamental Perspectives (qv), and move among any of four Fundamental Life Paths (qv). (See Identity, Broadening.)	P6a, PPR7a, D5	
ILP	(See Integral Life Practice.)	Appx A9a	Same
Impasses	Relatively pernicious Impediments, where the Actualization Cycle (qv) is stymied, obstructed, blocked, or stuck. Intractable problems, hang-ups, dysfunctions. (See Challenges, Restoration Growth.)	D7b, PPR4	Blocks, Pathologies
Impediments	All the ways the growth process can go wrong. Either Challenges or Impasses.	D7	Pathologies
Impediments, Actualization	(See Challenges.)	D7a, PPR3	
Impediments, Restoration	(See Impasses.)	D7b, PPR4	Pathology
Implementation	(See Guidance and Orchestration, Integration.)	PF1-12	Integration
Improvement & Translation	Horizontal Growth that occurs as we: Improve on the abilities we have acquired at that Stage, then translate our competence to other related abilities. (See Growth, Horizontal.)	PPR6a	Translation
Improvement Within Type	The form of Growth whereby the individual retains the characteristics of a particular Personality Type, but exhibits a healthier or more mature version of that Type.	P3b, PPR6c	Translation
Improvements	The ways in which one Model of Human Development is more inclusive, organized, balanced, differentiated, clear, consistent, unambiguous, explicit, complete, or correct than another.	Appx A6	

Term/Concept	Definition	Primary occurrence	Wilber equivalent
Improvements, High-Confidence	Occasions where the authors are at least 90% sure their position is an Improvement (qv) over some other position.	Appx A6	
Improvements, Major High-Confidence	Occasions where the authors view a given High-Confidence Improvement as addressing some major issue.	Appx A6	
Inclusiveness	Growth that occurs as we broaden the scope of our Identity to include: Social classes, racial and Ethnic Types, Gender Types, and other forms of diversity. (See Identity, Broadening.)	P6b, PPR7b, D5	Same
Individual	Characteristics pertaining to a single person. (See Self, Individual.)	P2a	
Inner Saboteur	(See Sub-Personality, Pernicious. See Gremlin.)	P4	Sub-Personality
Integral	A Model demonstrating that the sets of Stages offered by several Investigators are all aspects of a single overarching set of Stages. A Model that includes and integrates all the Domains and Sectors of ADAPT.	OV, Appx A2	Same (combining all Parameters of AQAL)
Integral Life Guide	A Growth Professional who weaves together all the diverse strands of Dimensions, Participants, Processes, Pathfinders, and Systems to implement a comprehensive experience of Growth.	PF10	Full-Spectrum Therapist, Four-Quadrant Therapist
Integral Life Practice	Ken Wilber's flagship collection of Specific Processes (qv) for implementing personal growth (primarily Actualization Growth). ILP. (By comparison, see Integral Transformative Practice.)	Appx A9a	Same
Integral Operating System	Ken Wilber's broadest, most comprehensive Model of Human Growth, incorporating all the Parameters from *Integral Psychology* and elsewhere – of which AQAL is a very abbreviated portion. (See AQAL, Ken Wilber.)	Appx A2	Not to be confused with Wilber's use of the same term to describe the application of AQAL to personal growth.
Integral Psychology	Ken Wilber's classic study on Human Development. Demonstrates that: The many different Developmental Sequences used to describe Human Growth are in fact elements of one grand Sequence.	Appx A2	same
Integral Theory	The effort to merge and synthesize all systems of Development (ranging from biological growth, to psychological development, to human evolution) into one grand system that summarizes the fundamental nature of reality. (See Integral.)	Appx A2	Same
Integral Transformative Practice	The program of Growth originated by Murphy and Leonard, under whose influence Integral Life Practice was developed. (See Integral Life Practice.)	Appx A9a	Same
Integration	Assimilating a Breakthrough or positive experience into one's personality and self-image. Phase 4 of the Actualization Cycle (qv).	PPR3a	
Integration	The consolidation of the new Experienced Self (qv) with the old Observed Self (qv). Phase 4 of the Transition Cycle (qv).	PPR1a	Same
Inter-Passage Growth	The Life Trajectory (qv) the Self passes through -- from internal, to external, and back to internal. (See Persona, Pre-/Trans- Fallacy.)	D6b, PPR8b	U-Shaped Pattern of Development.
Internal	Characteristics pertaining to the inside of a person. (See Internal Body, Internal Developmental Sequence.)	D1+2b, D5, Appx A7	Same
Involution	The descending arc of life, where we 'involve' toward Fulfillment, Grounding, Authenticity, and Compassion. (See Evolution.)	PPR8, D6b, S7	Same
IOS	(See Integral Operating System, AQAL.)	Appx A2	Same
Issues	The topics or themes we address at each Stage of life and within each Arena. (See Arenas, Lines, Studies.)	D4	

C2. Glossary of Terms. Page 211

Term/Concept	Definition	Primary occurrence	Wilber equivalent
ITP	(See Integral Transformative Practice.)	Appx A9a	Same
Journal	A personalized, quality notebook where readers record their responses to the their Explorations (qv) – generally reserving one or more separate pages for each Exploration.	PL2-3	Same
Journey	(See Life Journey Archetype.)	Appx B2	
Labyrinth	A maze of confused passageways, which may ultimately lead to a central sanctuary. Symbolic of the maze-like human interior. (See Thread.)	OV	
Layered	(See Self, Model of...)	Appx A7g-h	
Legacy	The Genetic, cultural, psychological, & material endowments we pass on to succeeding generations. (See Developmental Sequence, Life Passages.)	D1-2, D3a, Appx A8a	
Lesson	The material for study on a single concept, often covered in two facing pages. (See System; Session; Study Program.)	PL2, S, Appx C3	
Life Journey	(See Life Journey Archetype.)	Preface, OV, Appx B2	
Life Journey Archetype	The symbolic or archetypal version of the ADAPT Model. Derived from Campbell's Hero's Journey. (See Hero's Journey, ADAPT.)	Preface, OV, Appx B2	
Life Trajectory	The two Directions (qv) of orientation, played out of the course of a lifetime.	D6b, PPR8b	
Limitation	Un-actualized Potential or unrealized life Opportunities. The condition that results where Actualization Growth fails to take place. (See Challenges, Atrophy, Blight.)	D7a, PPR3	
Lines	(See Lines of Inquiry.)	D4	Same
Lines of Inquiry	The categories of development or investigation within each Arena. (See Arenas, Lines, Studies.)	D4, Appx A2	Line
Maturity	The objective of Growth in Psyche Passages (qv).	D3b	
Me-self	(See Self, Observed. By contrast, see I-Self.)	P1b	Same, Distal Self
Meaning of Life	The factors that give human life significance and purpose. The pinnacle of considerations regarding the Scope of Human Development. (See Human Development, Scope.)	IN1c, Preface	
Meanings of Life, Many	The fact that Life means different things to different people, and that people orchestrate their lives in accordance to the Meaning they attribute to it. (See Meaning of Life.)	IN1c	
Medical Model	See Therapeutic Model. (Also see Guidance Model.)	PPR4, PPR2	
Mentors	Practitioners from any profession (and others) that endeavor to help people grow. At least ten varieties: Teachers, professors, creative artists, specialty counselors, social workers, natural medicine practitioners, doctors, social activists, motivational speakers, managers and bosses. (See also: Counselor, Therapist; Spiritual Guide; Integral Life Guide.)	PF8, PF6-7, PF10	Same
Metamorphosis	The process of change that takes place as one transitions from one Stage to the next. (See Transition, Transition Cycle.)	PPR1a, D2	Same
Mid-Life	The point in life where we shift from the Ascending to the Descending Direction. (See Life Trajectory.)	D6b, PPR8b, S7b	Same
Mind-Oriented Practices	The practices of wellbeing, introspection, psychotherapy, and spirit that are directed toward mental clarity, awareness, and tranquility. (See Body-Oriented Growth Professions.)	PR31, D4b	
Modification	The change or modification that ADAPT makes in a given Wilber concept. Results in some form of Divergence. (See Divergence, Comparisons.)	Appx A6	
Moment of Truth	An important decision-point in life, where the path we choose will have a significant effect on our future. Often associated with important Challenges (qv).	IN2	

Term/Concept	Definition	Primary occurrence	Wilber equivalent
Monomyth	A pattern of narrative that appears again and again in many diverse cultures. (See Hero's Journey, Life Journey, Hero.)	Appx B1-3	Same
Moral Span	The range of people, animals, living things, and other entities we consider worthy of inclusion in any moral decision.	P6b, PPR7b, S6b	same
Morals	The social standards we derive from our Ethics (qv).	D4b8	same
Multi-Functionality	(See Self, Model of...)	Appx A7g-h	
Mystic	(See Translucent.)	D8, P7	Same
Mysticism	The practice of Awakening to Transcendent States (qv) of Consciousness. Four types: Nature, Deity, Formless, Non-Dual	D8, P7, PPR9, S8	Same
Myths	Epic stories that embody fundamental attributes of a Culture. Believed by Jung to derive from the Collective Unconscious (qv). (See Hero's Journey.)	PR17, Appx B1-3	Same
Navigation	See Guidance.	PF1-12	Same
Navigator, Internal	The inner Guide we form within ourselves by experiencing and internalizing all the modes of Guidance we receive from outside sources.	PF11	
Navigator/Captain	The Domain of Pathfinders, in its Archetypal form. (See Pathfinders.)	PF1-12	Navigation
Odyssey, Human	(See Human Odyssey.)	Preface, OV	
Odyssey, The	The poet Homer's classic epic on the return of the Hero Odysseus to his home in Ithaca after the Greek's triumph in Trojan War.	Appx B3	
Opportunity	A situation where Growth has the Opportunity (qv) to take place. (See Challenge, Potential.)	D7a	
Orchestration	The process of knitting together, coordinating, and unifying the various Domains into a cohesive growth process. (For comparison, see Guidance.)	PF1-12	Integration
Orientation, External	A focus on the outward activities and features of life. Direction, Ascending. (See Orientation, Internal.)	D6, PPR8, S7	Evolution
Orientation, Internal	A focus on the inward activities and features of life. Direction, Descending. (See Orientation, External.)	D6, PPR8, S7	Involution
Parameter	Any one of the major factors that describe and affect Growth. Either a Domain or a Sector. (See Domain, Sector.)	OV1, OV2	Same
Parenting	(See Child-Rearing.)	PF1	
Participant	Any of the seven elements of Identity that take part in the Growth process. The second Domain of ADAPT.	P1-7	Self
Participant, Individual	A Participant in the Growth process, experienced individually. (See Participants, Collective.)	P2a	Self
Participants, Collective	A Participant in the growth process, experienced collectively. Every human Group from two-person relationships, to families, to workgroups, to communities, to cultures. (See Participants, Individual.)	P2b	Culture only
Passages	The four major Sequences of Human Growth, corresponding to the four Realms.	D3-4	
Passages, Culture	The Sequence of Growth followed by whole Cultures. Similar to the Sequence for individuals, but often spread over eons of time. (See Spiral Dynamics.)	DD1+2b	Cultural Evolution
Passages, Life	The external phases of accomplishment or Achievement that occur as we progress through the biological Life Cycle.	D3-4a	Horizontal Translation
Passages, Psyche	The internal phases of mental Maturation that occur as we progress through the Stages of psychological Development.	D3-4b	Vertical Transformation

C2. Glossary of Terms. Page 213

Term/Concept	Definition	Primary occurrence	Wilber equivalent
Passages, Body	The internal phases of physical Enlivenment that occur as we awaken and connect the Energy Centers of our body.	D3-4c	
Passages, Spirit	The internal phases of spiritual Awakening that occur as we ascend through the Stages and States of spiritual Development, or as we Awaken to the Divine Presence.	D3-4d	Vertical Transformation
Pathfinders	The means by which the Processes are implemented, carried out, or put into effect. Accomplished by two general methods: Guidance and Orchestration.	PF1-12	Integration
Pathology	(See Impasse. Also see Medical Model vs. Guidance Model.)	D7b, PPR4	Same
Paths	The four Perspectives (qv), as applied to the types of life activity we choose to focus our attention on.	D5b, PPR7, S6	The Quadrants, applied
Peak Experience	A Temporary Altered State, especially where involving some extraordinary experience, insight, or revelation. (See State, Temporary; Trait.)	D8	Same
Persona	Our 'public face' -- the set of attributes and behaviors we construct to allow the Self to play a part in the drama of existence. An aspect of Personality Type (qv).	P3	Membership-Self, Rule/Role region
Personality Assessment System	A formal psychological test to determine a person's Personality Type. Examples: Jungian, Myers-Briggs. (See Type, Personality.)	P3f	same
Personality Type	(See Type, Personality.)	P3	same
Perspective Growth	The Process of growth whereby we consider, attend to, and develop all four Perspectives and their related Paths.	D5, P6a, PPR7a, S6a	Quadrants
Perspective Growth (System)	The System of Growth based upon the Process of Perspective Growth (qv).	S6a	Quadrants
Perspectives	The four basic perspectives from which any Growth experience can be interpreted – internal/individual (upper-left); internal/external (upper-right); internal/collective – i.e. cultural (lower-left); and external/collective – i.e. societal (lower-right). (For comparison, see Paths.)	D5a, P6a, PPR7a, S6a	Quadrants
Perspectives, Fundamental	A form of Perspective Growth (qv), whereby we learn to move fluidly among the four Perspectives (qv).	D5a, P6a, PPR7a, S6a	Quadrants
Phase	A group of Stages in the human life cycle. One of the steps in a System of Growth (qv). (See Developmental Sequence, External; Step.)	D1-2, S1-8	
Polarities	The fundamental opposites of the universe – male and female, mind and body, spirit and flesh, symbol and meaning, yang and yin, etc. Related by opposition, attraction/ repulsion, or oscillation. (See Directions.)	D6	
Potential	A conduit or path that presents the Opportunity (qv) for Growth.	D7a	
Pre-/Trans- Fallacy	Wilber's term: Either a Romantic Fallacy or an Inverse Romantic Fallacy. (See Romantic Fallacy.)	D8a-b	Same
Process	The means by which Growth takes place. Either General or Specific Processes. The third Domain of ADAPT.	PPR1-9, PR1-35	Methodology
Process, General	Any of the nine fundamental Processes that implement Growth in any Stage, Realm, or Arena. (For comparison, see Process, Specific.)	PPR1-9	
Process, Specific	Any of the 35 categories of techniques, therapies, practices, programs, activities, explorations, studies, and focused experiences that implement specific kinds of Growth in specific Stages, Realms, and Arenas. (See Process, General.)	PR1-35	Methodology
Processes, Comprehensive	The two Specific Processes that combine and coordinate many diverse growth Processes into a single, mutually-related Growth Experience. (See Processes, Specific.)	PR34-35	

Term/Concept	Definition	Primary occurrence	Wilber equivalent
Processes, Conscious Development	The five techniques, practices, and programs we use with conscious intention to promote Personal Growth, resolve psychological problems, and facilitate spiritual Enlightenment. (See Processes, Specific.)	PR29-33	
Processes, Formal Investigation	The six Specific Processes that engage our thinking and reasoning abilities to understand, affect, and utilize both tangible and abstract reality. (See Processes, Specific.)	PR18-23	
Processes, Foundational	The six fundamental Specific Processes upon which all future growth is built. (See Processes, Specific.)	PR1-6	
Processes, Physical World	The four Specific Processes that utilize encounters with material reality. (See Processes, Specific.)	PR7-10	
Processes, Self Expression	The five Specific Processes that express our inner reality in an outwardly-perceivable form. (See Processes, Specific.)	PR24-28	
Processes, Socio-Cultural	The seven Specific Processes that engage us with Groups of people. (See Processes, Specific.)	PR11-17	
Providence	The Guidance & Orchestration we receive from the Divine Presence (qv).	PF12, P7b, D8, PPR9, S8	Spirit
Psychotherapist	(See Therapist.)	PF6d	Same
Quantum Leap	A metaphor for the Transition (qv) – jumping from one Stage to the next.	D2	
Re-Experiencing	Reliving a past traumatic situation – revisiting it, bringing it to life, re-living it through memory. Phase 4 of the Restoration Cycle (qv).	PPR4a	
Re-Identification	The point at which the Self begins to identify with the subsequent Stage of development. Phase 3 of the Transition Cycle (qv).	PPR1a, 3a	
Re-Integrating	Viewing a traumatic situation from a healthier, more mature perspective – reinterpreting it, placing it in context, replacing it with a more balanced version of the original experience. Phase 5 of the Restoration Cycle (qv).	PPR4a	
Realization	The process whereby a possibility or an Opportunity (qv) for Growth becomes an actuality. (See Actualization.)	D7a	Actualization
Realm Growth	Growth that occurs within any of the four Realms (qv).	D3	
Realm of Everyday Life	What we do all day in the externals of our life: Get up, shower, get dressed, eat, go to work, etc. (See Life Passages, Arenas. See also Realms, External.)	D3-4a	Translation
Realm of the Body	Our Internal Body (Proprioceptive, Experienced, or Felt Body), the Body as experienced from the inside. The physical sensations and bodily feelings that accompany our mental life. (See Body Passages, Arenas. See also Realms, Internal.)	D3-4c	
Realm of the Psyche	The thoughts and emotions that go through our minds, while Everyday Life is taking place. (See Psyche Passages, Arenas. See also Realms, Internal.)	D3-4b	Transformation
Realm of the Spirit	The supernatural aspect of human life that exists beyond the concerns of everyday life, the mind, and the body. (See Spirit Passages, Arenas. See also Realms, Internal.)	D3-4d	Transformation
Realm, External	The Realm of the externals of one's life – Everyday Life. (See Realm, Internal; Developmental Sequence, External.)	D3a, D1+2b, Appx A7a	Translation
Realm, Internal	The Realms of the internals of one's life – Psyche, Body, Spirit. (See Realm, External; Developmental Sequence, Internal.)	D3b-d, D1+2b, Appx A7	Transformation

Term/Concept	Definition	Primary occurrence	Wilber equivalent
Realms	The four major spheres of human experience in which Growth and Development take place – Everyday Life, the Psyche, the Internal Body, and the Spirit.	D3-4	Realms, Planes, Domains, Spheres, Axes
Recognition	Becoming aware that a significant Opportunity (qv) for Growth exists. Phase 1 of the Actualization Cycle (qv).	PPR3a	
Resolution	Overcoming, surmounting, prevailing, mastering, or otherwise creating a positive outcome for any Impediment (qv).	PPR1a, 3a, 4a	Treatment
Restoration Cycle	A Cycle by which Restoration Growth (qv) can take place. Six Phases: Recognition, Resurrection, Confronting, Re-experiencing, Re-integrating. Re-structuring.	PPR4a	Therapy
Restoration Growth	The growth that takes place in resolving entrenched 'problems' -- so that normal Growth may resume. Often takes place through a six-phase Restoration Cycle (qv). (See Actualization Growth.)	PPR4a	Therapy
Restoration Growth (System)	The System of Growth based on the Process of Restoration Growth (qv).	S4, PPR4a	Therapy
Resurrecting	Becoming aware of the situation that created the Impediment – uncovering it, recollecting it, bringing it to the surface. Phase 2 of the Restoration Cycle (qv).	PPR4a	
Retrofit	(See Self, Model of...)	Appx A7g-h	
Role	(See Persona.)	P3	Persona, Type
Romantic Fallacy	The misconception where primitive, mythical Stages are interpreted as transcendent. The yearning for an earlier, more primitive, more innocent age – a return to Eden. (See Romantic Fallacy, Inverse; Pre-/Trans- Fallacy.)	D8a	Romantic worldview, Pre-/Trans- Fallacy
Romantic Fallacy, Inverse	The misconception where transcendent mystical States are interpreted as low-level pathologies or primitive states. (See Romantic Fallacy; Pre-/Trans- Fallacy)	D8b	Pre-/Trans- Fallacy
Scenario	A narrative that combines various Domains and Sectors to show how they work together to produce Growth. (See Domains, Sectors, Growth.)	OV3	
Sector	A single factpr of growth, within any of the five Domains. (See Domain, Parameter.)	OV2	Parameter
Self	The Individual or Collective Participant in the Growth process.	P1, P2	Same
Self System	The combination of the Experienced Self and the Observed Self. The interaction between those two factors that produces Growth.	P1	Same
Self, Experienced	The I-Self. The observing, subjective, inside Self that identifies with our current Stage of Development. (See Self, Observed.)	P1a	Proximate Self, Self-Sense
Self, Collective	The aspect of Self that identifies and grows as a Group. (See Self, Individual.)	P2b	Cultures only
Self, Immediate	The Experienced and Observed Selves together. (See Self, Overall.)	P1	Overall Self
Self, Individual	The aspect of Self that identifies and grows as an Individual. (See Self, Collective.)	P2a	Same
Self, Model of	The arrangement or structure of the Self's internal Realms – either as Archeology or as Architecture. (See Self, Archeology and Self, Architecture.)	Appx A7f-g	Archeology of Self
Self, Model of -- Archeology	The interior structure of Self -- where the Realms of Body, Psyche, and Spirit are stacked on one another, like layers of an archeological dig. (See Stacked Model. By comparison, see Multiple-Functionality Model.)	Appx A7f-g	Archeology of Self
Self, Model of -- Layered	(See Model of Self, Archeology.)	Appx A7f-g	Archeology of Self
Self, Model of -- Retrofit	(See Model of Self, Architecture.)	Appx A7f-g	

Term/ Concept	Definition	Primary occurrence	Wilber equivalent
Self, Model of -- Stacked	(See Model of Self, Archeology.)	Appx A7f-g	Archeology of Self
Self, Model of - Architecture	The interior structure of Self -- where the Realms of Body, Psyche, and Spirit are added as additional modes of functionality – like the retrofitting of an old building. (See Retrofit Model. By contrast, see Model, Archeology.)	Appx A7f-g	
Self, Model of - Multi- Functionality	(See Model of Self, Architecture.)	Appx A7f-g	
Self, Observed	The Me-Self. The detached, objective, outside Self. The Self from a prior Stage of development that we have transcended, or ceased to identify with. (See Self, Experienced.)	P1b	Distal Self, Self-System
Self, Overall	The Immediate Self (qv) plus the Witness (qv).	P1, P7b	Same
Sequence	(See Developmental Sequence.)	D1+2, Appx A8	
Session	In the Study Program (qv), the amount of material you should study at any one sitting. May include more than one Lesson (qv), but generally no more than one Exploration (qv). (See System; Lesson; Study Program.)	PL2, Appx C3	
Shadow Cycle	The five-phase distortion of the Transition Cycle (qv). Produces a pernicious Shadow Self (qv), which creates the Impasse (qv) that blocks the Growth process.	PPR2a, PPR4	
Shadow Self	Any disattached scrap of Identity that interferes with the Growth process. Any aspect of Self that causes or is caused by an Impasse (qv). (See Sub-Personality, Pernicious.)	P4, PPR2	Sub-personality, Shadow
Society	The Group (especially a large and pervasive Group), as defined by its external characteristics – organization, laws, roles, responsibilities, etc. (For comparison, see Culture.)	PR11-17, PF2, P2b	Same
Society, Agrarian	Cultures based on agriculture, whose activities of life revolve around the cycles of day, month, and season. (See Cultures, Static and Dynamic.)	DD1+2b	
Society, Bureaucratic	Highly centralized and regulated societies that offer few opportunities for individual initiative, growth, and change. (See Cultures, Static and Dynamic.)	DD1+2b	
Soul	(See Core Self.)	P7a	
Spiral	(See Spiral, Ascending.)	D1+2, PPR3, Appx A7f	Fulcrum
Spiral Dynamics	A popular and influential contemporary system of Culture Passages. From Beck and Cowan's book by the same name.	DD1+2b, P2b, PPR5	Same
Spiral, Ascending	Graphic depiction of a progressive series of Transition Cycles (qv). The major symbol for the Developmental Sequence, as it pertains to Succession Growth (qv). (By contrast, see Tree of Life.)	D1+2, PPR3, Appx A7f	
Spiritual Guide	A counselor, pastor, or master with the skills and experience to assist in navigating the higher realms of consciousness, or in awakening to the Divine Presence.	PF7	Same
Stacked Model	(See Model, Archeology. See Self, Model of...)	Appx A7g-h	Archeology
Stage	A level of development, maturity, enlivenment, or enlightenment through which we pass as we grow. (See Transition.)	D1, PPR6	Stage, Level, Wave, Sphere, Nest, Holistic Pattern
Stage Growth	Growth that occurs as we meet and master the Challenges (qv) presented by a particular Stage (qv) of Development. (See Horizontal Growth.)	D1, PPR6	Navigation

Term/Concept	Definition	Primary occurrence	Wilber equivalent
States, Permanent	Sustained and lasting States of mind. Traits. (For comparison, see Peak Experiences.)	D8	Same
States, Temporary	Fleeting, evanescent States of mind. (See States, Permanent; Peak Experiences.)	D8	Same
States, Altered	Non-normal or non-ordinary states of consciousness -- including everything from drug-induced states, to near-death experiences, to meditative states. (See States, Natural.)	D8	Same
States, Natural	The four normal or natural States of consciousness – waking/gross, dreaming/subtle, deep sleep/causal, and non-dual. (See States, Altered.)	D8	Same
States, Transcendent	According to Ken Wilber, the four levels of spiritual experience: Nature mysticism (psychic), deity mysticism (subtle), formless mysticism (causal), and non-dual mysticism. Also, any internal condition of higher consciousness.	D8	Same
Steps	Any of the Stages, Transitions, or States in a Developmental Sequence (qv). (See Phase; Fundamental Developmental Sequence.)	D1, Appx A7b	
Study	A scholarly investigation along a particular Line and within a particular Arena. (See Arena, Line, Issue.)	D4	Line
Study Program	The set of Lessons (qv) and Sessions (qv) necessary to understand one complete System (qv). Eight types, corresponding to the eight Systems. (See System-by-System.)	PL2, S, Appx C3	
Study Program, Quickstart	A quick way to familiarize yourself with the System-by-System (qv) approach for studying ADAPT. (See System; Lesson; Session.)	PL2, S, Appx C3	
Sub-Personality	Positive: 'Benign' mini-Identity that manifests itself in response to particular life situations. Negative: 'Pernicious' or malevolent mini-Identity that becomes an Impasse to future growth. (Also called Shadow Self, Inner Saboteur, Gremlin.)	P4	Same
Succession	(See Growth, Succession.)	Appx A7f	Ladder
System-by-System	A method of reading this book, whereby only those sections are read that pertain to a particular System of Growth (qv). A sequence of Lessons (qv) and Sessions (qv) for the study of the ADAPT Model, organized around the eight Systems of Growth (qv).	PL2, S, Appx C3	
System, Transportation	A set of factors that enable people or goods to be moved from one place to another. The symbolic version of the System of Growth (qv).	S	
Systems	The fifth Domain. The eight mechanisms by which the Dimensions, Participants, Processes, and Pathfinders work together to produce Growth. (See ADAPT, Domain, Scenario.)	S1-8, OV3	Integration
Systems of Growth	(See Systems.)	S, OV3	
Themes	The seven categories among which the 35 Specific Processes are divided – from the most fundamental to the most sophisticated. Themes of Emphasis. (See Specific Processes.)	PR1-35	
Theory of Everything	Ken Wilber's term to convey the comprehensiveness of his AQAL Model. As this book seeks to demonstrate, AQAL is actually a 'Theory of a Few Very Important Things.' (See Integral Theory.)	Appx A2	Same
Therapeutic Growth	See Restoration Growth, Therapy.	PPR4, PF6d, PR31, P4	Therapy
Therapeutic Model	An approach to Growth for people with 'problems' -- where the Growth processes are described as 'Therapies' or 'Treatments' of 'Neuroses,' 'Pathologies,' or 'mental illness'. Medical Model. (See Guidance Model.)	PPR4, PF6d, PR31, P4	
Therapist	A professionally-qualified practitioner -- such as a psychologist, psychiatrist, or counselor – who is trained in helping people with Restoration Growth (qv). (By comparison, see Counselor.)	PPR4, PF6d, PR31, P4	Same

Term/Concept	Definition	Primary occurrence	Wilber equivalent
Therapy	The process of helping people to overcome Impasses (qv). (By comparison, see Counseling.)	PPR4, PF6d, PR31, P4	Same
Thread	The clues to our path through the Labyrinth (qv). The guidance that enables us to find our way through our own interior.	OV	
Thread, Follow the	A method of reading and studying this book, whereby just one aspect is followed from beginning to end. Examples: Follow just the Archetypes, just the Cartoons, just the Tables, etc.	CL	
Together, Togetherness	The Domain of Systems, adjusted to fit the ADAPT acronym. (See System.)	OV1	Integration
Trait, Evolved	Traits that are expansive, open, flexible. (See Personality Type; Trait, Fixated.)	P3b, PPR6b	Translation
Trait, Fixated	Traits that are limited, restricted, rigid. (See Personality Type; Trait, Evolved.)	P3b, PPR6b	
Traits	Permanent features of one's character or Identity. (See Peak Experiences, Enneagram Types.)	P3b, PPR6b, D8	Same
Trajectory, Life	(See Life Trajectory.)	D6b	U-Shaped Pattern
Transcend & Include	The process whereby we transcend a prior Stage, but also include that Stage in our next Stage. (See Transcend & Include Cycle; Evolution & Involution.)	PPR8a, S7a	Same
Transcend & Include Cycle	The three-phase process by which Transcend & Include takes place. (See Transcend & Include; Evolution & Involution.)	PPR8a, S7a	
Transformation	Times when we are becoming something we have never been before. (See Discovery. For comparison, see Translation and Horizontal Growth.)	D2, PPR1	Same
Transition	A Quantum Leap that takes us from one Stage to the next. (See Stage.)	D2, PPR1	Translation
Transition Cycle	The four-phase process through which Transition (qv) takes place. We first Identify with a given Stage, then Differentiate ourselves from that Stage, then Identify with the next subsequent Stage, and finally Integrate the new Identification with the old. (See Shadow Cycle.)	PPR1a, D2	Fulcrum, Milestone, Round
Translation	The process of Horizontal Growth, where we apply skills learned in one field to a related field. (See Horizontal Growth. For comparison, see Transformation.)	PPR6, D1	Same
Translucent	Anyone with the deep capacity to experience the Divine Presence (qv). A Mystic. (See Transcendent States.)	D8, P7	Mystic
Treatments	The Methodologies that are applied to Impasses (qv) or Pathologies. (See Restoration Growth.)	D7b, PR 29, PR31, Appx A9b	Same
Tree of Life	The major symbol for the Developmental Sequence, as it pertains to Accumulation Growth (qv). The Great Tree. (For comparison, see Spiral, Ascending.)	D1+2, Appx A7f	
Tree, Great	(See Tree of Life, Great Tree.)	D1+2, Appx A7f	
Type	(See Personality Type.)	P3	Same
Type, Ethnic	The attitudes and modes of behavior that originate from one's Ethnic Group.	P3d, PPR6b, S5b	Same
Type, Gender	The attitudes and modes of behavior that originate from one's sexual Gender.	P3a, PPR6b, S5b	Same
Type, Improvement Within	The form of Horizontal Growth that occurs within a particular Personality Type. Includes Improvement within Enneagram Type from Fixated to Evolved. (See Growth, Horizontal; Types, Fixated & Evolved.)	P3, PPR6a	

Term/Concept	Definition	Primary occurrence	Wilber equivalent
Type, Personality	A set of identifiable Traits that occurs with regularity in human populations. At least seven varieties: Gender, Enneagram, Birth-Order, Ethnic, Comic, Personality Assessment, Archetype. (See Persona.)	P3	Type
Types, Birth Order	Differences in Personality resulting from the order of birth within one's family – especially first, last, and middle child. (See Type, Personality.)	P3c, PPR6b, S5b	
Tyranny	Highly controlled or oppressive societies that offer few opportunities for individual initiative, growth, and change. (See Cultures, Static & Dynamic.)	DD1+2b	
Vertical Transformation	The process of Growth from one Stage to the next. (For comparison, see Horizontal Translation.)	D1+2, PPR3	Same
Waking Up	(See Awakening. For comparison, see Growing Up.)	PPR9, D8, P7, PF12	Same
Wellness Model	(See Guidance Model. By contrast, see Medical Model.)	PPR3	
Wheel of Life	The 12 Arenas of Life Passages -- arranged as a pie chart, with concentric circles indicating levels of development.	D4a	
Whole Life Counselor	(See Integral Life Guide.)	PF10	Integral Therapist, Full-Spectrum Therapist, Four-Quadrant Therapist
Wilber-centric	An approach to Integral Theory that is purported to have an excessive or idolatrous reverence for the opinions and dicta of Ken Wilber. (See AQAL-phobic.)	Appx A4	
Wilber, Ken	A gifted systems theorist. Founder and foremost proponent of the academic discipline of Integral Theory. One of two major influences on this book. (See Integral Theory, Joseph Campbell.)	Appx A	Same
Witness	The Divine Presence (qv) in its Transcendent form. The all-pervasive Seer or I-I-Self. Our Essence, True Self, Transcendent Self, or True Nature. The pervasive, overarching Being that presides over all aspects of our existence -- observing, cherishing, guiding, and protecting us. (By comparison, see Core Self.)	P7b, D8, PPR9, PF12	Same. Ultimate Subject, Pure Consciousness, Antecedent Self, Emptiness

Appendix C3. Reading System-by-System:
The Study Programs

The most thorough and rewarding way to read this book is **System-by-System**. Reading this way will introduce you to each topic in its proper order – and will also give you the clearest understanding of the mechanisms by which Human Growth actually takes place.

To read System-by-System, you will follow what we call a **Study Program**. A Study Program is a set of readings from this book ('**Lessons**') that explain all the factors pertaining to a particular System. Since there are eight Systems, there are eight corresponding Study Programs (plus the Quickstart Program). Following the sequence of the first Study Program, turn to the first Domain of this book, *Dimensions*, and read the designated sections. Then do the same for the other three basic Domains -- *Participants*, *Processes*, and *Pathfinders*. By completing these four sets of readings, you will learn how the System works and how it applies in your own life.

Complete the Study Programs in the following order:

- Begin with the **Quickstart Study Program** for **System 1**. (p. 225)
- Next, complete the **Full Study Program** for **System 1**. (p. 227)
- After that, progress through the **Study Programs** in the following order: **2**, **3**, **4**, **5**, **8**.
- Save **Study Programs 6** and **7** for last, because they are somewhat abstruse and esoteric.

Divide your reading and study time into **Sessions** of 30 minutes to one hour. Complete one full Session (including no more than one Exploration) at a sitting. Keep a **Journal**, and write down your responses to each of the Explorations. Share your Journey with a partner, with a guide, with a discussion group, or with your social network. Absorb this book gradually over a leisurely period that could extend for several months.

Self-Contained Programs. "Like this Giant Tortoise, each **Study Program** is a self-contained unit. First, make a commitment to complete the 3-week Quickstart System. When you're ready for more, just commit to one additional Program at a time."

S1-8. The Complete ADAPT Study Program

The complete **ADAPT Study Program** consists of eight Systems – plus the Quickstart Program. The Study Programs vary in length – requiring between one and seven weeks to complete. All told, the Program takes approximately 18 weeks, or four months, to complete.

Each of the eight Systems is self-contained and stand-alone. It is not necessary to complete the entire series in order to benefit from the Program. Commit to one System at a time, and complete it. Then give yourself time to digest and reflect. When you feel ready, resume your study with the next System. Don't force it. Continue only when it feels interesting, informative, and fun.

THE ADAPT STUDY PROGRAMS

In general, this book is designed so that one new **Concept** (or sub-concept) is presented every two facing pages. The material pertaining to a particular Concept is called a **Lesson**. The combination of one or more Lessons to be completed at a sitting is called a **Session**. (Sessions of more than one Lesson all have the same number [5a, 5b, etc.] & are enclosed with a double-line box.) Some Lessons are duplicated from System to System, because those Lessons apply to each of those Systems. Sessions that appear for the first time in the learning sequence are called **New Sessions**.

Study Program	Lessons	Sessions	New Sessions	Weeks to Complete
1. Individual Growth, Quickstart (p. 225)	26	13	13	3
1. Individual Growth, Full (p. 227)	24	23	23	4 (in addition to Quickstart)
2. Collective Growth (p. 233)	18	12	6	1
3. Actualization Growth (p. 237)	24	19	12	2
4. Restoration Growth (p. 241)	16	12	8	1-2
5. Horizontal Growth (p. 247)	20	17	10	2
6. Perspective Growth (p. 253)	24	19	7	1-2
7. Evolution & Involution (p. 258)	26	18	3	1
8. Spiritual Growth (p. 263)	26	20	9	2
TOTAL				**18 weeks**

The various sections of the Domains of Specific Processes (PR) and Pathfinders (PF) pertain to any System and therefore can be read in virtually any order. Readings for those Domains are therefore suggestive only. For the sake of clarity, in each of the following eight sections, we repeat the descriptions of the eight Systems from Section S of the Main Text.

*At this point, do not be concerned to understand the many new terms and concepts you will encounter. They will be explained in the course of this book. *** The Study Plans on the following pages can appear complicated at first. However, they are only lists of pages, showing the recommended order in which various sections should be read.

Page 222. ADAPT Study Programs

Study Program S1. Individual Growth

Individual Growth is Growth that takes place in individual people.

SYSTEM 1: INDIVIDUAL GROWTH

- **Dimensions**
  - The **Stages** (D1) and **Transitions** (D2)
    Build upon one another to form a **Developmental Sequence** (D1+2).
  - The Developmental Sequence occurs
    Within a variety of **Arenas** (D4) in each of four **Realms** (D3).

- **Participants**
  - The Stages & Transitions are navigated by a **Self System** (P1),
    Consisting of the **Experienced & Observed Selves** (P1a-b).
  - The **Individual Self** (P2a) that experiences all this Growth
    Is constructed from 11 **Functional Constituents** (P5).

- **Processes**
  - The Self System progresses from Stage to Stage by the mechanism of the **Transition Cycle** (PPR1).
  - A series of Transition Cycles comprise the General Process of **Actualization Growth** (PPR3).
  - Individual Growth can be facilitated by any of 35 **Specific Processes** (PR1-35).

- **Pathfinders**
  - Individual Growth can be **Guided** and **Orchestrated** by any of the 12 **Pathfinders** (PF1-12).
  - The Pathfinders can be of three types – for instance, **Parents & Family** (**Collective**, PF1), **Long-Term Partner** (**Individual**, PF5), and **Internal Navigator** (**Internal**, PF11).

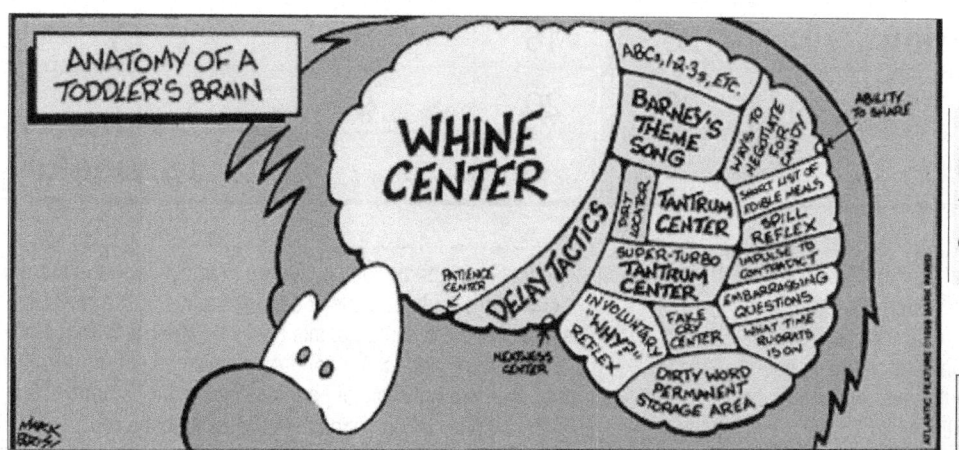

Becoming an Individual. "Now that I'm a Toddler, I've got very definite ideas that fill my brain."

Individual Growth System. Implicit in Wilber's *Embedding Cycle*.

S1. Individual Growth. Page 223

ERIC'S INDIVIDUAL GROWTH

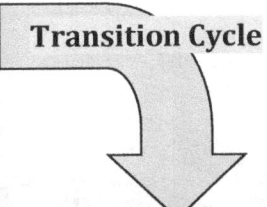

Baby

Transition Cycle

Toddler

"Little Eric is an Individual Person (P2a),
who has an Experienced Self (P1a)
and is developing an Observed Self (P1b).
He Transitions (D2a)
from Baby Stage to Toddler Stage (D1a)
by means of a Transition Cycle (PPR1)."

"In learning to walk,
Eric uses the Process of Physical Activity (PR8),
and is aided by his Daddy (PF1).
The whole process
is an experience in Nurture & Bonding (PR1)."

Page 224. ADAPT STUDY PROGRAMS

S1a. DIAGRAM OF SYSTEM 1

The **Yellow Circle** depicts the components of System 1, **Individual Growth**. Read clockwise, beginning at the upper-left.

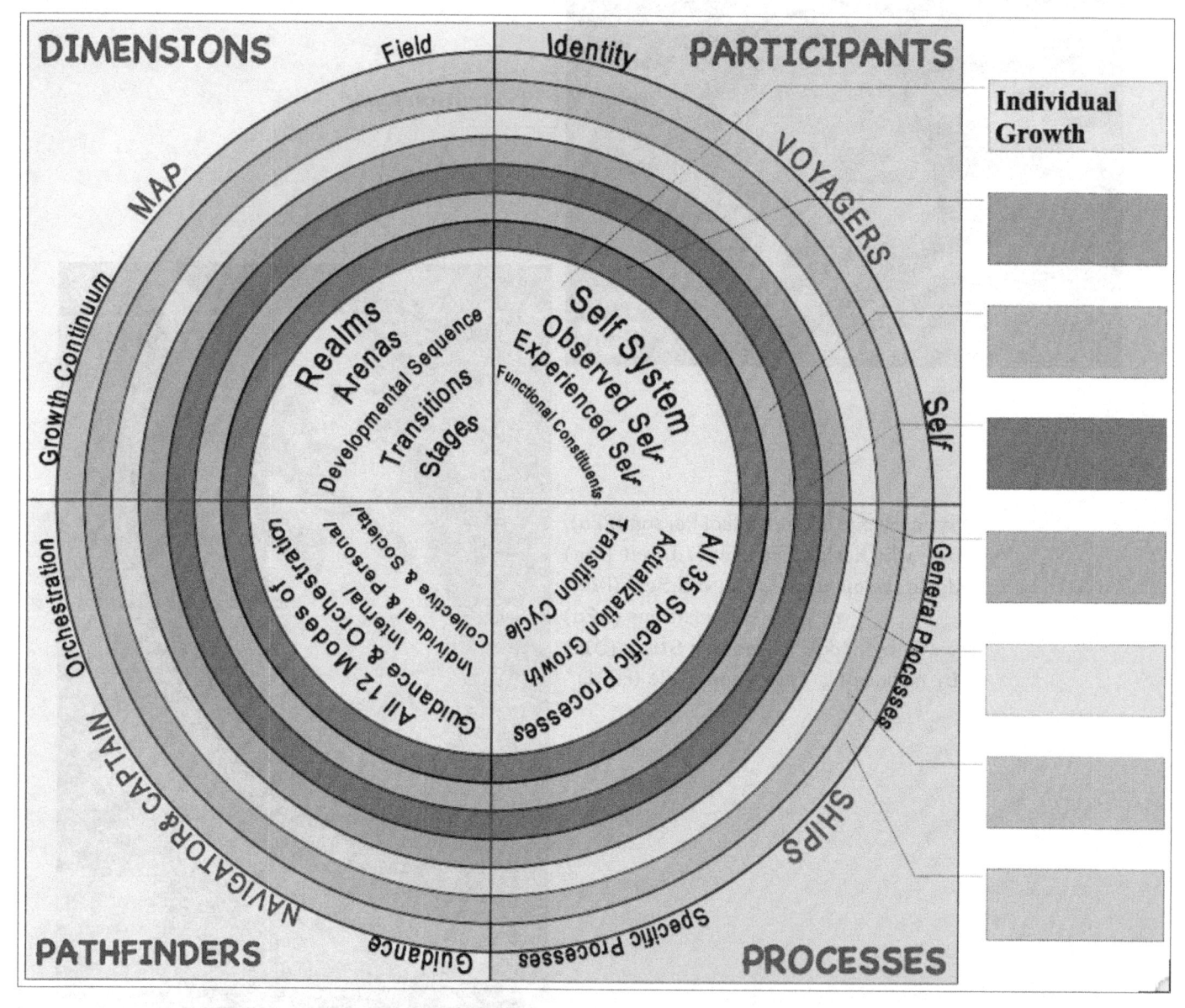

DIMENSIONS — Field / Identity — **PARTICIPANTS**

MAP / VOYAGERS

Growth Continuum

Realms / Arenas / Developmental Sequence / Transitions / Stages

Self System / Observed Self / Experienced Self / Functional Constituents

All 12 Modes of Guidance & Orchestration / Internal & External / Collective & Personal

All 35 Specific Processes / Actualization Growth / Transition Cycle

Orchestration

NAVIGATOR & CAPTAIN / SHIPS

PATHFINDERS — Guidance / Specific Processes — **PROCESSES**

Individual Growth

Self

General Processes

My Individual Growth. "I used to be a nerdy kid. Now I'm a hip, aware teenager."

S1b. Quickstart Study Program for Individual Growth

This **Quickstart Study Program** is an abbreviated version of the Full Study Program for System 1. This series of Lessons serves as an introduction to the Systems of ADAPT. It will teach you the basic Dimensions, Participants, Processes, and Pathfinders -- and show how they function together to produce Growth.

The pertinent sections of the ADAPT Model are shown in the right column. Lesson numbers are shown in the left column. Where the Lesson numbers are followed by letters and enclosed in a double-line box, those Lessons should all be included in a single Session. (Lessons 1a-c, for example, will all be part of your first Session.) Spend ample time on the Exploration. Allow somewhere between 30 minutes and one hour to complete all the reading, writing, and study for each Session. In general, limit yourself to just one Session at a sitting (including no more than one Exploration).

This Quickstart Program consists of 26 Lessons spread over 13 Sessions. You should allow yourself approximately three weeks to complete it. Once you are finished, you may proceed to the Full Study Program for System 1 (page 227).

QUICKSTART STUDY PROGRAM: INDIVIDUAL GROWTH (#1)
(continued next page)

LESSON	Dimensions
1a	**D1-8. DIMENSIONS INTRO.** The various areas of our life where our Growth takes place – and the various features of that Growth.
1b	**D1. STAGES.** The levels of development, maturity, enlivenment, or enlightenment through which we pass as we grow.
1c	**D1a. Stages of Life Passages.** The Stages of Everyday Life.
2	**D1b. Stages of Life Passages: Earlier Childhood.** The four Stages after Conception – Gestation, Infancy, Toddler, and Young Childhood. Plus Heritage before birth.
3a	**D2. TRANSITIONS.** The quantum leaps that take us from one Stage to the next.
3b	**D2a. Transitions of Life Passages.** The Transitions of Everyday Life.
4	**D2b. Transitions of Life Passages: Earlier Childhood.** The four Transitions before entering school – Conception, Birth, Crawling/Walking, Onset of Terrible Two's.
5a	**D1+2. DEVELOPMENTAL SEQUENCE.** A series of alternating Stages and Transitions.
5b	**D1+2a. Developmental Sequence of Life Passages.** The alternating Stages and Transitions of Everyday Life.
6a	**D3. REALMS.** The four major spheres of human experience where Growth can occur – Everyday Life, Psyche, Body, Spirit.
6b	**D3a. Life Passages.** The external phases of accomplishment or achievement that occur as we progress through the biological Life Cycle.
7a	**D4. ARENAS.** The specific areas of activity within each Realm where Growth takes place.
7b	**D4a. Arenas of Life Passages.** The spheres of activity in which we live our Everyday Life.

QUICKSTART STUDY PROGRAM: INDIVIDUAL GROWTH (#1) (cont.)

Participants, Processes, Pathfinders

LESSON	
8a	**P1-8. PARTICIPANTS INTRO.** The aspects of Identity, or Self, that partake in the Growth process.
8b	**P1. SELF SYSTEM.** A combination of the Experienced Self and the Observed Self – the two entities that engage in a dialectic by which the Self grows.
9a	**P2. INDIVIDUAL & COLLECTIVE SELVES.** The two forms of Identity that can participate in the Growth process.
9b	**P2a. Individual Self.** The aspect of Self that identifies and grows as an Individual.
10a	**PPR1-9, PR1-35. PROCESSES INTRO.** The Methods and Techniques that move us along the Growth Continuum.
10b	**PPR1-9, GENERAL PROCESSES.** Processes that are always in effect whenever Growth takes place.
10c	**PPR1. TRANSITION CYCLE.** The four-phase process of Metamorphosis by which we Transition from one Stage to the next.
11a	**PR1-35. SPECIFIC PROCESSES.** Methods and Techniques that promote specific kinds of Growth in specific situations.
11b	**PR1-6. FOUNDATIONAL.** Processes that are fundamental to all other Processes of Growth.
12a	**PF1-12. PATHFINDERS INTRO.** The means by which our Growth process is put into effect – combining Guidance & Orchestration.
12b	**PF1-4. COLLECTIVE & SOCIETAL GUIDANCE.** Guidance & Orchestration in the Growth process provided by the Society and Culture we grow up in.
12c	**PF1. PARENTS & FAMILY.** The original, the most influential, most beneficial Guides of our Journey of Growth.
13a	**PF5-10. INDIVIDUAL & PERSONAL GUIDANCE.** Guidance & Orchestration in the Growth process we receive from Guides who we choose ourselves, or who work with us personally.
13b	**PF5. LONG-TERM PARTNER.** The special person we choose to share our Journey through life.

Getting a Quick Start. "This **Quickstart Study Program** will introduce you to the most basic components of the ADAPT Model – and show you how they all work together to produce Growth."

S1c. Full Study Program for Individual Growth

This **Full Study Program** will teach you how Stages and Transitions combine to produce Growth in Individuals. Because this System is so fundamental, it is the longest and most challenging of the Study Programs. However, it also yields the most insights and conveys the greatest benefits. This Program consists of 50 Lessons spread over 36 Sessions (24 New Lessons and 23 New Sessions, after Quickstart). After Quickstart, you should allow yourself approximately four additional weeks to complete it.

FULL STUDY PROGRAM: INDIVIDUAL GROWTH (#1)
(continued next page)

Lesson	DIMENSIONS
1a	**D1-8. DIMENSIONS INTRO.** The various areas of our life where our Growth takes place – and the various features of that Growth.
1b	**D1. STAGES.** The levels of development, maturity, enlivenment, or enlightenment through which we pass as we grow.
1c	**D1a. Stages of Life Passages.** The Stages of Everyday Life.
2	**D1b. Stages of Life Passages: Earlier Childhood.** The four Stages after Conception – Gestation, Infancy, Toddler, and Young Childhood. Plus Heritage before birth.
3	**D1c. Stages of Life Passages: Later Childhood.** The period of our life when we are normally in school. Middle Childhood and Adolescence.
4	**D1d. Stages of Life Passages: Earlier Adulthood.** The period when we establish a life for ourselves, independent of the home we grew up in. Young Adulthood and Middle Adulthood.
5	**D1e. Stages of Life Passages: Later Adulthood.** The three final Stages before Death – Mature Adulthood, Elderhood, and Senescence. Plus Legacy after death.
6a	**D2. TRANSITIONS.** The quantum leaps that take us from one Stage to the next.
6b	**D2a. Transitions of Life Passages.** The Transitions of Everyday Life.
7	**D2b. Transitions of Life Passages: Earlier Childhood.** The four Transitions before entering school – Conception, Birth, Crawling/Walking, Onset of Terrible Two's.
8	**D2c. Transitions of Life Passages: Later Childhood.** The two school-related Transitions before leaving home. Entering School and Coming-of-Age.
9	**D2d. Transitions of Life Passages: Earlier Adulthood.** The two Transitions when we establish an independent life for ourselves. Nudged-from-the-Nest and Making-the-Grade.
10	**D2e. Transitions of Life Passages: Later Adulthood.** the final four Transitions of our life – Mid-Life Passage, Passing-the-Baton, Debility or Illness, and Death.

Individual Growth Through Discovery.
"I explore the world around me – and learn from what I discover."

Page 228. ADAPT Study Programs

FULL STUDY PROGRAM: INDIVIDUAL GROWTH (#1) (cont.)

DIMENSIONS (cont.)

LESSON	
11a	**D1+2. DEVELOPMENTAL SEQUENCE.** A series of alternating Stages and Transitions.
11b	**D1+2a. Developmental Sequence of Life Passages.** The alternating Stages and Transitions of Everyday Life.
12	**D1+2b. Developmental Sequences: External & Internal.** The alternating Stages and Transitions of all four Realms.
13	**D1+2c. Internal Developmental Sequence: The Chakras.** The seven-Stage Developmental Sequence for Psyche, Body, and Spirit.
14a	**D3. REALMS.** The four major spheres of human experience where Growth can occur – Everyday Life, Psyche, Body, Spirit.
14b	**D3a. Life Passages.** The external phases of accomplishment or achievement that occur as we progress through the biological Life Cycle.
15	**D3b. Psyche Passages.** The internal phases of mental Maturation that occur as we progress through the Stages of Psychological Development.
16	**D3c. Body Passages.** The internal phases of physical Enlivenment that occur as we activate and connect the Energy Centers of our body.
17	**D3d. Spirit Passages.** The internal phases or modes of spiritual Enlightenment that occur as we awaken ourselves to the Divine Presence or open ourselves to the Holy Spirit.
18	**D3b-d. Internal Realms.** The Development within the Internal Realms of Psyche, Body, and Spirit.
19a	**D4. ARENAS.** The specific areas of activity within each Realm where Growth takes place.
19b	**D4a. Arenas of Life Passages.** The spheres of activity in which we live our Everyday Life.
20	**D4a1. Wheel of Life.** The graphic depiction of the Arenas of Life Passages.
21	**D4a2. Career & Calling: A Sequence of Growth.** The combination of Stages, Transitions, Realm, and Arena that produces Growth in Career & Calling.
22	**D4b. Arenas of the Psyche.** The themes of Psychological Development that characterize our mental life.
23	**D4b1. Psyche Arenas: Sequences of Growth.** Growth in four Arenas of the Psyche.
24	**D4c. Arenas of the Body.** The regions or functions of the body where we experience Growth internally.
25	**D4c1. Body Arenas: Sequences of Growth.** Growth in four Arenas of the Body.
26	**D4d. Arenas of the Spirit.** The various modes by which we achieve Transcendent States and experience the Divine Presence.
27	**D4d1. Spirit Arenas: Sequences of Growth.** Growth in four Arenas of the Spirit.

Individual Growth Through Cause/Effect. "When I press the keys, a sound comes out. Wow! There is an **effect** that I myself can **cause**!"

S1. Individual Growth. Page 229

FULL STUDY PROGRAM: INDIVIDUAL GROWTH (#1) (cont.)

PARTICIPANTS, PROCESSES, PATHFINDERS

LESSON	
28a	**P1-8. PARTICIPANTS INTRO.** The aspects of Identity, or Self, that partake in the Growth process.
28b	**P1. SELF SYSTEM.** A combination of the Experienced Self and the Observed Self – the two entities that engage in a dialectic by which the Self grows.
29a	**P2. INDIVIDUAL & COLLECTIVE SELVES.** The two forms of Identity that can participate in the Growth process.
29b	**P2a. Individual Self.** The aspect of Self that identifies and grows as an Individual.
30	**P5. FUNCTIONAL CONSTITUENTS OF SELF.** The 11 fundamental components from which the Self is built. The fundamental mechanisms that enable the Self to grow.
31a	**PPR1-9, PR1-35. PROCESSES INTRO.** The Methods and Techniques that move us along the Growth Continuum.
31b	**PPR1-9, GENERAL PROCESSES.** Processes that are always in effect whenever Growth takes place.
31c	**PPR1. TRANSITION CYCLE.** The four-phase process of Metamorphosis by which we Transition from one Stage to the next.
32	**PPR3. ACTUALIZATION GROWTH.** The normal progression of Growth from Stage to Stage.
33a	**PR1-35. SPECIFIC PROCESSES.** Methods and Techniques that promote specific kinds of Growth in specific situations.
33b	**PR1-6. FOUNDATIONAL.** Processes that are fundamental to all other Processes of Growth.
34a	**PF1-12. PATHFINDERS INTRO.** The means by which our Growth process is put into effect – combining Guidance & Orchestration.
34b	**PF1-4. COLLECTIVE & SOCIETAL GUIDANCE.** Guidance & Orchestration in the Growth process provided by the Society and Culture we grow up in.
34c	**PF1. PARENTS & FAMILY.** The original, the most influential, most beneficial Guides of our Journey of Growth.
35a	**PF5-10. INDIVIDUAL & PERSONAL GUIDANCE.** Guidance & Orchestration in the Growth process we receive from Guides who we choose ourselves, or who work with us personally.
35b	**PF5. LONG-TERM PARTNER.** The special person we choose to share our Journey through life.
36a	**PF11-12. INTERNAL GUIDANCE.** Guidance & Orchestration in the Growth process we provide within ourselves.
36b	**PF11. INTERNAL NAVIGATOR.** The Guide we form within ourselves by internalizing the Guidance we receive from outside.

Individual Growth. "Study Program #1 will introduce you to **Stages** & **Transitions** – the two major components of the most basic form of Growth."

Stages Transitions

Study Program S2. Collective Growth

Collective Growth is Growth that takes place in **Groups** of people – ranging in size from **Couples** to whole **Cultures**.

SYSTEM 2: COLLECTIVE GROWTH

- **Dimensions**
  - The series of **Stages** (D1) and **Transitions** (D2) can also occur Collectively, In the form of a **Collective Developmental Sequence** (DD1+2).

- **Participants**
  - **Collective Participants** (P2b) include **Groups** of any size – from **Couples** and **Families**, to **Generations** and **Cultures**.

- **Processes**
  - **Collective Growth** (PPR5) may take place through the same mechanisms as **Individual Growth** (PPR1-4, PPR6-8).
  - However, there are also special **Collective Processes** of Growth (PPR5), Such as the **Generation Cycle** (PPR5b).
  - Growth can be implemented by all 35 **Specific Processes**, But especially by **Socio-Cultural Processes** (PR11-17).

- **Pathfinders**
  - Collective Growth can be **Guided** and **Orchestrated** by any of the 12 **Pathfinders** (PF1-12), But especially by the **Collective & Societal Modes** (PF1-4).

Our Collective Growth. "We used to be two teenagers dating. Now we're a happily married couple."

Collective Growth System. Implicit in Wilber's *Cultural Evolution*.

Ray & Dottie's Collective Growth

Developmental Sequence ⬇

"Ray & Dottie are a Couple (P2b)
who have gone through several Stages (D1)
and Transitions (D2) together
of a Collective Developmental Sequence (DD1+2)
in the Arena of Relationships (D4a)
within the Realm of Everyday Life (D3a)."

"In the course of a lifelong Marriage (PPR5),
they've navigated some difficult Transition Cycles (PR1)
with the aid of a strong Partnership (PF5),
the positive examples of their own Parents (PF1),
and an occasional Marriage Counselor (PF6a)."

Page 232. ADAPT Study Programs

S2a. Diagram of System 2

The **Orange Circle** depicts the components of System 2, **Collective Growth**. Read clockwise, beginning at the upper-left.

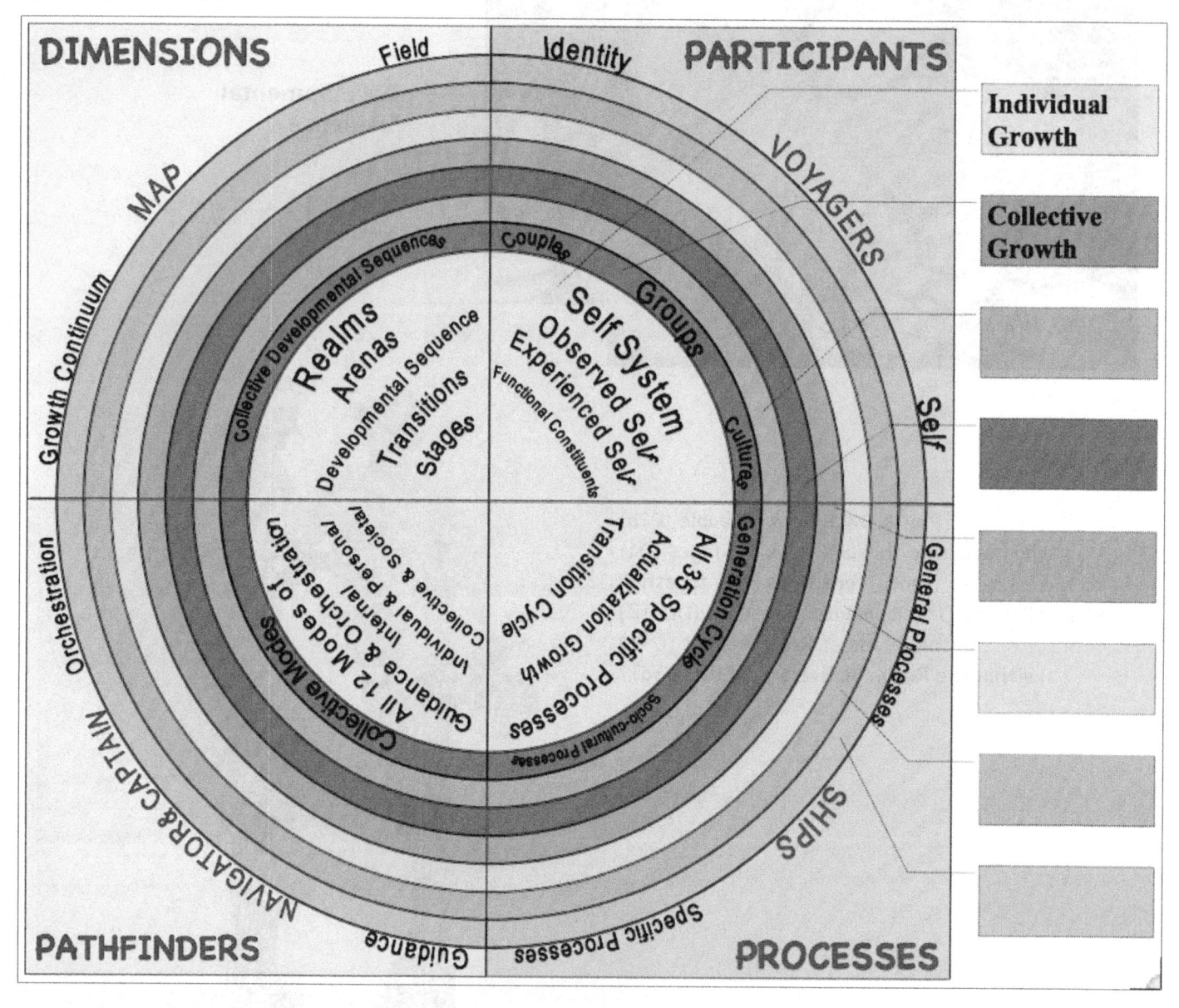

DIMENSIONS — Field, MAP, Growth Continuum
PARTICIPANTS — Identity, VOYAGERS, Couples, Groups, Cultures, Generation Cycle, Socio-cultural Processes, Self
Inner rings (top half): Realms, Arenas, Developmental Sequence, Transitions, Stages / Self System, Observed Self, Experienced Self, Functional Constituents / Collective Developmental Sequences
Inner rings (bottom half): Collective Modes, All 12 Modes of Guidance & Orchestration, Internal & External, Collective & Societal / All 35 Specific Processes, Actualization Growth, Transition Cycle
PATHFINDERS — Orchestration, NAVIGATOR & CAPTAIN, Guidance
PROCESSES — Specific Processes, SHIPS, General Processes

Legend:
- Individual Growth
- Collective Growth

My Cultural Development. "I'm growing by jumping from a simpler Culture to a more advanced one: I used to be a farm boy from the Corn Belt. Now I'm hustling to make my mark in the Corporate World."

S2b. Study Program for Collective Growth

This Study Program will teach you how Stages and Transitions combine to produce Growth in Groups of people. Viewed from a broader span of time, this Program will also show how Cultures evolve over time through the Generation Cycle. The Program consists of 18 Lessons spread over 12 Sessions, including six New Sessions. You should allow yourself approximately one week to complete it.

STUDY PROGRAM: COLLECTIVE GROWTH (#2)

DIMENSIONS, PARTICIPANTS, PROCESSES, PATHFINDERS

Lesson	
1	**D1. STAGES.** The levels of development, maturity, enlivenment, or enlightenment through which we pass as we grow.
2	**D2. TRANSITIONS.** The quantum leaps that take us from one Stage to the next.
3a	**DD1+2. COLLECTIVE DEVELOPMENTAL SEQUENCE.** A series of alternating Stages and Transitions for Groups of people.
3b	**DD1+2a. Developmental Sequence of Relationships.** The alternating Stages and Transitions for the Relationships Arena of Everyday Life.
4	**DD1+2b. Developmental Sequence for Cultures.** The alternating Stages and Transitions for whole Cultures & Civilizations.
5a	**P2. INDIVIDUAL & COLLECTIVE SELVES.** The two forms of Identity that can participate in the Growth process.
5b	**P2b. Collective Self.** The aspect of Self that identifies and grows as a Group.
6	**PPR1. TRANSITION CYCLE.** The four-phase process of Metamorphosis by which we Transition from one Stage to the next.
7a	**PPR5. COLLECTIVE GROWTH.** Growth that occurs among Groups of people – ranging from Couples to Cultures.
7b	**PPR5a. Generations.** The period of life, normally about 20-25 years, between the time one is born and the time one first procreates.
7c	**PPR5a1. Generation Cycle.** The four-phase cycle through which Cultures evolve over time.
8a	**PR1-35. SPECIFIC PROCESSES.** Methods and Techniques that promote specific kinds of Growth in specific situations.
8b	**PR11-17. SOCIO-CULTURAL.** Processes that engage us with groups of people – from pairs to whole cultures.
9a	**PF1-4. COLLECTIVE & SOCIETAL GUIDANCE.** Guidance & Orchestration in the Growth process provided by the Society and Culture we grow up in.
9b	**PF1. PARENTS & FAMILY.** The original, the most influential, most beneficial Guides of our Journey of Growth.
10	**PF2. SOCIETY & CULTURE.** The set of role models and the lessons on living life we receive from our Society & Culture.
11	**PF3. HOLISTIC GROWTH SITUATION.** A cluster of experiences that offers many diverse opportunities for Growth in a single integrated activity.
12	**PF4. AUTHORITIES.** People with exceptional wisdom whose work sheds light on and contributes to our Growth.

Collective Growth. "Study Program #2 will introduce you to **Groups** – the Participants in any Collective form of Growth."

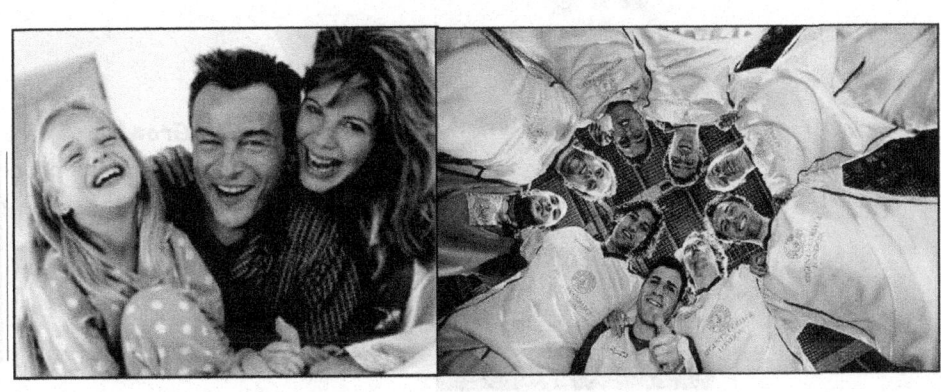

Study Program S3. Actualization Growth

Actualization Growth is Growth for relatively healthy people – Growth that proceeds forward from one Stage to the next.

SYSTEM 3: ACTUALIZATION GROWTH

❈ Dimensions

- Actualization Growth proceeds forward through the **Stages** (D1) and **Transitions** (D2)
  Of a **Developmental Sequence** (D1+2).
- At each Transition, **Impediments** (D7) in the form of **Challenges** (D7a) are confronted and overcome.
- When Challenges are not engaged and overcome (PPR4),
  They become **Limitations** -- and may eventually result in **Blight** (D7b).

❈ Participants

- The Stages & Transitions are navigated by a **Self System** (P1)
  Consisting of the **Experienced & Observed Selves** (P1a-b).
- Actualization Growth can occur for both **Individuals** and **Groups** (P2a-b).

❈ Processes

- In Actualization Growth, our **Human Potential** is brought to realization (PPR3)
  Through a series of **Actualization Cycles** (PPR3a),
  Using a broad assortment of the 35 **Specific Processes** –
  Including **Physical World** (PR7-10), **Socio-Cultural** (PR11-17), **Self-Expression** (PR24-28), and **Comprehensive Processes** (PR34-35).

❈ Pathfinders

- Actualization Growth may be **Guided** and **Orchestrated** by any of the 12 **Pathfinders** (PF1-12),
  But especially by a **Counselor** or **Coach** (PF6a), **Mentor** (PF8), **Integral Life Guide** (PF10), or cherished **Authorities** (PF4) --
  Sometimes in the supportive environment of a **Holistic Growth Situation** (PF3) or **Growth Center** (PF9).
- Over the course of time, an **Internal Navigator** (PF11) is gradually formed.

Our Actualization Growth. "Through a series of successful Transitions, we've progressed from a happy young couple to a deeply committed older couple."

Actualization Growth System. Implicit in Wilber's *Integral Life Practice*.

Stephanie's Actualization Growth

"As a Woman (P3a)
in the world of Corporate Competition (PF3)
Stephanie faced a series of Impediments (D7)
in the form of Challenges (D7a) --
which propelled her through
a spiral of Actualization Growth (PR3)."

Actualization Growth

"Stephanie attributes her Success (PR14)
to strong Work Habits (PR12),
an Ethic of Service and Commitment (PR15),
and an ability not to
take herself Too Seriously (PR26)."

"She never would have made it
without the support of her Partner (PF5),
the encouragement from her Life Coach (PF6a),
and the Managers and Bosses (PF8)
who recognized her potential (PR3)."

Page 236. ADAPT Study Programs

S3a. Diagram of System 3

The **Pink Circle** depicts the components of System 3, **Actualization Growth**. Read clockwise, beginning at the upper-left.

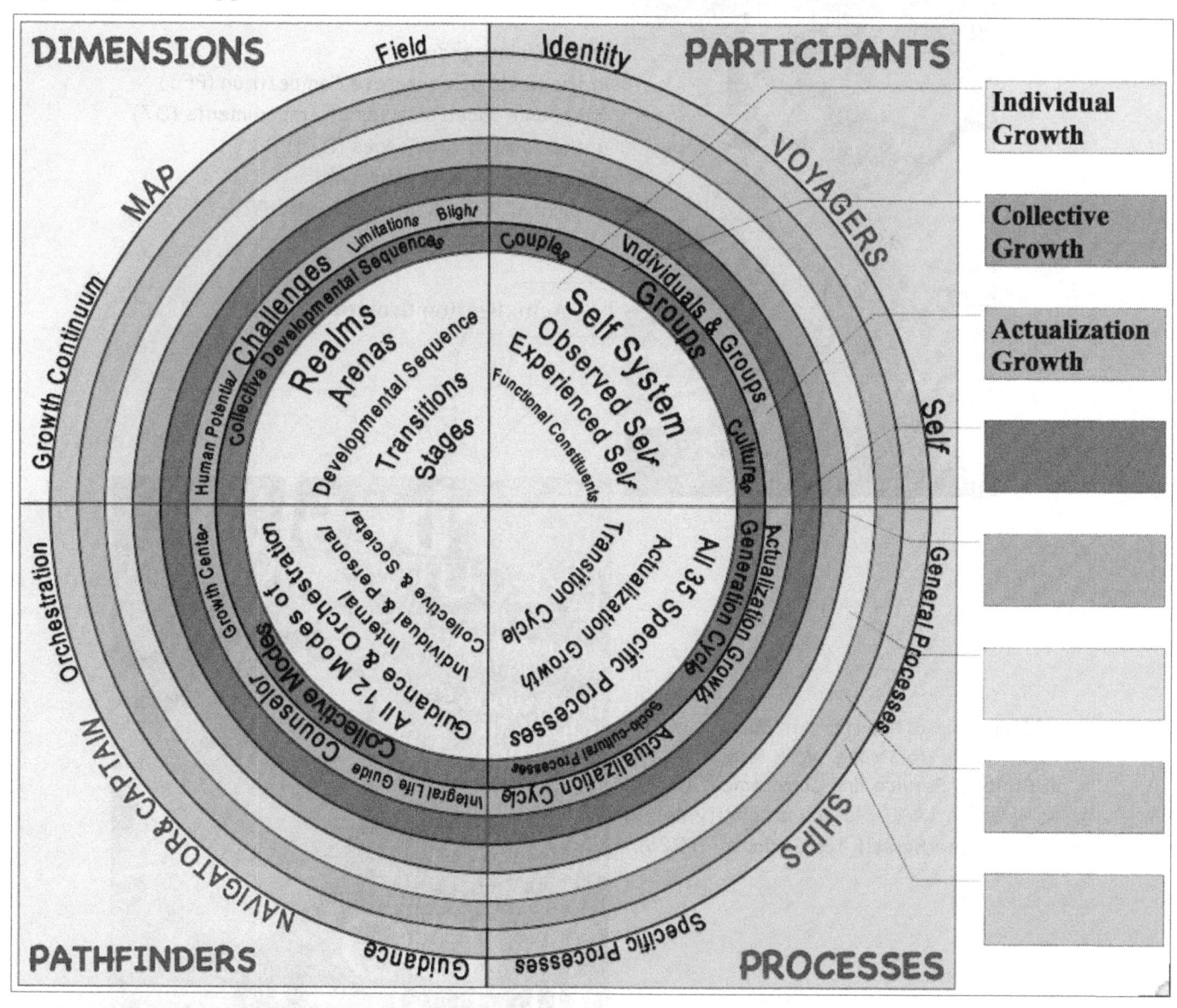

DIMENSIONS — Field | Identity — **PARTICIPANTS**

- MAP
- Growth Continuum
- Orchestration
- NAVIGATOR & CAPTAIN

Inner rings (clockwise from upper-left):
- Challenges — Limitations — Blight
- Realms
- Arenas
- Developmental Sequence
- Transitions
- Stages
- Human Potential
- Collective Developmental Sequences
- Growth Center

- Couples
- Individuals & Groups
- Self System
- Observed Self
- Experienced Self
- Functional Constituents
- Groups
- Cultures

- Actualization Generation Cycle
- All 35 Specific Processes
- Actualization Growth
- Transition Cycle
- Socio-cultural Processes
- Actualization Cycle

- Collective Modes of
- All 12 Modes of
- Guidance & Orchestration
- Internal & Personal
- Collective & Societal
- Counselor
- Integral Life Guide

PATHFINDERS — Guidance | Specific Processes — **PROCESSES**

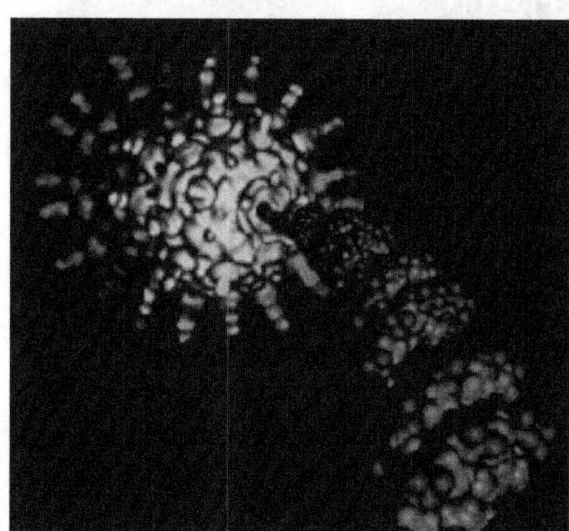

- VOYAGERS
- Self
- General Processes
- SHIPS

Legend (right side):
- Individual Growth
- Collective Growth
- **Actualization Growth**

Actualization Growth. "In Study Program #3, you will be introduced to the **Developmental Sequence** – a series of healthy Transition Cycles that produce Actualization Growth."

S3b. STUDY PROGRAM FOR ACTUALIZATION GROWTH

This Study Program will teach you how both Individuals and Groups can maximize their Human Potential – by overcoming Challenges through a series of successful Transition Cycles. The Program consists of 24 Lessons spread over 19 Sessions, including 12 New Sessions. You should allow yourself approximately four weeks to complete it.

STUDY PROGRAM: ACTUALIZATION GROWTH (#3)

DIMENSIONS, PARTICIPANTS, PROCESSES, PATHFINDERS

LESSON	
1	**D1. STAGES.** The levels of development, maturity, enlivenment, or enlightenment through which we pass as we grow.
2	**D2. TRANSITIONS.** The quantum leaps that take us from one Stage to the next.
3	**D1+2. DEVELOPMENTAL SEQUENCE.** A series of alternating Stages and Transitions.
4a	**D7. IMPEDIMENTS.** The two major ways the Growth process can be impeded or obstructed – Challenges & Impasses.
4b	**D7a. Challenges.** Everyday obstacles faced by relatively healthy people. Overt difficulties, demanding tasks, tests of one's abilities or resolve.
5	**P1. SELF SYSTEM.** A combination of the Experienced Self and the Observed Self – the two entities that engage in a dialectic by which the Self grows.
6a	**P2. INDIVIDUAL & COLLECTIVE SELVES.** The two forms of Identity that can participate in the Growth process.
6b	**P2a. Individual Self.** The aspect of Self that identifies and grows as an Individual.
6c	**P2b. Collective Self.** The aspect of Self that identifies and grows as a Group.
7	**PPR1. TRANSITION CYCLE.** The four-phase process of Metamorphosis by which we Transition from one Stage to the next.
8a	**PPR3. ACTUALIZATION GROWTH.** The normal progression of Growth from Stage to Stage.
8b	**PPR3a. Actualization Cycle.** The four-phase cycle whereby we overcome Challenges.
9	**PR7-10. PHYSICAL WORLD.** Processes that engage us with material reality.
10	**PR11-17. SOCIO-CULTURAL.** Processes that engage us with groups of people – from pairs to whole cultures.
11	**PR24-28. SELF-EXPRESSION.** Processes that enable us to express our inward reality in outward form.
12	**PR34-35. COMPREHENSIVE.** Processes combine and integrate many diverse Growth Processes into a single immersion experience.
13	**PF3. HOLISTIC GROWTH SITUATION.** A cluster of experiences that offers many diverse opportunities for Growth in a single integrated activity.
14	**PF4. AUTHORITIES.** People with exceptional wisdom whose work sheds light on and contributes to our Growth.
15a	**PF6. COUNSELOR OR THERAPIST.** A Growth Practitioner specially trained to implement some aspect of our Growth.
15b	**PF6a. Counselor or Coach.** Growth Practitioner specially trained to implement some aspect of Actualization Growth for people with Challenges.
16	**PF8. MENTORS.** People other than Counselors, Therapists, Spiritual Guides, etc. who endeavor to help us grow.
17	**PF9. GROWTH CENTER.** A place where people gather together to cultivate a particular aspect of their Growth.
18	**PF10. INTEGRAL LIFE GUIDE.** A Growth Practitioner whose work encompasses all five Domains of the ADAPT Model.
19	**PF11. INTERNAL NAVIGATOR.** The Guide we form within ourselves by internalizing the Guidance we receive from outside.

Study Program S4. Restoration Growth

Restoration Growth is Growth for people with deep-seated problems. Restoration Growth proceeds backward to resolve problems from prior Stages, so that forward-directed Actualization Growth (S3) can resume.

SYSTEM 4: RESTORATION GROWTH

❈ **Dimensions**
- Restoration Growth proceeds backward to previous **Stages** (D1) or **Transitions** (D2),
  Where **Impediments** (D7) in the form of **Impasses** (D7a) have occurred.

❈ **Participants**
- Those Impasses may be embodied in a pernicious **Shadow Self** (P4).
- Restoration Growth can occur for both **Individuals** and **Groups** (P2a-b).

❈ **Processes**
- The Shadow Self was formed by a distortion of the **Transition Cycle** (PPR1),
  Called the **Shadow Cycle** (PPR2).
- In Restoration Growth, our Human Potential (PPR3) is restored through one or more **Restoration Cycles** (PPR4a) --
  Using primarily the **Conscious Development Processes** (PR29-33).

❈ **Pathfinders**
- Restoration Growth may be **Guided** and **Orchestrated** (PF1-12) primarily by a trained **Therapist** (PF6d) --
  Sometimes with the aid of a **Spiritual Guide** (PF7),
  And sometimes only through the intervention of **Providence** (PF12).

My Restoration Growth. "As a troubled Young Adult, I need to revisit and resolve some traumatic childhood episodes -- so that I can resume normal Actualization Growth."

Restoration Growth System. Implicit in Wilber's *Pathologies* and *Treatments*.

S4. Restoration Growth. Page 239

RACHEL'S RESTORATION GROWTH

"As a Baby (D1),
Rachel was neglected and abused (PR1) --
which caused her normal Transition Cycle (PPR1)
to distort into a pernicious Shadow Cycle (PPR2)."

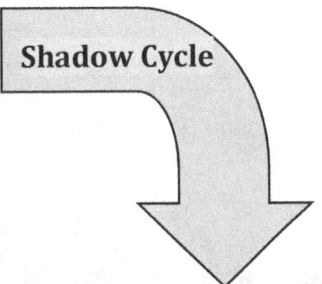

Shadow Cycle

Baby

"By the time Rachel became a Toddler (D1),
her resulting Shadow Self (P4)
had created entrenched Impediments (D6)
in the form of Impasses (D6b)
that made her sullen and withdrawn."

Toddler

"Now, as an Adult (D1),
with the help of her Therapist (PF6d),
and the support of her Integral Life Guide (PF10),
Rachel must Revisit Her Feelings as a baby (PR31),
and Restore her sense of Self-worth (PPR4) --
so that she may Resume a Happy, Growing Life (PPR3).

Page 240. ADAPT Study Programs

S4a. Diagram of System 4

The **Magenta Circle** depicts the components of System 4, **Restoration Growth**. Read clockwise, beginning at the upper-left.

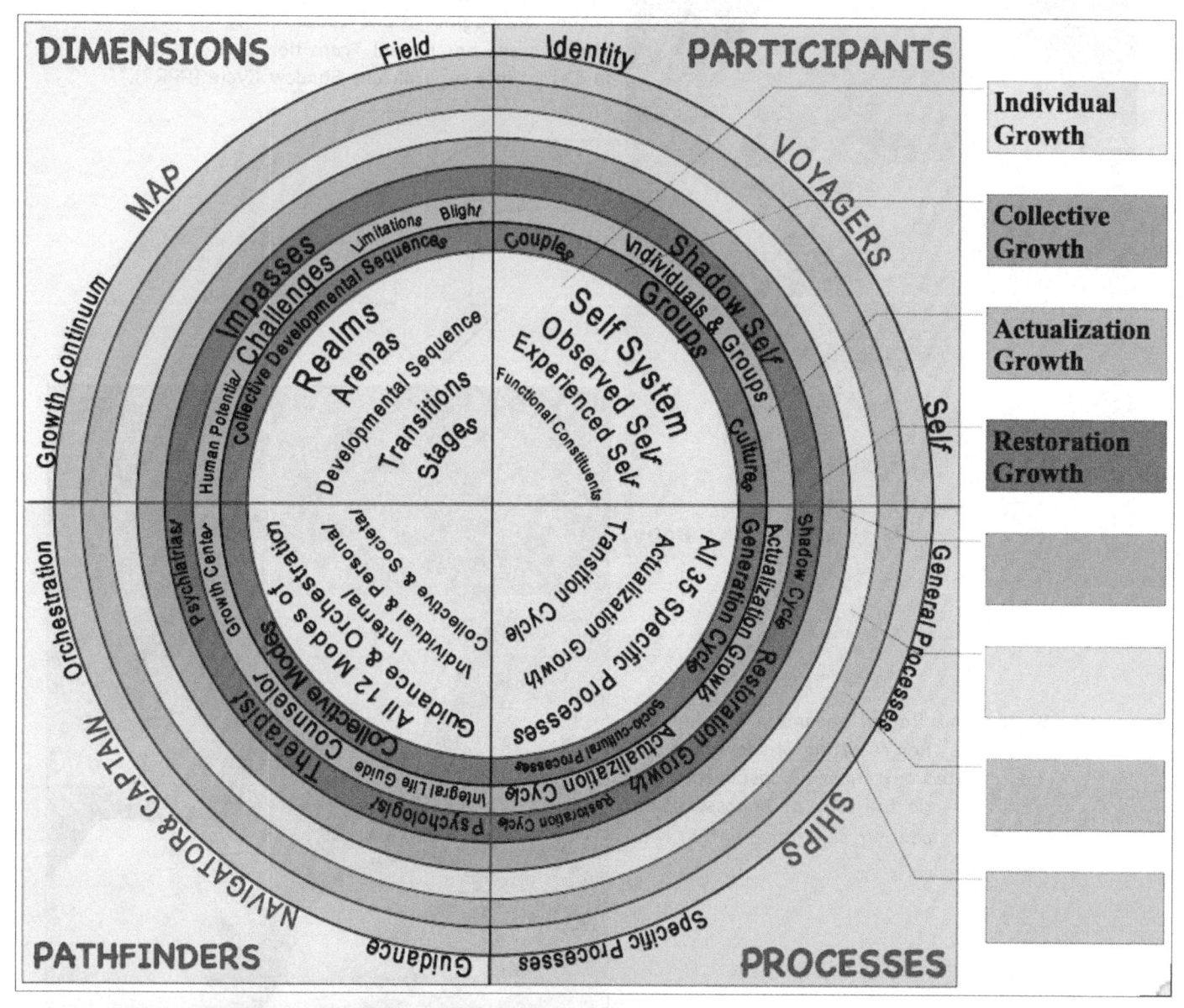

DIMENSIONS — Field / MAP / Growth Continuum / Orchestration

PARTICIPANTS — Identity / VOYAGERS / Self

- Individual Growth
- Collective Growth
- Actualization Growth
- Restoration Growth

PATHFINDERS — NAVIGATOR & CAPTAIN

PROCESSES — SHIPS / General Processes / Specific Processes / Guidance

Inner rings (clockwise from upper-left):
- Impasses — Limitations, Blight
- Challenges
- Realms / Arenas
- Human Potential / Collective Developmental Sequence
- Developmental Sequence / Transitions / Stages
- Internal & personal / Collective & Societal
- All 12 Modes of Guidance & Orchestration
- Collective Modes / Counselor / Therapist / Psychologist / Psychiatrist / Growth Center / Integral Life Guide
- Restoration Cycle / Actualization Cycle / Socio-cultural Processes
- Actualization Growth / Generation Cycle / Restoration Growth / Generation Cycle
- All 35 Specific Processes
- Actualization / Transition Cycle
- Self System / Observed Self / Experienced Self / Functional Constituents
- Shadow Self / Individuals & Groups / Couples / Groups / Cultures

America's Restoration Growth. "As a troubled Culture (racial strife, etc.), America needs to revisit and resolve past injustices (slavery, discrimination) -- so that normal, healthy Cultural Development can resume."

S4b. STUDY PROGRAM FOR RESTORATION GROWTH

This Study Program will teach you how Individuals (and sometimes Groups) can overcome an entrenched Impasse through a successful Restoration Cycle – often with the assistance of a Therapist or Integral Life Guide. The Program consists of 16 Lessons spread over 12 Sessions, including eight New Sessions. You should allow yourself approximately one to two weeks to complete it.

STUDY PROGRAM: RESTORATION GROWTH (#4)

LESSON	DIMENSIONS, PARTICIPANTS, PROCESSES, PATHFINDERS
1	**D1. STAGES.** The levels of development, maturity, enlivenment, or enlightenment through which we pass as we grow.
2	**D2. TRANSITIONS.** The quantum leaps that take us from one Stage to the next.
3a	**D7. IMPEDIMENTS.** The two major ways the Growth process can be impeded or obstructed – Challenges & Impasses.
3b	**D7b. Impasses.** Submerged or Subconscious difficulties encountered by people with entrenched 'problems.' Blocks, Hang-ups, or Pathologies that cause the Growth process to become obstructed, thwarted, repressed, distorted, split off, repressed, or damaged.
4	**P2. INDIVIDUAL & COLLECTIVE SELVES.** The two forms of Identity that can participate in the Growth process.
5a	**P4. SHADOW SELF.** Our Inner Saboteur or Gremlin -- any disattached scrap of Identity that impedes or distorts the Growth process.
5b	**P4a. Pathologies & Treatments.** The typical Pathologies and modes of Treatment at each Stage of Development.
6	**PPR2. SHADOW CYCLE.** A malfunction of the Transition Cycle, which can produce a pernicious Shadow Self that is the source of neuroses.
7a	**PPR4. RESTORATION GROWTH.** Revisiting past Stages to resolve Impasses, so that normal Actualization Growth can resume.
7b	**PPR3b. Restoration Cycle.** The four-phase cycle whereby we overcome Impediments.
8	**PR29-33. CONSCIOUS DEVELOPMENT.** Techniques, practices, and programs designed specifically to promote Personal Growth, resolve psychological problems, and facilitate spiritual enlightenment.
9a	**PF6. COUNSELOR OR THERAPIST.** A Growth Practitioner specially trained to implement some aspect of our Growth.
9b	**PF6d. Therapist.** Growth Practitioner specially trained to implement some aspect of Restoration Growth for people with Impasses.
10	**PF7. SPIRITUAL GUIDE.** A spiritual master or teacher, who can guide us in Awakening to the Divine Presence.
11	**PF12. PROVIDENCE.** The Guidance & Orchestration we receive from the Divine Presence.

Restoration Growth. "In Study Program #4, you will be introduced to the **Shadow Self** – a dis-attached scrap of identity that impedes or distorts our Growth process."

Study Program S5. Horizontal Growth

Horizontal Growth is Growth that occurs within a **Stage**. (In contrast to **Vertical Growth** [as in Systems 1-4], which takes us from Stage to Stage.) There are three modes of Horizontal Growth: **Improvement & Translation** (S5a, this page) and **Equivalence** (S5b, page 244) are discussed below. **Improvement Within Type** (S5c) is discussed under Enneagram Types (P3b).

SYSTEM 5a. IMPROVEMENT & TRANSLATION

❖ Dimensions

- Within a given **Stage** (D1),
  And within a given **Realm** (D3) and **Arena** (D4),
  An **Impediment** (D7)
  In the form of a **Challenge** (D7a) presents itself.

❖ Participants

- Progress within the Stage is navigated by the **Self System** (P1),
  Consisting of a mild form of **Experienced & Observed Selves** (P1a-b).
- Such progress can occur in both **Individuals** and **Groups** (P2a-b).

❖ Processes

- The Self System progresses <u>within</u> the Stage through a mild form of the **Transition Cycle** (PPR1).
- Progress occurs through **Improvement** of already existing skills and abilities,
  As well as **Translation** to similar or related skills and abilities (PR6a).
- Such progress is a type of **Actualization Growth** (PPR3).
- Horizontal Growth can be facilitated by any of 35 **Specific Processes** (PR1-35),
  Especially **Socio-Cultural** (PR11-17) and **Formal Investigation Processes** (PR18-23) –
  Processes that tend to put a premium on conformity, improvement within an established social role, and improvement in technical skills and knowledge.

❖ Pathfinders

- Improvement & Translation can be **Guided** and **Orchestrated** by any of the 12 **Pathfinders** (PF1-12),
  Especially **Society & Culture** (PF2) and **Authorities** (PF4) --
  Influences that tend to put a premium on obedience, and following the dictates of an established precedent.

My Improvement & Translation. "I've become better and better at walking. Now I'm learning to run, hop, and skip."

Horizontal Growth System. Implicit in Wilber's *Horizontal Translation*.

S5. Horizontal Growth.   Page 243

SAMANTHA'S IMPROVEMENT & TRANSLATION

"While in the Earlier Childhood Stage of Development (D1),
in the Realm of the Psyche (D3b)
in the Arena of Cognitive Development (D4b),
Samantha, an Individual little girl (P2a),
Learns to Read (D4b),
and develops a love of reading."

Improvement

"As Samantha matures within that Stage (D1),
she passes through mild Transition Cycles (PR1).
Her reading skills continue to Improve (PR6a)
so she can Read Longer and More Difficult Books (D4b).
She Looks Back with pleasure (P1b)
to those early Reading Experiences (D1)
that brought her to This Point (D1)."

Translation

"Now that Samantha is an excellent reader (D1),
she can Translate those abilities (D2)
to related skills like Writing and Spelling (D4b).
She is aided by Specific Processes
like Language & Communication (PR24).
Her progress is supported by a loving Mom (PR1),
dedicated Teachers (PR8),
and a Creative Grade School (PR9d)."

System 5b. Equivalence

- ❀ **Dimensions**
    - ❖ Equivalence takes place within each of **Stage** (D1) of Development,
    And within a given **Realm** (D3) and **Arena** (D4),

- ❀ **Participants**
    - ❖ Different **Personality Types** (P3) proceed each Stage in their own **Styles**.
    - ❖ Male and female **Gender Types** (P3a) are perhaps the prime form of Equivalence.
    - ❖ **Enneagram Types**, **Birth Order Types**, and **Ethnic & Cultural Types** (P3b-d) also exhibit this form of Growth.
    - ❖ Such progress can occur in both **Individuals** and **Groups** (P2a-b).

- ❀ **Processes**
    - ❖ Each Personality Type progresses through the usual **Transition Cycles** (PPR1) of the Developmental Sequence (D1+2),
    But in **Styles** that are **Horizontally Equivalent** (PPR6b).
    - ❖ Such progress is another aspect of **Actualization Growth** (PPR3).
    - ❖ Horizontal Growth can be facilitated by any of 35 **Specific Processes** (PR1-35) -- But Personality Types are especially shaped by **Socio-Cultural Processes** (PR11-17) that emphasize a prescribed social role.

- ❀ **Pathfinders**
    - ❖ Equivalence Growth can be **Guided** and **Orchestrated** by any of the 12 **Pathfinders** (PF1-12),
    Especially **Society & Culture** (PF2) and **Authorities** (PF4) --
    Influences that put a premium on conformity and following established precedents.

Our Equivalence. "We're both at the Young Adult Stage. Because we're different Enneagram Types (and Gender Types), we have very different ways of expressing it."

BARACK & MICHELLE'S EQUIVALENCE GROWTH

"The Obamas are a Couple (P2b)
who have differing Enneagram Types (P3b) --
and who go through the Stages (D1) and Transitions (D2)
in Styles that are Horizontally Equivalent (PPR6b).
Barack probably began as a convivial #9.
While Michelle may have been an ambitious #8 (P3b)."

Equivalence

"Their marriage underwent some Impediments (D7)
in the form of Challenges (D7a)."

Equivalence

"When they emerged from the pressures of Early Adulthood (D1),
Barack had morphed into an upwardly-mobile #3, while Michelle had shaped herself into a supportive and maternal #2 (P3b).
Their progress was aided by a Common Goal (PR14), but hampered by Public Scrutiny (PR25).
Their Relationship (PF5) may have been supported by some Counseling (PF6a),
And by the traditional Role Models of our Culture (PF2)."

Page 246. ADAPT Study Programs

S5a. Diagram of System 5

The **Purple Circle** depicts the components of System 5, **Horizontal Growth**. For each of the two sub-Systems, read clockwise, beginning at the upper-left.

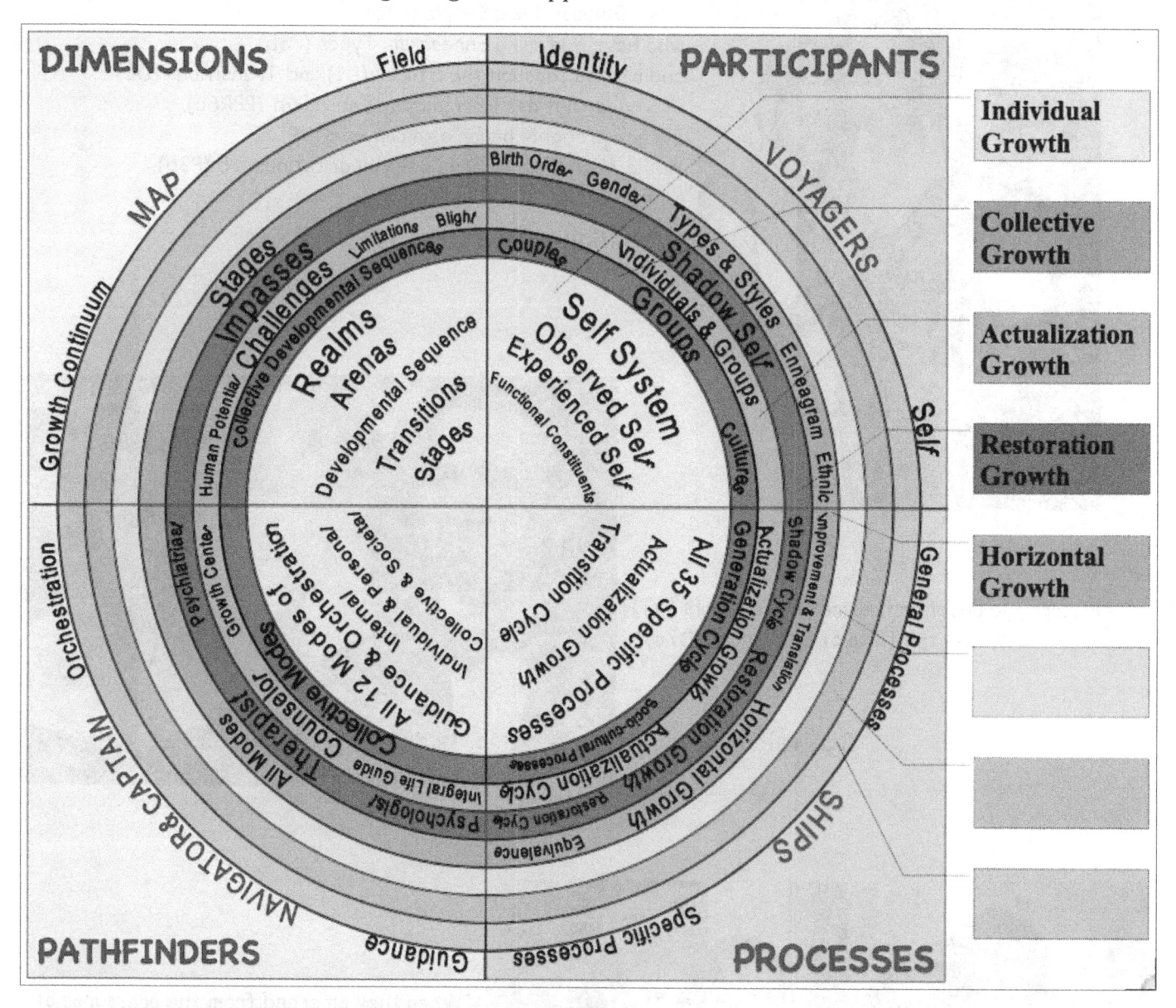

DIMENSIONS — Field | Identity — **PARTICIPANTS**

MAP / VOYAGERS

Growth Continuum — Birth Order, Gender, Types & Styles

Stages, Impasses, Challenges, Limitations, Blight — Couples, Individuals & Groups, Shadow Self

Realms, Arenas — Self System, Observed Self, Experienced Self — Groups, Enneagram, Cultures, Ethnic

Human Potential, Collective Developmental Sequences, Developmental Sequence, Transitions, Stages — Functional Constituents

Self

Orchestration, Psychiatrist, Growth Center, All Modes, Therapist, Counselor, Collective Modes, All 12 Modes of Guidance & Orchestration, Internal & Collective & Personal & Societal — Transition Cycle, Actualization Growth, All 35 Specific Processes, Socio-cultural Processes, Integral Life Guide, Psychologist — Actualization Cycle, Generation Cycle, Shadow Cycle, Improvement & Translation, Actualization Growth, Horizontal Growth, Restoration Growth, Generation Growth, Restoration Cycle, Equivalence

General Processes / SHIPS

NAVIGATOR & CAPTAIN / **PATHFINDERS** — Guidance / Specific Processes — **PROCESSES**

Legend:
- Individual Growth
- Collective Growth
- Actualization Growth
- Restoration Growth
- Horizontal Growth

Horizontal Growth. "In Study Program #5, you will be introduced to **Enneagram Types** – Personality Types that go through the same Stages of Growth, but in very different Styles."

S5b. Study Program for Horizontal Growth

This Study Program will teach you how both Individuals and Groups can grow within a Stage – primarily through the use of Improvement & Translation, but also through Equivalent Styles. The Program consists of 20 Lessons spread over 17 Sessions, including ten New Sessions. You should allow yourself approximately two weeks to complete it.

STUDY PROGRAM: HORIZONTAL GROWTH (#5)

Lesson	DIMENSIONS, PARTICIPANTS, PROCESSES, PATHFINDERS
1	**D1. STAGES.** The levels of development, maturity, enlivenment, or enlightenment through which we pass as we grow.
2	**D3. REALMS.** The four major spheres of human experience where Growth can occur – Everyday Life, Psyche, Body, Spirit.
3	**D4. ARENAS.** The specific areas of activity within each Realm where Growth takes place.
4	**D7. IMPEDIMENTS.** The two major ways the Growth process can be impeded or obstructed – Challenges & Impasses.
5	**D7a. Challenges.** Everyday obstacles faced by relatively healthy people. Overt difficulties, demanding tasks, tests of one's abilities or resolve.
6	**P1. SELF SYSTEM.** A combination of the Experienced Self and the Observed Self – the two entities that engage in a dialectic by which the Self grows.
7	**P2. INDIVIDUAL & COLLECTIVE SELVES.** The two forms of Identity that can participate in the Growth process.
8a	**P3. PERSONALITY TYPES & PERSONAE.** <u>Personality Type</u>: A profile of Personality that recurs in human populations with significant regularity. <u>Persona</u>: Our public face. Enables us to play a part in the drama of existence.
8b	**P3a. Gender Types.** The attitudes and modes of behavior that originate from one's sexual Gender.
9a	**P3b. Enneagram Types.** The nine Personality Types based upon the Enneagram system.
9b	**P3b1. Enneagram Traits.** The progression from Fixated to Evolved Traits within an Enneagram Type.
10	**PPR1. TRANSITION CYCLE.** The four-phase process of Metamorphosis by which we Transition from one Stage to the next.
11	**PPR3. ACTUALIZATION GROWTH.** The normal progression of Growth from Stage to Stage.
12a	**PPR6. HORIZONTAL GROWTH.** Growth that occurs within a Stage.
12b	**PPR6a. Improvement & Translation.** Growth within a Stage, where we: a) Improve on the abilities we have acquired at that Stage; b) Translate our competence to other related abilities.
13	**PPR6b. Equivalence.** Where two people with different Personality Types proceed through the Stages in Styles that are Horizontally Equivalent.
14	**PR11-17. SOCIO-CULTURAL.** Processes that engage us with groups of people – from pairs to whole cultures.
15	**PR18-23. FORMAL INVESTIGATION.** Processes that engage our thinking and reasoning capacities.
16	**PF2. SOCIETY & CULTURE.** The set of role models and the lessons on living life we receive from our Society & Culture.
17	**PF4. AUTHORITIES.** People with exceptional wisdom whose work sheds light on and contributes to our Growth.

Equivalence Growth. Male and Female Gender Types (P3a) go through the same Stages & Transitions of Growth (S1-2), but in different Styles

Study Program S6. Perspective Growth

Perspective Growth is Growth that occurs as we shift or broaden the **Perspectives** (D5) from which we view and orchestrate our lives. There are two modes of Perspective Growth – **Fundamental Perspectives** (S6a, this page) and **Inclusiveness** (S6b, page 250).

SYSTEM 6a. FUNDAMENTAL PERSPECTIVES

❀ Dimensions
- ❖ Within a given situation, we can take any of four **Fundamental Perspectives** (D5a).
- ❖ Each Perspective implies a particular **Path** (P5b) of action and endeavor.
- ❖ Fundamental Perspectives may pertain to any **Stage** (D1) of Development, In any **Realm** (D3) or **Arena** (D4).

❀ Participants
- ❖ By taking such Perspectives, we assume **Multiple Identities** (P6a), Identities that **Shift** (P6a) from one Perspective to another.
- ❖ Perspective Shift occurs primarily in **Individuals** (P2a), But may also occur in **Groups** (P2b).

❀ Processes
- ❖ Perspective Shift occurs through the General Process of **Perspective Growth** (PPR7a), Where we Shift fluidly from one Perspective to another.
- ❖ Perspective Growth can be facilitated by any of 35 **Specific Processes** (PR1-35), But is especially affected by **Self Expression Processes** (PR24-28) --
- ❖ Where **Creativity** in all forms can encourage Multiple Perspectives.

❀ Pathfinders
- ❖ Perspective Growth can be **Guided** and **Orchestrated** by any of the 12 **Pathfinders** (PF1-12), Especially **Society & Culture** (PF2), **Integral Life Guide** (PF10), and **Internal Navigator** (PF11) --
Influences that help us Shift our Perspectives.

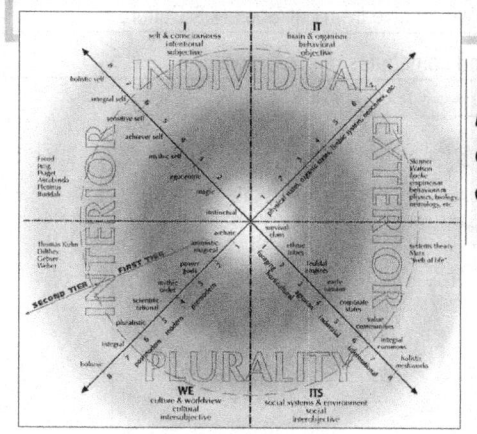

My Four Perspectives. "When I make any big life decision, I try to consider my inner and outer needs, as well as my individual and collective concerns."

Perspective Growth System. Implicit in Wilber's *Quadrants*.

System 6 is somewhat abstruse and esoteric. Comments and suggestions from readers are welcome.

S6. Perspective Growth. Page 249

BERNARD'S FUNDAMENTAL PERSPECTIVES

"Bernard, a solitary Individual (P2a),
Was a narrow-minded Introvert (P4),
Who saw life as a collection of Facts [individual/external],
That had to fit a Pattern [collective/external] (D5a)."

Expanded Perspectives

"When Bernard embraced all four Perspectives (D5a)
He became able to Shift Fluidly (PPR7a)
From one Perspective to another."

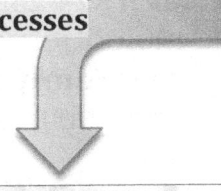

Expanded Processes

"Bernard was especially aided in his progress
By Self Expression Processes (PR24-28),
Such as Expressive Arts (PR28),
And Conscious Development Processes (PR29-33),
Such as Introspection & Self-Awareness (PR30).
These Processes often took place in
A Holistic Environment (PF3) or Growth Center (PF9),
Sometimes under the direction of an Integral Life
Guide (PF10)."

System 6b. Inclusiveness

❁ **Dimensions**
- ❖ We can practice Inclusiveness
  Within any **Stage** (D1) of Development --
  But primarily in **Realms** of **Everyday Life** (D3a) and the **Psyche** (D3b).

❁ **Participants**
- ❖ In our attitudes toward others (P2b),
  we can limit our Identification to our own private, personal **Self** (P2a).
- ❖ Or we can **Broaden** our Perspective (P6a) to include other **Individuals** (P2a),
  And also other **Groups** (P2b) –
  Including **Genders**, **Ethnic Groups**, and other forms of **Diversity** (P3).

❁ **Processes**
- ❖ Inclusiveness occurs through the General Process of **Perspective Growth** (PPR7b),
  Where we fluidly **Broaden** our **Identity** (P6b), wherever appropriate.
- ❖ Inclusiveness can be facilitated by any of 35 **Specific Processes** (PR1-35),
  But especially **Socio-Cultural Processes** (PR24-28) --
  Which encourage cooperation and mutual respect.
- ❖ And also by **Nurture & Bonding** (PR1) and **Family Dynamics** (PR6),
  Processes where Interconnectedness and Unity are the healthy norm.

❁ **Pathfinders**
- ❖ Inclusiveness Growth can be **Guided** and **Orchestrated** by any of the 12 **Pathfinders** (PF1-12),
  Especially **Society & Culture** (PF2), **Holistic Growth Situations** (PF3), and **Growth Centers** (PF9) --
  Influences that give us opportunities to Broaden our Perspectives.

My Inclusiveness. "As I've matured, I've learned to appreciate people with backgrounds and interests very different from my own."

SHEILA'S INCLUSIVENESS

"When Sheila was a Teenager (D1),
She was a spoiled, self-absorbed Rebel (P2a),
Concerned only with her own Material Needs D3a),
And her own Emotional Thrills (D3b)."

Inclusiveness

"When, as a Young Adult (D1),
Sheila went through
some deep Soul-Searching (PR30),
She decided to join the Peace Corps (PR34).
There, she discovered people (P2b)
With needs much greater than her own (D3a-b).
When her Empathy expanded to encompass a
whole Village (PPR7b),
She experienced true happiness (D8)
for the first time
Finally, her Soul had come to rest (PPR9)."

"Sheila was fortified and encouraged in her Journey
By the inspiring example of Mother Teresa (PF4),
By the supportive Environment of the Peace Corps (PR34),
And by her attentive Supervisor (PF8),
Who helped bring forth the care
that was in her heart (PR30).

Page 252. ADAPT Study Programs

S6a. Diagram of System 6

The **Blue Circle** depicts the components of System 6, **Perspective Growth**. For both sub-Systems, read clockwise, beginning at the upper-left.

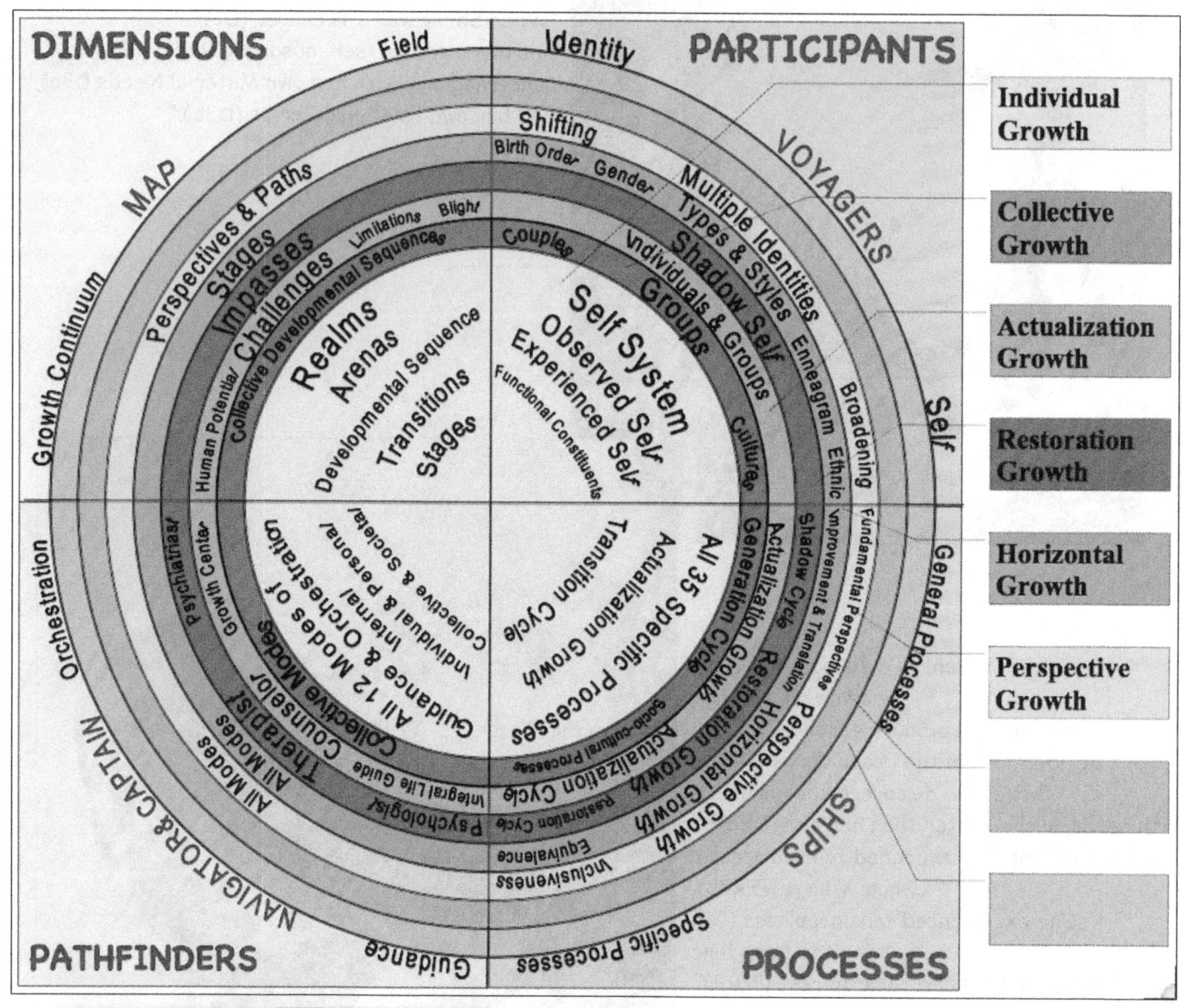

DIMENSIONS — Field | Identity — **PARTICIPANTS**

- MAP
  - Perspectives & Paths
  - Stages
  - Impasses — Limitations — Blight
  - Challenges
  - Realms — Human Potential — Collective Developmental Sequences
  - Arenas — Developmental Sequence
  - Transitions — Internal & Personal / Collective & Social
  - Stages — Functional Constituents
- Growth Continuum

- VOYAGERS
  - Shifting
  - Birth Order — Gender
  - Multiple Identities
  - Types & Styles
  - Shadow Self — Enneagram
  - Individuals & Groups — Ethnic
  - Couples — Cultures
  - Groups
  - Self System — Observed Self — Experienced Self

- Self — Broadening

- **PATHFINDERS**
  - Orchestration
  - Psychiatrist — Growth Center
  - Therapist — All Modes
  - Counselor — Collective Modes
  - Guidance & Orchestration of All 12 Modes
  - Psychologist — Integral Life Guide
  - Guidance

- **PROCESSES**
  - Specific Processes
  - Inclusiveness — Equivalence
  - Restoration Cycle
  - Actualization Cycle
  - Socio-cultural Processes
  - Actualization Growth — Generation Cycle — Restoration Growth — Horizontal Growth — Perspective Growth
  - Shadow Cycle — Improvement & Translation
  - Fundamental Perspectives
  - General Processes
  - All 35 Specific Processes
  - Actualization Cycle — Transition Cycle
  - SHIPS

Labels (right side):
- Individual Growth
- Collective Growth
- Actualization Growth
- Restoration Growth
- Horizontal Growth
- Perspective Growth

NAVIGATOR & CAPTAIN

Perspective Growth. "In Study Program #6, you will be introduced to **Perspectives & Paths** — the four Fundamental Perspectives from which we can view any life situation, and the four corresponding Paths our own life can take.

S6b. Study Program for Perspective Growth

This Study Program will teach you how both Individuals and Groups can expand their Perspectives on people and life situations – both by Shifting and by Broadening their Identity. The Program consists of 24 Lessons spread over 19 Sessions, including seven New Sessions. Allow yourself approximately one to two weeks to complete it. Since this topic is a somewhat abstruse and esoteric, you should delay it until after System 8, Spiritual Growth.

STUDY PROGRAM: PERSPECTIVE GROWTH (#6)

DIMENSIONS, PARTICIPANTS, PROCESSES, PATHFINDERS

Lesson	
1	**D1. STAGES.** The levels of development, maturity, enlivenment, or enlightenment through which we pass as we grow.
2	**D3. REALMS.** The four major spheres of human experience where Growth can occur – Everyday Life, Psyche, Body, Spirit.
3	**D3a. Life Passages.** The external phases of accomplishment or achievement that occur as we progress through the biological Life Cycle.
4	**D3b. Psyche Passages.** The internal phases of mental Maturation that occur as we progress through the Stages of Psychological Development.
5a	**D5. PERSPECTIVES & PATHS.**
5b	**D5a. Perspectives of Growth.** The four basic points-of-view, or aspects of existence, from which any Growth experience can be observed.
6	**D5b. Paths of Growth.** The four Perspectives, as applied to the types of life activity we choose to focus our attention on.
7	**P2. INDIVIDUAL & COLLECTIVE SELVES.** The two forms of Identity that can participate in the Growth process.
8a	**P3. PERSONALITY TYPES & PERSONAE.** <u>Personality Type</u>: A profile of Personality that recurs in human populations with significant regularity. <u>Persona</u>: Our public face. Enables us to play a part in the drama of existence.
8b	**P3a. Gender Types.** The attitudes and modes of behavior that originate from one's sexual Gender.
9a	**P6. MULTIPLE IDENTITIES.** Situations where healthy Individuals can assume more than one Identity – either by Shifting or by Broadening their Identity.
9b	**P6a. Shifting Identity.** We can view our life from any of four Fundamental Perspectives, and follow any of four Fundamental Life Paths.
10	**P6b. Broadening Identity.** We can grow by becoming more Inclusive as to who or what we Identify or Empathize with.
11a	**PPR7. PERSPECTIVE GROWTH.** Growth that occurs as we broaden the Perspectives from which we view and orchestrate our lives.
11b	**PPR7a. Fundamental Perspectives.** When we broaden our viewpoint, interests, and actions to incorporate all four Fundamental Perspectives.
11c	**PPR7b. Inclusiveness.** When we become more Inclusive as to who or what we identify or empathize with.
12	**PR1-6. FOUNDATIONAL.** Processes that are fundamental to all other Processes of Growth.
13	**PR11-17. SOCIO-CULTURAL.** Processes that engage us with groups of people – from pairs to whole cultures.
14	**PR24-28. SELF-EXPRESSION.** Processes that enable us to express our inward reality in outward form.
15	**PF2. SOCIETY & CULTURE.** The set of role models and the lessons on living life we receive from our Society & Culture.
16	**PF3. HOLISTIC GROWTH SITUATION.** A cluster of experiences that offers many diverse opportunities for Growth in a single integrated activity.
17	**PF9. GROWTH CENTER.** A place where people gather together to cultivate a particular aspect of their Growth.
18	**PF10. INTEGRAL LIFE GUIDE.** A Growth Practitioner whose work encompasses all five Domains of the ADAPT Model.
19	**PF11. INTERNAL NAVIGATOR.** The Guide we form within ourselves by internalizing the Guidance we receive from outside.

Study Program S7. Evolution & Involution

Evolution & Involution is Growth in two Directions – both Upward <u>and</u> Downward (or Outward and Inward). There are three modes of Evolution & Involution – **Transcend & Include** (S7a, this page), **Trajectories** (S7b, page 256), and **Gender-Type Growth** (Discussed under P3a, Gender Types; PP6b, Equivalence; and S5b, Horizontal Equivalence.).

SYSTEM 7a. TRANSCEND & INCLUDE

❂ Dimensions

- ❖ Transcend & Include directs us Upward & Outward in an **Ascending Direction** (D6a),
  But also Downward & Inward in a **Descending Direction** (D6a).
- ❖ Such Growth pertains to any **Stage** (D1) of Development,
  In any **Realm** (D3) or **Arena** (D4).

❂ Participants

- ❖ Transcend & Include occurs primarily in **Individuals** (P2a),
  But may also occur in **Groups** (P2b).
- ❖ Along the way, we may need to face our **Shadow Self** (P4).

❂ Processes

- ❖ In the Ascending Direction of **Evolution** (PPR8),
  We **Transcend** a prior Stage, and **Include** it in the subsequent Stage (PPR8a).
- ❖ When we fail to Include, we split off or **Disconnect** from the prior Stage (PPR2).
- ❖ In that case, the Descending Direction of **Involution** is needed to **Reconnect** us with our **Roots** (PPR4).
- ❖ Along the way, we may encounter at **Shadow Cycle** (PPR2),
  And need to engage in **Restoration Growth** (PPR4).
- ❖ Transcend & Include can employ any of the 35 **Specific Processes** (PR-35),
  Especially **Conscious Development** (PR29-33) –
  Since much of this Growth is done with conscious intention.

❂ Pathfinders

- ❖ Transcend & Include can be **Guided** and **Orchestrated** by any of the 12 **Pathfinders** (PF1-12),
  Especially **Counselor or Therapist** (PF6a-b) or **Integral Life Guide** (PF10).

My Transcend & Include. "I'm far more comfortable with myself – now that I'm reconnecting with the Inner Child I had formerly disowned."

Evolution & Involution Growth System. Implicit in Wilber's *Evolution & Involution*, or *Height & Depth*.

System 7 is somewhat abstruse and esoteric. Comments and suggestions from readers are welcome.

RANSOME'S TRANSCEND & INCLUDE

"As a Young Boy (D1),
Ransome was a spunky, fun-loving Kid (P2a),
Who enjoyed Getting in Trouble (D7a),
In the Classroom or on the Playground (D3a-b)."

Evolution: Disconnection

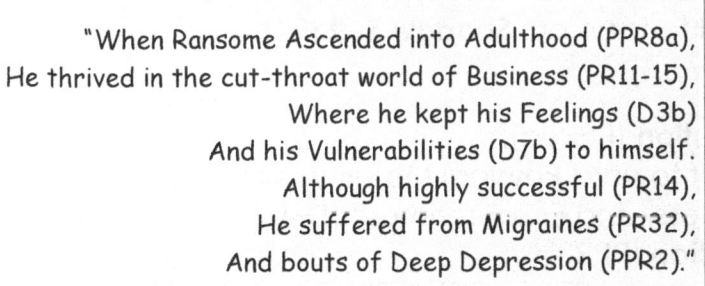

"When Ransome Ascended into Adulthood (PPR8a),
He thrived in the cut-throat world of Business (PR11-15),
Where he kept his Feelings (D3b)
And his Vulnerabilities (D7b) to himself.
Although highly successful (PR14),
He suffered from Migraines (PR32),
And bouts of Deep Depression (PPR2)."

Involution: Reconnection

"Ransome finally Broke Out of his Mental Prison (PPR4),
When he Descended into the Depths of his Soul (PPR8b),
And rediscovered his feisty, loveable Inner Child (P4) --
With the support of his Long-Term Partner (PF5),
His Therapist (PF6d), his Spiritual Guide (PF7),
And the improved Emotional Compass (PR30)
of his Internal Navigator (PF11).

System 7b. Life Trajectories

❁ Dimensions

- ❖ Life Trajectories is a **Developmental Sequence** (D1+2)
  That takes place over the course of a Lifetime.
- ❖ In our Earlier Life (D1),
  Our Trajectory directs us Upward & Outward in an **Ascending Direction** (D6b, PPR8b) –
  Often encountering **Challenges** (D7a) along the way.
- ❖ In our Later Life (D1),
  Our Trajectory directs us Downward & Inward in a **Descending Direction** (D6b, PPR8b).
- ❖ Between the two, there is a difficult **Transition** (D2) called **Mid-Life** (D7b) –
  Which often involves **Confronting** (PPR4) a major impasse (D7b).
- ❖ Such Growth can pertain to any **Realm** (D3) or **Arena** (D4).

❁ Participants

- ❖ Transcend & Include occurs primarily in **Individuals** (P2a),
  But may also occur in **Organizations** and other types of **Groups** (P2b).
- ❖ Along the way, we may need to face our **Shadow Self** (P4).

❁ Processes

- ❖ In our earlier Direction of **Evolution** (PPR8a),
  We trace an Ascending arc of toward Physical Maturity, Achievement, Psychological Maturity, Aliveness, and Enlightenment (D6b).
- ❖ In our later Direction of **Involution** (PPR8b),
  We follow a Descending arc toward Physical Stability, Fulfillment, Grounding, Authenticity, and Compassion (D6b).
- ❖ Along the way, we may encounter an **Impasse** (D7b),
  And need to engage in **Restoration Growth** (PPR4).
- ❖ Life Trajectories can employ any of the 35 **Specific Processes** (P1-35),
  Especially **Conscious Development** (PR29-33) –
  Since much of this Growth can be done with conscious intention.

❁ Pathfinders

- ❖ Transcend & Include can be **Guided** and **Orchestrated** by any of the 12 **Pathfinders** (PF1-12),
  Especially **Counselor or Therapist** (PF6a-b) or **Integral Life Guide** (PF10).
- ❖ The wisdom and experience we have gained over the course of our lifetime builds our **Internal Navigator** (PR11).

S7. Evolution & Involution. Page 257

MOSES'S LIFE TRAJECTORY

"As a Young Boy (D1),
Moses leads a privileged life (D3a),
As a Prince (P2a) in the court of the Pharaoh (PF8).
Moses's Evolution continues in an Ascending Direction (D6b),
Until he kills a Guard (P4) in defense of the Hebrews (P2b) --
Which forces him to flee from Egypt (D2)."

Evolution: Prince becomes outlaw.

"As a Mature Adult (D1),
Moses's Mid-Life Crisis (D2ad) begins
When God orders him to return to Egypt (P2b)
to confront Pharaoh (PPR4a).
After punishing Pharaoh with ten Plagues (PR32),
the confrontation culminates
in the parting of the Red Sea (D2),
And the destruction of Pharaoh's army (PPR4)."

Transition: Confrontation with Pharaoh.

Involution: Brings Hebrews home.

"After the Exodus from Egypt (D2),
Moses's Involution begins in a Descending Direction (D6b).
The Hebrews wander forty years in the Wilderness (PPR2),
Until a new Generation (P2b) of young people grows up (PPR5a),
Who never knew the subjugation of slavery (D7b).
Moses's Journey ends (D1)
With his arrival on the brink of the Promised Land (PPR3).

S7a. Diagram of System 7

The **Green Circle** depicts the components of System 7, **Evolution & Involution**. For each of the three sub-Systems, read clockwise, beginning at the upper-left.

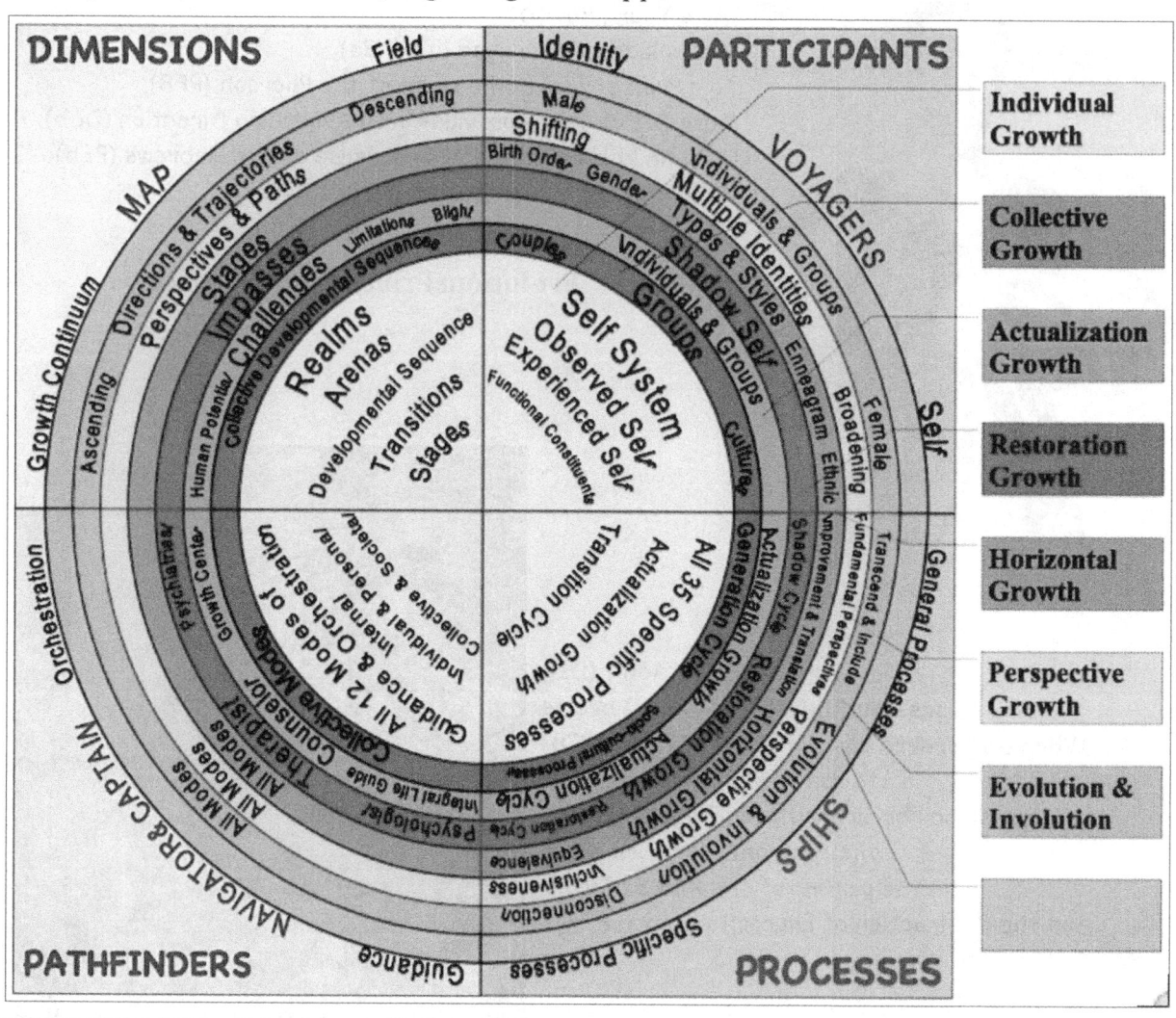

Diagram: A circular diagram divided into four quadrants labeled DIMENSIONS (upper-left), PARTICIPANTS (upper-right), PATHFINDERS (lower-left), and PROCESSES (lower-right). Concentric rings contain labels including: Field, Identity, Descending, Male, Shifting, Birth Order, Gender, Individuals & Groups, Multiple Identities, Types & Styles, Shadow Self, Couples, Individuals & Groups, Groups, Self System, Observed Self, Experienced Self, Functional Constituents, Realms, Arenas, Transitions, Stages, Developmental Sequence, Collective Development, Human Potential, Ascending, Growth Continuum, MAP, Directions & Trajectories, Perspectives & Paths, Stages, Impasses, Challenges, Limitations, Blight, VOYAGERS, Female, Broadening, Enneagram, Ethnic, Cultures, Fundamental Perspective, Transcend & Include, Self, General Processes, Evolution & Involution, SHIPS, Specific Processes, Disconnection, Inclusiveness, Equivalence, Restoration Cycle, Evolution & Involution, Horizontal Growth, Perspective Growth, Actualization Cycle, Generation Cycle, Restoration Growth, Actualization Growth, Shadow Cycle, Improvement & Translation, All 35 Specific Processes, Transition Cycle, Collective & Societal, Internal & Personal, Individual & Personal, Guidance & Orchestration, All 12 Modes of Collective Mode, Counselor, Therapist, Integral Life Guide, Psychologist, All Modes, All Modes, Psychiatrist, Growth Center, Orchestration, NAVIGATOR, CAPTAIN, Guidance.

Legend (right side): Individual Growth; Collective Growth; Actualization Growth; Restoration Growth; Horizontal Growth; Perspective Growth; Evolution & Involution.

S7b. Study Program for Evolution & Involution (facing page)

This Study Program will teach you how both Individuals and Groups can participate in Growth that is not only upward and outward, but also downward and inward. Such Growth occurs primarily through Transcending a prior Stage and then Including it in the next – or by following a Trajectory of Evolution & Involution over the course of a lifetime. The Program consists of 26 Lessons spread over 18 Sessions, including three New Sessions. You should allow yourself approximately one week to complete it. Since this topic is a somewhat abstruse and esoteric, you should delay it until after System 8 (Spiritual Growth) and System 6 (Perspective Growth).

> **Evolution & Involution.** "In Study Program #7, you will be introduced to **Life Trajectories** – the arc of Evolution & Involution that we trace over the course of a lifetime."

STUDY PROGRAM: EVOLUTION & INVOLUTION (#7)

DIMENSIONS, PARTICIPANTS, PROCESSES, PATHFINDERS

LESSON	
1	**D1. STAGES.** The levels of development, maturity, enlivenment, or enlightenment through which we pass as we grow.
2	**D2. TRANSITIONS.** The quantum leaps that take us from one Stage to the next.
3	**D1+2. DEVELOPMENTAL SEQUENCE.** A series of alternating Stages and Transitions.
4	**D3. REALMS.** The four major spheres of human experience where Growth can occur – Everyday Life, Psyche, Body, Spirit.
5	**D4. ARENAS.** The specific areas of activity within each Realm where Growth takes place.
6a	**D6. DIRECTIONS & TRAJECTORIES.** The two major vertical Directions our Growth can take – Ascending & Descending.
6b	**D6a. Directions of Growth.** In each of the four Realms, we can orient our life activities in two major Directions – Ascending and Descending.
6c	**D6b. Trajectories of Growth.** The Directions of Growth are played out over the full course of a lifetime.
7a	**D7. IMPEDIMENTS.** The two major ways the Growth process can be impeded or obstructed – Challenges & Impasses.
7b	**D7a. Challenges.** Everyday obstacles faced by relatively healthy people. Overt difficulties, demanding tasks, tests of one's abilities or resolve.
7c	**D7b. Impasses.** Submerged or Subconscious difficulties encountered by people with entrenched 'problems.' Blocks, Hang-ups, or Pathologies that cause the Growth process to become obstructed, thwarted, repressed, distorted, split off, repressed, or damaged.
8	**P2. INDIVIDUAL & COLLECTIVE SELVES.** The two forms of Identity that can participate in the Growth process.
9a	**P3. PERSONALITY TYPES & PERSONAE.** Personality Type: A profile of Personality that recurs in human populations with significant regularity. Persona: Our public face. Enables us to play a part in the drama of existence.
9b	**P3a. Gender Types.** The attitudes and modes of behavior that originate from one's sexual Gender.
10	**P4. SHADOW SELF.** Our Inner Saboteur or Gremlin -- any disattached scrap of Identity that impedes or distorts the Growth process.
11	**PPR2. SHADOW CYCLE.** A malfunction of the Transition Cycle, which can produce a pernicious Shadow Self that is the source of neuroses.
12a	**PPR4. RESTORATION GROWTH.** Revisiting past Stages to resolve Impasses, so that normal Actualization Growth can resume.
12b	**PPR3b. Restoration Cycle.** The four-phase cycle whereby we overcome Impediments.
13a	**PPR8. EVOLUTION & INVOLUTION.** The twin processes of Directional Growth – Ascending and Descending.
13b	**PPR8a. Transcend & Include.** When we Transcend a prior Stage, but Include it in the next Stage.
14a	**PPR8b. Life Trajectories.** The progression from Evolution, through Mid-Life, to Involution over the course of a lifetime.
14b	**PPR8c. Gender Types.** The tendency toward Evolution in males, toward Involution in females.
15	**PR29-33. CONSCIOUS DEVELOPMENT.** Techniques, practices, and programs designed specifically to promote personal Growth, resolve psychological problems, and facilitate spiritual enlightenment.
16	**PF6. COUNSELOR OR THERAPIST.** A Growth Practitioner specially trained to implement some aspect of our Growth.
17	**PF10. INTEGRAL LIFE GUIDE.** A Growth Practitioner whose work encompasses all five Domains of the ADAPT Model.
18	**PF11. INTERNAL NAVIGATOR.** The Guide we form within ourselves by internalizing the Guidance we receive from outside.

Our Underworld. "In Evolution & Involution (S7), we ascend to the Heavens and descend into our own personal Underworld."

Study Program S8. Spiritual Growth

Spiritual Growth is Growth that occurs as we **Awaken** to the **Divine Presence**.

SYSTEM 8: SPIRITUAL GROWTH

❋ Dimensions
- In Spiritual Growth, we ascend
- Within the **Internal Realm** (D3b-d) of **Spirit Passages** (D3d),
- By way of the **Spirit Arenas** (D4d)
- To higher and **Transcendent States** (D8) of our consciousness.
- Spiritual Growth can occur at any **Stage** (D1) of Development.
- Even Spiritual Growth is subject to **Impediments** (D7) –
  Especially the **Romantic Fallacy** (D8a)
  And the **Inverse Romantic Fallacy** (D8b).

❋ Participants
- As we ascend, we become increasingly **Attuned** (PPR9)
  to the **Divine Presence** (P7).
- In its **Immanent** form, the Divine Presence is the **Core Self** (P7a).
- In its **Transcendent** form, the Divine Presence is the **Witness** (P7b).
- Spiritual Growth occurs primarily with **Individuals** (P2a),
  But may also occur within **Groups** (P2b).

❋ Processes
- Spiritual Growth is a Process of **Awakening** (PPR9) to a truth that is <u>unchanging</u> and eternal.
- (In contrast to **Development** [as in Systems 1-7], which is a process of <u>change</u> and Metamorphosis (PPR1).
- Such Growth is often aided through **Spiritual Practices** (PR33),
  As well as by **Comprehensive Processes** (PR34-35) --
  Processes that focus on Growth of the Psyche (D3b) and Spirit (D3d).

❋ Pathfinders
- Spiritual Growth can be **Guided** and **Orchestrated**
  By a **Spiritual Guide** (PF7), by an **Integral Life Guide** (PF10),
  Or by **Authorities** (PF4), such as **Sacred Writings** (PR17, PR27) --
  Sometimes in the supportive environment of a **Meditation Center** (PF9a).
- Ultimately, such Growth does not occur solely through one's own efforts, But through the influence of Divine Grace, or **Providence** (PR12).

Spiritual Growth System. Implicit in Wilber's *Waking Up*.

Subjective or Objective? "Are Transcendent States just internal, subjective States of Mind? Or are they external, objective encounters with some sort of Divine Presence? Or both?"

JEAN VALJEAN'S SPIRITUAL GROWTH (*Les Miserables*)

"Jean Valjean, a poor Young Man, (P2a)
Who is one of the Wretched of the Earth (P2b),
Is imprisoned for 19 years (D7b)
For stealing a loaf of bread (D3a)."

Awakening to Grace

"Upon his parole, Valjean seeks refuge for the night with Bishop Myriel (PF9),
Where he steals two silver candlesticks (PR17),
And slinks out into the night (PPR2).
When Valjean is apprehended, the Bishop insists He <u>gave</u> the candlesticks to Valjean (PR33).
Valjean is thereby Awakened (PPR9) to the tangible evidence of God's Grace (PF12)."

Life of Service

"Once Valjean is Awakened (PPR9) to the pervasive Goodness (PF12)
Of a Higher Power (P7), he dedicates his life
To Alleviating Suffering and Serving Humanity (PR15).
His most noble act is to save precious, little Cosette (PPR4),
Daughter of the tragic Fantine (P4), who was brought to ruin (PPR2)
By the deplorable conditions in Valjean's factory (PF3)."

Page 262. ADAPT STUDY PROGRAMS

S8a. DIAGRAM OF SYSTEM 8

The **Gold Circle** depicts the components of System 8, **Spiritual Growth**. Read clockwise, beginning at the upper-left.

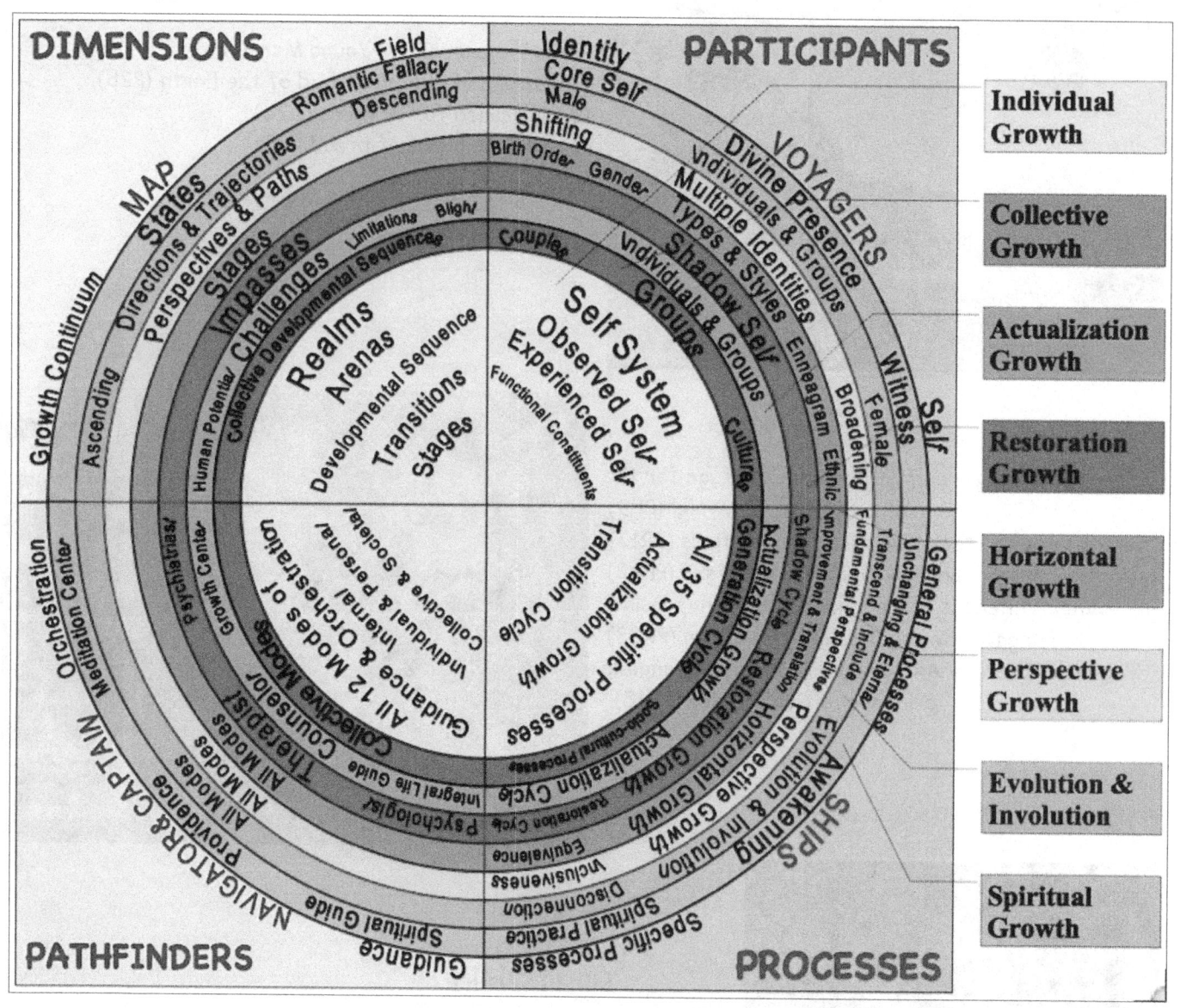

DIMENSIONS — Field, Romantic Fallacy, Descending, MAP, States, Directions & Trajectories, Perspectives & Paths, Stages, Impasses, Challenges, Limitations, Blight, Realms, Arenas, Human Potential, Collective Developmental Sequence, Developmental Sequence, Transitions, Stages, Ascending, Growth Continuum

PARTICIPANTS — Identity, Core Self, Male, Shifting, Birth Order, Gender, VOYAGERS, Individuals & Groups, Multiple Identities, Types & Styles, Shadow Self, Individuals & Groups, Couples, Groups, Self System, Observed Self, Experienced Self, Functional Constituents, Enneagram, Ethnic, Cultures, Broadening, Female, Witness, Self

PROCESSES — Divine Presence, Shadow Cycle, Actualization Cycle, Restoration Cycle, Horizontal Growth, Perspective, Evolution & Involution, Awakening, -SHIPS, Spiritual Practice, Disconnection, Inclusiveness, Equivalence, Socio-cultural Processes, Collective & Social, Internal & Personal, All 35 Specific Processes, Actualization Growth, Transition Cycle, Specific Processes, Guidance, Fundamental Perspectives, Transcend & Include, Unchanging & Eternal, General Processes, Generation Cycle

PATHFINDERS — NAVIGATOR & CAPTAIN, Providence, Meditation Center, Orchestration, Psychiatrist, Growth Center, Counselor, Therapist, Psychologist, Integral Life Guide, Spiritual Guide, All Modes, All 12 Modes of Guidance & Orchestration, Collective Modes

- **Individual Growth**
- **Collective Growth**
- **Actualization Growth**
- **Restoration Growth**
- **Horizontal Growth**
- **Perspective Growth**
- **Evolution & Involution**
- **Spiritual Growth**

Spiritual Growth. "In Study Program #8, you will be introduced to the **Core Self** & the **Witness** – the twin aspects of the Divine Presence, the spiritual entity that orchestrates and presides over our lives."

Core Self

Witness

S8b. Study Program for Spiritual Growth

This Study Program will teach you how both Individuals and Groups can experience Transcendent States and Awaken to the Divine Presence. The Program consists of 26 Lessons spread over 20 Sessions, including 9 New Sessions. You should allow yourself approximately two weeks to complete it.

Study Program: Spiritual Growth (#8)

Dimensions, Participants, Processes, Pathfinders

Lesson	
1	**D1. STAGES.** The levels of development, maturity, enlivenment, or enlightenment through which we pass as we grow.
2	**D3. REALMS.** The four major spheres of human experience where Growth can occur – Everyday Life, Psyche, Body, Spirit.
3a	**D3d. Spirit Passages.** The internal phases or modes of spiritual Enlightenment that occur as we awaken ourselves to the Divine Presence or open ourselves to the Holy Spirit.
3b	**D3b-d. Internal Realms.** The Development within the Internal Realms of Psyche, Body, and Spirit.
4a	**D4. ARENAS.** The specific areas of activity within each Realm where Growth takes place.
4b	**D4d. Arenas of the Spirit.** The various modes by which we achieve Transcendent States and experience the Divine Presence.
4c	**D4d1. Spirit Arenas: Sequences of Growth.** Growth in four Arenas of the Spirit.
5	**D8. TRANSCENDENT STATES.** The higher levels of consciousness experienced by mystics and translucents.
6	**D8a. Romantic Fallacy.** Interpreting primitive, archaic, or mythical Stages as Transcendent Stages or States.
7	**D8b. Inverse Romantic Fallacy.** Mistaking Transcendent Stages and States for low-level Stages or Pathologies.
8	**P2. INDIVIDUAL & COLLECTIVE SELVES.** The two forms of Identity that can participate in the Growth process.
9a	**P7. DIVINE PRESENCE.** The spiritual entity that presides over our lives – in its two manifestations: the Core Self and the Witness.
9b	**P7a. Core Self.** Our pure Identity, unaffected by material concerns, physical discomforts, or psychological obsessions and compulsions.
10	**P7b. Witness.** The pervasive, overarching Presence that presides over all aspects of our existence -- observing, cherishing, guiding, and protecting us.
11	**PPR9. SPIRITUAL GROWTH.** The process of Awakening to universal spiritual truths that are unchanging and eternal.
12	**PPR9a. Growing Up vs. Waking Up.** Growing Up is changing from one Stage to the next. Waking Up is awakening to truths that are unchanging and eternal.
13a	**PR29-33. CONSCIOUS DEVELOPMENT.** Techniques, practices, and programs designed specifically to promote Personal Growth, resolve psychological problems, and facilitate spiritual enlightenment.
13b	**PR33. Spiritual Practices.** Structured techniques and programs used to achieve higher States of consciousness, and/or a connection with the Divine Presence.
14	**PR34-35. COMPREHENSIVE.** Processes combine and integrate many diverse Growth Processes into a single immersion experience.
15	**PF4. AUTHORITIES.** People with exceptional wisdom whose work sheds light on and contributes to our Growth.
16	**PF7. SPIRITUAL GUIDE.** A spiritual master or teacher, who can guide us in Awakening to the Divine Presence.
17a	**PF9. GROWTH CENTER.** A place where people gather to cultivate a particular aspect of their Growth.
17b	**PF9a. Monastery or Meditation Center.** Place where people with a special sensitivity to spiritual matters gather to develop those powers.
18	**PF10. INTEGRAL LIFE GUIDE.** A Growth Practitioner whose work encompasses all five Domains of the ADAPT Model.
19	**PF11. INTERNAL NAVIGATOR.** The Guide we form within ourselves by internalizing the Guidance we receive from outside.
20	**PF12. PROVIDENCE.** The Guidance & Orchestration we receive from the Divine Presence.

Appendix C4.
Resources For Personal Evolution

This section describes many books and other resources that illuminate and substantiate the ADAPT Model and the Life Journey Archetype. It is more than an annotated bibliography. It is an illustration of the depth and range of the ADAPT Model itself – as well as an indication of what work needs to be done to flesh out this important field.

Each Resource is categorized according to the Parameter of ADAPT it primarily pertains to. The various additional ADAPT Parameters to which a particular entry applies are shown in **[bold brackets]**. Within a given Parameter, items are listed roughly in order of importance to this study. The various categories of Resources are shown on the facing page.

In the interest of space, most of the bibliographical resources from Wilber's and Campbell's works are not included. For instance, we list few of the Developmental Sequences from Wilber's Famous Tables, the Appendices to *Integral Psychology*. Refer to those works for information on those important studies. For like reasons, few studies on the Specific Processes are included here; those will be found in our book-length study *The Processes of Human Development* (IntegralWorld.net), and in our forthcoming revision of that study. Generally, for authors other than Wilber and Campbell, only one book is listed -- usually the book that is best known or most pertinent. This is not a complete bibliography, but only suggestive of the many resources that illuminate the themes of this book. Although all these perspectives are interesting, we do not necessarily agree with all their beliefs or contentions.

We have endeavored to list many important and unusual big-perspective books that the reader is unlikely to find elsewhere. Entries are chosen for their pertinence and importance to the topic, but also for their intellectual stimulation and readability. Our emphasis here is less on erudition, and more on inspiration. We want to stimulate your eagerness to explore this fascinating field.

The Resources of ADAPT

Treat this Appendix as a subject for study – just like any other section of this book. *** Begin by reading these two introductory pages. From the table of contents on the facing page, choose one category of Resources to explore in detail: Dimensions, for example. *** Read over the Dimensions section, and scan the graphics for additional clues. Then select one Resource for further exploration: *Frames of Mind* by Howard Gardner, for example. *** Before actually reading this book, see how much you can learn about it from various sources. For instance, explore internet resources like Amazon – asking question like these: What is the book's general content and thesis? How extensive and positive are the reviews? Use the 'Look Inside' feature to explore the book's contents. As you sample the author's writing, what most engages your attention? *** Investigate other sources for information on the author, Howard Gardner. From Wikipedia or Amazon's Author Page, what is Mr. Gardner's background? What else has he written? If a series, how does the author expatiate on his theme? What books, concepts, or insights is he most acclaimed for? How pertinent is Gardner's work to the ADAPT Model or Life Journey Archetype? *** After all this exploration, how interested are you in reading the book itself? Do you feel better qualified to decide whether the book is worth buying? Are you now better equipped to understand the book, once you have bought it? *** As time permits, select another category of Resources, and explore it in similar fashion. Continue exploring various Resources so long as your interest continues, or until you have completed all eight categories. *** In addition to the items listed here, what other books and Resources have you found valuable in your own personal Journey? Which categories of ADAPT do they pertain to? What do they add to the Resources you already find here? Please pass along your suggestions to the authors of this book.

RESOURCES FOR PERSONAL EVOLUTION

Books and other resources that illuminate and substantiate the ADAPT Model and the Life Journey Archetype.

❁ **Hugh & Kaye Martin: Books and Studies** (page 266).
Book-length studies on Human Development by Hugh & Kaye Martin on Integral-World.net. Books and educational materials for the Animal Kingdom (AK) Language Arts Program.

❁ **Ken Wilber: Books and Other Resources** (page 268).
Books and other resources by Ken Wilber that pertain to Human Development. Studies of Wilber's life and work. Models of Human Development that supplement, or are an alternative to, Wilber.

❁ **Joseph Campbell: Books and Other Resources** (page 271).
Books by Joseph Campbell and Carl Jung that pertain to Human Development. Studies of Campbell's life and work. The Hero's Journey, the Archetypal Characters & Symbols, the Life Journey in Epics & Literature.

❁ **Dimensions of Human Growth** (page 274).
Individual and Collective Developmental Sequences. Contemporary Cultural Evolution, Historical Surveys and Analyses, Timelines of History. Cultural Development in Literature & the Arts. Contrarian views of history. Realms and Arenas: Life, Psyche, Body, Spirit, Internal.

❁ **Participants in the Growth Process** (page 284).
Personality Types: Gender, Enneagram, Birth Order. Shadow Self, Divine Presence.

❁ **General Processes of Growth** (page 286).
Transition Cycle, Restoration Growth, Evolution & Involution, Awakening.

❁ **Specific Processes of Growth** (page 288).
Programs for Actualization Growth. Natural Nutrition, Holistic Health, Sexuality & Sensuality, Relationships & Marriage, Family Dynamics, Natural Environment, Skills, Archetype & Myth, Language & Communication, Stories & Literature, Expressive Arts, Body Therapies, Introspection & Self-Awareness, Psychotherapies, Psycho-Biologic Techniques, Spiritual Practices, Holistic Environments.

❁ **Pathfinders in the Growth Process** (page 298).
Holistic Growth Situations, Authorities. Growth Centers: Meditation Centers, Alternative Universities, Human Potential Centers, Personal journeys.

> The Resources in this section (Appx C5) are the Authorities (PF4) upon whose work this book is based.

Hugh & Kaye Martin: Books, Studies, Educational Materials

The authors' book-length studies on IntegralWorld.net . To access these studies, follow the links at: http://www.integralworld.net/readingroom.html#HM.) Along with the authors' books and educational materials for the Animal Kingdom (AK) Language Arts Program.

❦ **THE FUNDAMENTAL KEN WILBER: WHAT KEN WILBER REALLY SAYS ABOUT HUMAN GROWTH.**
A study of the entire spectrum of fundamental principles that constitute Ken Wilber's Integral Operating System. Organized using the Parameters of ADAPT, this topical anthology places Wilber's various pronouncements on each subject side-by-side, so they can be compared and evaluated. Reveals through extensive excerpts from Wilber's own work at least 76 instances [now 87 major instances] where Wilber's Model needs substantial reexamination, and perhaps revision. In the course of the analysis, this study demonstrates that Wilber himself employs a version of the ADAPT Model in his explorations of human development.
Best exploration of Ken Wilber's positions on Human Growth. Best anthology of key quotes from Wilber's <u>Integral Psychology</u> – organized using the Parameters of ADAPT.

❦ **THE PROCESSES OF HUMAN DEVELOPMENT: THE 33 FUNDAMENTAL METHODS BY WHICH PEOPLE GROW.**
Explores at length the 33 [now 35] techniques, programs, therapies, and activities that transport us on our lifelong journey of personal development. Investigates the seven key Process types: Foundational Processes that are fundamental to all subsequent growth; Physical World Processes that engage us with material reality; Socio-Cultural Processes that involve us with groups of people; Formal Investigation Processes that engage our thinking and reasoning powers; Self-Expression Processes that enable us to express our inward reality in outward form, Conscious Development Processes that are specifically designed to promote growth and resolve problems; Comprehensive Processes that combine and integrate many other Growth Processes. We find that the nine Modules of Wilber's Integral Life Practice must be substantially extended and articulated to provide a optimally-effective program for personal and professional Growth.
Best summary of the Specific Processes by which Human Growth is implemented. Best application of ADAPT to parenting and raising children. Revised and updated version in progress.

❦ **THE PROCESSES ACCORDING TO ESALEN: USING THE WORLD'S GREATEST GROWTH CENTER TO BUILD YOUR OWN INTEGRAL GROWTH PROGRAM.**
Shows how the offerings of Esalen Institute, the fabled Growth Center on California's Big Sur coast, can be used to build a highly effective program for personal and professional Growth. Describes in detail the features, the ambience, and the offerings of Esalen – and traces Esalen's intimate involvement with the development of the Human Potential Movement, and with Ken Wilber and Integral Theory in particular. Esalen's offerings for each of the 35 ADAPT Processes are evaluated and found generally superior to those of Wilber's Integral Institute. In a very personal reflection, Hugh Martin describes how Esalen helped him prevail in his battle against terminal cancer.
Best application of the ADAPT Model to Personal Growth. Best application of ADAPT to organizational analysis and consulting. Best personal memoir on the life-changing importance of the ADAPT Model. Best introduction to the wonders of Esalen.

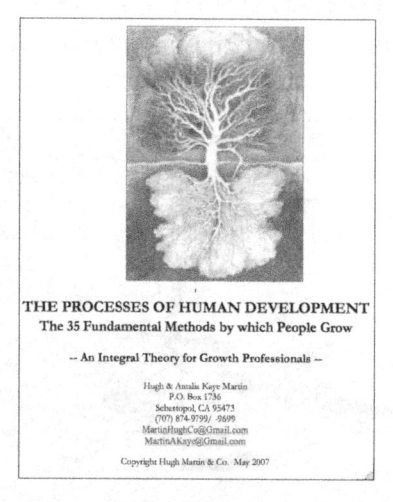

- **ARRAYS OF LIGHT: KEN WILBER'S TABLES OF CORRESPONDENCE.**
  Presents a redesigned version of Wilber's famous Tables (from the Appendix of *Integral Psychology*) that is more informative, more accessible, more appealing, and more useful. Wilber's Tables are the fundamental underpinning of his work. They are the platform he uses to summarize the evidence that supports and substantiates his theories of integral develop. If the Tables are not well-organized, understandable, accurate, representative, and complete, Wilber's whole system stands on shaky ground. This study endeavors to remedy the deficiencies in those Tables and to elevate recognition of their importance.
  Best study of the developmental correspondences that are the foundation of Wilber's system. Best explication of Wilber's Famous Tables from Integral Psychology.

- **THE HUMAN GROWTH CONTINUUM: THE EIGHT DIMENSIONS OF PERSONAL DEVELOPMENT.**
  Investigates in detail the eight Dimensions that define the landscape of our life journey. Explores the Stages of development through which we grow, the Transitions that take us from Stage to Stage, the States of consciousness at the highest levels of our awareness, the Realms and Arenas where life experience takes place, the Quadrants and Vectors that define the perspectives and directions of our experience, the Impediments to the Growth process (and their Resolutions), and the Coordination that weaves together the diverse strands of our Growth journey. We find that Wilber's four Dimensions of Quadrants, Levels, Lines, and States must be significantly expanded and differentiated to adequately describe the topography of the 'Growth Continuum.'
  Details of the Dimensions are superseded by the book you are now reading.

- **AQAL, THE NEXT GENERATION: BUILDING A MODEL OF HUMAN DEVELOPMENT THAT IS TRULY A 'THEORY OF EVERYTHING'.**
  An abbreviated, academic, earlier version of the book you are now reading. Presented at the July 2010 JFK University Integral Conference.

Ken Wilber: Books and Other Resources

Born in 1949, Ken Wilber has a pre-med background at Duke University and a degree in biochemistry from the University of Nebraska. He dropped out of the academic world to devote full time to studying a curriculum of his own making and writing books on his investigations. With 22 books on spirituality and science, and translations into more than 25 languages, Wilber is now the most highly-regarded writer on consciousness studies in the world, and is a central figure in the emerging field of transpersonal psychology. Even his first book, written at age 23, garnered reviews like these: "In one stroke, Wilber has established himself as the foremost scholar on psychology and consciousness studies" -- Dr. Kenneth Ring. "Quite simply, this is the most important book written on consciousness in modern times" -- Dr. Thomas Bearden. "Wilber will likely do for consciousness what Freud did for psychology" – Jean Houston. For the fundamental and pioneering nature of his work, Wilber has been called "the Einstein of consciousness research."

One of the most insightful and comprehensive thinkers of our time. Hip and accessible. A major inspiration for this study. Our emphasis is on Wilber's books that focus extensively on various aspects of Human Growth.

BOOKS BY KEN WILBER

- **INTEGRAL PSYCHOLOGY [IP] – CONSCIOUSNESS, SPIRIT, PSYCHOLOGY, THERAPY.** Boston, MA (2000): Shambala Publications.
Truly integrative model of consciousness, psychology, and therapy. Drawing on Eastern and Western, ancient and modern, Wilber creates a psychological model that includes waves and streams of development, states of consciousness, and conditions of self -- following the course of each from subconscious to self-conscious to superconscious. Includes Wilber's Famous Tables -- correlations of over one hundred psychological and spiritual schools of thought. *Best overview of Wilber's positions on Human Development.*

- **A BRIEF HISTORY OF EVERYTHING.** Boston, MA (1996): Shambala Publications.
The course of evolution as the unfolding manifestation of Spirit, from matter to life to mind -- including the higher stages of spiritual development where Spirit becomes conscious of itself. An exhilarating ride through the Kosmos in the company of one of the great thinkers of our time. Friendly, conversational, and accessible. *The best casual introduction to Wilber's AQAL Model.*

- **INTEGRAL SPIRITUALITY: A STARTLING NEW ROLE OF RELIGION IN THE MODERN WORLD.** Boston, MA (2006): Shambala Publications.
Formulates a theory of spirituality that honors the truths of modernity and postmodernity, while incorporating the essential insights of the great religions. *Wilber's best book on spirituality.*

- **UP FROM EDEN: A TRANSPERSONAL VIEW OF HUMAN EVOLUTION.** Garden City, NY (1981): Anchor Press/Doubleday.
Chronicles humanity's cultural and psycho-spiritual evolutionary journey over some six million years from its primal past into its dazzling cosmic future: At each historic period, asks three key questions: 1.) What are the major forms of transcendence available at this time? 2.) What substitutes for transcendence are created when the above methods fail? 3) What are the costs of these substitutes? Dramatic reformulation of history and anthropology. Companion to *The Atman Project*. Although early, *ranks among the most original and visionary of all Wilber's works.*

- **THE ATMAN PROJECT: A TRANSPERSONAL VIEW OF HUMAN DEVELOPMENT.** Wheaton, IL (1980): A Quest Book/Theosophical Publishing House.
Posits that every person intuits that he or she is God, but corrupts that intuition by applying it to his or her "small-s self," and will then do whatever's necessary to confirm that distorted intuition. "Through substitute seeking (Eros) and substitute sacrifices (Thanatos) individuals propel themselves through the ocean of equally driven souls, and the violent friction of these overlapping Atman Projects sparks that nightmare called history." Important early study on the quest for individual and cultural identity. *Along with Up From Eden, ranks among the most original and visionary of all Wilber's works.*

- **SEX, ECOLOGY, SPIRITUALITY: THE SPIRIT OF EVOLUTION.** Boston, MA (1995): Shambala Publications.
  The first volume of Wilber's projected magnum opus.
- **GRACE AND GRIT: SPIRITUALITY AND HEALING IN THE LIFE AND DEATH OF TREYA KILLAM WILBER.** Boston, MA (2001): Shambala Publications.
  Deeply moving account of Treya's five-year struggle with cancer – and the journey of Ken and Treya to spiritual healing.

OTHER VALUABLE WILBER RESOURCES

- **INTEGRAL OPERATING SYSTEM.** Louisville, CO (2005): Sounds True Publications.
  Casual, conversational audio introduction to the components of AQAL by Wilber himself.
- **INTEGRAL INSTITUTE.** www.IntegralInstitute.org.
  Wilber's virtual Growth Center for Integral Studies. Great idea that emerged before its time. Operations now suspended.

STUDIES ABOUT WILBER

- **Visser, Frank 2003. KEN WILBER – THOUGHT AS PASSION.** Albany, NY: SUNY Press.
  Excellent and readable guide to Wilber's life and work. Outlines his theories and uncovers his personal life, showing how his experiences influenced and shaped his writing.
- **Reynolds, Brad 2004. EMBRACING REALITY** – The Integral Vision of Ken Wilber. New York, NY: Tarcher/ Penguin.
  The first and only complete guide to Wilber's work – including thorough and faithful summaries of each book. Written with the support and guidance of Wilber himself.
- **Reynolds, Brad 2006. WHERE'S WILBER AT?: KEN WILBER'S INTEGRAL VISION IN THE NEW MILLENNIUM.** St. Paul, MN: Paragon House.
  Further explorations of Wilber's major concepts, and a report on developments in the Integral movement.

ALTERNATIVE MODELS OF HUMAN DEVELOPMENT

- **Smith, Andrew P. 2008. THE DIMENSIONS OF EXPERIENCE: A NATURAL HISTORY OF CONSCIOUSNESS.** Bloomington, IN: Xlibris. [D1+2, D3bd, PR2a, PPR3, PF11, S3]
  The first complete history of Consciousness ever written. How Consciousness evolved, beginning with the simplest forms of life. How dimensions of experienced space and time, together with increasing awareness of self and other, emerged in association with hierarchical complexity of information processing entities. Deserves to be resurrected from obscurity.
- **Wade, Jenny 1996. CHANGES OF MIND: A HOLONOMIC THEORY OF THE EVOLUTION OF CONSCIOUSNESS.** Albany, NY: SUNY. [D1+2, D3bd, PR2a, PPR3, PF11, S3]
  Draws on a wide range of sources from the fields of developmental psychology, brain research, new-paradigm studies, and mysticism to create a developmental model that begins before birth and ends after death.

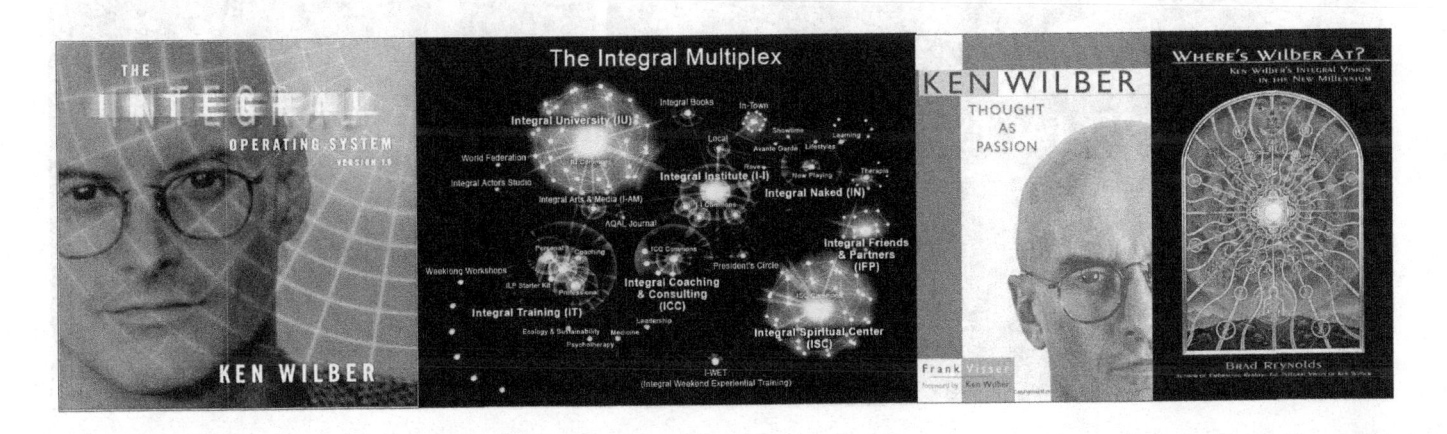

Page 270. Wilber + Campbell Appendices

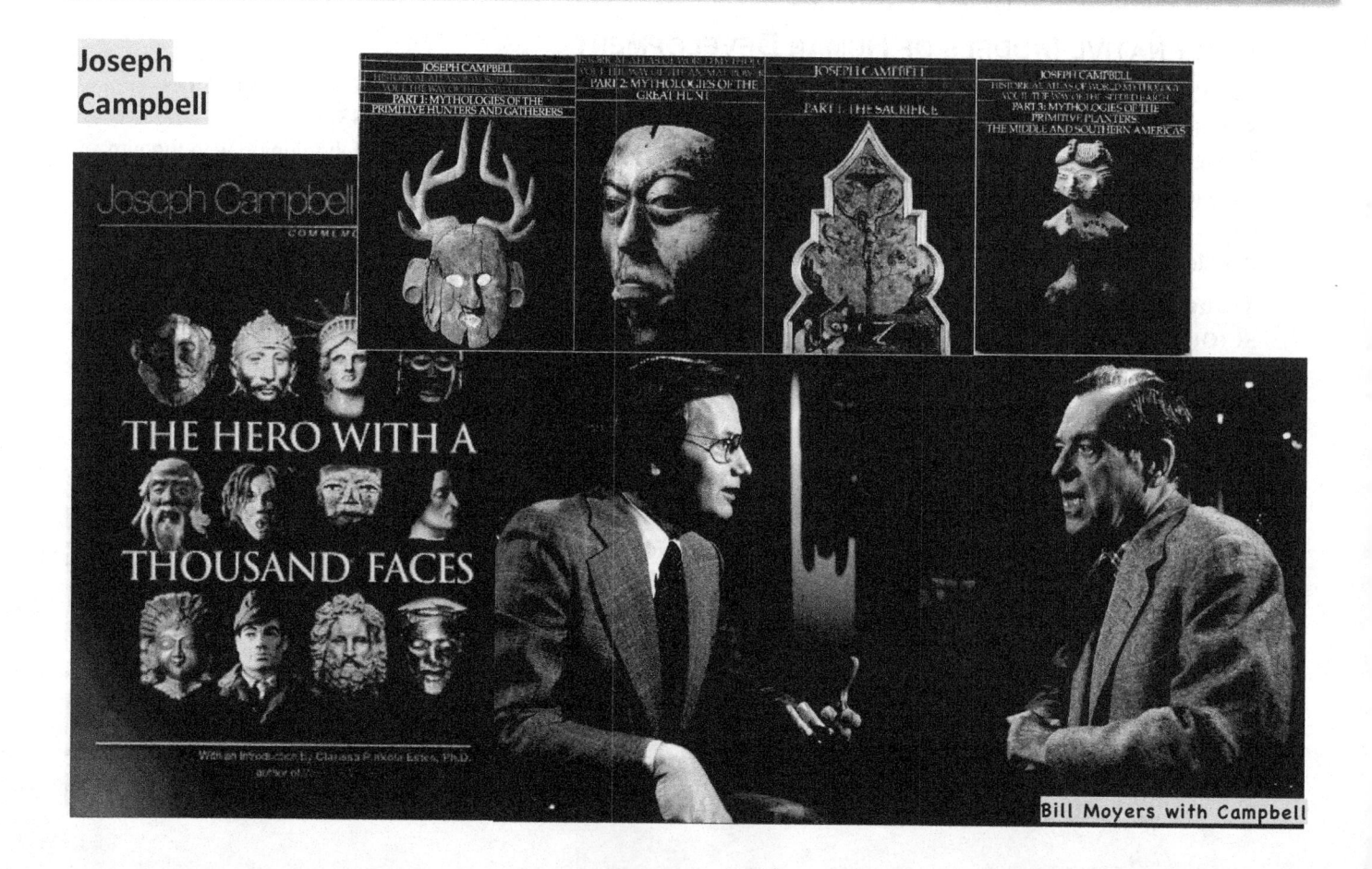

Ken Wilber

Joseph Campbell

Bill Moyers with Campbell

Joseph Campbell: Books and Other Resources

Joseph Campbell is an American author and teacher best known for his work in the field of comparative mythology. He was born in New York City in 1904, and from early childhood he became interested in mythology. He loved to read books about American Indian cultures, and frequently visited the American Museum of Natural History in New York, where he was fascinated by the museum's collection of totem poles. Campbell was educated at Columbia University, where he specialized in medieval literature, and continued his studies at universities in Paris and Munich.

While abroad he was influenced by the art of Pablo Picasso and Henri Matisse, the novels of James Joyce and Thomas Mann, the poetry of W. B. Yeats and T. S. Eliot, and the psychological studies of Sigmund Freud and Carl Jung. These encounters led to Campbell's theory that all myths and epics are linked in the human psyche, and that they are cultural manifestations of the universal need to explain social, cosmological, and spiritual realities.

In 1933, Campbell joined the literature department at Sarah Lawrence College, a post he retained until 1972. In 1944, he co-authored *A Skeleton Key to Finnegan's Wake* – Joyce's complex novel, from which Campbell first drew the concept of the 'monomyth.' Campbell's first original work, *The Hero with a Thousand Faces*, came out in 1949, and over time has been acclaimed as a classic. In this study of the "myth of the hero," Campbell asserted that there is a single pattern of heroic journey and that all cultures share this essential pattern in their various heroic myths. In his book he also outlined the basic conditions, stages, and results of the archetypal hero's journey. In 1988, shortly after Campbell's death, a series of television interviews with Bill Moyers, *The Power of Myth*, introduced Campbell's ideas to millions of viewers. According to Newsweek Magazine, "Campbell has become one of the rarest of intellectuals in American life: a serious thinker who has been embraced by the popular culture."

BOOKS BY JOSEPH CAMPBELL

- **HISTORICAL ATLAS OF WORLD MYTHOLOGY** (series). New York, NY (1988): HarperCollins.
  Campbell's multi-volume magnum opus: Our seemingly disparate spiritual traditions are neither discrete nor unique, but rather "ethnic manifestations" of those "elemental ideals" that have forever characterized the human psyche. Only partially completed before Campbell's death.

- **THE HERO WITH A THOUSAND FACES.** Princeton, NJ (1972): Princeton University.
  Outlines the Hero's Journey, a universal motif of adventure and transformation that runs through virtually all of the world's mythic traditions. Also explores the Cosmogonic Cycle, the mythic pattern of world creation and destruction. Campbell's most revolutionary and influential work.

- **THE POWER OF MYTH** with Bill Moyers (book and DVD set). New York, NY (1988): Doubleday
  Displays Campbell's unique ability to take a contemporary situation, such as the murder and funeral of President John F. Kennedy, and help us understand its impact in the context of archetypal mythology. Engaging question-and-answer format, creating an easy, conversational approach to complicated and esoteric topics.

- **THE MASKS OF GOD** (series). New York, NY (1991): Penguin.
  The primitive roots of mythology, examined in light of the most recent discoveries in archaeology, anthropology, and psychology.

About Joseph Campbell

❊ **Campbell, Joseph and Phil Cousineau, ed 2014. THE HERO'S JOURNEY: JOSEPH CAMPBELL ON HIS LIFE AND WORK.** Novato, CA: New World Library.
Campbell's only spiritual autobiography – a beautifully crafted collection of conversations, interviews, and outtakes from the Hero's Journey documentary. Reveals and illuminates Campbell's personal and intellectual journey in warm, relaxed format.

❊ **Larsen, Stephen and Robin Larsen 1991. A FIRE IN THE MIND: THE LIFE OF JOSEPH CAMPBELL.** New York, NY: Doubleday.
From the Big Sur and Robinson Jeffers to the mystery world of James Joyce's Finnigan's Wake, the Larsens take us to all the places in mind and location that Campbell frequented. His long-time connections to great novelists like John Steinbeck, and to modern thinkers like Michael Murphy of the Esalen Institute, reveal the eclectic panorama that was this great, and sometimes under-appreciated, man's purview.

Writings of Carl Jung

❊ **Jung, Carl Gustav 1968. MAN AND HIS SYMBOLS.** New York, NY: Dell. [D4d, P3g, PPR9, PR17, PF2, Appx B1]
Illustrated throughout with revealing images, this is the first and only work in which Jung explains to the layperson his enormously influential theory of symbolism as revealed in dreams and myths.

❊ **Jung, Carl Gustav 1981. THE ARCHETYPES AND THE COLLECTIVE UNCONSCIOUS.** Princeton, NJ: Princeton University. [D4d, P3g, PPR9, PR17, PF2, Appx B1]
In-depth studies of two concepts that are most pertinent to *The Human Odyssey*.

❊ **Jung, Carl Gustav and Joseph Campbell, ed. 1976. THE PORTABLE JUNG.** New York, NY: Penguin. [D4d, P3g, PPR9, PR17, PF2, Appx B1]
Jung's pioneering studies of the structure of the psyche -- including the works that introduced the Collective Unconscious, the Shadow, the Anima and Animus, and Synchronicity. Selected by Joseph Campbell -- with an extended, in-depth introduction.

Appx B1. The Hero's Journey

❊ **Vogler, Christopher 2007. THE WRITERS JOURNEY: MYTHIC STRUCTURE FOR WRITERS.** Studio City, CA: Michael Wiese Productions. [D4d-6, P3g, PPR9, PR17, PF2, Appx B1]
Explores the powerful relationship between mythology and storytelling in a clear, concise style. Required reading for movie executives, screenwriters, playwrights, scholars, and fans of pop culture.

❊ **Gilligan, Stephen and Robert Dilts 2009. THE HERO'S JOURNEY: A VOYAGE OF SELF DISCOVERY.** Williston, VT: Crown House. [D4d-6, P3g, PPR9, PR17, PF2, Appx B1]
How to discover your calling. How to embark on the path of learning and transformation that will reconnect you with your spirit, change negative beliefs and habits, heal emotional wounds and physical symptoms, deepen intimacy, and improve self-image and self-love. Transcript of four-day workshop.

Appx B1f. Archetypal Characters & Symbols

❊ **Bolen, Jean Shinoda 2000. GODDESSES IN EVERYWOMAN: POWERFUL ARCHETYPES IN WOMEN'S LIVES** (+series). New York, NY: Harper. [D4d-7, P3ag, PPR9, PR17, PF4-11, Appx B1]
The Personality Types introduced as seven archetypal goddesses with whom any woman can identify. Just as women used to be unconscious of the powerful effects that cultural stereotypes had on them, they were also unconscious of powerful archetypal forces within them that influence what they do and how they feel, and which account for major differences among them. This book awakens that awareness.

❊ **Archive for Research in Archetypal Symbolism (ARAS) 2010. THE BOOK OF SYMBOLS: REFLECTIONS ON ARCHETYPAL IMAGES.** Cologne, Germany: Taschen. [D4d, P3g, PR17]
Extensive and subtle outline of the major symbols and their meanings. No pat definitions of the kind that tend to collapse the symbol. The still vital symbol remains partially unknown, compels our attention, and unfolds in new

C4. Resources for Personal Evolution. Page 273

meanings and manifestations over time. How to move from the visual impression of a symbolic image in art, religion, life, or dreams -- then directly experiencing that symbol in all its personal and psychological resonance.

✺ **Chevalier, Jean and Alain Gheerbrant 1997. THE PENGUIN DICTIONARY OF SYMBOLS.** New York, NY: Penguin. **[D4d, P3g, PR17]**
Extensive outline of all the major symbols and their meanings. Draws together folklore, literary and artistic sources. Focuses on the symbolic dimension of every color, number, sound, gesture, expression or character trait that has benefitted from symbolic interpretation. Contributions from 15 scholars -- including anthropology, ethnology, psychotherapy, and art history.

APPX B3. THE LIFE JOURNEY: EPICS & LITERATURE

✺ **Reese, Edward and Frank R. Klassen, eds 1980. THE REESE CHRONOLOGICAL BIBLE.** Bloomington, MN: Bethany House. **[DD1+2, P7, PPR9, PR33, PF12, S8]**
Places all the passages of the King James Bible in the chronological order in which the events occurred. In the majestic language of Shakespeare's time -- a mode of verbal expression that has never been equaled.

✺ **Rouse, W. H. D., trans. 2007. THE ODYSSEY OF HOMER.** New York, NY: Signet. **[D, P, PPR, PR17, PF, Appx B3]**
The great epic in a novelistic style that is supremely entertaining and accessible.

✺ **Rouse, W. H. D., translator. Nadia May, reader. THE ODYSSEY OF HOMER.** Ashland, OR: Blackstone Audiobooks. **[D, P, PPR, PR17, PF, Appx B3]**
The Rouse translation read by one of the great audio interpreters.

✺ **Fagles, Robert and Bernard Knox, trans. 1997. THE ODYSSEY OF HOMER.** New York, NY: Penguin. **[, P, PPR, PR17, PF, Appx B3]**
Captures the energy and poetry of Homer's original in a bold, contemporary idiom, and gives us an *Odyssey* to read aloud, to savor, and to treasure for its sheer lyrical mastery. With textual commentary.

Dimensions

D1+2. Developmental Sequences

D1+2. Individual Developmental Sequences

✪ **Armstrong, Thomas 2007. The Human Odyssey: Navigating the Twelve Stages of Life.** New York, NY: Sterling. **[DD1+2, D3, P2a, PPR3, S1]**
The broad sweep of human life -- combining scientific and psychological knowledge combined with personal accounts, literary passages, myths and legends, and psycho-spiritual perspectives. A comprehensive, groundbreaking view of our development.

DD1+2b. Collective Developmental Sequences: Cultural Stages

✪ **Beck, Don Edward and Christopher C. Cowan 2005. Spiral Dynamics: Mastering Values, Leadership, and Change.** Malden, MA: Wiley-Blackwell. **[DD1+2b, P2b, PPR5, PR16, PF2, S2]**
In seven Stages, tracks our historic emergence from clans to tribes to networks and holograms. Reveals the hidden codes that shape human nature, create global diversities, and drive evolutionary change.

✪ **Strauss, William and Neil Howe 1992. Generations: The History of America's Future, 1584 to 2069** (+series). New York, NY: Wm. Morrow. **[DD1+2b, P2b, PPR5, PR16, PF2, S2]**
Plots a recurring cycle in American history -- a cycle of spiritual awakenings and secular crises -- from the founding colonists through the present day and well into this millennium. Masterwork on the four-stage Generation Cycle by which cultures evolve.

✪ **Neumann, Erich 1949. The Origins and History of Consciousness** (+works). Princeton, NJ: Princeton University Press. **[DD1+2b, D4b-9, P2b, PPR5, PR16, PF2, S2]**
Synthesizes Jung's ideas into a unified theory of psychology around his own new concept of "centroversion" -- the integrative force of the organism, its survival instinct in the widest sense. Shows how ego-consciousness -- the self-aware "I" of the modern human being -- is the preeminent organ of centroversion, with own evolutionary history.

✪ **Gebser, Jean 1986. The Ever-Present Origin. Part One: Foundations of the Aperspectival World. Part Two: Manifestations of the Aperspectival World** (+works). Athens, OH: Ohio University. **[DD1+2, D4b-9, P2b, PPR5, PF2, S2]**
Five structures of Consciousness -- Archaic, Magical, Mythical, Mental, and Integral (Aperspectival) – that unfold in a sequential but non-linear fashion, and have different kinds of characteristic ways of experiencing self, other, and world.

✪ **Voegelin, Eric 2001. Order and History: Israel and Revelation** (+series). Columbia, MO: University Of Missouri. **[DD1+2, D4b-9, P2b, PPR5, PF2, S2]**
The uniqueness of Israel: The recognition by human beings of their existence under a world-transcendent God, and the evaluation of their actions as conforming to or diverging from the Divine will. Redemption comes from a source beyond itself. Beginnings of a monumental five-volume series covering the entire span of human history – one of the most original and influential philosophers of our time.

✪ **Sheldrake, Rupert 2012. The Presence of the Past: Morphic Resonance and the Memory of Nature** (+works). Rochester, VT: Park Street. **[PPR3, PR23, PF12, S3]**
All self-organizing systems, from crystals to human society, inherit a collective memory that influences their form and behavior. This collective memory works through Morphic Fields -- which organize the bodies of plants and animals, coordinate the activities of brains, and underlie conscious mental activity. All human beings draw upon and contribute to a collective human memory. Even our individual recollections depend on morphic resonance, more than physical storage in the brain. Controversial theory that revolutionizes our conception of matter and reality.

C4. Resources for Personal Evolution. Page 275

DD1+2b. Collective Developmental Sequences: Contemporary Cultural Evolution

- **Ray, Paul H. and Sherry Ruth Anderson 2000. THE CULTURAL CREATIVES – HOW 50 MILLION PEOPLE ARE CHANGING THE WORLD.** New York, NY: Harmony/Random House. **[DD1+2b, P2b, PPR5, PR16, PF2, S2]**
  An emerging Generation whose values embrace a curiosity and concern for the world, its ecosystem, and its peoples; an awareness of and activism for peace and social justice; and an openness to self-actualization through spirituality, psychotherapy, and holistic practices. Valuable survey of the exciting transformation at work in today's culture.

- **Phipps, Carter 2012. EVOLUTIONARIES: UNLOCKING THE SPIRITUAL AND CULTURAL POTENTIAL OF SCIENCE'S GREATEST IDEA.** New York, NY: Harper. **[DD1+2b, P2b, PPR5, PR16, PF2, S2]**
  The concept of Evolution is far more profound than Darwin and Dawkins. A far-reaching movement of visionary scientists, philosophers, and spiritual thinkers is forging a new understanding of the Evolution of Human Culture that honors science, reframes culture, and radically updates spirituality.

- **Ardagh, Arjuna 2005. THE TRANSLUCENT REVOLUTION – HOW PEOPLE JUST LIKE YOU ARE WAKING UP AND CHANGING THE WORLD.** Novato, CA: New World Library. **[DD1+2b, P2b, PPR5+9, PR16+33, PF7, S8]**
  Radical positive change is taking place throughout our global society, resulting in increasing numbers of people from diverse and divergent backgrounds who are awakening to a state of deeper purpose, joy, compassion, self-fulfillment, and service to others. Excellent survey of the spiritual transformation that is accompanying our culture's psychological changes.

- **Florida, Richard 2003. THE RISE OF THE CREATIVE CLASS: AND HOW IT'S TRANSFORMING WORK, LEISURE, COMMUNITY, AND EVERYDAY LIFE** (+series). New York, NY: Basic Books. **[D4a, DD1+2, P2b, PPR5, PR16, PF2, S2]**
  Examines an emerging class whose economic function is to create new ideas, new technology, and new creative content. Shares common characteristics such as creativity, individuality, diversity, and merit.

Dimensions (cont.)

DD1+2b. Arenas of Cultural Development: Historical Surveys and Analyses

- **Burke, James 1986. THE DAY THE UNIVERSE CHANGED: COMPANION TO THE PBS TELEVISION SERIES** and DVD set (+works). New York, NY: Little Brown. [D2, DD1+2b, P2b, PPR5, PR19, PF4, S2]
  The moments in history when a change in knowledge radically altered man's understanding of himself and the world around him. Brings the Evolution of Culture stunningly alive.

- **Kuhn, Thomas S. 2012. THE STRUCTURE OF SCIENTIFIC REVOLUTIONS** (+works). Chicago, IL: University of Chicago. [D2, DD1+2b, P2b, PPR5, PR23, PF4-2, S2]
  Challenges long-standing linear notions of scientific progress. Argues that transformative ideas don't arise from the day-to-day, gradual process of experimentation and data accumulation -- but that the revolutions in science -- breakthrough moments that disrupt accepted thinking and offer unanticipated ideas -- occur in inspired quantum leaps. Landmark event in the history and philosophy of science.

- **Rothbard, Murray N. 2002. A HISTORY OF MONEY AND BANKING IN THE UNITED STATES: THE COLONIAL ERA TO WORLD WAR II** (+works). Auburn, AL: Ludwig von Mises Institute. [DD1+2b, D4a-3, P2b, PPR5, PR19, PF2, S2]
  Traces inflations, banking panics, and money meltdowns from the Colonial Period through the mid-20th century. Shows how government's systematic war on sound money is the hidden force behind nearly all major economic calamities in American history.

- **Thomas, Hugh 1982. A HISTORY OF THE WORLD.** New York, NY: HarperCollins. [DD1+2b, D4a, PPR5, PR20, PF3, S2]
  History as it arises from the technological achievements of mankind. No endless barage of dates or wars. The story of the survival of the human race. From one of the great modern historians.

- **Graeber, David 2011. DEBT: THE FIRST 5000 YEARS.** Brooklyn, NY: Melville House. [DD1+2b, D4a-3, PPR4, PR15, PF2, S2]
  For more than 5,000 years, humans have used elaborate credit systems to buy and sell goods -- beginning long before the invention of coins or cash. This created a society divided into debtors and creditors. Even the language of the ancient works of law and religion (words like "guilt," "sin," and "redemption") derives in large part from ancient debates about debt, and shapes even our most basic ideas of right and wrong.

DD1+2b. Cultural Developmental Sequences: Timelines of History

- **TIMELINES OF WORLD HISTORY 2011.** New York, NY: DK Publishing. [DD1+2b, P2b, PPR5, PF2, S2]
  The pageant of history displayed in the inimitable DK multi-modal style. A feast for the eyes and the mind.

- **Scarre, John 1993. SMITHSONIAN TIMELINES OF THE ANCIENT WORLD: A VISUAL CHRONOLOGY FROM THE ORIGINS OF LIFE TO AD 1500.** New York, NY and London: DK Publishing. [DD1+2b, P2b, PPR5, PF2, S2]
  From the beginnings of the Earth and the emergence of mankind in Africa, through to Egypt and the pyramids, the fall of the Roman Empire, the voyages of discovery, and the height of the Inca Empire -- everything through A.D. 1500. Superbly illustrated with museum artifacts, archaeological finds, artists' reconstructions, and maps.

- **Trager, James 1992. THE PEOPLE'S CHRONOLOGY: A YEAR-BY-YEAR RECORD OF HUMAN EVENTS FROM PREHISTORY TO THE PRESENT.** New York, NY: Henry Holt. [DD1+2b, P2b, PPR5, PF2+4, S2]
  The pageant of history presented through its most fascinating facts and occurrences. As stimulating and entertaining as a tome like this can be.

C4. Resources for Personal Evolution. Page 277

- **Gonick, Larry 1997. Cartoon History of the Universe** (+series). New York, NY: Doubleday. **[DD1+2b, P2b, PPR5, PF2, S2]**
  An entertaining and informative illustrated guide that makes world history accessible, appealing, and funny.

- **Grun, Bernard and Eva Simpson 2005. The Timetables of History: A Horizontal Linkage of People and Events.** New York, NY: Touchstone Books. **[DD1+2b, P2b, PPR5, PF2+4, S2]**
  The pageant of history presented in an informative, factual style.

- **Bunch, Bryan and Alexander Hellemans 2004. The History of Science and Technology: A Browser's Guide to the Great Discoveries, Inventions, and the People Who Made Them from the Dawn of Time to Today.** Boston, MA: Houghton Mifflin Harcourt. **[DD1+2b, P2b, PPR5, PR23, PF4-2, S2]**
  From the first stone tools to the first robot surgery, this easy-to-read reference book offers more than seven thousand concise entries organized within ten major historical periods and categorized by subject, such as archaeology, biology, computers, food and agriculture, medicine and health, materials, and transportation.

Dimensions (cont.)

DD1+2b. Cultural Developmental Sequences: Literature & The Arts

- **Steer, John and Antony White 1994. ATLAS OF WESTERN ART HISTORY: ARTISTS, SITES, AND MOVEMENTS FROM ANCIENT GREECE TO THE MODERN AGE.** New York, NY: Facts on File (Infobase). **[DD1+2b, D4b-7, P2b, PPR5, PR28, PF4-7, S2]**
  Uses color reproductions, maps and other illustrations to illuminate the movements, trends and artists that have influenced Western artistic tradition for more than 2000 years. Fixes art history to actual sites -- making it easier for students, historians and art lovers to make sense of the vast waves of artistic movement.

- **Hobbs, Jack A. and Robert L. Duncan 1991. ARTS, IDEAS, AND CIVILIZATION.** Upper Saddle River, NJ: Prentice Hall. **[DD1+2b, D4b-7, P2b, PPR5, PR28, PF4-7, S2]**
  A stimulating, perceptive, and sumptuous survey of the major developments of Western Civilization, as expressed in literature, art, and music.

- **Myers, Bernard S. 1968. ART AND CIVILIZATION.** New York, NY: McGraw Hill. **[DD1+2b, D4b7, PPR5, PR28, PF2]**
  Traces the history of art, not just for its own sake, but as a reflection of the progression of Civilization from prehistory to the modern day.

- **McCrum, Robert et al 1986. THE STORY OF ENGLISH: A COMPANION TO THE PBS TELEVISION SERIES** (+PBS series). New York, NY: Viking Press (Penguin). **[DD1+2b, P2b, PPR5, PR24, PF4, S2]**
  A stimulating and comprehensive record of spoken and written English -- from its Anglo-Saxon origins some two thousand years ago to the present day, when English is the dominant language of commerce and culture with more than one billion English speakers around the world. Companion to the popular PBS series.

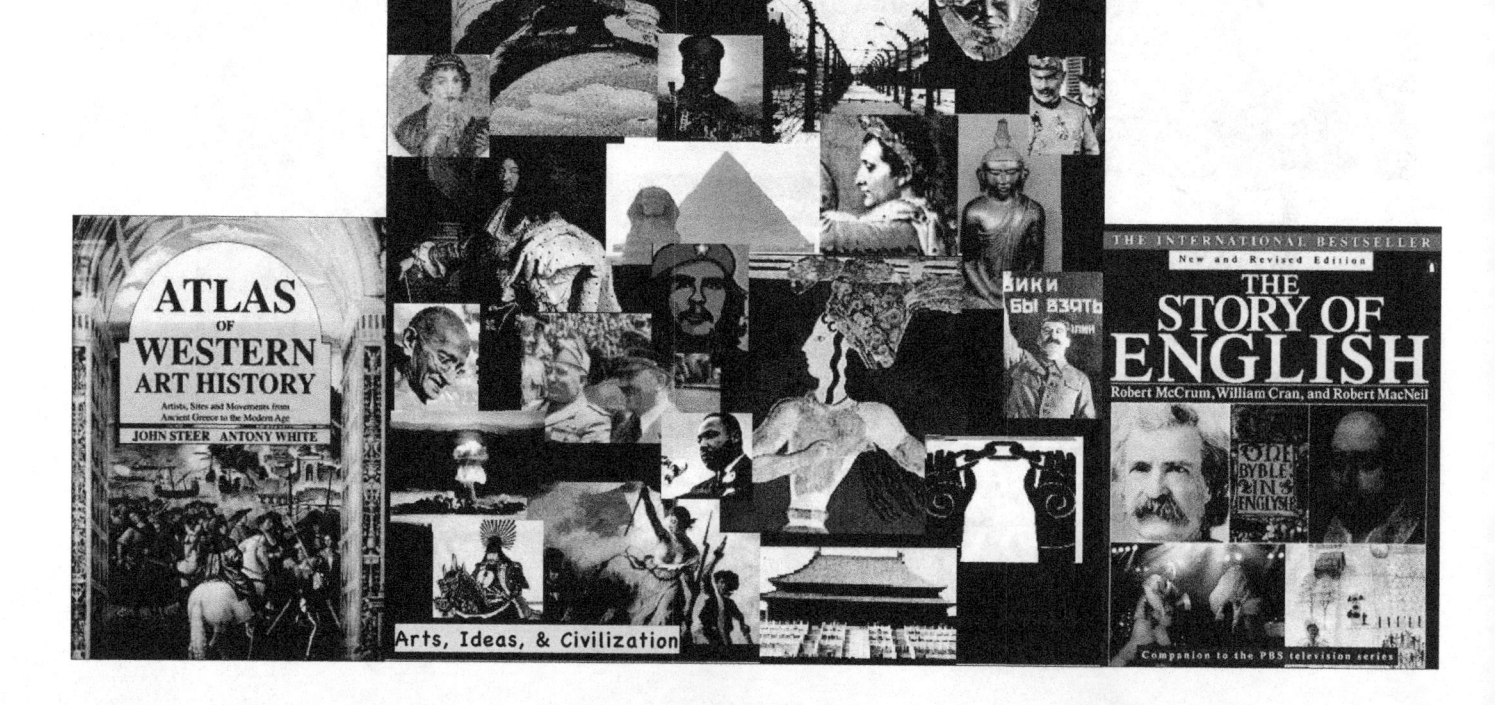

DD1+2b. Cultural Developmental Sequences: Contrarian Views of History

- **Peckham, Morse 1962. BEYOND THE TRAGIC VISION: THE QUEST FOR IDENTITY IN THE NINETEENTH CENTURY.** New York, NY: George Braziller. [DD1+2b, P2b, PPr5, PR27-28, PF4, S2]
Sees four stages in the nineteenth century's effort to solve the problem of finding a ground for human identity: The period of discovery and analogy from man to nature (Romanticism), the period of Transcendentalism, the period of Objectism (Realism or Naturalism), and the period of Stylism (Aestheticism). At the end of this process, Nietzsche asserts that human identity exists but has no grounds in nature or the divine.

- **Buchanan, Patrick J. 2008. CHURCHILL, HITLER, AND "THE UNNECESSARY WAR": HOW BRITAIN LOST ITS EMPIRE AND THE WEST LOST THE WORLD** (+works). New York, NY: Crown Publishing (Random House). [DD1+2b, P2b, PPR5, PF2, S2]
If not for the blunders of British statesmen—Winston Churchill first among them -- the horrors of two world wars and the Holocaust might have been avoided and the British Empire might never have collapsed into ruins. Half a century of murderous oppression of scores of millions under the iron boot of Communist tyranny might never have happened, and Europe's central role in world affairs might have been sustained for many generations.

- **Menzies, Gavin 2003. 1421: THE YEAR CHINA DISCOVERED AMERICA** (+works). New York, NY: William Morrow (HarperCollins). [DD1+2b, P2b, PPR5, PR16, PF2, S2]
The fascinating argument that the Chinese discovered the Americas a full 70 years before Columbus. Asserts that the Chinese circumnavigated the globe, desalinated water, and perfected the art of cartography. Most of the renowned European explorers actually sailed with maps charted by the Chinese.

- **Mann, Charles C. 2005. 1491: NEW REVELATIONS OF THE AMERICAS BEFORE COLUMBUS** (+series). New York, NY: Alfred A. Knopf. [DD1+2b, P2b, PPR5, PR16, PF2, S2]
Contrary to what so many Americans learn in school, the pre-Columbian Indians were not sparsely settled in a pristine wilderness; rather, there were huge numbers of Indians who actively molded and influenced the land around them. Those who came later found an emptied landscape -- the ravages of what was likely the greatest epidemic in human history, introduced inadvertently by Europeans to a population without immunity.

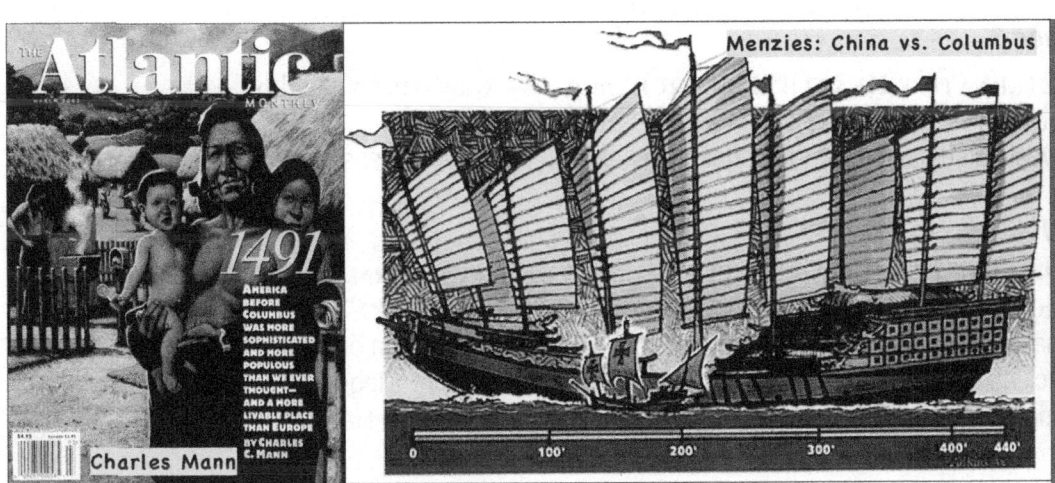

Dimensions (cont.)

D3. REALMS

D3a. Life Passages

✸ **Sheehy, Gail 2006. PASSAGES: PREDICTABLE CRISES OF ADULT LIFE** (+series). New York, NY: Ballantine. **[D3a, D1+2, P2a, PPR3, S3]**
Brilliant road map of adult life that shows the inevitable personality and sexual changes we go through in our 20s, 30s, 40s, 50s, and beyond. Freed developmental studies from being limited to childhood.

✸ **Levinson, Daniel J. 1978. THE SEASONS OF A MAN'S LIFE** (+ WOMAN'S LIFE 1997). New York, NY: Knopf. **[D3a, D1+2, P2a, P3a, PPR3, kS3]**
Explores and explains the periods of personal development through which all human begins must pass, and which together form a common pattern underlying all human lives. Breakthrough study that ranks with Kinsey and Erikson.

✸ **Gardiner, Harry W. and Corinne Kosmitzki 2010. LIVES ACROSS CULTURES: CROSS-CULTURAL HUMAN DEVELOPMENT.** Upper Saddle River, NJ: Pearson. **[DD1+2b, D3a, PPR3+5, PR16, PF2, S3]**
Cultural similarities and differences in human development throughout the world over the entire human lifespan.

D3b. Psyche Passages

✸ **Erikson, Erik 1950. CHILDHOOD AND SOCIETY.** New York, NY: Norton. **[D3a-b, D1+2, P2a, PPR3-4, PF1-2, S3-4]**
Vastly influential study of the eight pivotal Stages of life: Trust vs. mistrust. Autonomy vs. Shame and Doubt. Initiative vs Guilt. Industry vs Inferiority. Identity crisis and role confusion. Intimacy vs. Isolation. Generativity vs. Stagnation. Ego integrity vs. despair.

✸ **Maslow, Abraham H. 1968. TOWARD A PSYCHOLOGY OF BEING.** New York, NY: Wiley **[D3a-b, D1+2, P2a, PPR3, S3-4]**
The theory of self-actualization and the hierarchy of human needs -- the cornerstones of modern humanistic psychology. Uses studies of psychologically healthy people to demonstrate that human beings are by nature loving, noble and creative, and that they are capable of pursuing the highest values and aspirations.

✸ **Piaget, Jean and Barbel Inhelder 1958. THE GROWTH OF LOGICAL THINKING FROM CHILDHOOD TO ADOLESCENCE: AN ESSAY ON THE CONSTRUCTION OF FORMAL OPERATIONAL STRUCTURES** (+works). New York, NY: Basic Books. **(D1+2, D4b-6, P2a, PPR3, PF21, PF9-4, S3]**
The classic study on the development of logical intelligence. Sets forth a description of the changes in logical operations between childhood and adolescence. Describes the formal structures that mark the completion of the operational development of intelligence.

D3c. Body Passages

✸ **Easley, Norman. ALTERNATIVE HEALTH RESEARCH:** http://www.alternativehealth-research.com/index.html. **[D3b-c, P2a, PPR3-4, PR32, PF8-5, S3-4]**
The most thoroughly-investigated studies on the connection between bodily processes and psycho-spiritual health.

D3d. Spirit Passages

✸ **Metzner, Ralph 1998. THE UNFOLDING SELF: VARIETIES OF TRANSFORMATIVE EXPERIENCE.** Pioneer Imprints.com: Pioneer Imprints. **[D2, D1+2, D3d, P1, PPR9, PR33, PF7, S8]**
Examines the transformations that people undergo in the process of their expansion of consciousness. Conveys subtle concepts and fascinating breadth through an engrossing tapestry of myth, allegory, cross-references and historical context. An original collaborator on psychedelics with Leary and Alpert at Harvard.

C4. Resources for Personal Evolution. Page 281

- **Moss, Robert 2010. The Secret History of Dreaming** (+works). Novato, CA: New World Library. **[D3d, D8, P7, PPR9, PF12, S8]**
  Traces the strands of dreams through archival records and well-known writings, weaving remarkable yet true accounts of historical figures who were influenced by their dreams. A new way to explore the history of consciousness -- combining the storytelling skills of a novelist, the research acumen of a scholar of ancient history, and the personal experience of a master active dreamer.

- **Myss, Caroline 1997. Anatomy of the Spirit: The Seven Stages of Power and Healing** (+works). New York, NY: Harmony Books. **[D1+2, D3c-d, P7, PR33, PF4, S8]**
  Presents Myss's breakthrough model of the body's seven centers of spiritual and physical power. Synthesizes the ancient wisdom of three spiritual traditions -- the Hindu chakras, the Christian sacraments, and the Kabbalah's Tree of Life. Demonstrates the seven stages through which everyone must pass in the search for higher consciousness and spiritual maturity.

D3b-d. Internal Passages & Chakras

- **Judith, Anodea 2004. Eastern Body, Western Mind: Psychology and the Chakra System as a Path to the Self.** Berkeley, CA: Celestial Arts. **[D1+2b, D3bcd, P2, PPR9, PR33, PF7, S8, Appx A9c]**
  Uses the Chakra system as a map upon which to chart our Western understanding of individual development. Each chapter focuses on a single Chakra, starting with a description of its characteristics, then exploring its particular childhood developmental patterns, traumas and abuses, and how to heal and maintain balance. A classic.

- **Lockhart, Maureen 2010. The Subtle Energy Body: The Complete Guide.** Rochester, VT: Inner Traditions (Bear & Co.). **[D3b-d, P7, PPR9, PR33, PF7, S8]**
  Ancient traditions have long maintained that the human being is a complex of material and nonmaterial systems, or energy bodies. The "subtle body" is an energetic, psycho-spiritual entity of several layers of increasing subtlety and metaphysical significance, through which the aspirant seeks knowledge of the self and the nature of God. The component parts of the subtle body serve as a map of the different levels of consciousness.

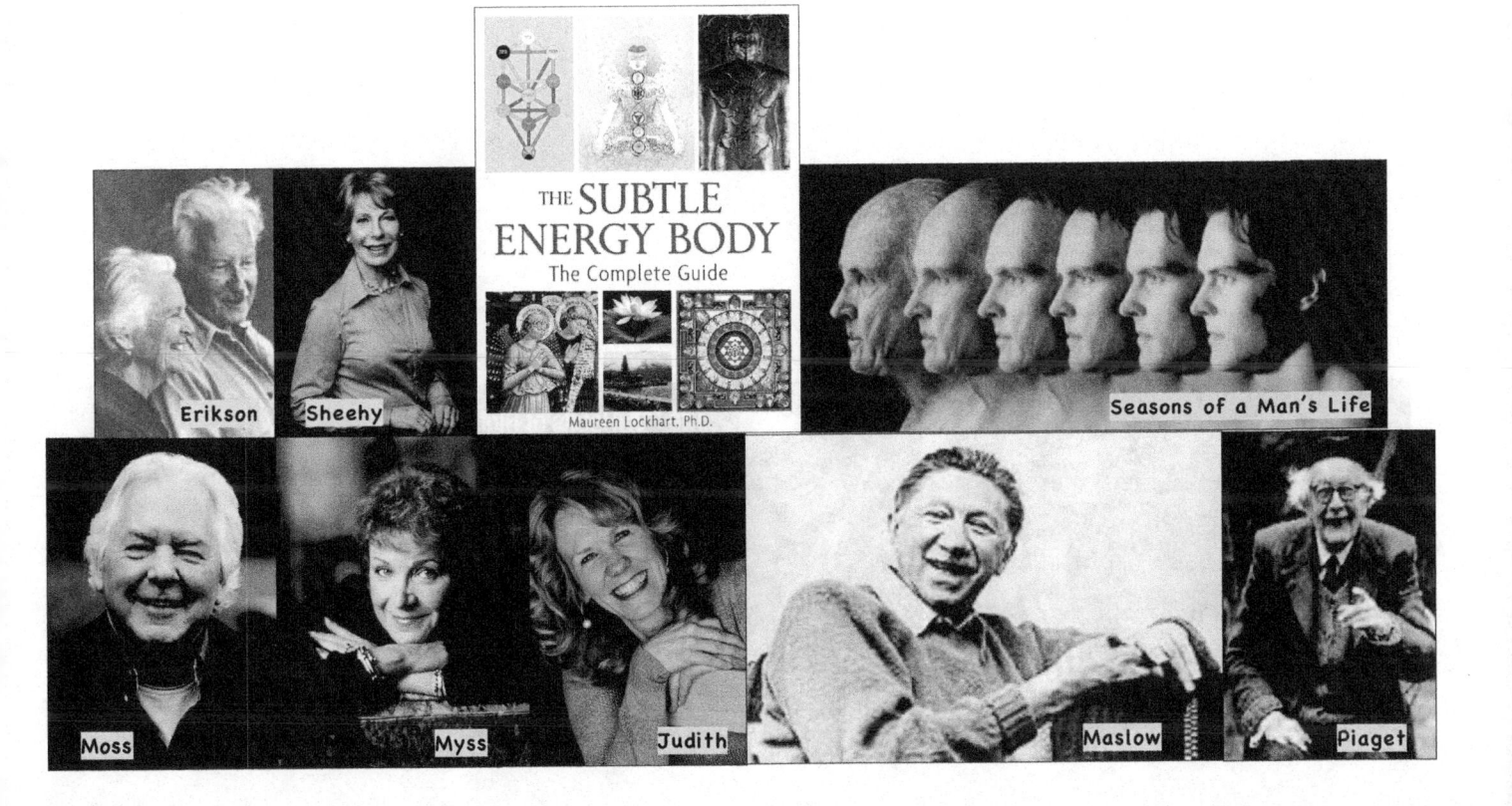

D4. ARENAS: D4A. LIFE ARENAS

❈ **Covey, Stephen R. 1990. THE 7 HABITS OF HIGHLY EFFECTIVE PEOPLE: POWERFUL LESSONS IN PERSONAL CHANGE** (+works). New York, NY: Simon & Schuster. **[D4a-2, P2, PPR3, PR14, PF6c-2, S3]**
Before you can adopt the seven habits of success, you must make a "paradigm shift" -- a change in perception and interpretation of how the world works. Affects how you perceive and act regarding productivity, time management, positive thinking, developing your "proactive muscles," etc. Covey takes you through this change.

❈ **Kinder, George 1999. THE SEVEN STAGES OF MONEY MATURITY: UNDERSTANDING THE SPIRIT AND VALUE OF MONEY IN YOUR LIFE.** New York, NY: Delacorte Press. **[D4a-3, P2a, PPR3, PR13, PF6c-3, S3]**
Drawing on ancient Buddhist wisdom and years of financial practice, Kinder creates a program that guides us through the seven stages of a revolutionary journey -- one designed to help us uncover the roots of our attitudes about money, and attain true peace, freedom, and security in our financial lives.

❈ **Boldt, Lawrence G. 2009. ZEN AND THE ART OF MAKING A LIVING: A PRACTICAL GUIDE TO CREATIVE CAREER DESIGN.** New York, NY: Penguin Books. **[D4a-2, P2a, PPR3, PR13, PF6c-2, S3]**
Like a traditional career guide, this book includes resumé advice and worksheets for narrowing down and sticking with your goals. Takes off from there to guide the reader on a quest for spiritual fulfillment through work -- something you won't find elsewhere.

❈ **Gallwey, W. Timothy 1999. THE INNER GAME OF WORK: FOCUS, LEARNING, PLEASURE, AND MOBILITY IN THE WORKPLACE** (+works). New York NY: Random House. **[D4a-2, P2a, PPR3, PR13, PF6c-2, S3]**
Teaches you how to stop working in the conformity mode and start working in the mobility mode. How having a great coach can make as much difference in the boardroom as on the basketball court. How to find that coach and, equally important, how to become one.

❈ **Jarow, Rick 1995. CREATING THE WORK YOU LOVE: COURAGE, COMMITMENT, AND CAREER.** Rochester, VT: Destiny Books. **[D4a-2, P2a, PPR3, PR13, PF6c-2, S3]**
A unique alternative approach to work -- using self-reflective exercises based on the seven chakras, to help you determine the elements you need to create a life filled with meaning and purpose.

D4. ARENAS: D4B. PSYCHE ARENAS

- **Csikszentmihalyi, Mihalyi 1993. THE EVOLVING SELF: A PSYCHOLOGY FOR THE THIRD MILLENNIUM** (+works). New York, NY: HarperCollins. **[D1+2, D4b-4, P1, PPR1, PF2, S2]**
Genetically programmed behaviors that once helped humans adapt and multiply now threaten our survival. These traits include obsessions with food and sex, addiction to pleasure, excessive rationality, and a tendency to focus on the negative. Urges readers to find ways to reduce the oppression, exploitation, and inequality that are woven into the fabric of society.

- **Gadpaille, Warren J. 1975. CYCLES OF SEX.** New York, NY: Scribner's. **[D1+2, D3abc, D4abc, PPR3, PR4, PF5, S3]**
Landmark study of psychosexual development over the entire human lifespan. Hard to find, but deserves to be resurrected.

- **Gardner, Howard 1983. FRAMES OF MIND: THE THEORY OF MULTIPLE INTELLIGENCES.** New York, NY: Basic Books. **[D3b, D4b, P2a, PPR3, PR, PF4, S3]**
There is not one thing called intelligence, but rather several different types of intelligence that work (and play) together inside each person's overall intellectual development.

- **Goleman, Daniel 2005. EMOTIONAL INTELLIGENCE: WHY IT CAN MATTER MORE THAN IQ** (+series). New York, NY: Bantam. **[D3b, D4b-3, P2a, PPR3, PR30, S3]**
Emotional Intelligence consists of self-awareness, altruism, personal motivation, empathy, and the ability to love and be loved. Produces people who truly succeed in work as well as play -- people who build flourishing careers and lasting, meaningful relationships.

Daniel Goleman | Howard Gardner | MIHALY CSIKSZENTMIHALY

Participants

P3. TYPES & PERSONAE

P3a. Gender Types

- **Gilder, George 1992. MEN AND MARRIAGE** (+works). Gretna, LA: Pelican. [P2, P3a, PPR3-4, PR30, PF1, S1-2]
  Examines the deterioration of the traditional family, the well-defined sex roles it offered, and how this change has diverted the focus of our society. Men will only fulfill their paternal obligations when the nesting instinct of women leads them to do so. This civilizing influence, balanced with proper economic support, is essential for maintaining a productive and caring society. Landmark work on restoring healthy parental relationships and non-dysfunctional families.

- **Warren, Farrell 1986. WHY MEN ARE THE WAY THEY ARE: THE MALE-FEMALE DYNAMIC** (+series). New York, NY: McGraw-Hill. [P2, P3a, PPR3-4, PR30, PF1, S1-2]
  The politically-incorrect, contra-feminist bestseller: Women believe that they must have a sensitive, caring man -- yet he must also be an Alpha male. The impossibility of meeting such contradictory demands confuses men and women, and sets them up for disappointment and pain in relationships.

- **Luke, Helen 1996. THE WAY OF WOMAN: AWAKENING THE PERENNIAL FEMININE** (+works). New York, NY: Image (Doubleday). [P2, P3a, PPR3, PR17, PF1, S1-2, Appx B1]
  Draws from the riches of the Bible, mythology, folklore, Greek tragedies, and modern poetry to reconnect women with lost feminine images, symbols, and values. The book that speaks deeply to women.

P3b. Enneagram Types

- **Riso, Don R. and Russ Hudson 1999. THE WISDOM OF THE ENNEAGRAM – THE COMPLETE GUIDE TO PSYCHOLOGICAL AND SPIRITUAL GROWTH FOR THE NINE PERSONALITY TYPES.** New York, NY: Bantam. [D1, D3b, P3b, P6, PPR6, PR30, S5]
  The nine Enneagram Types. How to figure out which type you are. How to observe your Type's fixations and let go of the need to act out automatic and dysfunctional behavioral responses. Identifies red flags of self-illusion and provides practical suggestions for spiritual Growth. Clearest discussion of the Enneagram types and their potential for personal evolution.

- **Maitri, Sandra 2001. THE SPIRITUAL DIMENSION OF THE ENNEAGRAM: NINE FACES OF THE SOUL** (+works). New York, NY: Tarcher. [D1, D3bd, P3b, P6, PPR9, PR33, S8]
  A member of the first group of students to whom Claudio Naranjo presented the Enneagram system in the U.S. almost three decades ago. With Almaas, has preserved the legacy of this original transmission.

- **Naranjo, Claudio 1994. CHARACTER AND NEUROSIS: AN INTEGRATIVE VIEW.** Gateways/IDHHB. [D1, D3b, P3b, P6, PPR6, PR30, S5]
  Goes far beyond mere personality typing: The Enneagram Types as windows into nine forms of character structure and neurosis. The most faithful and profound interpreter of Ichazo's original work. Esoteric and provocative.

- **Almaas, A.H. 1998. FACETS OF UNITY – THE ENNEAGRAM OF HOLY IDEAS** (+works). Berkeley, CA: Diamond. [D1, D3bd, P3b, P6, PPR9, PR33, S8]
  Not directed toward the psychological Types, but to the higher spiritual realities they reflect. The disconnection from each Holy Idea leads to the development of its corresponding fixation. Unlocking the fixation frees us from its limitations. Key originator of modern Enneagram work, along with Ichazo and Naranjo.

- **Rohr, Richard and Andreas Ebert 2001. THE ENNEAGRAM: A CHRISTIAN PERSPECTIVE.** New York, NY: Crossroad. [D1, D3bd, P3b, P6, PPR9, PR33, S8]
  Shows both the basic logic of the Enneagram and its harmony with the core truths of Christian thought from the time of the early Church forward.

- **Searle, Judith 2001. THE LITERARY ENNEAGRAM: CHARACTERS FROM THE INSIDE OUT.** Tucson, AZ: Editorial Department. [D1, D3bd, P3b, P6, PPR6, PR27, S5]
  Offers a fresh version of the standard Great Books course -- using characters from literature to show the inner dynamics of the nine Enneagram personality types and their variations.

P3c. Birth Order Types

- **Leman, Kevin 2009. THE BIRTH ORDER BOOK: WHY YOU ARE THE WAY YOU ARE.** Grand Rapids, MI: Revell Books. [D1, D3b, P3c, PPR6, PR6, S5]
  Fascinating and often funny look at how birth order affects personality, marriage and relationships, parenting style, career, and children. Much-beloved classic.

P4. Shadow Self

- **Rowan, John 1990. Subpersonalities: The People Inside Us.** New York, NY: Routledge. [D7, P4, PPR2, PR30, PF6d, S4]
  We all have a number of inner personalities that express themselves in different situations. By recognizing them, we can come to understand ourselves better and improve our relationships with others. Intriguing study of the characters and demons that populate our interiors.

- **Carson, Rick 1983. Taming Your Gremlin: A Surprisingly Simple Method for Getting Out of Your Own Way.** New York, NY: HarperCollins. [D7a, P4, PPR2, PR30, PF6a, S4]
  An easy-to-understand, unique, and practical system for banishing the nemesis within -- blending Taoist wisdom, the Zen Theory of Change, and sound psychology.

P7. Divine Presence

- **Rushdoony, Rousas J. 1990. Systematic Theology (+works).** Portland, OR: Ross House (Exodus). [D3d, P7, PPR9, PR33, PF12]
  Theology belongs in the pulpit, the school, the workplace, the family, everywhere. Without a systematic application of theology, people too often approach Scripture with a smorgasbord mentality, picking and choosing what pleases them. Important message, whether you are religious or not: Apply your Worldview consistently throughout the entire spectrum of your life.

- **Yogananda, Paramahansa 2004. The Second Coming of Christ: The Resurrection of the Christ Within You (+works).** Los Angeles, CA: Self Realization Fellowship. [D3d, D8, P7, PPR9, PR33, PF12]
  A profoundly enriching journey through the four Gospels. Verse by verse, he illumines the universal path to oneness with God taught by Jesus to his immediate disciples but obscured through centuries of misinterpretation. How to become like Christ; how to resurrect the Eternal Christ within yourself.

- **Shermer, Michael 2000. How We Believe: Science, Skepticism, and the Search for God** (+works). New York, NY: Henry Holt. [D4d, P7, PPR9, PR19, PF4, S8]
  Offers fresh insights into age-old questions -- including how and why humans put their faith in a higher power, even in the face of scientific skepticism.

General Processes

PPR1. Transition Cycle

- **Kegan, Robert 1982. The Evolving Self – Problem and Process in Human Development** (+works). Cambridge, MA: Harvard University [D1+2, P1, P2a, PPR3, S3].
  Each meaning-making Stage is a new solution to the lifelong tension -- between the universal human yearning to be connected, attached, and included, on the one hand, and to be distinct, independent, and autonomous on the other. Landmark work on human development from a Western academic perspective. Source for the ADAPT Model's Transition Cycle.

PPR4. Restoration Growth

- **Conger, John P. 1988. Jung and Reich: The Body as Shadow.** Berkeley, CA: North Atlantic Books. [D3bc, D7, P4, PPR4, PR29+31, PF6d, S4]
  Jung and Reich: Outlines each man's personality and compares their lives and their work, emphasizing points of convergence between them. Puts Jung's mystical and psychological approach to spiritual disciplines in dialog with Reich's controversial theories of "genitality" and character armor. The result is a heady "what if?"

PPR8. EVOLUTION & INVOLUTION

- **Almaas, A.H. 1998. INNER JOURNEY HOME: THE SOUL'S REALIZATION OF THE UNITY OF REALITY** (+works). Berkeley, CA: Diamond. **[D1+2, D8, P7, PPR8+9, PF7, S7+8]**
What is the soul, and how do we come to know it? What is its journey in life, and what stages and obstacles are encountered along the way? The centerpiece of the Diamond Approach spiritual path.

- **Gerzon, Mark S. 1996. LISTENING TO MIDLIFE.** Boston, MA: Shambhala. **[D6b, P4, PPR8b, PR30, PF11, S3-4]**
Challenges us to see Midlife as a metamorphosis, a period of transition and quest, during which we learn to live our unlived lives.

- **Hillman, James 2000. THE FORCE OF CHARACTER -- AND THE LASTING LIFE.** New York, NY: Ballantine. **[D6b, P4, PPR8b, PR30, PF11, S3-4]**
Our culture treats aging like a disease to be avoided or ameliorated. But as our physical capacities diminish, our capacities of character are allowed to rise to the surface.

- **Hollis, James 1993. THE MIDDLE PASSAGE.** Toronto, Canada: Inner City. **[D6b, P4, PPR8b, PR30, PF11, S3-4]**
The conflicts and disturbances that happen at Mid-Life are wonderful wake-ups that new directions are needed to achieve a meaningful life. When we travel the Middle Passage consciously, we render our lives more meaningful, and the second half of life immeasurably richer. Sensitive discussion by acclaimed Jungian analyst.

PPR9. AWAKENING

- **Merton, Thomas 1948. THE SEVEN STOREY MOUNTAIN** (+works). New York, NY: Harcourt Brace. **[D8, P7, PPR9, PR33, PF7, S8]**
The growing restlessness of a brilliant and passionate young man whose search for peace and faith leads him, at the age of twenty-six, to take vows in one of the most demanding Catholic orders, the Trappist monks. At the Abbey of Gethsemani, Merton is liberated by "the four walls of my new freedom."

- **Moore, Thomas 1996. THE RE-ENCHANTMENT OF EVERYDAY LIFE** (+works). New York, NY: HarperCollins. **[D3bd, PPR9, PR15, PF7, S8]**
Shows that a profound, enchanted engagement with life is a necessity for our personal and collective survival. Addresses specific aspects of daily life: Clothing, food, furniture, architecture, ecology, language, and politics. Describes the renaissance these can undergo when there is a genuine engagement with beauty, craft, nature, and art in both private and public life.

- **Warren, Rick 2002. THE PURPOSE DRIVEN LIFE: WHAT ON EARTH AM I HERE FOR?.** Grand Rapids, MI: Zondervan. **[D3ad, PPR9, PR15, PF7, S8]**
Written around five purposes: Worship, fellowship, discipleship, ministry and mission. The bestselling hardback non-fiction book in history, and the second most-translated book in the world, after the Bible.

A. H. Almaas

Robert Kegan

Specific Processes

PR1-35. PROGRAMS FOR ACTUALIZATION GROWTH

- Wilber, Ken and Terry Patton, et al 2008. INTEGRAL LIFE PRACTICE: A 21ST-CENTURY BLUEPRINT FOR PHYSICAL HEALTH, EMOTIONAL BALANCE, MENTAL CLARITY, AND SPIRITUAL AWAKENING. Boston, MA: Integral Books. [D, P2a, PPR3+9, PR33, PF10, S3]
The definitive explication of Integral Life Practice (ILP) – Wilber's set of Specific Processes designed to develop physical health, spiritual awareness, emotional balance, mental clarity, relational joy, and energy level, within a framework that integrates all aspects of one's life.

- INTEGRAL LIFE PRACTICE STARTER KIT. Louisville, CO (2006): Sounds True Publications.
Structured, easy-to-follow audio introduction to the major modules of ILP.

- Leonard, George B. and Michael Murphy 1995. THE LIFE WE ARE GIVEN: A LONG-TERM PROGRAM FOR REALIZING THE POTENTIAL OF BODY, MIND, HEART, AND SOUL. New York, NY: Tarcher. [D, P2a, PPR3+9, PR33, PF10, S3]
Integral Transformative Practice (ITP) -- a balanced and comprehensive long-term program for personal development. Step-by-step instructions for joining body, mind, heart, and soul in an evolutionary adventure that can transform our interiors and our Culture. Murphy's ITP and Wilber's ILP have been significant influences on each other.

- Brand, Stewart 1981. THE NEXT WHOLE EARTH CATALOG: ACCESS TO TOOLS (+series). New York, NY: Random House. [D2, DD1+2, P2, PPR3+5, PF4, S2+3]
The definitive manual on how the Emerging Culture is being created, and will be created. Major landmark.

PR2. NATURAL NUTRITION

- Pitchford, Paul 1993. HEALING WITH WHOLE FOODS: ASIAN TRADITIONS AND MODERN NUTRITION. Berkeley, CA: North Atlantic Books. [D3c, P2a, PPR3+4, PR2, PF6c-5, S3]
A wealth of information on health, diet, alternative medicine, natural food presentation, and recipes, researched by an expert in the field. Readers will learn how to apply Chinese medicine and the five-element theory to a contemporary diet; treat illness and nervous disorders through diet; and make the transition to whole vegetable foods.

- Smith, Lendon 1983. FEED YOUR YOURSELF RIGHT (+works). New York, NY: McGraw Hill. [D3c, P2a, PPR3, PR2, PF6c-5, S3]
Authoritative advice from a much-beloved pediatrician: Planning a healthy diet and outlines specific nutritional programs for such major problems as alcoholism, obesity, allergies, arthritis, cancer, high-blood pressure, etc.

- Cousens, Gabriel 1993. SPIRITUAL NUTRITION: SIX FOUNDATIONS FOR SPIRITUAL LIFE AND THE AWAKENING OF KUNDALINI (+works). Berkeley, CA: North Atlantic Books. [D3c, P2a, PPR3+8, PR2, PF7, S3]
Combines the best of ancient spiritual wisdom with invaluable illuminations and practical applications offered by modern spiritual seekers. Whether you are ready to adopt a 100% live-food diet, or you simply wish to steadily improve and strengthen your diet and spiritual life, this book is a valuable tool.

PR3. HOLISTIC HEALTH

- Northrup, Christiane 1994. WOMEN'S BODIES, WOMEN'S WISDOM: CREATING PHYSICAL AND EMOTIONAL HEALTH AND HEALING (+works). New York, NY: Bantam Books (Random House). [D3c, P3a, PPR3+4, PR3, PF6c-5, S3]
The bible of women's health -- now with the latest developments and advances: More fulfilling sex life; healing terminal illnesses; dissolving PMS and easing menstrual cramps; decreasing the risk of birth defects; how to birth naturally, despite the current induction and C-section epidemic; cellular inflammation, the root cause of all chronic degenerative diseases; the "fountain of youth molecule," etc.

❂ **Pizzorno, Joseph 1996. TOTAL WELLNESS: IMPROVE YOUR HEALTH BY UNDERSTANDING THE BODY'S HEALING SYSTEMS** (+works). New York, NY: Prima Lifestyles (Crown, Random House). **[D3c, P2a, PPR3+4, PR3, PF6c-5, S3]**
How to pinpoint exactly what our bodies need to be healthy. Covers each of the major body systems, describing how they work, how to recognize when something is not working correctly, and how to make it work again. How to use lifestyle modifications and natural medicines to reestablish optimal health, often through self-treatment techniques.

❂ **Balch, James and Phyllis Balch 2000. PRESCRIPTION FOR NUTRITIONAL HEALING : PRACTICAL A-Z REFERENCE TO DRUG-FREE REMEDIES USING VITAMINS, MINERALS, HERBS, AND FOOD SUPPLEMENTS** (+series). New York, NY: Avery Publishing (Penguin). **[D3c, P2a, PPR3+4, PR3, PF6c-5, S3]**
The most comprehensive guide to natural health -- with cutting-edge findings in alternative and preventative therapies, vitamins, supplements, herbs, etc.

❂ **Ody, Penelope 1993. THE COMPLETE MEDICINAL HERBAL: A PRACTICAL GUIDE TO THE HEALING PROPERTIES OF HERBS, WITH MORE THAN 250 REMEDIES FOR COMMON AILMENTS.** New York, NY and London: DK Publishing. **[D3c, P2a, PPR3+4, PR3, PF6c-5, S3]**
A dictionary of 130 herbs, all well illustrated both as growing plants and in prepared forms. Charts describe a wide range of ailments and the appropriate home remedies. Includes excellent instructions on preparing herbs for use.

❂ **Golan, Ralph 1995. OPTIMAL WELLNESS: WHERE MAINSTREAM AND ALTERNATIVE MEDICINE MEET.** New York, NY: Wellspring (Ballantine Books). **[D3c, P2a, PPR3+4, PR3, PF6c-5, S3]**
Empowering self-care guide that challenges the "crisis/disease" orientation of modern medicine -- prescription drugs, expensive surgery, and high-tech intervention. Points the way to a more comprehensive system of health care that heals the whole person. The "Ten Common Denominators" of illness that most frequently threaten optimal health. Master Symptom Survey, which reveals the hidden conditions that erode good health.

❂ **Zimmer, Carl 1979. PARASITE REX: INSIDE THE BIZARRE WORLD OF NATURE'S MOST DANGEROUS CREATURES.** New York, NY: Atria (Simon & Schuster). **[D3c, P4, PPR4, PR3, PF8-5, S1]**
The array of amazing creatures that invade their hosts, prey on them from within, and control their behavior. Can change DNA, rewire the brain, make men more distrustful or women more outgoing, and turn their hosts into the living dead.

PR4. Sexuality & Sensuality

Anand, Margo and M. E. Maslednikov 1989. The Art of Sexual Ecstasy: The Path of Sacred Sexuality for Western Lovers (+series). New York, NY: Jeremy P. Tarcher (Penguin). **[D3d, D4a10, D4b2, D8, PPR9, PR33, PF7, S9]**
Landmark book on human sexuality. Makes the sacred lovemaking techniques of Tantra fully comprehensible to Western readers. Elegantly illustrated. Helps the reader to acquire new attitudes, to broaden his or her range of experience, to revitalize and strengthen relationships.

PR5. Relationships & Marriage

Schnarch, David 1998. Passionate Marriage: Keeping Love and Intimacy Alive in Committed Relationships (+works). New York, NY: Henry Holt. **[D4a9, D4b2, PPR3, PR5, PF5, PF6c7]**
Differentiation -- the often threatening process of defining yourself as separate from your partner, which inevitably draws you closer to your partner than you ever dreamed possible. Doesn't just cure sexual dysfunction, but helps couples reach the mind-blowing heights of their sexual potential.

PR6. Family Dynamics

Hellinger, Bert. 1998. Love's Hidden Symmetry: What Makes Love Work in Relationships (+series). Phoenix, AZ: Zeig, Tucker & Theisen. **[D3b, P2b, PPR5, PR6, PF6d, S2]**
A flowing combination of narrative, anecdotes, transcripts and didactic material, illustrating how members of families carry each others traumas and misunderstandings, often for generations, and how these are resolved through re-establishing the proper "orders of Love". Much broader and deeper than "How To Have A Good Relationship". It is about the unacknowledged rules of love and relationship and the restoration of integrity to family and relationship systems.

PR10. Natural Environment

Muir, John and Edward Way Teale, ed. 1975. The Wilderness World of John Muir (+works). New York, NY: Mariner Books (Houghton Mifflin). **[D8, P4-9, PPR7, PR35, PF3, S8]**
Gives our generation a picture of an America still wild and unsettled only one hundred years ago. The best of Muir's writing from all of his major works, selected by a man who himself is a great nature writer. Magnificent, thrilling, exciting, breathtaking, and awe-inspiring.

Thoreau, Henry David and Jeffrey S. Cramer, ed. 2004. Walden: A Fully Annotated Edition (+works). New Haven, CT: Yale University Press. **[D8, P4-9, PPR7, PR35, PF3, S8]**
The great classic. By immersing himself in nature, Thoreau hoped to gain a more objective understanding of society through personal introspection. Part personal declaration of independence, social experiment, voyage of spiritual discovery, satire, and manual for self-reliance.

Stamets, Paul 2005. Mycelium Running: How Mushrooms Can Help Save the World (+works). Berkeley, CA: Ten Speed Press. **[D3a, P2b, PPR5, PR10, PF3, S2]**
A manual for healing the earth and creating sustainable forests through mushroom cultivation, featuring mycelial solutions to water pollution, toxic spills, and other ecological challenges. Part of a larger trend toward using living systems to solve environmental problems and to restore ecosystems.

Fukuoka, Masanobu 1987. The Road Back to Nature: Regaining the Paradise Lost (+works). Japan Press. **[D3a, P2b, PPR5, PR10, PF3, S2]**
No-till, no-fertilizer, no-weeding, no-pruning, no-herbicide farming system based on recognizing the complexity of living organisms that shape an ecosystem and deliberately exploiting those complexities. Not just as a means of producing food, but an aesthetic and spiritual approach to life, the ultimate goal of which was "the cultivation and perfection of human beings".

PR11. Skills

❀ **McGuinness, Diane 1997. WHY OUR CHILDREN CAN'T READ AND WHAT WE CAN DO ABOUT IT** (+works). New York, NY: The Free Press (Simon & Schuster). **[D4a-1, D4b-6, P1, PPR3, PR11+12, PF9-3, S3]**
The ultimate case for phonics. Maintains that any child can be taught to read fluently if given proper principles and instruction. Dramatically reveals how dyslexia and behavior problems such as ADD stem not from neurological disorders but from flawed curriculum and methods of instruction.

PR17. Archetype & Myth

❀ **Graves, Robert 1955. THE GREEK MYTHS** (+works). New York, NY: Penguin Books. **[D4-7, P3+7, PPR9, PR17, PF4-11, S8]**
Classic volume encompassing many of the greatest mythic stories ever told—stories of the gods, heroes, and extraordinary events that inspired Homer, the Greek tragedians, and much of subsequent European literature. Uses a novelist's skill to weave a crisp, coherent narrative of each myth. Provides commentaries with cross-references, interpretations, and explanations based on solid scholarship.

❀ **Chinen, Allan 1992. ONCE UPON A MIDLIFE: CLASSIC STORIES AND MYTHIC TALES TO ILLUMINATE THE MIDDLE YEARS** (+series). New York, NY: Jeffrey P. Tarcher (Penguin). **[D4d-6, P3g, PPR8b, PR17, PF4-5, S7b]**
In fairytales, the Prince and Princess marry and live happily ever after. But what really happens then? The unique stories in this book, collected from around the world, provide the answer. They portray men and women at midlife, and offer timeless wisdom for surviving and growing in this often turbulent time.

❀ **Renault, Mary 1962. THE BULL FROM THE SEA** (+works). New York, NY: Pantheon Books (Knopf). **[D8, P3g, PR17, PF4-11, S2]**
Reconstructs the legend of Theseus, the valiant youth who slew the Minotaur, became king, and brought prosperity to Attica. Central volume of a trilogy. A myth analogous to the journey through our soul's interior.

PR24. Language & Communication

- **Barnhart, Robert K. and Sol Steinmetz, eds. 1988. Chambers Dictionary of Etymology.** New York, NY and Edinburgh: Chambers Harrap Publishers. **[D4a-1, P2, PPR5, PR24, PF2]**
Explores the development of meaning, spelling, and pronunciation of over 25,000 English words. Traces words back to their Proto-Germanic or Indo-European roots, and include words borrowed from other languages, as well as the sources and dates of their first recorded use. Celebrated volume that is the reference of choice in etymological matters.

- **Burke, Kenneth 1968. Language As Symbolic Action: Essays on Life, Literature, and Method** (+works). Berkeley, CA: University of California Press. **[D4b-7, PPR7a, PR24, PF4, S6b]**
Humankind is a "symbol-using animal." What we call "reality" is actually "a clutter of symbols about the past combined with whatever things we know mainly through maps, magazines, newspapers, and the like about the present -- a construct of our symbol systems."

- **Lakoff, George and Mark Johnson 1980. Metaphors We Live By.** Chicago, IL: University of Chicago Press. **[D4b-7, P1, PPR7a, PR24, S6a.]**
Metaphor is a fundamental mechanism of mind, one that allows us to use what we know about our physical and social experience to provide understanding of countless other subjects. Because such metaphors structure our most basic understandings of our experience, they are "metaphors we live by" -- metaphors that can shape our perceptions and actions without our ever noticing them.

PR27. Stories & Literature

- **Frye, Northrup 1957. Anatomy of Criticism** (+works). New York, NY: Princeton, NJ (Princeton University Press). **[D4b-7, PPR7a, PR27, PF4, S6b]**
Magisterial work proceeding on the assumption that criticism is a structure of thought and knowledge in its own right. Four brilliant essays on historical, ethical, archetypical, and rhetorical criticism, employing examples of world literature from ancient times to the present. Reconceived literary criticism as a basic way "to produce, out of the society we have to live in, a vision of the society we want to live in."

- **Magill, Frank 1991. Masterpieces of World Literature** (+series). New York, NY: Collins Reference. **[D4b-7, PPR7a, PR27, PF4, S6b, Appx B1]**
Philosophy and fantasy, plays and poems, essays and epics -- 270 literary classics that range from The Divine Comedy and Death Comes for the Archbishop to The Aeneid and The Grapes of Wrath are summarized and analyzed. Just one of the series -- in a long line of essential reference works.

PR28. Expressive Arts

- **Battistini, Mathilde 2005. Symbols and Allegories in Art** (+Guide to Imagery series). Malibu, CA: Getty Museum. **[D3bd, D4b-7, D6s, P7, PPR8, PR28, PF4-7, S6a]**
The hidden meanings in works of art. From antiquity, when the gods and goddesses were commonly featured in works of art, through to the twentieth century, when Surrealists drew on archetypes from the unconscious, artists have embedded symbols in their works. Four sections featuring symbols related to time, man, space (earth and sky), and allegories or moral lessons. Presented in entertaining, accessible, multi-modal style. Part of the definitive, multi-volume survey on the history and meaning of art.

- **Mathieu, William A. 2010. Bridge of Waves: What Music Is and How Listening to It Changes the World** (+works). Boston, MA: Shambhala Publications. **[D4b-7, P5-8, PPR8, PR28, PF4-6, S7]**
Music bridges mind and heart, self and other, and affirms our place in the world. The author asks you to question what music is and how it works -- how to understand its value in your life, in the life of your community, and in the evolution of the cosmos.

C4. Resources for Personal Evolution. Page 293

- **Maltin, Leonard 2010. LEONARD MALTIN'S CLASSIC MOVIE GUIDE: FROM THE SILENT ERA THROUGH 1965** (+series). New York, NY: Plume (Penguin). **[D4a-5, P3, PR28, PF4-4, S6]**
  With entries spanning across the decades, this comprehensive guide has expanded star and director indexes, and capsule reviews of the great and obscure -- films that turn up on Turner Classic Movies in the wee hours of the morning.

PR29. BODY THERAPIES

- **Murphy, Michael 1992. THE FUTURE OF THE BODY – EXPLORATIONS INTO THE FURTHER EVOLUTION OF HUMAN NATURE.** New York, NY: Tarcher. **[D3c, P5, PPR3-4, PR29, PF6ad, S3-4]**.
  Scientifically sophisticated survey and investigation of a huge range of somatic processes and modalities. Magnum opus by the illustrious co-founder of Esalen.

- **Juhan, Dean 1987. JOB'S BODY – A HANDBOOK FOR BODYWORK.** Barrytown, NY: Barrytown, Ltd. **[D3c, P2a, PPR3-4, PR29, PF6ad, S3-4]**
  Detailed theoretical and practical explanations of numerous bodywork modalities. The human response to touch from the micro-cellular level, through to system responses, all the way to the origins of the body/mind split in western philosophy. The interactivity, interconnectedness, and interdependence of all aspects of the human body, mind and spirit. Classic work that is often required reading for massage certification.

- **Brennan, Barbara Ann 1998. HANDS OF LIGHT – A GUIDE TO HEALING THROUGH THE HUMAN ENERGY FIELD.** New York, NY: Bantam Books. **[D3c, P5, PPR3-4, PR30, PF6ad, S3-4]**
  Our physical bodies exist within a larger "body" -- a human energy field or aura, which is the vehicle through which we create our experience of reality, including health and illness. It is through this energy field that we have the power to heal ourselves. Remarkable delineation of the Subtle Bodies from a hands-on bioenergetic practitioner with extraordinary sensitivities to non-material phenomena.

PR30. Introspection & Self-Awareness

✺ **Cameron, Julia 2002. The Artist's Way** (+series). New York, NY: Tarcher. **[D2, D4b-7, PPR1, PR28, PF11, S3]**
A comprehensive twelve-week program to recover your creativity from a variety of blocks, including limiting beliefs, fear, self-sabotage, jealousy, guilt, addictions, and other inhibiting forces, replacing them with artistic confidence and productivity. Beautifully crafted and profoundly empowering. Major influence on the Explorations of this book.

✺ **Garfield, Patricia 2001. The Universal Dream Key** (+works). New York, NY: HarperSanFrancisco. **[D8, PPR9, PR17, PR30, PF7, S8]**
All dreams fall into 12 archetypes -- despite significant differences in dreamers and their cultures. Most dreams are common, easily recognizable narratives ("Being Chased or Attacked"), though a few may be less familiar to Western readers ("Being Menaced by a Spirit"). Each "negative" dream has a corresponding positive or healing version.

✺ **Progoff, Ira 1992. At Journal Workshop: Writing to Access the Power of the Unconscious and Evoke Creative Ability** (+series). New York, NY: Tarcher. **[P2a-4, PPR3, PR30, PF11, S3]**
The classic on journal-writing: A structured format that enables you to get to know the inner core of your life on ever-deeper levels and gain a fuller perspective on who and where you are. This book's technique of Explorations.

PR31. Psychotherapies

✺ **Perls, Frederick S., Ralph Hefferline, and Paul Goodman 1977. Gestalt Therapy: Excitement and Growth in the Human Personality.** Gouldsboro, ME: Gestalt Journal Press. **[D7b, P4, PPR4, PR29+31, PF6d, S4]**
Synthesizing psychoanalysis, western philosophy, and eastern meditation techniques, the book presents a new and vital perspective on mental health and illness, as well as a series of exercises and practices designed to bring us into closer contact with our daily experience and gain insight into the neurotic mechanisms by which we ward off excitement and Growth. Shifts from Freud and Jung's focus on our past -- memories, dreams, and subconscious -- to our present, here-and-now awareness. A major innovation in psychotherapy.

✺ **Berne, Eric 1996. Games People Play: The Basic Handbook of Transactional Analysis.** New York, NY: Ballantine. **[D7, P4, PPR4, PR30+31, PF6ad, S3-4]**
Because there is so little opportunity for intimacy in daily life, and because intense forms of intimacy are psychologically impossible for most people, the bulk of our social life is taken up with playing Games. We must learn either to become more intimate, or at least to play more beneficial social Games. Started a revolution in how people think of their own behavior.

✺ **Brennan, James F. 2002. History and Systems of Psychology.** Upper Saddle River, NJ: Pearson. **[D7b, P4, PPR4, PR31, PF6d, S4]**
Psychology's origins and development: Historical, cultural, social and philosophical. Textbook style.

PR31. Surveys and Compendia of Therapies

✺ **Corsini, Raymond J. and Danny Wedding, eds. 2013. Current Psychotherapies.** Independence, KY: Cengage Learning. **[D7b, P4, PPR4, PR31, PF6d, S4]**
Excellent introductions to a wide selection of the over-400 psychotherapies popular today. Helps readers learn, compare, and apply the major systems of psychotherapy in a way that will be meaningful in their own practices. Companion book of case histories.

✺ **Corsini, Raymond J. 2001. Handbook of Innovative Therapy.** Hoboken, NJ: Wiley. **[D7b, P4, PPR4, PR31, PF6b]**
Textbook and manual covering a large variety of innovative and esoteric therapies: natural high, covert conditioning, mindbody communication, imaginal cognition, deep psychobiology, eidetic therapy, provocative therapy, intensive marathon, primal therapy, etc.

C4. Resources for Personal Evolution. Page 295

- **Schneider, Kirk J., James F. T. Bugental, and J. Fraser Pierson, eds. 2002. THE HANDBOOK OF HUMANISTIC PSYCHOLOGY: LEADING EDGES IN THEORY, RESEARCH, AND PRACTICE.** Thousand Oaks, CA: Sage. **[D7, P2a, PPR3, PR31, PF6a-d, S3-4]**
Essays and studies on therapies, philosophies, and research that do justice to the highest reaches of human achievement and potential: personal construct psychotherapy, transpersonal psychology, credulous approach, peace psychology, organizational development theory, inner experiencing, constructivist therapy, Abraham Maslow, Rollo May, etc.

- **Cain, David J. and Julius Seeman, eds. 2001. HUMANISTIC PSYCHOTHERAPIES: HANDBOOK OF RESEARCH AND PRACTICE.** Washington, DC: American Psychological Association (APA). **[D7, P2a, PPR3, PR31, PF6a-d, S3-4]**
Comprehensive overview of the history, defining characteristics, and evolution of Humanistic Psychotherapies -- including client-centered, Gestalt, existential, and experiential. Shows these approaches to be equivalent or superior to more traditional methods in treating a wide range of psychopathology.

- **Corey, Gerald 2005. THEORY & PRACTICE OF COUNSELING & PSYCHOTHERAPY.** Independence, KY: Cengage Learning. **[D7, P4, PPR3-4, PR31, PF6ad, S3-4]**
Introduces students to the major theories of counseling (psychoanalytic, Adlerian, existential, person-centered, Gestalt, reality, behavior, cognitive-behavior, family systems, feminist, and postmodern approaches, etc.) and demonstrates how each theory can be applied to one particular case.

- **Messer, Stanley B. and Alan S. Gurman, eds. 2011. ESSENTIAL PSYCHOTHERAPIES: THEORY AND PRACTICE.** New York, NY: Guilford. **[D7b, P4, PPR4, PR31, PF6d, S4]**
Overview of core approaches to treating individual and relational disorders. Covers treatments with deep historical roots (such as dynamic and humanistic approaches), those associated with empirical traditions (such as behavioral and cognitive-behavioral approaches), as well as those at the cutting edge (such as third-wave behavioral treatments). Brings order and reason to the literally hundreds of specific techniques espoused in the literature.

PR32. Psycho-Biologic Techniques

❂ **Gerber, Richard 1995. Vibrational Medicine: New Choices for Healing Ourselves** (+series). Rochester, VT: Bear & Co. **[D3bc, P5, PPR8, PR32, S7]**
Encyclopedic treatment of energetic healing, covering subtle-energy fields, acupuncture, Bach flower remedies, homeopathy, radionics, crystal healing, electrotherapy, radiology, chakras, meditation, and psychic healing. How various energy therapies work. New insights into the physical and spiritual perspectives of health and disease.

❂ **Hunt, Valerie V. 1995. Infinite Mind: The Science of Human Vibration** (+series). Malibu, CA: Malibu Publishing. **[D3bc, P5, PPR8, PR32, S7]**
Shows that the mind and emotions are not restricted to the brain and nervous system, but rather originate in the aura, out of which the body is originally formed. Important implications in the field of communication with the so-called dead, and in healing diseases which originate in imbalances in the energy field before viruses, bacteria, genetic defects and other factors do their damage.

❂ **Hadady, Letha 1996. Asian Health Secrets: The Complete Guide to Asian Herbal Medicine.** New York, NY: Crown Publishing (Random House). **[D3c, P2a, PPR3+4, PR3, PF6c-5, S3]**
Brings the ancient knowledge of Chinese, Indian, and Tibetan herbal medicine to Westerners. Tools for self-diagnosis emphasize treating the person, rather than the illness, to ensure a healthy harmony of body, mind, and spirit. Herbs are recommended for a gamut of problems, ranging from eating disorders, arthritis, and PMS to sexual dysfunction and depression.

PR33. Spiritual Practices

❂ **Walsh, Roger and Frances Vaughn 1999. Essential Spirituality: The 7 Central Practices to Awaken Heart and Mind.** Hoboken, NJ: Wiley. **[D8, P2, PPR3+9, PR33, PF7, S8]**
Each of the great spiritual traditions has both a common goal -- recognizing the sacred and divine that exist both within and around us -- and seven common practices to reach that goal. Filled with stories, exercises, meditations, myths, prayers, and practical advice to integrate these seven principles into one truly rewarding way of life.

❂ **Smith, Houston 1991. The World's Religions: Our Great Wisdom Traditions.** New York, NY: Harper. **[D8, P2b, PPR9, PR33, PF4-11, S8]**
Core beliefs and inherent beauty of the world's seven great religions: Hinduism, Buddhism, Taoism, Confucianism, Islam, Judaism, and Christianity. The common wisdom that they all share alike. Famous and masterly study of comparative religions.

❂ **Walsh, Roger and Frances Vaughn, eds. 1993. Paths Beyond Ego: The Transpersonal Vision.** New York, NY: Jeffrey P. Tarcher. **[D8, P2a, PPR3+9, PR33, PF7, S8]**
From the material view, the physical world is the ultimate, if not the only reality -- and the behaviors and experiences can be understood through the researches of neuroscience and psychodynamic formulations. Life is a finite game. From the transpersonal view, the physical world and all its laws represent only one of an indeterminable number of possible realities whose qualities we can apprehend only through the evolution of our consciousness. In this view, consciousness pervades all realities and is the primary source or creative principle of existence, including the energy-matter of the physical world. Life is an infinite game. Fifty essays exploring the emerging field of transpersonal psychology.

❂ **Kabat-Zinn, Jon 2006. Coming to Our Senses: Healing Ourselves and the World Through Mindfulness.** (+series). New York, NY: Hyperion. **[D3d, P2a, PPR4+9, PR7+33, PF11, S3+8]**
Examines the mysteries and marvels of our minds and bodies, describing simple, intuitive ways in which we can come to a deeper understanding, through our senses, of our beauty, our genius, and our life path in a complicated, fear-driven, and rapidly changing world. From the preeminent authority on mindfulness meditation.

C4. Resources for Personal Evolution. Page 297

❀ **Khalsa, Shakta Kaur 1998. KUNDALINI YOGA: THE FLOW OF ETERNAL POWER - A SIMPLE GUIDE TO THE YOGA OF AWARENESS AS TAUGHT BY YOGI BHAJAN** (+works). New York, NY: G.P. Putnam (Penguin). **[D3d, D8, P7, PPR9, PR33, PF7, S8]**
Offers an accessible introduction to the ancient practice of Kundalini Yoga, which if practiced regularly, can strengthen the nervous system, balance the glandular system, and harness the energy of the mind and emotion as well as the body. Covers Kundalini yogic philosophy and lifestyle in detail.

PR34. HOLISTIC ENVIRONMENTS

❀ **Mollison, Bill 1988. PERMACULTURE: A DESIGNER'S MANUAL** (+works). Tyalgum, AU: Tagari. **[D3ad, P2, PPR5, PR35, PF3, S2]**
The conscious design and maintenance of agriculturally productive ecosystems that have the diversity, stability, and resilience of natural ecosystems. The harmonious integration of landscape and people -- providing their food, energy, shelter, and other material and non-material needs in a sustainable way. Without a permanent agriculture, there is no possibility of a stable social order.

❀ **Savory, Allen 1988. HOLISTIC RESOURCE MANAGEMENT: A MODEL FOR A HEALTHY PLANET** (+works). Washington, DC: Island Press. **[D3ad, P2, PPR5, PR35, PF3, S2]**
On the most fundamental level, environmental problems are caused by human management decisions, rather than the commonly blamed culprits -- environmental degradation, overpopulation, poor farming practices, or lack of financial support. A revolutionary decision-making framework.

❀ **Hemenway, Toby 2001. GAIA'S GARDEN: A GUIDE TO HOME-SCALE PERMACULTURE.** White River Junction, VT: Chelsea Green Publishing. **[D3ad, P2, PPR5, PR35, PF3, S2]**
Application of Mollison's permaculture principles to the backyard garden. A fusion of the practical and the visionary -- using the natural intelligence of Earth's symbiotic communities to strengthen and sustain ecosystems in which humans are a partner, not a competitor.

Richard Gerber, M.D. — Vibrational Medicine

Yellow Sub Meets Maharishi

Valerie Hunt

Gaia's Garden — Toby Hemenway

Kabat-Zinn

Roger Walsh

Houston Smith

Permaculture: A Designers' Manual — Bill Mollison

Page 298. Wilber + Campbell Appendices

Pathfinders

PF3. HOLISTIC GROWTH SITUATIONS

❀ **Jardine, Ray 1999. BEYOND BACKPACKING: RAY JARDINE'S GUIDE TO LIGHTWEIGHT HIKING** (+series). AdventureLore Press. **[D4a-6, P2, PPR7b, PR10, PF3, S4]**
The definitive guide to high-performance, low-load backpacking: The "Ray Way" to backcountry bliss.

❀ **Fletcher, Colin 1968. THE COMPLETE WALKER: THE JOYS AND TECHNIQUES OF HIKING AND BACKPACKING** (+works). New York, NY: Alfred A. Knopf (Random House). **[D4a-6, P2, PPR7b, PR10, PF3, S4]**
The Hiker's Bible. Covers everything: shoes (from full-scale boots to trail runners to hiking sandals), socks, packs, tents, clothing, weather, food, cooking, stoves, lights, hats, animals. Extensive experience. Witty, wry humor and very honest accounts of his own dumb mistakes.

❀ **Weaver, William Woys 1997. HEIRLOOM VEGETABLE GARDENING: A MASTER GARDENER'S GUIDE TO PLANTING, SEED SAVING, AND CULTURAL HISTORY.** New York, NY: Henry Holt. **[D3a, P2b, PPR5, PR10, PF3, S2]**
Encyclopedic guide to the history and cultivation of some of America's most treasured heirloom vegetables. How to connect with the living wisdom of the past.

PF4. AUTHORITIES

- **Bronowski, Jacob 1962. WESTERN INTELLECTUAL TRADITION: FROM LEONARDO TO HEGEL** (+works). New York, NY: Harper Perennial. **[DD1+2b, P2b, PPR5, PF4, S2]**
Shows how arts and sciences fed off each other, and in turn the sciences fed philosophy, which in turn produced the subspecialty of political philosophy we know as political science. Ties each development to a sequence of writers who helped lead from one major thinker to the next.

- **Clark, Gordon S. 1997. THALES TO DEWEY** (+series). Unicoi, TN: Trinity Foundation. **[D3b, P2a, PPR9, PR19, PF4-10, S2]**
A summary of the great philosophers from a presuppositional perspective, showing where each goes astray. Argues for Revelation as the ultimate source of knowledge.

- **Buckingham, Will et al 2011. THE PHILOSOPHY BOOK (BIG IDEAS SIMPLY EXPLAINED)** (+series). Brooklyn, NY: Melville House Publishing. **[D4b-9, P2b, PPR5, PR19, PF4-10, S2]**
Uses innovative graphics and creative typography to help demystify hard-to-grasp concepts for those new to philosophy. Cuts through the haze of misunderstanding, untangling knotty theories, and shedding light on abstract concepts. Breathes new life to a subject that is often regarded as esoteric and academic.

- **Dowley, Tim and Paul Marsh 1981. EXPLAINING THE GOSPELS: AN ILLUSTRATED INTRODUCTION.** Colorado Springs, CO: David C. Cook Publishers. **[P7, PPR9, PR33, PF4, S8]**
Excellent, richly-illustrated introduction and explanation of the first four books of the New Testament -- books that recount the life and teachings of Jesus Christ.

- **Murray, Charles 2003. HUMAN ACCOMPLISHMENT: THE PURSUIT OF EXCELLENCE IN THE ARTS AND SCIENCES, 800 B.C. TO 1950.** New York, NY: HarperCollins. **[DD1+2b, P2b, PPR5, PF4, S2]**
The giants in the arts and what sets them apart from the merely great. The differences between the great achievement in the arts and those in the sciences. The meta-inventions, 14 crucial leaps in human capacity to create great art and science. The patterns and trajectories of accomplishment across time and geography.

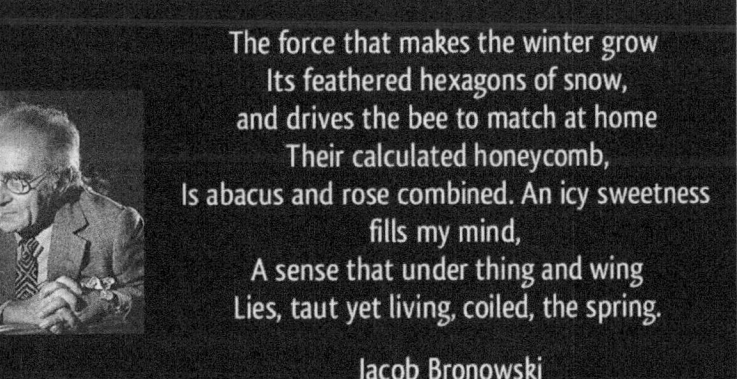

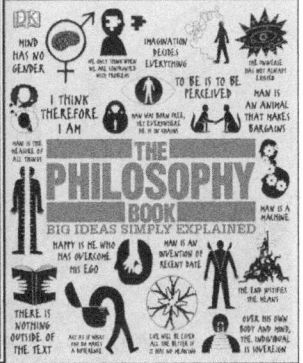

> The force that makes the winter grow
> Its feathered hexagons of snow,
> and drives the bee to match at home
> Their calculated honeycomb,
> Is abacus and rose combined. An icy sweetness
> fills my mind,
> A sense that under thing and wing
> Lies, taut yet living, coiled, the spring.
>
> Jacob Bronowski

PF9. GROWTH CENTERS

PF9a. Meditation Centers [D8, P7, PPR9, PR33, PF9a, S8]

A Growth Center that concentrates on Spiritual Practices. A place where people with special sensitivities to spiritual matters gather to develop those capacities. The modern version of the monastery.

- **TASSAJARA ZEN MOUNTAIN CENTER**, 39171 Tassajara Road, Carmel Valley, CA 93924. 415-865-1899. www.sfzc.org/Tassajara.
Founded by S.F. Zen Center's Shenryu Suzuki in 1967 as the first Zen monastery outside of Asia. Offers retreats and practice periods for outside guests only during the five summer months. Buried deep in the remote Ventana Wilderness east of Carmel, CA. Best place to totally detach yourself from the cares and vexations of daily life.

- **GREEN GULCH FARM ZEN CENTER**, 1601 Shoreline Highway, Muir Beach, CA 94965. 415-383-3134. www.sfzc/ggf.
Zen practice center founded in 1972 by Suzuki disciple Richard Baker. Offers practice workshops and retreats, plus popular Sunday Program that includes zazen instruction, lecture, sitting, and homemade vegetarian lunch. Secluded valley with zendo, gardens, and farm opening out onto spectacular Muir Beach, north of San Francisco. Great place to experience the flavor of the Zen lifestyle.

- **SPIRIT ROCK MEDITATION CENTER**, P.O. Box 169, Woodacre, CA 94973. 415-488-0164. www.SpiritRock.org.
The teachings of the Buddha in the Vipassana tradition of mindful awareness. Silent meditation retreats, classes, trainings, and Dharma study. Tranquil rural setting north of San Francisco.

PF9b. Alternative Universities [P2a, PPR3, PR29-33, PF9b, S3+8]

Colleges and graduate programs that concentrate on alternative psychology and/or spiritual studies.

- **CALIFORNIA INSTITUTE FOR INTEGRAL STUDIES (CIIS)**, 1453 Mission Street, San Francisco, CA 94103. 415-575-6100. www.CIIS.edu.
  Long and honorable history, extending back to 1950's origins with Alan Watts and Aurobindo. Primarily graduate programs in psychology, philosophy, religion, cultural anthropology, transformative studies and leadership, integrative health, women's spirituality, counseling, community mental health, and the arts.

- **NAROPA UNIVERSITY**, 2130 Arapahoe Ave., Boulder CO 80302. 303-444-0202. www.naropa.edu
  Founded in 1974 by renowned Tibetan Buddhist master Chogyam Trungpa – with faculty that has included such luminaries as Allan Ginsburg, Ken Wilber, and John Cage. Offers over two dozen residence and distance-learning degrees in an exceptionally broad range of alternative fields. Bachelor's: Contemplative psychology, early childhood education, environmental, music, peace, Eastern arts, writing, performance, etc. Master's: Art therapy, religious studies, somatic counseling, transpersonal psychology, wilderness, poetics, etc.

- **FIELDING GRADUATE UNIVERSITY**, 2112 Santa Barbara Street, Santa Barbara, CA 93105. 800-340-1099, 805-687-1099. www.Fielding.edu.
  Quality distance-learning graduate programs in education, organizational development, and psychology. Organizational management master's program with an integral studies concentration. Also, an integral studies certificate program. Integral programs developed in association with Ken Wilber.

- **JOHN F. KENNEDY UNIVERSITY**, Pleasant Hill, California. 94523-4817. 800-696-5358, 925-969-3300. www.Jfku.edu.
  Major alternative university. Undergraduate-completion programs, graduate and doctorate degrees, and certificates in the fields of psychology, law, management, liberal arts, holistic studies, and museum studies. Integral Studies program currently suspended.

- **SAYBROOK UNIVERSITY**. 747 Front Street, 3rd Floor, San Francisco, CA 94111-1920. 800-825-4480. www.Saybrook.edu.
  A premier institution for humanistic studies. Offers advanced degrees in psychology, mind-body medicine, organizational transformation, and related human sciences.

- **SOFIA UNIVERSITY** (formerly Institute for Transpersonal Psychology), 1069 East Meadow Circle, Palo Alto, CA, 94303. 650-493-4430. www.Itp.edu.
  A leader in transpersonal research and transpersonal education. Master's and doctoral programs in psychology and spirituality.

PF1-12. Personal Journeys [D3bcd, P2a, PPR3, PR29-33, PF3+9f, S3]

- **Schwartz, Tony 1995. WHAT REALLY MATTERS: SEARCHING FOR WISDOM IN AMERICA.** New York, NY: Bantam.
  The story of the author's four-year, human-potential odyssey through many processes of psychology and spirit. Discovers the best teachers and techniques for inner development, and identifies the potential pitfalls and false gurus he meets along the way. Includes chapters on Esalen and Wilber.

PF9f. Growth Centers – Descriptions [D3bcd, P2a, PPR3, PR29-33, PF9ef, S3]

- **Anderson, Walter Truett 1983. THE UPSTART SPRING: ESALEN AND THE HUMAN POTENTIAL MOVEMENT: THE FIRST TWENTY YEARS.** Upper Saddle River, NJ: Addison Wesley. [PPR3, PR31, PF9f]
  A charming, gossipy multiple biography of the curious gurus who spawned Esalen. The best book to capture the flavor of the Esalen experience – particularly in its early days.

- **Kripal, Jeffrey J. 2007. ESALEN: AMERICA AND THE RELIGION OF NO RELIGION.** University of Chicago Press. [PPR5, PR31, PR2, PF9f]
  How two maverick thinkers sought to fuse the spiritual revelations of the East with the scientific revolutions of the West -- combining the very best elements of Zen Buddhism, Western psychology, and Indian yoga into a utopian vision that rejected the dogmas of conventional religion. Emphasizes Esalen's theories and socio-religious implications, rather than the Esalen experience itself.

PF9f. Human Potential Growth Centers [D3bcd, P2a, PPR3, PR29-33, PF9ef, S3]

Places to experience a wide variety of Processes in idyllic settings.

- **ESALEN INSTITUTE**, 55000 Highway One, Big Sur, CA. 831-667-3000. www.Esalen.org.
  The *grande dame* of all human potential centers, and still reigning queen. More than a Growth Center or an educational institute: A world-wide network of seekers who look beyond dogma to explore deeper spiritual possibilities; forge new understandings of self and society; and pioneer new paths for change.

- **BREITENBUSH HOT SPRINGS** PO Box 578 Detroit, OR 97342. 503-854-3320. www.Breitenbush.com.
  A remote forest retreat in the Oregon Cascades -- blessed with abundant hot springs, a glacier-fed river, tranquil and majestic mountains -- where one can discover a vast and personal connection with the natural world in any season. Magical retreat for Growth programs, or just personal rejuvenation.

- **THE FINDHORN FOUNDATION (AND UNIVERSITY)**, The Park, Findhorn Bay, Moray IV36 3TZ, Scotland, UK. +44 (0)1309 691620. www.Findhorn.org.
  One of Britain's largest and best-established intentional communities. A Northern Scotland eco-village offering workshops and residential programs for over 3000 visitors per year. Best place to regress back to the Golden Days of the 1960's.

- **HOLLYHOCK**, Cortez Island, British Columbia, Canada. 800-933-6339. www.Hollyhock.ca.
  Canada's major Growth Center, still connected to her counterculture roots. Exists to inspire, nourish and support people who are raising their own consciousness and making the world a better place.

- **OMEGA INSTITUTE**, 150 Lake Drive, Rhinebeck, NY 12572. 845-266-4444. www.Eomega.org
  The major Growth Center on the East Coast of the US. Nurtures dialogues on the integration of modern medicine and natural healing. Offers programs that connect science, spirituality, and creativity. Special attention to sustainability, women's leadership, veterans care, and service -- issues that must be addressed in order for our society to heal and flourish.

C4. Resources for Personal Evolution. Page 303

The ADAPT Model

The Life Journey Archetype

Invitations to Enchantment
These Quick Reference Guides are your Maps to the twin Enchanted Realms of Concept and Symbol.

Appendix C5.
QUICK REFERENCE GUIDES:
The Domains & Sectors of ADAPT

For easy reference, this Appendix presents diagrams and thumbnail descriptions of each Domain and Sector of the ADAPT Model and the Life Journey Archetype:

- ❂ **C5a. The Parameters of ADAPT:**
  Dimensions, Participants, Gen. Processes, Pathfinders (page 306)
  Thumbnail descriptions of all the major Parameters for the four basic Domains of ADAPT on one two-page spread.

- ❂ **C54b. The Parameters of ADAPT:**
  Systems, Specific Processes (page 308)
  Thumbnail descriptions of all the major Parameters for the two auxiliary Domains of ADAPT on one two-page spread.

- ❂ **C5c. The Life Journey Archetype:**
  Dimensions, Participants, Gen. Processes, Pathfinders (page 310)
  Thumbnail descriptions of all the major Sectors for the four Domains of the Life Journey Archetype on one two-page spread.

- ❂ **C5d. ADAPT Circle Diagram** (page 312)
  Circle Diagram displaying all the Domains and major Sectors of the ADAPT Model. The four quadrants of the Diagram represent the basic four Domains. The eight concentric circles are the eight Systems of Growth. The items within each circle are the Sectors for that System. The items outside the circles pertain to all eight Systems. [For comparable Circle Diagrams of Ken Wilber's AQAL and Integral Operating System (IOS), see Appendix A1.]

The Anatomy Lesson. "These Diagrams are an Anatomy of the entire ADAPT Model. They show you what's under the skin."

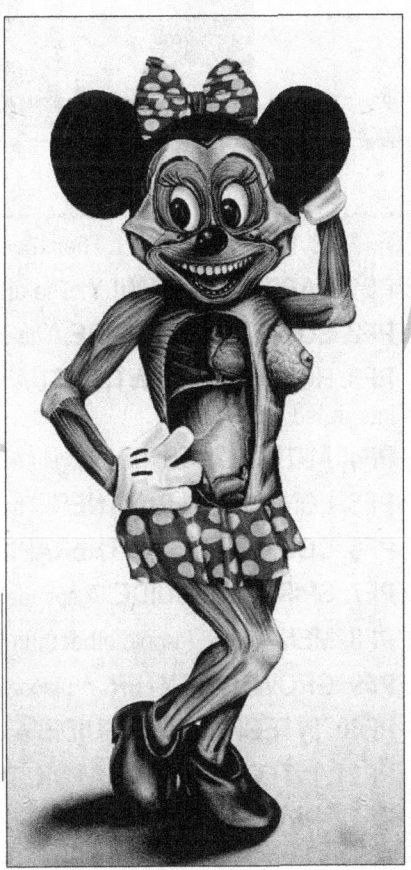

DIMENSIONS

HUMAN GROWTH. Moving and progressing along the Growth Continuum.

D1-8. DIMENSIONS. The various areas of our life where our Growth takes place – and the various features of that Growth. ***
GROWTH CONTINUUM. The set of eight Dimensions of Growth.

D1. STAGES. The levels of development, maturity, enlivenment, or enlightenment through which we pass as we grow.

D2. TRANSITIONS. The quantum leaps that take us from one Stage to the next.

D1+2. DEVELOPMENTAL SEQUENCE. An alternating series of Stages and Transitions.

D3. REALMS. The four major spheres of human experience where Growth can occur – Everyday Life, Psyche, Body, Spirit.

D4. ARENAS. The specific areas of activity within each Realm where Growth takes place.

D5. PERSPECTIVES & PATHS. The four basic points-of-view from which any Growth experience can be observed.

D6. DIRECTIONS & TRAJECTORIES. The two major vertical Directions our Growth can take – Ascending & Descending.

D7. IMPEDIMENTS. The two major ways the Growth process can be impeded or obstructed – Challenges & Impasses.

D8. TRANSCENDENT STATES. The higher levels of consciousness experienced by mystics and translucents.

The ADAPT Model of Human Development

PATHFINDERS

PF1-12. PATHFINDERS. The means by which the Processes are put into effect – combining Guidance & Orchestration.

PF1. PARENTS & FAMILY. The original, the most influential, most beneficial Guides of our Journey of Growth.

PF2. SOCIETY & CULTURE. The set of role models and the lessons on living life we receive from our Society & Culture.

PF3. HOLISTIC GROWTH SITUATION. A cluster of experiences that offers many diverse opportunities for Growth in a single integrated activity.

PF4. AUTHORITIES. People with exceptional wisdom whose work sheds light on and contributes to our Growth.

PF5. LONG-TERM PARTNER. The special person we choose to share our Journey through life.

PF6. COUNSELOR OR THERAPIST. A Growth Practitioner specially trained to implement some aspect of our Growth.

PF7. SPIRITUAL GUIDE. A spiritual master or teacher, who can guide us in Awakening to the Divine Presence.

PF8. MENTORS. People other than Counselors, Therapists, Spiritual Guides, etc. who endeavor to help us grow.

PF9. GROWTH CENTER. A place where people gather together to cultivate a particular aspect of their Growth.

PF10. INTEGRAL LIFE GUIDE. A Growth Practitioner whose work encompasses all five Domains of the ADAPT Model.

PF11. INTERNAL NAVIGATOR. The Guide we form within ourselves by internalizing the Guidance we receive from outside.

PF12. PROVIDENCE. The Guidance & Orchestration we receive from the Divine Presence.

PARTICIPANTS

P1-8. PARTICIPANTS. The aspects of Identity, or Self, that partake in the Growth process.

P1. SELF SYSTEM. A combination of the Experienced Self and the Observed Self – the two entities that engage in a dialectic by which the Self grows.

P2. INDIVIDUAL & COLLECTIVE SELVES. Individual Self: The aspect of Self that identifies and grows as an Individual. Collective Self: The aspect of Self that identifies and grows as a Group.

P3. PERSONALITY TYPES & PERSONAE. Personality Type: A profile of Personality that recurs in human populations with significant regularity. Persona: Our public face. Enables us to play a part in the drama of existence.

P4. SHADOW SELF. Our Inner Saboteur or Gremlin -- any disattached scrap of Identity that impedes or distorts the Growth process.

P5. FUNCTIONAL CONSTITUENTS OF SELF. The fundamental components from which the Self is built. The fundamental mechanisms that enable the Self to grow.

P6. MULTIPLE IDENTITIES. Situations where healthy Individuals can assume more than one Identity – either by Shifting or by Broadening their Identity.

P7. DIVINE PRESENCE. The spiritual entity that presides over our lives – in its two manifestations: the Core Self and the Witness.

SYSTEMS (next diagram)

S1-8. SYSTEMS OF HUMAN GROWTH. The eight mechanisms by which the Dimensions, Participants, Processes, and Pathfinders function together to produce Growth.

SPECIFIC PROCESSES (next)

PR1-35. SPECIFIC PROCESSES OF HUMAN GROWTH. The specific Methods and Techniques that move us along specific parts of Growth Continuum.

GENERAL PROCESSES

PPR1-9, PR1-35. PROCESSES. The Methods and Techniques that move us along the Growth Continuum.

PR1-9. GENERAL PROCESSES. The fundamental Processes that are always in effect whenever Growth takes place.

PPR1. TRANSITION CYCLE. The four-phase process of Metamorphosis by which we Transition from one Stage to the next.

PPR2. SHADOW CYCLE. A malfunction of the Transition Cycle, which can produce a pernicious Shadow Self that is the source of neuroses.

PPR3. ACTUALIZATION GROWTH. The normal progression of Growth from Stage to Stage.

PPR4. RESTORATION GROWTH. Revisiting past Stages to resolve Impasses, so that normal Actualization Growth can resume.

PPR5. COLLECTIVE GROWTH. Growth that occurs among Groups of people – ranging from Couples to Cultures.

PPR6. HORIZONTAL GROWTH. Growth that occurs within a Stage.

PPR7. PERSPECTIVE GROWTH. Growth that occurs as we broaden the Perspectives from which we view and orchestrate our lives.

PPR8. EVOLUTION & INVOLUTION. The twin processes of Directional Growth – Ascending and Descending.

PPR9. AWAKENING. The process of Waking Up to universal spiritual truths that are unchanging and eternal.

SYSTEMS OF GROWTH

<u>S1-8. SYSTEMS OF GROWTH.</u> Mechanisms by which the Dimensions, Participants, Processes, and Pathfinders work together to promote Growth.

S1. INDIVIDUAL GROWTH. Growth that takes place in Individual people.

S2. COLLECTIVE GROWTH. Growth that takes place in Groups of people.

S3. ACTUALIZATION GROWTH. Forward-directed Growth that proceeds from one Stage to the next.

S4. RESTORATION GROWTH. Backward-directed Growth that resolved Impasses in prior Stages, so that forward-directed Growth can resume.

S5. HORIZONTAL GROWTH. Growth that occurs within a Stage. Includes three types: a) Improvement & Translation, b) Equivalence and c) Improvement Within Type.

S6. PERSPECTIVE GROWTH. Growth that occurs through shifting or broadening one's Identity. Includes two types: a) Fundamental Perspectives, and b) Inclusiveness.

S7. EVOLUTION & INVOLUTION. Growth in two Directions – both Upward & Downward (or Outward & Inward). Includes three types: a) Transcend & Include, b) Life Trajectories, and c) Gender-Type Growth.

S8. SPIRITUAL GROWTH. Growth that occurs through Awakening to the Divine Presence.

ADAPT Auxiliary Domains: SYSTEMS & SPECIFIC PROCESSES

SPECIFIC PROCESSES

<u>PR1-35. SPECIFIC PROCESSES.</u> The specialized Methods and Techniques that move us along particular Stages, Realms, and Arenas of the Growth Continuum.

<u>PR1-6. FOUNDATIONAL.</u> The fundamental experiences upon which all future Growth is built.

PR1. NURTURE & BONDING. Activities that satisfy our needs for basic physical and emotional sustenance.

PR2. NATURAL NUTRITION. Activities that provide natural, whole foods – containing all the building blocks for physical and mental development, without the toxic residue.

PR3. HOLISTIC HEALTH. Treatment practices that mobilize the body's natural capacity to maintain wellness and heal itself.

PR4. SENSUALITY & SEXUALITY. The pervasive experience of bodily pleasure in a moderate or intense state of arousal.

PR5. RELATIONSHIPS & MARRIAGE. <u>Relationship</u>: A close association between two people. <u>Marriage</u>: A Relationship with a formal commitment to remain together for the long term.

PR6. GROUP & FAMILY DYNAMICS. Experiences that promote connection, appreciation, and mutual support among group or family members.

<u>PR7-10. PHYSICAL WORLD PROCESSES.</u> Encounters with material reality.

PR7. SENSORY EXPERIENCE. Activities that engage our five senses in experiences with the physical and mental world.

PR8. PHYSICAL ACTIVITY. Activities that engage various parts of our bodies in vigorous, natural movement.

PR9. LIFE EXPERIENCE. Experiences that engage us with the challenging situations and activities of everyday life.

PR10. NATURAL ENVIRONMENTS. Experiences that enable us to observe, study, imitate, appreciate the world of nature.

<u>PR11-17. SOCIO-CULTURAL PROCESSES.</u> Engage us with Groups of people, ranging from couples to Cultures.

PR11. SKILLS. Activities that teach us how to make something or to do something.

SPECIFIC PROCESSES (cont.)

PR12. HABITS & PROGRAMMING. Activities that transform transient actions into routine patterns of behavior.

PR13. RESPONSIBILITY. The capacity to respond dependably to a perceived need.

PR14. ENTERPRISE & LEADERSHIP. Enterprise: Self-initiated activities that provide goods or services in exchange for compensation. Leadership: Activities that prepare us to create and guide an Enterprise.

PR15. VALUES, ETHICS, SERVICE. Values: The guiding principles upon which we base our life. Ethics: The codes of behavior we derive from a system of Values. Service: The efforts we make on behalf of others, as a result of our Ethics.

PR16. ACCULTURATION. Experiences that initiate us into the ceremonies and traditions of our own or other Cultures.

PR17. ARCHETYPE & MYTH. Myths, legends, or creative works that exemplify foundational, archetypal features of a Culture.

PR18-23. FORMAL INVESTIGATION PROCESSES. Engage our Thinking and Reasoning abilities to understand, affect, and utilize both tangible and abstract reality.

PR18. ORDER, STRUCTURE, SYSTEMS. Activities that promote a sense of Order, develop the capacity to Structure increasingly-complex wholes, and apply those Structures to functional Systems.

PR19. EXPLANATIONS. Activities that define, explain, discuss, clarify, or give reasons for, any phenomenon we encounter.

PR20. TECHNOLOGIES. Activities that describe, explain, demonstrate, or operate, any practical device or mechanism.

PR21. LOGIC & REASONING. The explicit skills of developing formally-reasoned explanations and arguments.

PR22. PLANNING & ORCHESTRATION. The skills of planning and orchestrating the components of some anticipated event.

PR23. SCIENCE & PROOF. Activities that enable us to systematically test Explanations for real-world phenomena.

P24-28. SELF EXPRESSION PROCESSES. Express our inner reality in an outward form.

PR24. LANGUAGE & COMMUNICATION. Activities that enable us to formulate, articulate, and convey inchoate thoughts and feelings through language and other forms of communication.

PR25. RECORDED EXPERIENCES. Activities that capture highlights and representative vignettes of quintessential life moments in permanent form.

PR26. HUMOR, COMEDY, FUN. Activities that entertain us, amuse us, and help keep life in perspective.

PR27. STORIES & LITERATURE. Story- or literature-based illustrations of enriching and instructive life situations.

PR28. EXPRESSIVE ARTS. Activities that express our inner world of thought and emotions through observable media.

PR29-33. CONSCIOUS DEVELOPMENT PROCESSES. Techniques, practices, and programs designed specifically to promote personal growth, resolve psychological problems, and facilitate spiritual enlightenment.

PR29. BODY THERAPIES. Body-centered techniques used to promote physical, psychological, and spiritual transformation.

PR30. INTROSPECTION & SELF-AWARENESS. Inner-directed explorations of thoughts, emotions, and physical feelings.

PR31. PSYCHOTHERAPIES. Mind-oriented techniques that are designed to resolve mental difficulties, promote psychological well-being, and develop one's inner potential.

PR32. PSYCHO-BIOLOGIC TECHNIQUES. Techniques and programs that use Natural Medicine and Natural Nutrition Processes to achieve psychological (as well as physiological) balance and well-being.

PR33. SPIRITUAL PRACTICES. Techniques and programs that use structured spiritual practices to achieve higher States of consciousness, and/or a connection with the Divine.

PR34-35. COMPREHENSIVE PROCESSES. Combine and coordinate many diverse Growth Processes into a single, mutually-related Growth experience.

PR34. HOLISTIC ENVIRONMENTS. Personality Type: A profile of Personality that recurs in human populations with significant regularity. Persona: Our public face. Enables us to play a part in the drama of existence.

PR35. INTEGRAL PROGRAMS. Our Inner Saboteur or Gremlin -- any disattached scrap of Identity that impedes or distorts the Growth process.

Page 310. Wilber + Campbell Appendices

DIMENSIONS

HUMAN GROWTH. The JOURNEY we take across the turbulent seas and exotic lands of life.

D1-8. GROWTH CONTINUUM. The MAP of our Life Journey. *** **DIMENSIONS.** The COORDINATES of that Map.

D1. STAGES. The ISLANDS or WAY STATIONS we visit in the course of our Journey -- our STOPOVERS or PORTS OF CALL.

D2. TRANSITIONS. The OPEN SEAS and ROUTES OF PASSAGE our Ship will take between one port of call and the next.

D1+2. DEVELOPMENTAL SEQUENCE. Our entire LIFE JOURNEY until our Ship reaches its final destination.

D3. REALMS. The four regions where our Life Journey takes place – EVERYDAY LIFE, ENCHANTMENT, ORDEALS, HEAVENS.

D4. ARENAS. The various AREAS OF ACTIVITY at every Port of Call – waterfront, downtown, residential area, countryside.

D5. PERSPECTIVES. The four POINTS OF VIEW from which our story can be told. *** **PATHS.** The four DIRECTIONS of Journey.

D6. DIRECTIONS. The two VERTICAL PATHS our Journey can take – upward to the Heavens, or downward to the Underworld.

D7. IMPEDIMENTS. The two major OBSTACLES between us and our destination – CHALLENGES & IMPASSES.

D8. TRANSCENDENT STATES. The supremely ILLUMINATING MOMENTS when we commune with the gods.

The Life Journey Archetype

PATHFINDERS

PF1-8. PATHFINDERS. The means by which our Voyage is GUIDED AND ORCHESTRATED. **Guidance.** DIRECTING our Ship – the task of the NAVIGATOR. **Orchestration.** ARRANGING AND COORDINATING our Voyage -- the responsibility of the CAPTAIN.

PF1. PARENTS & FAMILY. The voices of our HERO'S ORIGINS. The reverberations of his Troubled Past.

PF2. SOCIETY & CULTURE. The influence exerted by any SOCIETY our Hero encounters in the course of his adventures.

PF3. HOLISTIC GROWTH SITUATION. Any SELF-CONTAINED LIVING ENVIRONMENTS where our Hero pauses or dwells.

PF4. AUTHORITIES. HEROES and LEGENDS from times past. SACRED WRITINGS and Ancient Sayings that hold important truths.

PF5. LONG-TERM PARTNER. The FAITHFULNESS or TREACHERY AND DECEIT of the person on whom our Hero most relies.

PF6. COUNSELOR OR THERAPIST. Anyone with SPECIAL GIFTS that enable our Hero overcome CHALLENGES or IMPASSES.

PF7. SPIRITUAL GUIDE. Anyone who connects our Hero with the SPIRIT WORLD, or aids our Hero with supernatural insights.

PF8. MENTORS. People other than Parents, Counselors, or Spiritual Guides who AID OUR HERO in the course of his travels.

PF9. GROWTH CENTER. The HARMONIOUS KINGDOMS or BEWITCHING KINGDOMS where our Hero pauses or dwells.

PF10. INTEGRAL LIFE GUIDE. The WISE COUNSELOR who possesses an intimate knowledge of our Hero's four Worlds.

PF11. INTERNAL NAVIGATOR. Our HERO'S CHARACTER, once he has absorbed the lessons from his many Ordeals & Trials.

PF12. PROVIDENCE. The continuing presence and influence of some DIVINE BEING in our Hero's life. The Great LOOM OF FATE.

PARTICIPANTS

P1-8. PARTICIPANTS. The crew, passengers, and other VOYAGERS who take part in our Life Journey.

P1. SELF SYSTEM. Our HERO -- the CENTRAL CHARACTER, the adventurer who triumphs over challenges and hardships.

P2. INDIVIDUAL SELF. INDIVIDUAL CHARACTERS – Hero, Sidekick, Mentor, Spiritual Guide, Main Villain.
*** **COLLECTIVE SELF.** GROUP CHARACTERS – the Ship's Crew, Townsfolk, Invading Army, Gang of Villains.

P3. PERSONALITY TYPES. The stereotyped 'CHARACTERS' we find aboard Ship – the Forceful Leader, Dutiful Helper, Jovial Carouser, Reclusive Thinker, Cooperative Mate, Free Spirit, Jokester, Voice Of Prophecy, Slouch.

P4. SHADOW SELF. The MISFIT or TROUBLEMAKER, who disrupts things and causes the Journey to go wrong -- the Grumbler, Slacker, Rebel, Plotter, Saboteur, Mutineer, Stowaway.

P5. FUNCTIONAL CONSTITUENTS. The various members of the SHIP'S CREW, characterized by their FUNCTION aboard ship – the Captain, Navigator, Helmsman, Surgeon, Cook, Carpenter, Midshipman, Mate.

P6. MULTIPLE IDENTITIES. The fluid, changing, SHAPE-SHIFTING IDENTITIES -- when our Hero assumes a disguise, when a character turns into an animal, when a god appears in human form.

P7. DIVINE PRESENCE. The SPIRITUAL ENTITY who orchestrates the Hero's World. *** **Core Self.** The FAMILIAR SPIRIT – takes a personal interest in the Hero's life. *** **Witness.** The PERVASIVE SPIRIT -- presides over the Hero's World from afar.

The ADAPT Model in Symbolic form

GENERAL PROCESSES

PPR1-9. PROCESSES. The SAILING SHIPS, and other MEANS OF CONVEYANCE, that carry us along the channels, trade routes, and open seas of our Growth. *** **General Processes.** The MEANS OF PROPULSION that can power any Ship – Sails, Oars, Animal Power, Steam Engine, Diesel. *** **Specific Processes.** The specific KINDS OF SHIPS – from rowboats to ocean liners.

PPR1. TRANSITION CYCLE. The Process by which we travel from ONE ISLAND TO THE NEXT – embarking, sailing, arriving at port.

PPR2. SHADOW CYCLE. When our NORMAL PASSAGE from one port to the next goes awry – adverse winds, storms, a mutiny.

PPR3. ACTUALIZATION GROWTH. The NORMAL PROGRESS OF OUR VOYAGE – from one Island to the next, then the next, etc.

PPR4. RESTORATION GROWTH. GETTING BACK ON TRACK after our Ship has been blown off course.

PPR5. COLLECTIVE GROWTH. The challenges and adventures that all the Voyagers SHARE TOGETHER.

PPR6. HORIZONTAL GROWTH. The explorations that take us to VARIOUS PARTS OF THE ISLAND -- waterfront, shops, pubs.

PPR7. PERSPECTIVE GROWTH. Our story is told from MULTIPLE PERSPECTIVES -- thereby giving increased clarity and depth.
*** **Inclusiveness.** A VARIETY OF CHARACTERS are presented sympathetically -- so that we can feel affinities with them all.

PPR8. EVOLUTION & INVOLUTION. Metaphorically, the GREAT TREE that grows Upward & Outwards, but also Downward & Inwards. *** **Transcend & Include.** That same Tree adding new RINGS OF GROWTH to the Original Tree at its core.

PPR9. SPIRITUAL GROWTH. The WISDOM our Hero receives from a Higher Being -- during a dream, vision, visitation.

C5d. Circle Diagram:
The ADAPT Model Of Human Development

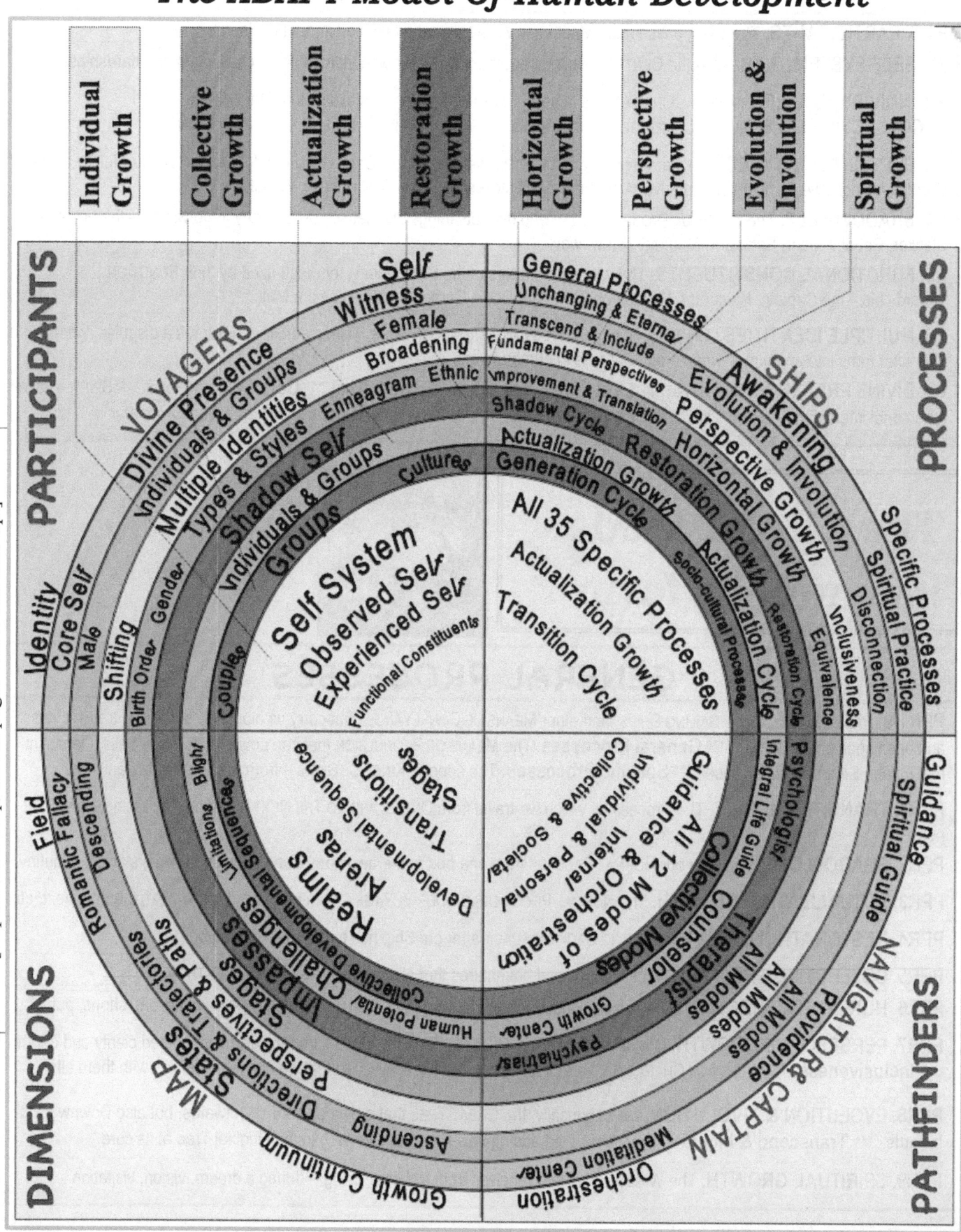

[Explanation on previous page. View this side up.]

PARTICIPANTS — Individual Growth, Collective Growth, Actualization Growth, Restoration Growth, Horizontal Growth, Perspective Growth, Evolution & Involution, Spiritual Growth — **PROCESSES**

VOYAGERS
- Self
- Witness
- Divine Presence
- Female / Male
- Multiple Identities — Individuals & Groups
- Types & Styles — Broadening
- Enneagram — Ethnic
- Shadow Self
- Individuals & Groups — Cultures
- Groups — Couples

SHIPS / Processes
- General Processes
- Unchanging & Eternal
- Transcend & Include
- Fundamental Perspectives
- Improvement & Translation
- Shadow Cycle
- Actualization Growth — Restoration Growth — Horizontal Growth
- Generation Cycle
- Awakening — Evolution & Involution — Perspective Growth
- Specific Processes
- Spiritual Practice
- Disconnection
- Inclusiveness
- Equivalence
- Socio-cultural Processes
- Restoration Cycle
- Actualization Cycle

Self System
- Observed Self
- Experienced Self
- Functional Constituents

All 35 Specific Processes
- Actualization Growth
- Transition Cycle

Identity — Core Self — Shifting — Birth Order — Gender
Field — Romantic Fallacy — Descending — Blight — Limitations — Developmental Sequences — Collective Development — Human Potential — Growth Center — Psychiatrist

Realms / Arenas / Transitions / Stages
- Collective & Societal
- Individual & Personal
- Internal
- Guidance & Orchestration
- All 12 Modes of
- Collective Modes
- Counselor
- Therapist
- All Modes
- Providence
- Orchestration — Mediation Center

PATHFINDERS
- Guidance
- Spiritual Guide
- Integral Life Guide
- Psychologist
- NAVIGATOR & CAPTAIN

DIMENSIONS
- MAP — States — Stages & Paths — Impasses — Challenges
- Directions & Trajectories — Perspectives
- Ascending
- Growth Continuum

Your Own Hero's Journey. Like Pinocchio, your Whole Life can spread out before you like one Grand Vision.

Your Own Starry Night. Like Van Gogh, you can immerse yourself in rapturous contemplation of the Glory that is all around you.

Your Moment of Truth
When your impulses sweep you toward a brighter future and a new beginning,
will you go with the flow?

Made in the USA
Monee, IL
17 June 2024